Frank talk

The inside Stories of ZAPPA's oTher people

Andrew Greenaway

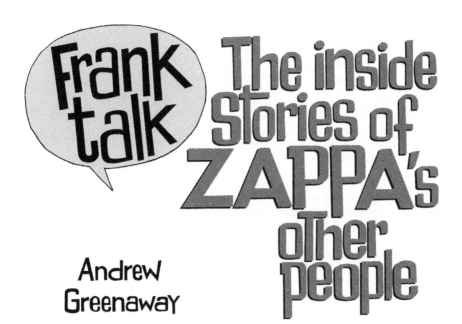

Frank talk

The inside Stories of ZAPPA's oTher people

Andrew Greenaway

WP
WYMER
PUBLISHING
Bedford, England

First published in Great Britain in 2017
by Wymer Publishing
Bedford, England
www.wymerpublishing.co.uk
Tel: 01234 326691
Wymer Publishing is a trading name of Wymer (UK) Ltd

ISBN 978-1-908724-67-0

Edited by Jerry Bloom.

Typeset by Wymer
Printed and bound by
Lightning Source, UK, USA & Australia

A catalogue record for this book is available from the British Library.

Cover design by Antero Valério

This book is dedicated to:

Julie – *love of my life*

Thanks to:
Julie & Chris & Emma & Lizzy
All of the Greenaway tribe and outlaws.

My Zappanale & Moo-ah buddies:
"Uncle" Ian Day and "Canadian" John Campbell.

My former Ministry drinking pals:
Jazzman Dave and Bebirdo.

My German bro: Amaretto Mick Zeuner.

My ZappaCast chums:
Scott Parker, Mick Ekers and Scott Fischer.

My Music Emporium partner: Baker Lee.

My Cal Schenkel: Antero Valério

André Cholmondeley and Bob Dobbs, for facilitating and
participating in two of the interviews.

And finally, to all of my interviewees: this book is what it is
because of you – I just had the good sense to speak with y'all!

PREAMBLE

In the same way that I didn't set out to write a book about Frank Zappa's ill-fated 1988 world tour (it just sort of fell into my lap), I never imagined myself as an interviewer: of musicians, no less. Me, who can't play a note!

But over time I have sort of become just that: a person that Frank might've despised – someone who can't write, doing interviews with people who can't think, in order to prepare articles for people who can't read. Well, that's everybody here well and truly slagged off!

When I saw some of the interviews contained in this volume being quoted in various books, it struck me that maybe I should do something more with them than letting them fester online.

With two of my subjects already dead and one passing away just last year, it seemed time was nigh to stick them all together in one place. That time is now and that place is here.

I have substantially re-edited and expanded the interviews in a bid to present never before seen glimpses of Zappa's work ethic, his personal life and his legendary band auditions.

Of course there's one obvious omission from the interviewees: the man himself. But I hope you'll agree that his voice comes across loud and clear through the reminiscences of those who knew him best – and in the copious annotations that I have appended to them.

It's important to note that this book is not all about Frank. Within these pages you'll also learn more about all those guys so beautifully caricatured within. It would be rude not to talk to them about their own activities, wouldn't it? Especially when some have gone on to have very fine careers in their own right.

So their stories can also be found within these pages, providing much that you won't find in a conventional book on Zappa's life and work. But there's also plenty of material that should be.

In 1984, Frank stated that his *Them Or Us – The Book* was "the only real and official Frank Zappa book. All other books attempting to trade on my name are unauthorised and full of misinformation."

There is no doubt that with Frank no longer around to correct them, some of my interviewees have been economical with the actualité on occasion and my book may well contain some 'fake news'. But I hope it won't be deemed "tawdry", which is what Terry Gilliam told me he thought of the script Zappa adapted from his *Them Or Us* book. If readers find my book informative and mildly entertaining, that'll do me!

Rather than compile the interviews in the order in which they were conducted, I have instead chosen to arrange them alphabetically. Laying them out this way I felt gave the book a very interesting flow – as well as obscuring the lack of any improvement in my interviewing technique over the years. Happily, this also means my conversations with Frank's living relatives now conclude this tome.

I did actually come close to interviewing Frank himself once. Having organised an interview with his son Dweezil through the then UK distributors of Zappa Records, Music For Nations. I contacted them again when it became known that Frank would be passing through the UK in July 1991. The plan was that Fred Tomsett, the editor of the British fanzine *T'Mershi Duween* (1988-2000), would take the lead and I would ride shotgun.

We were conscious of Frank's dislike of interviews generally and the caustic wit he would often display in such situations (see Thorsten Schütte's excellent *Eat That Question* documentary for evidence of this). We were thus a little concerned that meeting our hero might drastically alter our opinion of him. In the event, it didn't happen.

To be honest, I don't think we should have worried as the 'fan' interviews he did undergo (notably with the guys from the US fanzine *Society Pages*) showed him to be very appreciative of their interest in his work and eked out some fantastic material. He also seemed to be in surprisingly good spirits during that particular visit: when BBC radio presenter Brian Hayes questioned how musical styles could crop up on opposite sides of the world, Zappa simply replied "Sailors."

His passing less than three years later robbed the world of not just great music, but also of someone of great wit and moral fortitude who potentially could have given the United States a far better President than the present incumbent.

My hope, dear reader, is that this book brings him back to life, albeit fleetingly and that you can hear FRANK TALK once more!

Andrew Greenaway
July 2017

THE INTERVIEWS

ARTHUR BARROW

Arthur "Tink" Barrow was Zappa's bass player from 1978 to 1980 and 'Clonemeister' (running band rehearsals in Zappa's absence) from 1979 to 1982. He made his recording debut on Zappa's rock opera, *Joe's Garage* – a "stupid little story about how the government is going to do away with music."

Barrow plays on many Zappa albums throughout the 1980s (most controversially, the 1985 remixes of *We're Only In It For The Money* and *Cruising With Ruben & The Jets*) as well as a number of posthumous releases (most notably, the live albums *Halloween* (2003), *Buffalo* (2007) and *Chicago '78* (2016)).

In the mid-1980s, Barrow worked extensively with Italian record producer Giorgio Moroder, including on soundtracks for films like *Scarface* (1983) and *Top Gun* (1986).

He is one of the few former band members to have published a memoir detailing his time with Zappa, beyond and before.[1]

In 2000, I started a website devoted to all things Zappa. In March 2001, out of the blue, I got an email from Barrow. Seizing the moment, I asked if he'd like to be subjected to some dumb questions – but not his least favourite one.[2]

Of course, he said yes!

---

[1] *Of Course I Said Yes! The Amazing Adventures Of A Life In Music* by Arthur Barrow (CreateSpace Independent Publishing Platform, 2016).

[2] Barrow joined Zappa's band on bass in June 1978, and went on tour in September. In *Of Course I Said Yes!* Barrow says the question is "Why were there two bass players in 1978?" In October, at the start of the US East Coast leg of the tour, Zappa brought bassist Patrick O'Hearn back into the line-up. Barrow says "I heard that the 'Mean Girls' in the band had been complaining to Frank about my playing. They were in touch with Pat, and influenced Frank to add Pat to the line-up. So there you have it; please don't ask me again. Pat is a nice guy, and we got along fine. He is a great player."

When you first started to play music, what was your main instrument?
Ukulele, tenor guitar and then guitar when I was about 13.

You saw taking up bass as the only way of getting into Frank's band – but you didn't just play bass with him, did you?
I also played keyboards and guitar with Zappa[3], if that's what you mean.

It is. You're generally perceived as just a bass player. But you contributed a whole lot more.
I also played bass with a lot of other people besides Frank.

I recently heard the full radio broadcast of a Zappa gig you did in Rotterdam in May 1980; your bass playing was quite wonderful.
Thank you!

Given that you obviously excelled at this instrument, why don't you do more stuff like *The Shadows*[4] or *Code Blue*[5] on your albums – most of your own songs are keyboard based, aren't they?
I think of my music as being composition based, not player based. I did plenty of fancy bass work with Frank, so listeners know I can do that. I think of the composition first, not how impressive my playing is. Weird, eh?

What is your least favourite eating utensil?
Chopsticks.

So a spoon's your favourite, right?
You must be English, judging by your spelling. But you're wrong; it's the fourk.

As *We're Only In It For The Money* was the first FZ album you got into, how did you subsequently feel about your involvement in the remix[6]?
I told Frank I thought it was a bad idea, but it was his music and he was

---

[3] Such as the organ solo on *If Only She Woulda* (from Zappa's *You Are What You Is*, 1981) and piano and guitar on *The Radio Is Broken* (from Zappa's *The Man From Utopia*, 1983).

[4] From Barrow's *Music For Listening* album (1991).

[5] From Barrow's *AB3* album (1999).

[6] In 1984, Zappa stated that the original master tapes for his early albums *We're Only In It For The Money* (1968) and *Cruising With Ruben & The Jets* (1968) were in a "wretched condition" and he'd had to re-record new drum and bass tracks, provided by Barrow and drummer Chad Wackerman, in order to reissue them.

the boss. It was a lot of fun, though. It is a bit odd to now be on an album that was my favourite in high school.

Aside from *St. Alfonzo's Pancake Breakfast*, what other pieces did you play for Zappa during your audition?
A lick in *Twenty-One*[7] that ended up in *Keep It Greasy*[8] was one. Also some sight reading and some jamming. Maybe *The Black Page*.[9]

You took over from percussionist Ed Mann as Clonemeister: how did he and the other band members react to your new appointment?
They hated it – which I can understand, after all, most of them had seniority over me. We all would have preferred that Frank conduct all the rehearsals and not have a Clonemeister.

I understand you continued as Clonemeister after you quit touring with Zappa – so how did that go down with guys like subsequent bassist Scott Thunes?
I had absolutely no problems with players during that time.

***Mo's Vacation* is one of my favourite unreleased Zappa tracks - as performed by yourself and Vinnie Colaiuta[10] in Poughkeepsie, September 1978. What was that like to learn?**
Pretty hard for me. A piece of cake for drummer Vinnie – he could sight read the sucker. I never really did play it right all the way through. There are sections in the bass part that are impossible, as far as I can tell. You should see all the coffee stains on my chart. I spent about 30 hours working on it when I first got it. I shedded on it during our week off in Munich.

So when did you last pick your feet in Poughkeepsie?[11]
Right before I shuffled off to Buffalo.

What can you tell me about the dawn raid when Tommy Mars[12] and Ike Willis were whisked off by the British police as Frank slept in a different hotel?
I don't recall that incident. What happened?

---

7 An instrumental that was finally released on the live album *Chicago '78* in 2016.

8 From Zappa's *Joe's Garage Acts II & III* album (1979).

9 From *Zappa In New York* (1978).

10 American session drummer who worked with Zappa from 1978 to 1981. His career has included long associations with Joni Mitchell and Sting.

11 A reference to the 1971 American crime thriller, *The French Connection*.

12 Keyboard player with Zappa from 1977 to 1982.

I was hoping you'd tell me. It received a fair bit of media attention at the time and I recall that Frank – even though he wasn't involved and as much as he hated drugs – slagged off the way our friendly Constabulary handled it. Were you one of the guys in the band who started the tradition of *The Jazz Discharge Party Hats*?[13]
No.

Any salacious tales from the road you'd care to divulge?
Hmmm, not particularly.

In the 1970s you were in a band with Don Preston. And Jimmy Carl Black made guest appearances on stage and in the studio during your tenure with Frank. What do you think of the Grandmothers?[14]
I heard them last year and they sounded pretty good. Jimmy Carl Black is very friendly and a fellow Texan. And I met Bunk Gardner[15] for the first time – another very nice cat.

Have you remained in touch over the years?
I talked to Don about a week ago – he had a question about a synth.

What about any of the other guys – aside from those involved with the Banned From Utopia.[16] Tell me something about your relationship (musical or otherwise) with Vinnie.
Haven't talked to him for a while. He's the best drummer I have ever heard, much less played with – it was an honour.

And Warren Cuccurullo?
Probably haven't talked to him in 20 years. We got along okay, though – no bad feelings or anything.

Steve Vai?
Been in touch by email lately – he was always a decent guy and sounds like he still is. A great player.

---

13 From Zappa's *The Man From Utopia* album (1983).

14 Band co-founded by Don Preston and Jimmy Carl Black in the early 80s.

15 Woodwind and tenor sax player with the Mothers.

16 Another band comprised of Zappa's former musicians who first performed a tribute concert several months after his death (as the Band From Utopia – a name suggested by Barrow) at the Jazz Open Festival in Stuttgart, Germany on 1st July 1994. While the Zappa Family Trust (ZFT) gave its approval to the release of a DVD and CD of this concert to be issued, the musicians later decided to rename the band because of Gail Zappa's concern that it sounded too close to Zappa's album *The Man From Utopia*. They changed it to the Banned From Utopia for a tour of North America in 1995, and have continued to tour under that name in various incarnations on and off ever since.

Shankar?

Awesome musician and a great guy. Not in touch, though. I would love to talk to him again one day. Frank wanted him to be in the band at one point, while Frank was producing his album. I spent many hours in a London hotel room trying to teach him some of the music. He transcribed a lot of it into his Indian form of music notation.

Bob Harris?

A nice guy, but not in touch.

Finally, Peter Wolf?[17]

Words cannot describe how I feel.[18]

Do you have any plans to release your recordings of that early band with Don, Bruce Fowler[19] and Vinnie?

Yes, I plan to release those along with other early stuff on a 'basement tapes' kind of collection.[20]

Zappa's planned *Crush All Boxes* album (that evolved into *You Are What You Is*) is well documented. But it's come to light that Frank originally had other plans for some of the material that appeared on the *Ship Arriving Too Late To Save A Drowning Witch* (1982) and *The Man From Utopia* (1983) albums. Were you aware of the mooted *Chalk Pie* album?

Vaguely.

When is the new ZFT[21] - approved Banned From Utopia album, *So Yuh Don't Like Modern Art*, coming out?[22]

I don't know – Bruce Fowler is in charge of that.

What's on it?

Tink/13 is great. It has some previously unheard sections that were rehearsed in 1980, but got kind of lost until I discovered some old

---

17 Keyboard player with Zappa from 1977 to 1978.

18 In a 1992 interview conducted by Tom Brown and Slev Uunofski for British Zappa fanzine T'Mershi Duween, Barrow had this to say about the reaction to his appointment as Clonemeister: "Unfortunately, the guys in the band that had seniority over me, resented having a punk like me tell them what to do. Particularly Peter Wolf. He really seemed to have it in for me."

19 Trombonist, with Zappa from 1972 to 1975 and again in 1988.

20 Released by Barrow in 2003, on his album *On Time*.

21 The Zappa Family Trust.

22 It was released in 2002.

charts I had written for it.

Who's on it?

The usual suspects – I don't know if Ray White[23] is guesting on it. Again, Bruce is producing – except for *Tink*; that's mine.

Are you gonna tour to promote it?

Hopefully!

Interview conducted on Tuesday 17th April 2001.

---

[23] Vocalist/guitarist with Zappa from 1976 to 1984.

LORRAINE BELCHER CHAMBERLAIN

In *The Real Frank Zappa Book[1]*, Zappa refers to "a girl I met in a restaurant in Hollywood" in 1964, before relaying the story of his bust at Studio Z in Cucamonga for 'conspiracy to commit pornography'. As any fule kno, the girl – referred to as "his buxom red-haired companion" in the Ontario Daily Report – was Lorraine Belcher.

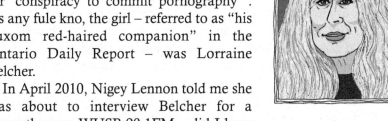

In April 2010, Nigey Lennon told me she was about to interview Belcher for a Zappathon on WUSB 90.1FM – did I have any questions for her? Of course, but not as many as I should have. Not helped by the 'official' airbrushing of history[2], I didn't appreciate that Zappa's friendship with Belcher lasted right up until just before his death.

The interview on WUSB was very entertaining – Belcher is a natural raconteur. With the possibility of an autobiography at some point in the future, the following gives just a brief glimpse into her amazing life.

Tell me a little about your background – and how, in all the towns in all the world, you walked into that particular 'gin joint' in 1964 and met Zappa!
I was born in Tacoma Washington. At age 15, I moved to Ohio to live with my real father, but after a few months returned home to find the house sold and empty. As a result, I ended up a ward of the court and was in a series of reform schools until four months after I turned 18. I flew to Santa Barbara then and enrolled in college. That lasted a year, after getting pregnant and then giving the child up for adoption.

It was a couple of months after giving birth that I met Frank in the

---

[1] Zappa's autobiography, written with Peter Occhiogrosso (Simon & Schuster, 1990).

[2] In a May 2016 comment on Moon Zappa's Facebook page. Belcher claims Zappa's wife Gail "insisted he not use my name, nor tell the truth about our relationship" in *The Real Frank Zappa Book*.

Carolina Pines, a coffee shop/late night hangout on Sunset & La Brea in Hollywood.

Tell us about that first meeting.
It was about 4 o'clock in the morning and my friend was talking to somebody in there s he knew – some guy – and I was getting a little bored. I looked across the room and sitting in a booth was Frank in a little striped t-shirt with a guy in iridescent green suit with iridescent green Bobby Rydell hair and another guy who turned out to be Captain Beefheart.[3]

I looked right at Frank and he – with his very intense gaze – looked right back at me and crooked his finger, beckoning me over. I gave him my back. But after a few minutes, I was getting a little bored, so I thought I'd take a peek at him again. He kind of tilted his head to the side and grinned at me and waved at me again to come over. I thought, 'Oh, what the hell,' and I got up.

As I was strolling across the restaurant, he was very smart and took another chair from another booth and put it on the outside of his booth so that I wouldn't get squeezed in with them. As I got there, Frank said, "Pleasure looking at ya!" And as I sat down I said, "Likewise." I thought he was fantastically attractive and so ridiculous looking! He had beautiful eyes and such an odd manner.

We sat their laughing and talking for at least an hour before my friend noticed I was gone. Anyway, he ended up driving us both to Cucamonga.

Did you say your friend was later one of a number of Suzy Creamcheeses?[4]
I always thought Lauren Irell was one of the early Suzy Creamcheeses. Later it was Pamela Zarubica. I could be wrong.

Did you know Pamela?
I met Pamela, yes. She always claimed to be the muse behind Lenny Bruce, Phil Spector and Frank Zappa. Like they would have been nothing without her. I found these claims to be embarrassing. I liked

---

[3] Stage name of Don Van Vliet (1941-2010), American singer/songwriter and early friend of Zappa's.

[4] Zappa said that Suzy Creamcheese - who was referenced on the album *Freak Out!* (1966) - was a figment of his imagination, "until people started identifying with it heavily. It got to weird proportions so that when we did our first tour of Europe, people were asking if Suzy Creamcheese was along with us. So I procured the services of another girl named Pamela Zarubica."

her, but felt she was mostly hype. I was in awe of anyone having that much self-confidence... or maybe self-delusion.

So, did you immediately embark on a sexual relationship with Frank in Cucamonga?

I slept with Frank off and on for a couple of months before we ever had sex. Then, one morning, he woke me up and said, "I think it's time for your morning orgasm!" We went on from there. He was so patient and understanding and told me later it was well worth the wait.

What was Studio Z like?

Studio Z had blacked out storefront windows.

Upon entering, there was an office to the left, control room to the right, then double swinging doors which led to the recording area, which was a huge room. To the left were dilapidated couches, to the right a grand piano. Musical instruments and drum sets, cords running everywhere. Past the piano was a long rectangular area where he projected films on the back wall. Past the couches there was a wall with a window and door that led into the bedroom, which was festooned with a myriad of wacky items, including a huge aquarium filled with decapitated dolls...heads & arms filling it to the brim. On the back wall was a glittering jukebox. That was the door to the bathroom. You could open it up and had to duck to get in there. I thought it was quite cosy.

Who else was living there?

No one else lived there, except towards the end when my friend Theo, from reform school, moved in with her baby boy. That ended when the bust happened.

Was that the 'white girl with a black baby'?

Yes, Theo was the white girl with black baby, Todd.

Did you ever meet Paul Buff, the owner of Pal Recording Studios?[5]

I think I met Paul in the early days. But I couldn't begin to even tell you what he looked like, or any impressions! Boy, am I getting old...

Can you recall any of the sessions that occurred during you tenure at Studio Z?

No one recorded while I was there, as I frequently left for weeks at a

---

5 An independent studio in Cucamonga started by engineer/innovator Paul Conrad Buff (1936-2015) where *Wipe Out!* by The Surfaris was recorded - and where Zappa first learnt basic recording techniques: he later purchased the studio from Buff, renaming it Studio Z.

time to go stay in my little place in Laguna Beach. Mostly the Mothers would rehearse there.

The 'party tape' aside, did you appear on any Studio Z recordings?
Frank recorded me singing quite a bit at one point. He told me he thought I had a range somewhere between John Lee Hooker and Minnie Riperton and wanted me to sing with the Mothers. But the minute he wanted me to sing alone, with him at the piano, I would freeze and go off pitch. He wasn't patient enough to put up with that. I could only sing when he was out of the room – and he was listening to me sing through the mike, in the control room. Not good. So we gave up.

I did sing back-up in the studio sometimes over the years... on *The Mud Shark*,[6] with Mark Volman and Howard Kaylan. It was just fun fooling around with him at the recording studio... I don't know whatever made it in the mix besides *The Mud Shark*.

Did you overdub a live recording of that, or was that a separate studio recording?
Mark and Howard and I recorded over the live one, I think. We were in the studio adding tracks.

What are you memories of the Soul Giants/early Mothers?
I loved to listen to them rehearse, but didn't speak to them much except for Beefheart, Motorhead[7] and Jimmy Carl Black. I went to their gigs sometimes...at the Saints 'N Sinners in Riverside, I think. Frank was always frustrated at having to play anything like *Louie Louie* and would always go off the cover band plan, playing his own stuff. Then people would start yelling.

The bikers from a club called the Comancheros loved Frank's own material, though. They came to Studio Z many times to hang out with us. Great big scary guys playing marbles on the floor like children. Very funny.

Were you aware of Frank's brief tenure as a beat poet, writing under the pseudonym Vincent Beldon?
I seem to recall Frank telling me about various excursions into alternate artistic endeavours when I first met him... the Steve Allen show with the bicycle. But I can't excavate Vincent Beldon out of my brain, really,

---

6 From Zappa's *Fillmore East, June 1971* album (1971).

7 Jim "Motorhead" Sherwood (1942-2011), sax and tambourine player with the original Mothers.

even though that sounds familiar. I do have the original text he wrote of *Trouble Every Day*... he mailed it to me in Laguna Beach after reading it to me over the phone during the Watts Riots. I, too, had been watching the whole thing on TV. It's kind of wrinkled after all these years, but still such a fantastic piece. It stands as a great poem.[8]

Why did Frank refer to you as 'Pete' on the *Freak Out!* sleeve?
When I first met Frank, I told him my name was Lorre, spelled like Peter Lorre. He never called me Lorre and went on with Pete from then on.

Are there any references to you in any of Frank's songs?
No songs about me that I know of. I think it's because I asked him to once in the early days, wanting him to write some kind of love song. Frank hated love songs!

In the recent radio interview with Nigey, you told the wonderful story behind *Call Any Vegetable*[9] – care to relay that one more time for the world?
He told me that his wife[10] never made a sound during sex. This made him feel bad.

One day, after he'd been on the road to a meeting in LA for a while, he realised he'd forgotten something and turned around. When he got home he found his wife passed out on the bed with a potato carved like a dildo. He was originally very upset, since she'd apparently been so satisfied she had to take a nap! Then he asked her to tell him about the potato. She had apparently tried all the other vegetables and found the potato to be the most harmonious with the vaginal canal... pH balance, etc. It didn't produce any kind of infection or discharge and held up well.

That's why he wrote *Call Any Vegetable*.

And 'the bust' story?
We were really broke and one day this guy came by pretending to be a used car dealer. They were going to have a bachelor party for someone who was getting married and, originally, he wanted a pornographic film. But Frank said he didn't have the materials for that, but he could

---

[8] This exchange actually took place via email on 26th June 2011. Belcher was able to confirm that the same typewriter was used for both the Beldon poem, LA Night Piece, and the Watts Riot lyrics.

[9] From Zappa's *Absolutely Free* album (1967).

[10] Kay Sherman (m. 1960–64).

make a tape. So he said okay and he'd be back the next day to get it. So Frank pulled the bed out of the bedroom into the middle of the recording area and put up microphones. He said this is what we're gonna do: you're under age and I've picked you up in a bar and we've come to a motel. That was all I knew.

We were fully clothed, the lights were on and Theo played this background music. Frank said, "Well, little honey, have you graduated from high school yet?" And I looked at him and said, "NO, I graduate in June, but I'm gonna go to summer school." He didn't know what I was going to say, so he asked, "What are you going to study?" And I said, "Cosmetology!" And then we'd laugh.

It took about 45 minutes to an hour to record and then Theo said, "Okay, get down to business," and we'd start moaning and groaning and carrying on. And laughing! Frank stayed up half the night editing what was a great comedy tape into a nasty little heavy breathing and moaning tape that lasted about five minutes.

In the morning, there was a knock at the door and this guy goes into the control room with Frank. I was with Theo and her baby in the bedroom. Then suddenly, the doors burst open – it sounded like a herd of elephants coming across the room – and there was Frank leading them saying, "Pete, Theo - we're under arrest." I had nothing on and I grabbed the sheet and pulled it up over me. There were eleven men in the bedroom and Detective Willis steps forward and says, "Identify yourself." I said I'll identify myself after you get out of here and let me get dressed. So they backed off.

I managed to brush my teeth and do my hair and make-up. When I eventually stepped out from the jukebox, Willis right away asked me, "Tell me, have you ever engaged in oral copulation with Mr Zappa?" I laughed and said, "I know that's a felony in the state of California, but are you asking because it pertains to this little charade or for your own perverse curiosity?" I was very frightened, but I wasn't about to let him see that.

Frank, knowing that I had been in reform school was just devastated. He was so worried and he was apologising to me. I did that little finger burst thing and said, "Oh, what the hell!" And we started laughing. He had his arms around me as the photographer kicked the door open. That's where that photograph came from – it looked like we posed for it.

Then the band showed up to rehearse. They had them all in a line with their sleeves rolled up and I'll never forget Motorhead looking over at me saying, "Pete, they're looking for tracks!" He was so excited. Because he didn't do drugs, he thought that was really exotic!

So Frank spent ten days in Tank C,[11] and shortly thereafter you left Studio Z – where did you then live?
I lived in Laguna for a while. Frank closed Studio Z and moved to Echo Park, where I would stay with him sometimes. It was a chaotic time.

Then I moved to Seattle for a while. Frank couldn't find me. So he put out *Lumpy Gravy*, which was my nickname for him. There was a little cartoon guy inside the album cover saying, "write to us" with the address in New York. I had married some guy I'd only known for three weeks, to get away from the rock 'n' roll life in LA. I sent a little note to him saying, "I am married but still recognisable." And he called a few days later. When I picked up the phone, Frank said, "I thought you'd see that."

The Mothers then played Seattle three times in nine months. Frank and I would sit alone together backstage saying, "What are we going to do?" He had married Gail[12], who was pregnant with Moon[13]. So he came up with the brilliant idea of me divorcing my husband and moving in with them in LA. Shocking. Even more shocking was, I did it! But I said, "I want my own room."

We never touched each other the year I lived there with them. I moved back to Seattle for a few years, but we still saw each other, as I would fly down there sometimes for a visit.

It was five years before Frank and I were intimate again, which destroyed the relationship with Gail when she found out.

So what did Gail think about your friendship?
Gail acted very cool about me moving in. She was very friendly to me. I always tried to go on errands with her so Frank and I wouldn't be alone in the house, making her wonder. It was an unspoken deal: Frank was not to sleep with anyone in LA where she and the children lived and not me anywhere in the world.

We broke that deal five years later when I went on the road with him out of Seattle. When she found out, she was furious. We barely spoke after that. She would make cryptic remarks to me only in passing.

I saw her here in San Francisco in 2004 at a Zappa film festival at the

---

11 As referenced in *San Ber'dino* from Zappa's *One Size Fits All* album (1975).

12 Zappa's second wife (m. 1967-1993), Adelaide Gail Sloatman (1945-2015).

13 Gail and Frank's first child, Moon Unit Zappa born 28th September 1967.

Castro Theater. When she finished taking questions from the audience after the movie, I jumped out into the aisle as she was passing by to give autographs in the lobby. She cried out, "Pete!" and threw her arms around me. It was a Friday night and she was going directly back to LA, returning for Sunday night with Moon. She wanted me to return on Sunday night so I could see Moon again (whom I loved so much and hadn't seen since she was five).

I couldn't return, but I wrote to her several times. She never replied. I believe she wasn't so much thrilled to see me as shocked and said all that stuff because she was so stunned. I have given up trying to be in contact with her.

Did Frank ever talk to you about any other women in his life? We know about Nigey and Jenny Brown from Australia[14]. In his autobiography, Ozzy Osbourne mentions "some Japanese chick that Frank was hanging out with"[15] in the late 70s. He also allegedly had a one-night stand with Janis Joplin while Gail was pregnant with Moon[16].

He never spoke about anyone except that girl from Australia. At one point he was going to get an apartment in San Francisco, but never did it. I encouraged him to do whatever would make him happy, but he gave up.

When he and Gail met John Lennon, Gail got all mixed up with Primal Scream Therapy with them and said she was going to divorce Frank if he didn't do it too. That didn't last long. She gave up on both, of course.

After Cucamonga, did you have any further contact with Beefheart or Motorhead?

I used to see Beefheart and Motorhead all the time at Frank and Gail's house. Sometimes, when he and Don were in a feud, he would come and visit me in the back yard... he wouldn't come in the house, or maybe Frank wouldn't let him... I'm not sure. So we would just talk outside.

---

[14] In her *Flirting With Disaster* stand-up skit from June 2016, Moon describes her father as a bit of a cheater, adding, "When I was little, he moved this Australian lady named Jenny into the basement: he slept with her downstairs, and we slept upstairs. Meals were awkward. It was like a game of chicken between Jenny and my mother." In spite of this, Gail gives Brown an 'honourable mention' in the liner notes to the posthumous Zappa release *FZ:OZ* (2002).

[15] *I Am Ozzy*, written with Chris Ayres (Grand Central Publishing, 2010).

[16] See *Zappa: A Biography* by Barry Miles (Grove Press, 2004).

I moved to New York City in 1972 and saw Frank all the time, whenever he was in town... with or without the band. At those times, I saw Beefheart and Motorhead. I was in touch with Beefheart for many years, whenever he was in New York. I loved both of them.

I only connected with Motorhead again in 2001, when the Grandmothers were playing in San Francisco. It was a fantastic show and so great to see Don Preston and the boys again after all those years. Motorhead and I have been in touch ever since and I went to his wedding in Stockton a few years ago.[17]

When – and why – did your sexual relationship with Frank end?
My sexual relationship with Frank ended several times. Every time I had a serious boyfriend and during my marriage to the sculptor, John Chamberlain[18]. Frank waited patiently and we still spent time together during those periods but just didn't have sex. It was sort of a 'same time next year' relationship in later years.

He was always waiting for me to change my mind whenever I wouldn't sleep with him, knowing eventually I would.

When did you last speak to him?
The last time I was with him was when he played Springfield, Connecticut.[19] I was in NYC when I got his phone message and raced back to my house in Chester CT to change my clothes and zoom to his show there.

Afterwards, we spent the night in his hotel. I thought then that he looked tired.

Later, when they were going to do that big tribute for him at the Ritz[20] and he called asking me to join him in New York, as he was going alone, but still refused to tell me how bad he was.

I was in my bedroom packing to go in to meet him in the city when the news came on the TV. Moon and Dweezil were being interviewed, saying their father was too ill to travel. That came as such a shock to me. I remember sitting down on the bed in tears. I was living in a dream world, though, thinking he was going to live another twenty years. In

---

17 Motorhead sadly passed away on Christmas Day the following year.

18 An American sculptor, who passed away on what would have been Zappa's 71st birthday (21st December 2011).

19 See *Zappa The Hard Way* (Wymer Publishing, 2010) for Chamberlain's account of this final meeting.

20 *Zappa's Universe: A Celebration* took place on 7-9 November 1991 at The Ritz in New York. In 2012, I asked Gail Zappa about the likelihood of the concert video that PolyGram produced of this event in 1993 ever being expanded and reissued on DVD; her response was, "That project was done under intense duress, so it is not on my list of priorities."

fact, I still thought that for a long time afterwards. That's when I started writing him letters and tearing them up... his silence told it all.

Soon, I could write nothing, thinking about how Gail would hate to see my missives arriving in the mailbox while her husband was dying. I have regretted that ever since. I don't know why the hell I was thinking about her at such a time instead of writing to Frank!

I bought a card once to send to him during that year which said, "I heard you are sick..." and on the inside it said, "...if you die, can I have all your stuff?" Obviously a card for someone with a cold. I threw it away, of course, even though I knew he would have laughed. It was too close to the bone for me.

When I saw Gail at the Castro and she was onstage answering questions from the audience, I told Wilson[21] I was going to stand up and shout from my seat saying, "Gail! I'm kind of broke! Did Frank leave me anything in his will?" He was scared I might actually do it. I have a sick sense of humour, but I'm not that sick. I just like cooking these things up, but not actually following through. I learned of his passing one morning on the radio. I was alone and grieving. It was awful.

Aside from the meeting at the Castro Theater, have you had any other contact with Gail since his death?
She never replied to my few attempts at contact. Also, a few years ago when I was in LA, I drove to the house and buzzed the gate. Her assistant came down to talk with me and I handed her a note for Gail which I'd written in the car in case she wasn't home. She did not respond to that either.

Did you ever re-connect with your adopted child?
My child found me when he turned 19. I was thrilled. I raced to Sacramento to spend two weeks with him, then moved him to Connecticut to live with me for nearly a year. We are still in touch by email and visit one another once in awhile.

Do you have any other children?
I had three stepsons when I was married to John Chamberlain. The middle one, Jesse, died suddenly over ten years ago. We remained close all these years until recently, when I became a witness for Gerard Malanga[22] in a fraud lawsuit against John regarding some allegedly

---

[21] S. Clay Wilson, an American underground cartoonist, who married Chamberlain on 10th August 2010.

[22] American poet, photographer, filmmaker, curator and archivist.

phony Warhol's he sold as real[23]. It is a big scandal.

John has told the boys to have no contact with me, which breaks my heart. I can't believe they are following his orders! I love them and hope to hear from them again someday.

When did you first meet the great American underground cartoonist, S. Clay Wilson?

I met S Clay Wilson in 1968 in the Blue Moon Tavern in Seattle. We had mutual friends. We've been flirting ever since, but were never single at the same time until 2000, when I met up with him in Colorado, gave him a ride home to SF and never left. (I was on my way to southern California to live.)

We had visited one another many times over the years and spent hours on the phone despite our mates' disapproval. We have corresponded all this time and both of us saved every letter and postcard. I have all of our letters now in one box. I should do a book, as they are very funny and all of his are illustrated... even the envelopes.

Yes, you must write a book! How is he these days?

Wilson's traumatic brain injury was devastating. He bled in both hemispheres of his brain and was in a coma for three weeks. Then spent a whole year in the hospital. I brought him home on 10 November 2009.

He needs 24 hour care, as his short-term memory is shot and he cannot problem solve or do anything for himself. He is physically okay and I make him exercise every day. Once in awhile a friend will take him to lunch or a museum and I take him out walking every day. But he no longer reads (this house is filled with thousands of books).

He is drawing again, but not as often as even a few months ago, which worries me. I hate being a nag, so I encourage him to draw every day and have to let it go at that. Some days he will, most days he won't. It is hard to keep him entertained and engaged, but he still loves movies so we haunt the libraries for them and I have a Netflix account for new ones (which he rarely likes).

I have a caregiver come four afternoons a week so I can get away for a few hours on my own, usually to run errands. Taking care of someone in this condition can be overwhelming, as you never get a moment to yourself.

---

23 Andy Warhol, the American pop-artist who died on 22nd February 1987, wrote in his diaries (Warner Books, 1989) of his hatred for Zappa.

I made a webpage for people since I got him a Special Needs Trust. People can donate money to it on that site, or mail a cheque to our post office box. The address of the web page is www.sclaywilsontrust.com.

He can remember old friends, much of his knowledge about art and some of his life experiences. Often he surprises me with an incredibly sensitive observation. He doesn't like to talk on the phone much, as he cannot picture the person on the other end. He is still smart and sometimes playful, but he is severely challenged and changed in many ways. You used to have to fight to get a word in edgewise with him and now he is very quiet.

I hope people will open their hearts as well as their wallets, since he is no longer capable of earning a living.

Interview conducted on Friday 7th May 2010

Having remained in touch with Belcher (she's so funny – it's easy to see why Zappa was so fond of her!), seven years after our first interview I asked her further questions.

In his book, *Frankie & Bobby: Growing Up Zappa*, Bob Zappa describes the nineteen year old you as someone who would try to convince anyone who listened that you were a witch. What's your take on that?
At first, I wrote a nice note to Bobby, asking why he had written that condescending piece of fiction. He admitted that it was Frank who was always claiming I was a witch at that time.

Frank was always impressed by what he perceived to be my 'paranormal gifts'.

I woke him up in the night, telling him all four tyres on his car were flat. The next day, he went out to discover it was true. Someone had slashed them! We suspected the Baptist freaks across the street.

There were numerous episodes like that, where I would dream something, tell him and then it would happen. Including the bust for pornography... I woke him up in the night, asking if we could get arrested for that silly audio tape. Because I saw us getting put in handcuffs! He said he didn't know. Neither of us knew it was illegal. We went back to sleep and the cops burst in the doors the next morning, after Frank was paid the $100. So go figure.

I dreamt stuff all the time that happened. Frank talked about it, not me! He was fascinated by this side of me, because it really happened a lot.

I also asked Bobby why he wrote about me with such an attitude when I was actually the only person who was nice to him! And what right he had to say that my relationship with Frank ran its course, just fizzled out or something, when actually we weren't allowed to be together without a chaperone until I turned 21!

I was 19. I didn't have a job. We had no money. We always had to have Motorhead or Motorhead's mom with us! It was hard to keep asking that of them. I didn't know what else to do but go up to Seattle and stay with Theo.

Frank and I never fell out of love. Bobby never mentions how odd it must have been, years later, to come visit Frank – and Gail and Moon – and find me living there. Guess it hadn't 'fizzled out' after all?

Or did he forget he saw me? Even though Gail flounced through the house, spotted Bobby, flipped her hair at him and walked back out, saying nothing.

Essra Mohawk told me that when Frank got Gail pregnant with Moon, he asked her what he should do. She told him to marry Gail. Any thoughts on that?
Frank told me he hunted for me while Gail followed him all over the country, pointing at her growing belly, telling him he had to marry her. It was only later, after *Lumpy Gravy* came out, that I wrote that note after seeing his invitation to write to him on the inside cover.

He always told me he didn't love her. It was Moon: he couldn't leave her.

Essra also told me that when Frank awoke, he always said, "Another day, another dollar!" – every day.
Never! We were always sexy first thing, then allowed the realities of the day to begin. But also... in the early years, when we were together, we were poor!

Later, when he was on the road and we got to spend a few days together, he never once said anything like that. It would have just sounded... ridiculous? Not anything that was on his mind when waking up with me. It's an old cliché, of course and one Chamberlain used to say by changing it to, "Another day, another donut hole."

If Frank had said that, I'd have laughed!
Interview conducted on Wednesday 24th May 2017.

BRUCE BICKFORD

André Cholmondeley formed the ultimate Zappa tribute band, Project Object, in the early 1990s and has been touring with them – and Zappa alums including Ike Willis, Napoleon Murphy Brock, Ed Mann, Don Preston and Denny Walley – ever since.

For many years, the Zappa Family Trust has attempted to prevent Project Object from performing Zappa's music in his home country and in 2008, Dweezil Zappa posted a blog in which he described Cholmondeley, as "obnoxious". Addressing him directly, he added, "Your obsequious fawning over 'alumni' and your precious associations you have with them are embarrassingly shallow. Your attempts to draw attention to yourself as some sort of soldier fighting the good fight for Frank's music reveal what you really are - a depressing epigone starving for recognition."

I have been friends with Cholmondeley for over 15 years. His tireless efforts in promoting Zappa's music cannot be overestimated and Dweezil's description of him does not reflect the warm, witty, intelligent man I know.

In 2009, Cholmondeley very kindly offered to phone Bruce Bickford – the Seattle born maker of clay animated films, who's work is featured extensively in Zappa's *Baby Snakes* (1979), *The Dub Room Special!* (1982), *The Amazing Mr. Bickford* (1987) and *Video From Hell* (1987) videos – and ask him some questions on my behalf.

While doing so, their conversation naturally evolved and Cholmondeley asked a few of his own – making for one heck of an interview.

A few months later, I met Bickford at Zappanale[1] and apologised personally for asking (via Cholmondeley) how hairy his bottom was – a question he justifiably refused to answer.

---

[1] Annual music festival held in Bad Doberan, Germany, featuring various bands performing Zappa music and more.

How did you first meet Zappa and get to work with him?
I was in LA, in early 1973, looking for work... and I just kept going around town, to the animation houses. I showed the stuff to the people who did stuff for *200 Motels*[2] and they put me in touch with Cal Schenkel[3]. Then he arranged for me to meet Frank.

So you were familiar with Frank Zappa's music and his *200 Motels* movie, then?
Yeah.

Were you a big fan, had you seen him play live by then?
Yeah – I saw him play live in 1970.

So that was it? Schenkel introduced you and the rest is history, right? That was it: Frank immediately wanted to work with you?
He called me back a year later. I went back down with him and we started talking about making a movie. I moved down there from Seattle in June 1974 through 1980.

Did he pretty much just let you get on with it, or did he direct any of the claymations used in *Baby Snakes*?
Oh, he directed, um, 1% of it maybe [chuckles]. I was usually working totally alone.

Give us an example of one of your 'blues raps'.
An example of what it sounds like?

Yes.
Well, it's best when I have some people there... coz that gets me hyped up. I'll just give you the opening line [chuckles]. It goes like... well, you know, you have to act a little if you're gonna sing [laughing - drops his voice into semi-faux blues-guy vocals]: "Lemme tell you a li'l story about a place called Monster Road. Now you might think, there couldn't be a road named that. Well, the road was named for the people who originally lived there. They were the monsters, but that's another story. This story is about the road and about all the other weird stuff that goes on there." So, that's the opening line.

Well that's great!! We'll have to do one with some music. Maybe I'll

---

[2] Murakami-Wolf provided the animated scenes in Zappa's 1971 film.

[3] Artist who collaborated with Zappa on many of his best-known album covers.

dig up the tape from when you performed with Project Object in Seattle.[4] Do you have a favourite spoon?
Um... what's that for?

Well, I'm not sure... that's a deep reference! Maybe he's talking about that guy from Seattle – Spoonman?[5]
Well I met him once! I met him at that concert where they were playing with the Persuasions[6] and the Seattle Symphony. Steve Vai, I think, was there. Yeah, he was there – a bunch of old Zappa members.

[Author's note: That'd be *An Evening Of The Music of Frank Zappa* at the Avery Fisher Hall... but I simply meant do you have a favoured utensil consisting of a small shallow bowl at the end of a handle-type-of-cutlery – or flatware – kind-of-a-thing! But never mind!]

Warren Cuccurullo told Andrew he'd love to get you to animate his song, *Think Kartoonz*.[7] Is there a chance of that?
Well I met him, last time I was in LA. When was that? I think last August. He had some... well he was talking about animating the 9/11 image, or something like that. But it was very vague. He was very hard to, uh, communicate with. He just... he'd keep changing the subject on me [laughs]. Even though I knew what he wanted. He would just... and he never got back to me! Sometimes, someone else has to make the first step [laughs]!

Well, yeah! I hope that happens. I love Warren – his music and as an artist. I've met him a couple of times and I'm actually probably real interested in some of his 9/11 thoughts. But he's interesting, sometimes when you're trying to communicate with him! So, in other words, you would do it? But he's just gotta get in touch and kinda make things happen, huh?
Well, he's gotta want it. I mean, he's gotta want it bad! He's gonna want to get me interested. Coz what I do...if I'm gonna do anything, I want

---

4 This blues rap is one of the special features (titled *Seattle Rainbow - Halloween* 2003) on Bickford's *Cas'l'* DVD (2015)

5 Artis The Spoonman, an American street performer, who made a couple of guest appearances on stage with Zappa in 1981 and provides an uncredited spoon performance on Zappa's *Civilization Phaze III* album (1994).

6 An a cappella group that began singing together in Brooklyn in the mid-1960s. Zappa flew them to LA to record their eponymous debut album in 1970. The following year, they were the opening act for The Mothers and can be heard on the posthumous Zappa album, *Carnegie Hall* (2011). A cover of Zappa's *Love Of My Life* by The Persuasions' former lead vocalist, Jerry Lawson, appeared on the download-only *AAAFNRAAAAAM Birthday Bundle 21 Dec. 2011* album.

7 From Cuccurullo's album *Playing In Tongues* (2009).

to do it, I want to make something interesting, but good! It takes a hell of a lot of commitment. I don't just want to fiddle around. I want to have some kind of plan.

I'm just frustrated as hell. I'm working on my own stuff, coz it's all I can do. I can barely do that, coz it just takes so much organisation to get the right images and everything. But I'm going ahead with it and I'm gonna keep doing this... gonna keep doing my own projects until someone comes along who feels like gettin' serious.

Do you get a lot of requests like that – where people ask you about doing some animation and then they don't follow up?
Not a lot, because I'm not in the mainstream. But I get requests sometimes from these crackpots... and people who are sincere, but they overvalue their own product, ya know? They think their story or their music is really hot, when it's dog crap! They want my animation, but they're offering peanuts.

But you're not saying Warren's a crackpot, right?
No – he's got money!

And you like his music?
Yeah.

What do you think of *Wild Strawberries*?[8]
It was a movie... oh , look, they mentioned that in the documentary *Monster Road*. Or I must have mentioned the movie. It was something my dad liked. We were just talking about my dad a lot in the documentary and so that's where that came from. *Wild Strawberries* wasn't one of my favourite movies... I didn't understand it very good [laughs]. But it was one of my dad's favourites.

Do you think Bill Gates will ever help finance a war movie for you?
What kind of war movie?

I guess Andrew means one that you dramatise... with your animation.
It's up to Bill Gates. I have no influence.

Have you ever met Bill Gates?
No. I think Paul Allen[9] would be more accessible. But even then, you'd

---

8 Swedish film, written and directed by Ingmar Bergman (1957).

9 Co-founder of Microsoft with Gates.

have to go through all kinds of stuff. I've heard Paul Allen has these five rules when you go to talk with him: you can't look him in the eye; you can't shake hands with him; you can't ask him questions – he'll do the asking. Or – if you're talking about what you're doing , if you say 'Now I've got an idea for this', you don't go ahead and tell him the idea – you wait for him to say 'Okay, tell me the idea'. Then you get to tell it. He's gotta have these things set up – probably coz he gets hit by every kind of crackpot. Even rich crackpots! [laughs]. He's gotta have that filter to get down to business.

I would go for Steven Jobs. His company seems more supportive of art and artists. What are you working on right now? You've got proposals out... you're trying to get grants... getting your work out to Disney and others. Does that describe what you're working on right now? Can you add to that?
Well, that's about it. Doing illustrations, mainly. Then trying to back 'em up with some written descriptions of the scenes. I'm just getting the flavour of the exotic places in this pirate story [laughs] and trying to make it as ethnic as possible.

Right now you do have some real ethnic pirates... you've got these Somali guys.
Yeah! I've got some drawings of them.

Are you gonna throw in any Irish/Scottish ethnicity – the 'classic pirates'?
Well, yeah! Those guys come back from the past. But there's all these modern day pirates as well.

Sure! But you've got the classic, the *Pirates Of The Caribbean* type-guys – the Johnny Depp model, though they made him a lot nicer than most pirates act!
Yep – that period.

These illustrations you're doing – are they line drawings? Paintings? Sketches?
Mostly line drawings. But I'm colouring a few of them... and that's where the time... I mean, that's where the labour comes in. Well, or just simple line drawings or coloured stuff... it's just, equally, you know, time consuming.

Interview conducted in 2009.

JIMMY CARL BLACK

In the mid 1960s, Jimmy Carl Black was drumming for the Soul Giants, alongside vocalist Ray Collins and Roy Estrada on bass. When guitarist Ray Hunt quit, Collins contacted his old friend from Pal Studios (Zappa), who took over the band and renamed them the Mothers – promising them fame and fortune.

He achieved the former as 'the Indian of the group' who pops up throughout the *We're Only In It For The Money* album (1968).

Black plays on all of the 'original' Mothers albums recorded in the 1960s, appears in the movie *200 Motels* (1971) and can be heard on the posthumous live release *Road Tapes, Venue #1* (2012).

When Zappa split the original Mothers up in 1969, Black went on to form Geronimo Black and, later, the Grandmothers. Both would feature a number of former Zappa sidemen.

As 'Indian Ink', Black was the second drummer in the short-lived Magic Band that Captain Beefheart put together for his Knebworth Festival (UK) and Roxy (US) shows in July 1975.

In 1993, Black hooked up with Liverpool's Muffin Men, with whom he would tour for the rest of his days, playing Zappa, Beefheart and more.

I first met Black in October 1993, when the Jack & Jim Show (Black with Eugene Chadbourne on guitar, banjo and umbrella) played The Swan pub opposite Fulham Broadway underground station in London. He let me buy him a drink or two (yeah, drinking beer with one of the idols of my youth near the home of my favourite football team – nirvana).

A few months later, the Grandmothers played Dingwalls near Camden Lock. So there's me sat in the middle of this darkened room when up pops Jimmy – singles me out, comes over, says, "Hi Andy, how are ya?", put his arm around me... how special did that make me feel?

And thus started our friendship.

I had regular contact with Black via email and saw him whenever he toured the UK – including when the Grandmothers played the London Astoria on 13 March 1998.

I thought it would be nice to 'illustrate' a review I was writing for the resultant album, *Eating The Astoria* (2000), with a few quotes from the boys in the band. Black responded by saying, "Why don't you do an interview with me via email?" In for a penny and all that. I quickly tossed off... some questions and here is the result of the first of three interviews I would conduct with Black.

What sort of music were the Soul Giants playing prior to becoming The Mothers?

The Soul Giants were mainly an R&B band but we played a few current hits because we were playing in bars mostly. We did do a few songs by Frank. You know we had Ray Collins as the lead singer and he is one of the best R&B singers around, in my opinion.

Do you have any specific recollections of recording with the GTOs?[1]

I played the drums on most of that LP along with Roy on bass. I do remember that about that time, the Jeff Beck Band was hanging around at Frank's house and I believe that a couple of the members played on a little of the record. Ronnie Wood comes to mind.

Was there much animosity towards Frank when he disbanded the Mothers in 1969 – as you and Don returned on a number of subsequent occasions[2], I assume not from you until the lawsuit in 1985?[3]

Yes, there was some heavy feelings from the band at the time. It was not the disbandment but the way it was done. I called Frank on the phone for something or another and after about ten minutes of talking, he said that he had decided to break up the band and our salaries (they were

---

[1] The GTOs were an acapella girl group from the Los Angeles area. Their only album, *Permanent Damage* (1969), was produced by Zappa.

[2] Both Black and Preston appeared in Zappa's film, *200 Motels*. Preston would continue to perform live with Zappa on and off until 1974, while Black later contributed to the *You Are What You Is* album (1981).

[3] In his posthumous memoir *For Mother's Sake: The Memoirs And Recollections Of Jimmy Carl Black 1938-2008* (Inkanish Publications, 2013), Black talks of how he and other members of the original Mothers tried to ensure they were paid artist royalties when Zappa re-issued their early recordings on CD in the mid-1980s: "The whole lawsuit thing had started in 1985 but it didn't go to arbitration until 1990. Originally, the lawsuit was a Class Action Suit for $150,000. As the years went by, people started to drop out. I can't remember exactly how many of us there were at the beginning but at the end there was myself, Don, Bunk, Art Tripp, Ray Collins and Jim Fielder...that lawsuit cost Frank quite a bit of money."

really draws, since according to the contract at the time, we all were pardners) had stopped as of last week. It would have been better if he would have given a date, say like six months and then we all could have made better plans.

I felt the same way as the rest of the guys at the time, but didn't hold a grudge against Frank like some of the guys did. I did the later things with Frank, not for him but for myself.

Martin Lickert seems to think you enjoy a drink or three. He told me about some of Keith Moon's[4] antics during the recording of *200 Motels* – any stories from that period that you can recall and would care to relate?

He's right, I used to enjoy a drink or a hundred, but I don't drink anymore at all. I wouldn't be able to do all this touring if I was still tilting like I used to. So it's better that I don't drink at all now. I had a birthday while we were filming *200 Motels* and Ringo gave me a huge birthday cake and a couple of bottles and the whole crew enjoyed that party. Me, being as big of a Beatle fan as I was and still am, that was the best thing that ever happened to me. Ringo is a very nice man. Moony was crazy, but a great fellow to party with – and I did, mucho!

Do you recall your 'guest appearance' on the *Bongo Fury* tour in El Paso?[5] What were relations like between Zappa and Van Vliet at that time?

I sure do. I sang *So Fine* and *Lonely, Lonely, Nights* and had a great time with the guys. I didn't know all the guys in the band, but Denny Walley and George Duke[6] I knew from before. By the time Frank and Don got to El Paso, they weren't even speaking to each other anymore. Seems that Don was drawing too many pictures of Frank in his drawing book and Frank didn't like it. I saw some of the pictures and I thought they were pretty funny. Frank didn't. That is where Beefheart hired me to join the Magic Band.

How did the *Harder Than Your Husband*[7] session come about?

Denny Walley called me in 1980 and said Frank wanted me to call him.

---

4 As well as Starr, the film also featured the former Who drummer as a 'hot nun'.

5 Black appeared as a special guest on the Zappa/Beefheart/Mothers tour at the County Coliseum, El Paso, Texas on 23rd May 1975.

6 Keyboard player and singer, with Zappa between 1970 and 1975.

7 From Zappa's *You Are What You Is* album.

So I did and he asked me if I would like to come to California and record a new country type song that was going to be on his new album. I was living in Albuquerque, New Mexico at the time and said that I would like that very much.

So the next day there was an airplane ticket waiting for me at the airport and off I went. Frank put me up in a very nice hotel and then had his driver pick me up in his Rolls Royce and took me to his new studio in his house. I sang the song and he asked if I could stay a few more days so I could do some more tracks on the album and I did. I think I wound up recording four or five more songs on that album. It is one of my favourite albums of Frank's.

Any plans to release the live tracks from *Looking Up Granny's Dress*, from the Grandmothers European tour of 1981 on CD[8]?
No!

I have a tape of Zappa allegedly teaching Geronimo Black a tune called *Falling In Love Is A Stupid Habit*. He subsequently denied it was him – in which case, are you gonna record it as you won't have to pay any royalties to Gail!?
He wasn't teaching Geronimo Black that tune but he was playing it for me. He said that I could have the song and we even discussed the instruments that would sound good on it. It was Frank playing the piano in his studio with Andy Cahan[9] and me there. The year was 1981 and I was in California rehearsing for the first Grandmothers tour of Europe. I don't even have a copy of that tape anymore, but if you want to make me a copy, I might do the song. Although if I did it, I'll bet Gail would remember the song and probably not let me release it.

You told me that your son was a better-than-Dweezil guitarist. Is he pursuing a musical career?
I should have said as-good-as-Dweezil guitarist and I still think he is. Yes, he is pursuing a musical career with his two brothers and possibly his dad as vocalist. We have been writing songs for a CD that I've personally wanted to do for a long time. He wants to use the name Geronimo Black and I think he should since that is his name[10]. His

---

[8] As well as live versions of a number of Zappa songs, this 1982 album also included a version of the Ray Collins' song *Deseri* recorded at Pal Studios with Zappa on drums, issued without his permission. A CD reissue of the live material would almost certainly have resulted in legal action from the Zappa family.

[9] Keyboard player and member of Geronimo Black and the Grandmothers.

[10] Geronimo Black performed at the 20th Zappanale in the year after his father passed away (2009).

brother, Darrell, is on drums and his other brother, Gary, is on percussion and trumpet. They could also be called The Brothers of Intention.

Talking of guitarists, what led to Roland St. Germain's[11] departure from the Grandmothers?

He didn't like Don Preston because of personal reasons. Egos get in the way of music a lot of the time, if you know what I mean. I'm really glad he left because it brought us Sandro Oliva[12], which is much more in the style of what the Grannies are doing.

I think it would be good for the Grandmothers to play more original material – certainly stuff like *The Great White Buffalo* always gets a good reception – but you obviously can't abandon Frank's music completely. What about including a little more Beefheart, as you do with the Muffin Men?

In live performances we will always play a certain amount of Zappa music, but we don't want to record any more of it. After all, Frank did it pretty well, don't you think? I have a new Indian song called *Chief Old Fox* that I just wrote with my old writing pardner, Dawayne Bailey,[13] who co-wrote *The Great White Buffalo* with me and it sounds really good. We will record that one for sure. We might do some Beefheart music in the future; as you know, I really like doing and can do.

Do you know how the Captain is these days?

I really don't know how he is doing since I live here in Europe and don't go to the States very often. But when the Grannies tour of the States in August, September and October starts, maybe I'll find out and then I will be able to say for sure.[14]

What are Roy Estrada, Motorhead Sherwood and Ray Collins up to these days?

I don't know what Roy or Ray are doing or even exactly where they are,

---

[11] The Grandmothers' guitarist and musical director, circa 1993.

[12] Italian guitarist and composer who performed with The Grandmothers from 1994 to 2000.

[13] American guitarist who has toured and recorded with Bob Seger & the Silver Bullet Band and Chicago.

[14] Beefheart retired from making music in 1982 to concentrate on his art and drawings. He became increasingly reclusive and, by the early 1990s, was reportedly using a wheelchair as a result of contracting multiple sclerosis. He passed away on 17th December 2010 following complications with the disease.

but I'm in touch with Motorhead – and also Billy Mundi.[15] Motor lives in San Jose, California and Billy lives in Lake Oroville, California. Neither one is playing music now. I know Roy isn't anymore and hasn't in almost twenty years. Too bad, since he was a great bass player. Maybe we can get him to at least sing with us when we play in LA later this summer - if Bunk can find him.

I didn't realise that Steve B. Roney was also former Muffin Men drummer Stefano Baldasseroni. Does your partnership signal the end of JCB's career as a drummer?

Yes, Steve played the drums on *God Shave the Queen* CD with the Muffins in 1998 and did a great job on it, in my opinion. He is one of the best drummers I have ever heard. I have a lot of respect for him, even though he's just a kid. No, it doesn't signal the end of my drumming career, but I really don't want to do it much anymore. I still play with my blues band and take jobs if someone needs a drummer. I'm just tired of carrying them around and having to set up and tear down after the gig. Singing is much more satisfying to me and I really enjoy it.

Tell me about your upcoming live album with Sandro: *Junk Food*.

I don't know anything about that. We did a video about four years ago called *Junk Food*, but I don't know if Sandro recorded it or not. Maybe[16].

What are your plans for the future - any more UK dates with Jack, the Muffins or the Grannies?

I'm going to America on tour with the Grandmothers in August, September and October for a 60-city tour of the whole USA. Don Preston and Bunk Gardner will join Sandro, Steve, Ener Bladezipper[17] and me for that tour. I am going to do a tour next year with Eugene Chadbourne, but I don't know if it will be in England. I'm coming to the UK with the Muffins at the beginning of November before we go to Germany. The Grandmothers are planning a spring tour, but I'm not

---

[15] Joined The Mothers as second drummer alongside Black in 1966, later joining the 'supergroup' Rhinoceros. He briefly joined The Grandmothers in 2001 (effectively replacing Black). Mundi passed away on 29th March 2014 due to complications from diabetes, which had earlier caused him to have one of his legs amputated just below the knee.

[16] Sandro Oliva issued the album as a 'private limited edition' in 2003. It was recorded in Rome in 1996 by Oliva and his band The Blue Pampurio's, with Black appearing as a special guest.

[17] Dutch bass player, who performed with The Grandmothers from 1988 to 2000.

sure if it will include the UK. Maybe. I will do a tour with the Farrell/Black Band right after I return from the States.

Once again, if you're interested in what I'm up to, keep reading my website. And please, if you're interested in new CDs, I have them for sale in my little online mail order record shop. I want to thank Andy for letting me do this interview. Remember: Music makes the world go round, especially creative Music.

Interview conducted on Friday 23rd June 2000.

By 2003, Black was a regular feature of Muffin Men shows around Europe. The band decided to celebrate their thirteenth year of operation and were invited to play two sets at the annual Zappa Festival, Zappanale (one with Napoleon Murphy Brock and Ike Willis; one with Black). This prompted another brief chat with Black. Main Muffin man Roddie Gilliard was also on hand to join in the fun.

Ever had any close encounters with a Beatle?
As you know, I did the movie with Ringo Starr and it was a very heartening experience for me – being a huge Beatles fan. I really enjoyed spending the time I got with Ringo. He even gave me a birthday celebration on 1st February 1971 at Pinewood Studios, where the movie was filmed.

Roddie, the Muffin Men have performed with Jimmy, Ike Willis, Don Preston & Bunk Gardner – and it looks like you might get something on with Napoleon Murphy Brock. Any other Zappa alumni you'd like to play with?
Roddie Gilliard: The GTOs, Sal Marquez[18], Sugarcane Harris[19] or Burt Ward[20].

---

18 Trumpeter who recorded and toured with Zappa from 1972-73.

19 Violinist who performed with Zappa from 1969-70.

20 American television actor best known for his portrayal of Robin in the TV series *Batman* (1966-68). In 1966, Ward released a single for MGM Records called *Boy Wonder, I Love You*. It featured Ward reading fan letters over the musical backing of The Mothers of Invention, arranged and conducted by Zappa.

What has Inkanish Records[21] achieved in its first year of operation? And what do you hope it'll achieve in the future?
We've released three officially and about ten unofficially. And I'm still broke – I guess I don't have any 'commercial potential'. I will keep releasing things that I think should be out there for real music lovers.

I hope to release my sons' new CD, entitled *Geronimo Black*, when they finish it; that should be in the summer. I still want to do a new solo CD with the boys in the Muffins sometime this year as soon as I have the money together. It's really hard to do much when you don't have the money available for the project. Anyway, onward and upward!

How's your autobiography coming along[22]?
Talk to Rod. I know nothing.

Roddie, for fuck's sake – when're you gonna finish Jimmy's book!?
Roddie Gilliard: Oooh, you bitch. Suffice to say, there have been some developments in the last months, but graphic designers keep getting side tracked – too busy doing CD sleeves and building model railways.

Interview conducted on Sunday 2nd March 2003.

When I saw the Muffin Men at The Boardwalk in Sheffield in May 2008, Black and I had agreed it was about time we conducted another interview.

I last spoke with Black on the phone in August 2008, as he was preparing to leave hospital having been told he had inoperable lung cancer. He said he actually felt okay, but had been told that he wasn't. It seemed that it was just the chemo he'd been undergoing these past few years for his leukaemia that made him "feel like shit".

With my late friend Dave McMann, I helped organise a concert to raise funds for his mounting medical bills, which he was of course happy about. Sadly, he passed away just over a week before the concert

---

[21] In 2001, Black launched his own record label. Black's birth name was James Inkanish.

[22] Black had been talking about writing and publishing his autobiography for a number of years. He was still working on it when he succumbed to cancer in 2008. His last wish was that his book be finished, and it was finally published in 2013 as *For Mother's Sake: The Memoirs And Recollections Of Jimmy Carl Black 1938-2008* (Inkanish Publications). The first part of the book (the "Memoirs") was transcribed and edited by Gilliard from audio recordings made when Black was on the road with the Muffin Men, and covered the period up to 1994.

took place at the Bridge House II in London's Canning Town on 9 November 2008.

This interview was completed before our last telephone conversation. Much of it was used in the 'Recollections' part of Black's posthumous autobiography.

You've been battling leukaemia for a few years now?

I have had leukaemia since 2001 and have gone through five months of chemotherapy and this April I started and completed ten weeks of radiation therapy, which was a drag. The therapy wasn't bad; it was the after effects that weren't good. I am still reeling from that shit. Three weeks ago the doctors found a pretty big tumour on my right lung that looked like cancer to them. I went into the hospital two weeks ago and had three biopsies done on that tumour. All three tests came back saying that the tumour wasn't cancerous. The doctors can't believe it. On the 20th of this month, I am going back into the hospital and having an operation to either remove it or something. I have to say that this has not been a good year so far for me health wise. I hope it gets better from now on.

I'll drink to that. Do you plan to record the song you wrote late last year while undergoing chemotherapy?

I do plan to record the song and in fact the guy I have been playing with in Italy – his name is Bruno Marini[23] – has got the song now and is coming up with an arrangement for it. The music to the song was written by my old friend Tom Leavey. He was the bass player in the original Geronimo Black band and I think it will be a great song.

Talking about Geronimo Black, what are your memories of your first encounter with Denny Walley?

Denny is one of my all-time greatest friends. He was Tom Leavey's brother-in-law. The boys were married to a couple of sisters from Coney Island. I still think that Geronimo Black was a great band and always will. I am very proud of the music we played and of the musicians that played it.

The Zappanale this year should be very good with Denny being there. By the way, he just called me yesterday and wished me good tidings with my operation.

---

23 Black had previously recorded the album *Freedom Jazz Dance* (2008) with sax and Hammond organ player Marini.

You've just released a CD called *Freedom Jazz Dance* on the Italian Azzurra Music label with Bruno – how did that come about?

Bruno called me up last year and asked me to come to Verona, Italy and go into the studio and record this CD. I think that the CD came out very interesting since I have never done anything like it before. I really enjoyed playing with all the players that participated on the recording. Valentina Black – no relation – is a wonderful and absolutely beautiful woman and singer. Bruno arranged all the horn parts, which sound great and he also played flute and Hammond organ.

Tell me about the recording of *Strange News From Mars*.[24]

Strange News From Mars is a very interesting recording by Jon Larsen, who is a very talented guitarist and songwriter. I went to Oslo, Norway and went into the studio the second morning and did my talking parts and a little percussion on a few tracks. He then took the tracks to Los Angeles and got Arthur Barrow, Tommy Mars and Bruce Fowler to play on most of the songs. I really like the sound of the recording, as it sounds very Zappa-like.

I have since then gone back to Oslo and done another recording with Jon and the CD is called *The Jimmy Carl Black Story*[25]. It is due out anytime. I basically went into the studio one night and told my life story. It took me about one and a half hours to do it. He then used some blues players from Oslo and also some of the guys from the *Strange News* CD for the background music.

Of course, you played with Tommy Mars in Sardinia in 1995 – how did that happen?

Well, I got a call from Sandro Oliva saying that this promoter was interested in doing a night of Zappa music and would me and Ener Bladezipper be interested in playing with Sandro and Tommy Mars. I had met Tommy on a number of occasions through Denny Walley and Frank. I asked Ener, who was living in Amsterdam, if he wanted to do it and he said okay. The money was great so we did it.

As it turned out we had only two hours to rehearse and one of the songs we pulled off was *Brown Shoes Don't Make It*[26], the *Tinsel Town Rebellion* version because Tommy knew that way. All in all, it was a great concert and a great time in Sardinia.

---

[24] Album by Jon Larsen, released on Zonic Entertainment in 2007.

[25] Album by Jon Larsen, released on Zonic Entertainment in 2008.

[26] Originally on The Mothers' album *Absolutely Free* (1967), but re-recorded live by Zappa in 1979 for his *Tinsel Town Rebellion* album (1981).

How did your collaboration with Ella Guru[27] – on *The First Album*, a really nice, dreamy record – come about?

Those guys are big fans of The Muffin Men and always came to our gigs in Liverpool. I met John[28] at The Cavern when we played there and he asked me if I would be willing to sing on two tracks of their new CD. I said sure and I did. It is a very nice CD, although I wasn't expecting that type of recordings with the name Ella Guru. I thought that they played more like Captain Beefheart, but that wasn't the case.

And some of their song titles are a little misleading, too![29] Tell me about the Black Brown Stone Trio.

When I played that festival with Dr. Chadbourne in France in 2006, I met and played with Steven De Bruyn who is a harp player from Belgium. He later asked me if I was interested in coming to Brussels and recording a CD with him and a guy named Jos Steen in the Belgium National Radio studio. I said sure, so I went and recorded with them. The pay was good and they paid all my expenses from Germany. It is a very interesting recording that fans would enjoy.

As a Grandmother, how do you feel about the current line-up[30]?

You mean an original Grandmother. I really don't think about it too much. I think that it was wrong to fire Bunk the way that happened as he was also there from the beginning. I never have heard any music from this particular line-up so I can't say. I am sure that they play good, as Napi, Don and Roy are strong players. I don't know the other two guys.

What were the circumstances of Bunk's dismissal?

I really don't know since I was in Europe and they were in California. What Bunk told me was, he asked Roy something like "What about loyalty?" and Roy said and I quote Bunk, "Then was then and now is

---

27 Liverpool band who had Black provide guest vocals on their debut album in 2004.

28 The band's singer and guitarist, John Yates.

29 The album includes tracks called *This Is My Rock And Roll* and *My Favourite Punk Tune*.

30 After a lengthy tour of North America in 2000 - with Preston and Oliva both vying to be the band's musical director - The Grandmothers split in two: Preston initially formed a short-lived US version featuring Billy Mundi, before settling on a line-up that included Gardner, Estrada and Napoleon Murphy Brock; Black attempted to form an 'EU Grandmothers' with the remaining band members plus Zappa's sister Candy Zappa. In 2002, both bands planned to tour Europe which, according to Oliva, caused "a lot of confusion with promoters and venues that were already dealing with our tour." So the EU version called it a day. The Grandmothers West (with Preston, Gardner, Brock, Estrada and special guest Bob Harris) headlined Zappanale 13. Black did briefly guest with them, but was incensed at being sidelined by Preston, with whom he never worked again.

now." Unquote. In my opinion, that is pretty cold, especially saying that to one of the founding members of The Grandmothers. Roy certainly is not a founding member. The founding members of the Grandmothers are: Don Preston, Bunk Gardner and Jimmy Carl Black.

Of course, this is all hearsay to me since I wasn't there. I will say that I am very happy to be playing with The Muffin Men. I get my fill of Zappa music with them and they also do some of my songs. But then again, so did the Grannies.

What's your take on the *We're Only In It For The Money* remix? Why did Frank say the original drum and bass tracks were unusable and then was able to remaster and reissue it later?
I don't know why Frank said that the drum and bass tracks were ruined. He didn't remaster and reissue the correct version of the album. That was Rykodisc after they bought the catalogue from the ZFT. That is the version that the fans wanted and finally got. Unfortunately, it was not the case on *Cruising With Ruben And The Jets*[31]. I wished it were.

Those two guys that replaced the tracks on those albums got $10,000 each for doing that. We, being the Mothers Of Invention, on the other hand, got paid $300 dollars for doing both albums in 1967 while we were living in New York.

Dr Chadbourne mentioned a story that *We're Only In It For The Money* didn't actually feature the Mothers, but a bunch of session musicians. What was that all about?
That wasn't a story that he said. That was from an e-mail he got from Gail about us trying to release *Mom And Dad*[32] and *Willie The Pimp*[33] on the CD, *Hearing Is Believing*[34]. She told the guy from Boxholder Records that I wasn't even on *Mom And Dad* and in fact wasn't even on *We're Only In It For The Money* album. The good Doctor then asked her if Frank had hired Rich Little (a famous comedian, who does impressions) to do "Hi, boys and girls - I'm Jimmy Carl Black and I'm the Indian of the group". Well, that stopped her in her tracks.

It is ironic that she could say something like that when she wasn't

---

[31] In 2010, the ZFT reissued the original version of *Cruising With Ruben & The Jets* with Black and Estrada's parts intact on CD as part of the *Greasy Love Songs* album.

[32] From The Mothers' *We're Only In It For The Money* album (1968).

[33] From Zappa's *Hot Rats* album (1969).

[34] Album by The Jack & Jim Show, released in 2007.

even allowed to come down to the studio. I was there almost at every one of the sessions that happened at Mayfair Studios[35].

Have you heard the *MOFO*[36] CD set? Any surprises for you?

I have heard the CD as Roddie Gilliard gave it to me as a birthday present on my 69th birthday. I have to say that I really enjoyed the whole CD. It is great to hear all the tracks in various forms and then the whole thing together.

What about *Joe's Corsage*[37]?

I can't really comment on the *Joe's Corsage* since I have never heard it and didn't even know it was out.

Okay. How was Japan?

Japan was a wonderful trip for me, although I wasn't feeling very well. I had just finished ten weeks of radiation treatments about three weeks before I left for Japan. Actually, that was way too soon for me to go. Man, that shit really knocked the piss out of me. Here it is in August and I am still not completely recovered from that shit. Anyway, we were in Tokyo for eight days and played three gigs.

The first gig was a Captain Beefheart night and so we played mostly Beefheart songs. The second gig was a Zappa night, so we played mostly Zappa songs - and, by the way, we made sure that JASRAC the equivalent to the GEMA (collecting society for collective rights management) in Japan paid for the songs. The fourth gig was in Nagoya and we got an excellent recording of that show which is now out on CD. I really enjoyed the food over there and was surprised to find so many Mothers Of Invention fans at every show. It really made me feel good to know that I am still loved for the music that I was a part of.

The tour was a short one, which I was grateful for since the way I was feeling and my best friend, Eugene Chadbourne, was patient with me and did take pretty damn good care of me. I would like to go back sometime but, as you know, I don't know how much more time I have with all the shit medically going on with me. I hope a few years. When

---

35 At Zappa.com, Gail Zappa wrote the following note about 'the Mothers today', listed on the original sleeve of the *We're Only In It For The Money* album in 1968: "This is different than the actual players on this record - not unlike all the other people pictured on the album art who did not perform hereon. The actual players are Frank Zappa, Ian Underwood, Roy Estrada, Billy Mundi. Fuck off. Word."

36 A four disc *Making Of Freak Out* set released by the ZFT in 2006.

37 A compilation album issued by the ZFT in 2004 featuring early demos recorded by the Mothers.

I pass on, maybe people will start buying my music and that way help my sweet little wife through hard times. Greg Russo[38] is doing his part, thank God.

Yes, Greg's doing a marvellous job remastering and issuing some of your older material. What's next from Crossfire Publications?
While I was in Italy, this last time before I went into the hospital, I was in the studio and did my vocal parts to *Stolen Cadillac*[39] that will feature Candy Zappa also singing the other part of the song. That is one of the new songs on the next CD which, I think, is going to be called *If We Were Only Living In California*[40]. You can confirm that with Greg. It sounds to me like a great CD.

You know that I really let him have a free reign on what he puts on these CD. He always sends me the product for approval first but I really trust him and really enjoy working with him. He is a very dear friend of mine.

So, what of the *For Mother's Sake* book?!
I am working slowly now on the book as I only have two chapters left to do. I am going to finish it very soon as I don't know what will happen to me health wise in the near future.

How do you come up with the songs you cover in the Jack & Jim Show – DMX's *One More Road To Cross*, for example?
Jack usually just starts playing a new song and I pick up on it within a couple of bars and we have a new song in the set. We will then try to play it on every gig of that particular tour until it is the way he likes it. We have a new CD out called *Think 69*[41] from our very successful tour of the USA last year that has a new song called *Mr. Spooky*. That song came from my little granddaughter, Lisa Maria, here in Germany. She's five years old and that is what she calls me, Mr. Spooky. It is a very funny song and the people love it.

---

38 Author of the book, *Cosmik Debris: The Collected History & Improvisations Of Frank Zappa* and proprietor of Crossfire Publications, who have issued a large number of Black's recordings.

39 A 'Western swing' penned by Nigey Lennon. Black and Candy Zappa performed the song live at Zappanale in 2002, and finally got around to recording it six years later.

40 Issued as a download-only album by Crossfire Publications in August 2008.

41 Another album by The Jack & Jim Show released in 2007.

Will we see you at "that quote-unquote festival slash event slash what the fuck"[42] in Bad Doberan again?

Not this year, but the festival wants me to play possibly next year since it is the 20th anniversary of the festival and I would love to do that. I really would like to do it with the Jack And Jim Show.

What are your feelings about the Zappa Family Trust's recent 'aggressive action' against tribute bands?

Zappa Plays Zappa says that Dweezil is the real thing but in reality Frank is the real thing and everything else is tribute bands, period.

Yes, I have to admit it's all getting a bit silly: the ZFT bangs on about protecting 'the intent of the composer' on the one hand, then on the other licenses Frank's unreleased music to producers and artists; I can't believe he ever intended to wind up on Gene Simmons' Asshole[43].

How's Bunk these days – and what's he up to?

The last time I talked to him, which was about a month ago, he was doing very good. He's still teaching and he also has beaten prostate cancer and doing well. I would really love to play with him again, probably for the last time in this life, one more time. I wish it could be at the Zappanale 20. He would fit in perfectly with the Jack And Jim Show band since he has played with Chadbourne before.

A video clip by John Cline of you performing with Frank in Albuquerque in October 1980 has just appeared online – can you tell me a little about that?

John Cline is a good friend of mine from Albuquerque. I was living up there at the time I went to California and Frank's studio and recorded *Harder Than Your Husband*.

When they did the tour, one of the first gigs was in Albuquerque at the university. Frank asked me if I would sing the song live and, of course, I said I would. John then asked Frank for permission to videotape the song and to my surprise, Frank gave him permission. It really is a good video. I had never seen it until it appeared on YouTube[44].

---

[42] Zappanale, as described to *Der Spiegel* by Gail Zappa.

[43] The second solo album by the Kiss front man, released in 2004. It featured an extract from an unreleased live performance by Zappa licensed via the ZFT's short-lived Extraordinary Teamwork project. Simmon's incorporated Zappa's music into a song he titled *Black Tongue*, which also featured newly recorded background vocals by Gail, Moon, Dweezil and Ahmet Zappa.

[44] Cline posted his video at https://youtu.be/zatefH0-pjQ

Did your sons ever release their planned Geronimo Black CD?

Not yet, but I hope so soon. It is sort of out on my label, Inkanish Records, but not as an official release since I have no money to release it properly. They are going back into the studio soon and doing another CD that I hope will be released since Geronimo is writing a lot of new songs now. They are playing a lot at the moment. They play almost every weekend in El Paso.

How did you select the songs you covered on *How Blue Can You Get?*[45]

We just got together before the recording started and ask each other what songs each wanted to do and we went in and recorded them. We didn't want to do any original songs on this CD. Just songs we liked.

I understand you're about to be interviewed for a new documentary on *FZ & Mothers Of Invention in the 60s*, being produced by Chrome Dreams[46]?

Yeah, the boys are coming this afternoon to my house where we will do the interview. I didn't know it was being produced by Chrome Dreams. I thought it was Prism Films, although they are probably working together. It should be interesting since it looks like I am the only original Mother to be interviewed.

Do you know what prompted Walter Becker's[47] lobbying of the Rock and Roll Hall of Fame to get you included as a founding member of the Mothers?

I have no idea why except that I am very grateful to him. I am a big fan of Steely Dan. I wished all of the Mothers of Invention could and should have been inducted at the time Frank was inducted. I am sure that Gail was very happy that we weren't and, in fact, I wouldn't be surprised if she had something to do with it.

Any thoughts on the passing of the former Senator from North Carolina, Jesse Helms[48]?

One less member of the famed KKK gone. What else is there to say

---

[45] An album by The Jimmy Carl Black Band released in 2007, featuring Mick Pini on guitar and Roddie Gilliard on bass. It was a collection of songs recorded by Bob Dylan, Steve Miller, The Band, Lou Reed, Freddie & Albert King and more.

[46] The DVD *Frank Zappa And The Mothers Of Invention In The 1960s* was issued by Chrome Dreams in 2008 and included the last filmed interview with Black. It also included new interviews with fellow Mothers Don Preston, Bunk Gardner and Art Tripp.

[47] Co-founder, guitarist, bassist and co-songwriter of Steely Dan.

[48] A leader in the US conservative movement, described by the *Washington Post* as a "White Racist".

about that elixir?

Finally, can we talk a little bit more about your private life – how did you meet Moni?
I was playing a gig in Traunstein, Germany, with The Farrell/Black Blues Band and she was in the front row just staring at me. At the time, I didn't know just how big of a fan of the Mothers she was. She had been looking at my picture on all those album covers – she has all the original albums – for the last twenty-five years. She was absolutely beautiful and I couldn't believe such a beautiful woman would be interested in an old fart like me – I was fifty-eight, then.

I tried to get to know her after the concert but she didn't speak any English at that time and, of course, I didn't speak any German. So that was the beginning of our relationship. I have to say that eleven months later that year, I married that girl and am the happiest I have ever been in all my life - still. She takes very good care of me and she still loves Zappa music.

She loves going to the Zappanale and hopefully we will go next year. That would be a finale of my career as a guy that was fortunate enough to play in the best band in the world from the 1960s. I really believed that and still do.

Interview conducted on Thursday 7th August 2008.

TERRY BOZZIO

T erry Bozzio was Zappa's drummer from 1975 to 1978. His abilities on the kit so impressed Zappa, that he composed a piece of music for him with so many notes on the manuscript that he called it *The Black Page*.

Bozzio plays on many of the 'classic' late 1970s Zappa albums, appears in the movie *Baby Snakes* (1979) and can be heard on the posthumous lives releases *FZ:OZ* (2002), *Philly '76* (2009) and *Hammersmith Odeon* (2010).

In 1977, Bozzio joined The Brecker Brothers, recording the live album *Heavy Metal Be-Bop*.

After leaving Zappa, he played with Eddie Jobson's band, U.K.

In 1980, he formed the band Missing Persons with his vocalist then-wife, Dale, guitarist Warren Cuccurullo, bassist Patrick O'Hearn and keyboard player Chuck Wild.

Since then he has worked with the likes of Mick Jagger, Jeff Beck, Steve Vai, Dweezil Zappa, as well as recording and touring as a solo artist.

In 2006, Bozzio was one of the 'sternly accomplished special guests' on Dweezil's first Zappa Plays Zappa tour.

Shortly before a REMO sponsored drum Master Class on Sunday 27 September 1992, a slightly jet-lagged Bozzio spoke to an incredibly nervous me backstage at the Grand Theatre, Clapham Junction. Though our discussion was quite brief, Bozzio spoke openly and... er, Frankly.

First of all, how's your pickle?[1]
How's my pickle? It's just fine!

---

[1] A reference to the *Zappa In New York* album (1978), on which Zappa says to Bozzio, "Let go of your pickle!" during the improvised section of the track *Titties & Beer*.

Could you tell me a little bit about how you came to audition for Frank?

Well, basically: I heard from Eddie Henderson[2] – who I was playing with at the time – that George Duke had said that Zappa was looking for someone. Never heard his music. Three days before the audition, I decided to buy a couple of albums – *Live At The Roxy*[3] *(sic)* and *Apostrophe(')*[4]. Didn't sleep for the next three days. Flew myself down to LA. Went to Zappa's warehouse – you know, he had a big huge stage, sound and light equipment I'd never seen before. Most difficult music I'd ever seen spread all over the stage. There were about fifty drummers around. There were two Ludwig Octaplus sets set up. One drummer would set one kit up while the other one would audition. They were going back and forth, dropping like flies. So I thought I'd never get this gig, so I asked some friends if they'd heard about a Weather Report[5] audition, because I heard that they were looking for a drummer and I knew I wasn't gonna get this gig and they said, well Frank's drummer left…

Chester Thompson?[6]

…yeah, to join them. So that made me even more discouraged. But I thought, well I paid the money to come down here, I owe it to myself to try. The one thing I'd noticed was a lot of the drummers were sort of flaunting their chops. I thought the least I could do was go up there and listen and try and play with the guy.

So I did the best I could: sight-reading a very difficult piece, memorising a very difficult piece, jamming with a very odd time signature – like 19 – and then playing a blues shuffle. At the end of that, Frank said "You sound great, I'd like to hear you again – after I hear the rest of these guys." I turned to his road manager, his road manager turns to the twenty or so guys that were hanging around and they're all shaking their heads and the road manager turns around and says, "That's it, nobody else wants to play after Terry." So Frank turns to me and says "Looks like you've got the gig if you want it." So I was completely blown away.

---

2 American jazz trumpet and flugelhorn player, born the same year as Zappa (1940).

3 Zappa's album, *Roxy & Elsewhere* (1974).

4 Zappa's other album released in 1974.

5 American jazz fusion band, led by Austrian-born keyboard player Joe Zawinul and American saxophonist Wayne Shorter.

6 Drummer with Zappa from October 1973 to December 1974.

What had you been doing up until that point?

I'd gone to school; studied jazz and classical music for 2½-3 years. Played a rock show called *Godspell*[7]. Then started to play with all the jazz/Latin guys around San Francisco. I played with two or three guys who'd been with Herbie Hancock's[8] band, Eddie Henderson, Julian Priester[9], Al Jackson[10]. I was in a band called Listen with Andy Narell, the steel drum player. I was in Azteca with Sheila E's[11] father.

Later on you actually worked with Herbie Hancock and Dweezil – on the soundtrack to *Back To The Beach*[12].

Yeah, just on that session.

Is that what led to you playing on Dweezil's second album?[13]

I don't know if that led to it. Dweezil has been around in my life since he was like so high.

It says on the sleeve that you played "at short notice".

Yeah, Gail called me and said Dweezil would love me to play on some tracks on his album and I said "Sure".

Your time with Frank was during the Warner Bros lawsuit. I guess there was lots of rehearsing and experimentation going on – what songs do you particularly remember from that period?

From that period? I remember when Frank went through the lawsuit thing[14], he said he might not be able to pay us. We all said we we're willing to hang for a few months as long as the savings held out in the hopes that things would get better. Frank was really depressed at that time.

It was just me and Patrick O'Hearn and Eddie Jobson. I was gonna be the sort of lead singer and do the stuff that Napoleon did. It was a

---

7 1970s musical inspired by the Gospel of Matthew.

8 American keyboard player, bandleader and composer.

9 American jazz trombone player and composer.

10 American drummer, best known as a founding member of Booker T. & The M.G.'s.

11 American drummer and percussionist whose notable collaborators include Prince.

12 1987 comedy film starring Frankie Avalon and Annette Funicello. Herbie Hancock provided a cover of The Surfaris' instrumental hit (recorded at Pal Studios) *Wipe Out!*, with 'special appearances' by Dweezil and Bozzio. Their version was nominated for the Grammy Award For Best Rock Instrumental Performance, but lost out to Zappa's *Jazz From Hell*.

13 *My Guitar Wants To Kill Your Mama* (1988) features Bozzio on three tracks.

14 Warner Bros had initially refused to issue *Zappa In New York*, so Zappa claimed breach of contract and sued them. When he tried to get other labels to release it, Warners counter-sued.

very strange time, you know. Then he got Ray White – we auditioned lots of singers. I remember doing *Pound For A Brown*, er... oh God, *The Torture Never Stops...*

The *Zoot Allures* album was basically just you two with a few 'guest' musicians, including Captain Beefheart.
Yeah, he was in the first line-up I toured with.

One of the songs I liked from that period was *The Ocean Is The Ultimate Solution*, with you and Patrick O'Hearn.
Yeah, actually what happened was me and Dave Parlato and Frank jammed at the Record Plant for about thirty-five minutes – filled up two reels of tape. Zappa, out of all that material, edited it down to about thirteen minutes. He played it on a really interesting Fender 12-string that had a Barcus Berry in the neck. He had the bottom strings turned to Major 7ths... I think he had every string tuned to a different interval, so it was like a Major 7th then a Minor 7th. The next ones were, you know, a tri-tone Major 3rd and a Minor 3rd. He had the low strings panned left and the high strings panned right and the Barcus Berry panned centre; he had this glass-shattering 12-string sound, it was really unique. So we just jammed.

And then he... Patrick was playing with Joe Henderson at the Lighthouse and I went to see him play one night. He was staying at my house. I brought him home. He had this big bass in the car. He didn't want to leave it in the car, so he brought it inside. That was how Patrick auditioned for Frank. You know, Frank said, "You play that thing?" Patrick said "Yeah!" He goes "Whip it out" And he put him in the studio. Patrick had already played a gig at 2 or 3 in the morning and he had to play *The Ocean Is The Ultimate Solution* as sort of an audition. So he got the gig and played great bass through it and Frank put an electric guitar solo on there. It was fun.

Apparently a drum out-take from that was used for *Friendly Little Finger*, using his Xenochrony[15] technique, like on *Rubber Shirt*.
It wouldn't surprise me.

I've got to talk about *The Black Page* – he said that he wrote that because you were such a talented drummer and he knew you would

---

[15] A technique developed by Zappa whereby "various tracks from unrelated sources are randomly synchronized with each other to make a final composition with rhythmic relationships unachievable by other means."

be able to play it. Could you tell me a little about how you learnt it?
Well, basically he walked in and he said, "What do you think about this, Bozzio?" And I said "Wow, Frank. I'm impressed." He wrote it because we had done this 40-piece orchestra gig together.

The Abnuceals Emuukha Electric Symphony Orchestra[16]?
Yeah. He was always hearing the studio musicians in LA that he was using on that talking about the fear of going into sessions some morning and being faced with 'the black page'. So he decided to write his *Black Page*. Then he gave it to me and I could play parts of it right away. But it wasn't a pressure thing, it just sat on my music stand and for about fifteen minutes every day for two weeks before we would rehearse I would work on it. After two weeks I had it together and I played it for him. He said, "Great!" took it home, wrote the melody and the chord changes, brought it back in and we all started playing it.

There's a similar piece called *Mo's Vacation*, which you've described as "ten *Black Pages*". Did you actually play that live?
That was sort of what made *The Back Page* obsolete. You know, it was like *The Black Page*, but more of it! I always say with Zappa that the level of difficulty just doesn't get any worse, it's just like more of it to memorise and stuff. But *Mo's Vacation* had some really hard stuff in it as well.

I've heard a version with Vinnie Colaiuta.
Yeah, it was past me. When I left the band it was written maybe a year later or so.

He hasn't actually released that officially.
I thought it was on that album he did with the London Symphony.

Oh, that's the deluxe orchestral version, *Mo 'N Herb's Vacation*[17]. I'm thinking of the rock band rendition.
There's another piece – a page long – called *For C Instruments*. That's very difficult.

I think that's part of the 1st Movement of *Sinister Footwear*. In 1977, you played on the premiere performance of a song called *Envelopes*.
Right.

---

[16] Put together to present a series of orchestral pieces written by Zappa at Royce Hall, UCLA in September 1975, some of which can be heard on the *Orchestral Favorites* album (1979).

[17] From *London Symphony Orchestra, Vol I* (1983).

That's mainly Tommy Mars, with you coming in at the end – was that just an improvised solo?
Yeah, he used it a sort of a set-up piece for me to play a drum solo afterwards.

During your stint with Zappa you played with a whole host of interesting people – I think Flo & Eddie[18] guested at one point?
Yeah.

Beefheart, George Duke – there were also a couple of ladies: Norma Bell[19] and Bianca Odin[20]. He's just released one track with Bianca on[21], but we haven't actually had anything from Norma Bell so far.
Norma Bell was a woman who came from Detroit. She's a really good saxophone player. She played with Tommy Bolin[22] and, I think, Ralphe Armstrong who was being considered for the gig at the time. He was the Mahavishnu's bass player.[23] He suggested her. She played with us on stage somewhere like Detroit, where she lived and then Frank brought her along on the road. By the time we got back to LA at the end of the tour she had pretty much succumbed to, you know, hanging out with the wrong people and allegedly doing a lot of drugs. So Frank said, "Forget this!" She wasn't showing up for rehearsals. She didn't last very long. I don't think we recorded anything with her[24].

No. He's not very tolerant of people who use those naughty substances. You played some interesting places, though – you played Ljubljana and Zagreb. Do you recall those?
Yeah, definitely. I remember Zagreb was literally the smokiest gig I've ever played in my life. It was so smoky that as a comment on it I went out and played the show with an unlit cigarette hanging out of my mouth. The follow spots were like two beacons coming through the fog – like a lighthouse. I had never been in a hockey rink, with 10,000

---

18 Also know as. Mark Volman and Howard Kaylan.

19 Alto saxophonist and singer, with Zappa in November 1975.

20 Keyboard player and singer (also known and Lady Bianca or Bianca Thornton), with Zappa from October to November 1976.

21 A live version of *Wind Up Workin' In A Gas Station* with Odin appears on Zappa's *You Can't Do That On Stage Anymore Vol. 6* (1992).

22 Guitarist who played with the James Gang, Billy Cobham and Deep Purple before sadly passing away on 4th December 1976.

23 In 1975, Bell actually toured with Armstrong as a member of the Mahavishnu Orchestra.

24 Recordings with Bell later turned up on the posthumous Zappa albums, *Frank Zappa Plays The Music Of Frank Zappa: A Memorial Tribute* (1996) and *Joe's Menage* (2008).

people, filled with so much smoke in my life. It was probably horribly unhealthy. But the gig went over great. They didn't say a peep through the whole show – we thought we were dying a death – then they stood up and cheered for twenty or thirty minutes.

As we left, they were still cheering. It was ridiculous. Then we went to Ljubljana and I remember that I went out after the gig through the arena, which was pretty much empty – went up to the mixing board and was just saying hi to my friends on the crew and there was this guy asleep with his face welded onto the ice – out on drugs. I just remember those images.

In *The Real Frank Zappa Book* there's a few funny stories – I just wondered if you know who the 'fabulous musician' was who gratified a girl with a champagne bottle?
Oh no, I don't. It was probably way before my time[25]. It sounds like a pretty common thing to do!

Why did you leave Zappa?
I kind of... [laughs] it isn't really common, is it? In the rock 'n' roll sense it seems pretty tame compared to some of the stories I've heard. Why did I leave Frank? I auditioned with Group 87 to get a deal with CBS the day that we started to resume rehearsals again after a break in Spring of 1978. I went in, I'd cut my hair, I was wearing different clothes, I'd just played this audition and been offered a deal with a record company. We started to rehearse, me and Pat and Frank could tell I wasn't really into it. So he called me into his 'office', as he would say, we stepped behind the stage and he said, "I think it's time you go off and do your own thing." Like a good father would: "Son, it's time for you to strike out on your own."

But you went off then to join U.K.?[26]
Yeah, I spent about a year not doing much. I auditioned for Thin Lizzy, that didn't work out.

You also turned down Jethro Tull?
No, he [sic] didn't hear me play until I was with U.K., so that wasn't until 1980 that I got an offer from him. But in 1978, it was: I auditioned

---

[25] It was another drummer, Aynsley Dunbar, who was with Zappa from 1970 to 1971.

[26] A British progressive rock supergroup that included Eddie Jobson. Jobson had played violin and keyboards with Bozzio in Zappa's band from 1975 to 1977. Bozzio replaced drummer Bill Bruford in U.K.

for Thin Lizzy; did one final tour with the Brecker Brothers; then at the end of the year started off with U.K. I spent all of one year with them, then formed Missing Persons.

Of course, you did appear on *Joe's Garage* in 1979 as 'Bald-Headed John'. Have you got any stories about John Smothers[27]?
He's a great guy, a wonderful guy. Just a real character.

You also played on John Wetton's[28] solo album, *King's Road*?[29]
No. Unless he took this one cut off of what we did with U.K. and used it. Because we recorded a song in Japan at a sound check, a song John wanted to do – sort of a shuffle. I honestly don't know, but I thought that was Simon Kirke from Bad Company that played most of that album.

Could you tell me something about Group 87, the band that featured Peter Wolf and Patrick O'Hearn. Was that actually a proper band or just a one-off album?
It didn't feature Peter Wolf; he was sort of an additional musician. I opted to be an additional musician too because I wanted to make it more of a rock 'n' roll band and they wanted to make it more of an instrumental thing. So I said "Fine. I won't join the band but I'll make the album."

The album didn't get made until a break in 1979 when I was with U.K. It's Mark Isham[30], mainly. Patrick O'Hearn, mainly. Peter Maunu[31] wrote all the songs. I arranged a couple of things in there. I did some very inventive drum beats that I believed were to be the beginnings of my making a stylistic statement – I don't believe I made any stylistic statement until I left Zappa, in terms of innovative drum beats or anything I could call my own. Mark has gone on to be a super film score composer. Patrick is scoring for films. Pete's on *The Arsenio Hall Show*[32].

---

27 Zappa's bodyguard from 1972 to 1984. Bozzio appears as Bald-Headed John – demonstrating his 'mysterious command of the English language' – in *Dong Work For Yuda* on Zappa's *Joe's Garage Acts II & III* double album (1979).

28 John Kenneth Wetton (1949-2017) was an English singer, bassist and songwriter who has played with Family, King Crimson, Roxy Music, Wishbone Ash, U.K., Asia and more.

29 Actually a compilation album of various tracks recorded by Wetton between 1972 and 1980, largely comprised of material he has performed on with U.K. and King Crimson.

30 American trumpeter, synthesist, and film composer.

31 American session guitarist.

32 American syndicated late-night talk show, created by and starring comedian Hall.

Patrick O'Hearn seems to have pretty much given up playing bass to make 'new age' albums.

Yeah, he does those albums – he plays bass on those, but he's not a professional bass player anymore in terms of working for other people to make his living. He's a composer and he writes really beautiful music and plays for himself. I mean, he does odd other things that people might call him for.

Could you tell me a little about Missing Persons?

We had our fifteen minutes, as Andy Warhol would say. I think it was a really interesting and fun concept that was just something that would last about that long. I think it was excellent musicians in it; I have nothing but respect for the musicians.

My relationship with Dale was a tragedy. She had all her problems with drugs and alcohol. I had a lot of problems with being co-dependant with her. It was just a chemical firestorm. Anyway, we never really had a very good relationship and in the end that's what broke it all up.

Like Harry and Rhonda[33]?

No. I mean Harry and Rhonda was completely scripted out by Frank. I just read that stuff.

Chuck Wild was also featured on *Thing-Fish*, on 'Broadway piano'.

Yeah. Because we went up to Zappa's one night just to visit and he said, "Here, read this, read this, read this. Chuck, you play the piano." And that was that. We had a lot of fun.

How did you meet up with Jeff Beck for the *Guitar Shop*[34] album?

Well Jeff had been trying to contact me while I was still with Missing Persons and I was always busy. Then I was about to embark on a clinic tour and I got called that day to go down and jam with him and Mick Jagger on the *Throwaway*[35] video set. Evidently Jagger had auditioned a bunch of drummers and none of them was right and it was the night before it. I walked in and they liked me so that was that. I played drums on the video and was asked to play with Jagger, but I didn't really want

---

[33] Two characters from Zappa's album *Thing-Fish* (1984), played by Terry and Dale Bozzio.

[34] The English rock guitarist's 1989 instrumental rock album, also featuring keyboard player and composer Tony Hymas.

[35] The second single from the Rolling Stones lead singer's second solo album, *Primitive Cool* (1987).

to do it so I asked for a lot of money. It was a long time commitment, for very few gigs and a lot of rehearsals and it just didn't seem right. So I passed on that.

Jeff said, "I'd like to use you on my thing. What do you think?" His manager flew down a few times and we talked about forming some sort of band. Essentially, it was like Jeff's name but it was really a three-way writing thing. Tony Hymas wrote most of the music, I guess. I wrote a little. Jeff wrote a little.

That's your voice on *A Day In The House* and *Guitar Shop*, isn't it?
Yeah, just doing some vocal stuff. The tracks were just kind of lacking. Jeff's sort of odd to work with because he's not really a writer. You know, it's hard to sort of... er...

Is Punky really more fluid[36]?
No [laughs]. Jeff Beck is definitely the best guitar player I've ever played with. I mean, Frank is another great guitar player; he's got his own style. Jeff is just wonderful, though.

Yeah, I've been a fan of his for some time.
I think Zappa is, even [laughs].

You played on the soundtrack to the film *Twins*[37]. Did you actually appear in that film?[38]
I don't know if I appear. I know I did a close-up one morning. All I know was that was like three days in hell being wallpaper on a movie. But I made $5,000 and bought my tape machine.

You left Beck shortly after that?
No, no, no. We did the album; we did a tour of Japan, a tour of the States with Stevie Ray Vaughan and then a tour of Europe. Came to London, Jeff pulled out his back.

That's right.
Then we re-scheduled the Hammersmith gigs, did those. Went into the studio for three days and that's when Tony quit. Then Jeff and I tried to get something together with Roger Daltrey, which never happened.

---

36 Another reference to the *Zappa In New York* album. This time the track *Punky's Whips*, in which Bozzio sings of hearing that the lead guitar player from the group Angel (Punky Meadows) is "more fluid than Jeff Beck".

37 1988 American 'buddy film' directed by Ivan Reitman, starring Arnold Schwarzenegger and Danny DeVito.

38 Beck and Bozzio can indeed be glimpsed as part of singer Nicolette Larson's backing band in the film, performing *I'd Die For This Dance*.

Auditioned to sort of jam with Paul Young and Pino Palladino; that wasn't a good match. Then we started writing some stuff ourselves. I went home to LA, worked with Richard Marx and I haven't heard from Jeff since. I gave him a call yesterday; I hope to see him while I'm here but Jeff's sort of reclusive![39]

I understand you're now working with Steve Vai?
Yeah, I just finished making his album[40].

Is it actually a proper band?
I really don't know. He would like it to be. My definition of a band is an unconditional acceptance of all members. So far, what I'm doing is playing drums on Steve Vai's music. That I consider more of a session gig than being in a band with the guy[41].

Is that playing more structured songs than on his all instrumental *Passion And Warfare* album?[42]
Yeah, it's much more structured songs. There's a little bit of out stuff, but for the most part its sort of AOR heavy metal.

It was rumoured that you might turn up for the *Zappa's Universe* tribute concerts that happened last year.
I was in New York at the time and I heard about it there. I was doing a clinic tour and the day I played somebody asked me "Are you gonna go play at The Ritz for the Zappa's Universe thing?" I said, "What?!" And he said, "Dale's there, Steve's there," all these people there. I said, "No, I haven't been asked and I'm flying to Boston directly after this gig." So that was that.

Have you heard Dweezil's versions of *Broken Hearts Are For Assholes* and *I'm So Cute*[43]?
No!

---

[39] Bozzio has subsequently worked with Beck, including recording the *Live: B.B. King Blues Club & Grill, New York* album (2006).

[40] *Sex & Religion* released under the band name Vai in 1993.

[41] When Vai toured the album, Bozzio and bassist T. M. Stevens were replaced by drummers Abe Laboriel Jr. then Toss Panos, and former Zappa bass player Scott Thunes

[42] Vai's second solo album, released in 1990.

[43] Two songs originally from Zappa's *Sheik Yerbouti* album that Dweezil and his band "Z" would cover in concert in the early 1990s. Dweezil would again perform both songs with Zappa Plays Zappa several years later: a version of *I'm So Cute*, featuring Bozzio on drums and vocals, can be seen and heard on the ZPZ DVD (2007); and *Broken Hearts...* appears on his *Return Of The Son Of...* live album (2010).

On his new album, I understand there's a version of Cream's *White Room*[44] – did you play on that?

No!

What sort of stuff have you been playing?

I played on something called *Dan Halen* [laughs]. I played on a lot of bits and pieces of stuff that were really difficult and I had no time to get them together and I was really challenged by Dweezil[45].

He had been, you know... when you work with anybody with the last name Zappa you don't have a life, you know, you just play that music. It's great when you're young, but at this point in my life I'd rather do my own music.

I went in for one week and cut I guess eight or nine tracks with Dweezil of some of the most difficult stuff I've had to do since I left Frank. It was just ridiculous. It wasn't written out, I had like bits and pieces of the hard bits scribbled out by Mike or... er?

By Mike Keneally?

Mike Keneally, or what's his name?

Scott Thunes?

Yeah.

Because Dweezil doesn't actually write music, does he?

No. Dweezil doesn't know what he's doing; he just memorises it and tells everybody else to play it! Quite like Frank in a lot of ways, but Frank would write as well. But yeah, I think it was some really good stuff – some really interesting beats and grooves.

Yeah, I think Dweezil's really progressed over three albums – the last one was definitely the best to date.[46] When I saw him on tour last year I was really impressed. He played some of his dad's tunes as well. Which was nice.

Interview conducted on Sunday 27th September 1992.

---

44 At the time of writing, this song – if ever recorded by Dweezil! – remains unreleased.

45 Bozzio plays on the tracks: *Bellybutton*, *Rubberband* and *Them* on "Z's" *Shampoohorn* album (1993); and *Fwakstension* and *Therapy* on Dweezil's *Automatic* album (2000).

46 *Confessions* (1991).

NAPOLEON MURPHY BROCK

Napoleon Murphy Brock is a singer, saxophonist and flute player discovered by Zappa in Hawaii in 1973. The two worked together from 1973 to 1976 and then again in 1984.

Brock plays on many of the 'classic' mid-1970s Zappa albums, sings on *Thing-Fish* (1984), appears in the home video *A Token Of His Extreme* (2013) and Roxy-*The Movie* (2015) and can be heard on the posthumous lives releases *FZ:OZ* (2002) and *Roxy By Proxy* (2014).

Between 1976 and 1979, Brock sang on a number of solo albums by George Duke.

In 2006, Brock was one of the 'sternly accomplished special guests' on Dweezil Zappa's first Zappa Plays Zappa tour. In 2009, the band featuring Brock won the best rock instrumental performance Grammy for their rendition of Zappa's *Peaches En Regalia* from that tour.

Brock disappeared from the music scene for much of the 1990s. When I found out that he had gotten back into music and had been playing with the 10-piece Tampa Bay based Zappa cover band, Bogus Pomp, I half-heartedly investigated the possibility of interviewing him. I made a few contacts, but kind of put the idea on the back burner. Then he started playing with Ike Willis and Project Object and my interest was renewed – but once again, I didn't really pursue it as I knew that all good things come to those who bide their time.

In March 2002, Billy James (aka the ANT-BEE, who worked as Zappa's copyist in the 1980s and wrote the book *Necessity Is... The Early Years Of Frank Zappa & The Mothers Of Invention*) contacted me to say that Brock would be visiting England shortly and "would like to do an interview for your website - are you interested?" Silly question, really. Arrangements were quickly made and before I knew it I was sitting face-to-face with one of my teenage heroes at London's Institute of

Contemporary Arts in The Mall.

Looking incredibly fit and healthy (Brock, that is – not me), here's what went down.

How did you first get into music?
I've been into music all of my life. I started when I was about five – gospel, in church. My grandparents, who I lived with, were very religious – the Baptist church. Everyone in the family sang – that's what we did, they started us off very young. For some reason, they thought I should be singing in all the choirs. That was basically how I got started. I got to Junior high school and it was the same – you know, the choirs. Then in high school, it went full blown; I started playing the clarinet when I was a sophomore. Then I got into tenor saxophone. I was in the concert band, I sang in the jazz band, I was in a marching band, in the orchestra and I sang in all the choirs. I've been doing it since then.

I understand you were playing sax in a bar in Hawaii when Frank discovered you?
Well, actually, I was in a six-piece band[1] – we did our own little tours in different cities in the United States.

What sort of music were you playing?
We were playing cover music – you know, top 40, whatever was popular at the time. Then we mixed some jazz in with it if it was suitable for the venue we were playing. Dance music mostly, because people liked to dance and we liked to see them have a good time.

So how did the meeting with Frank come about?
As I understand it, he had just finished touring Australia and they were getting ready to go to Europe a week or two after that. He was taking a little break with his wife, Gail. They stopped off in Hawaii for a week or so. His road manager, Marty Perellis, set them up in a hotel and went out walking around in Hawaii – probably to see if he could get lucky or something! If you want a good time, what better place to do it than in Hawaii? Hawaii is literally paradise.

He came to a show of mine – outside a nightclub at the Coral Reef hotel – and got curious as to why there was a line of people waiting to

---

[1] Named Communication Plus, a recording of the band was officially released in 2011 titled *This Is What Frank Zappa Heard: Communication Plus – Live At The Red Noodle Waikiki, Hawaii.*

get into a place on a Wednesday night. He didn't recognise the name of the band, so he thought he'd get in line and come in and see why everybody was queuing up.

What was the name of your band?

Gregarious Movement[2]… 'happy people who like happy people who like happy people' something like that to define the word gregarious. We wanted to start a movement here. We were picking up happy people along the way and making other people who were sad happy. But mostly the music that we were playing was happy music.

Anyway, he came into the club and saw us playing – didn't recognise us, because no one knew about us except the club owners that hired us and the people who came to see us. He ran back to the hotel, woke Frank up and said, "Hey, get your clothes on: I just found your new lead vocalist." Because Frank had just fired Sal Marquez – they'd had some sort of squabble in Australia and he was without a lead vocalist, because Sal was the lead vocalist at the time. Frank got up, came by to the hotel, stood in line like anybody else and once he got in he sat at the back of the room – there weren't any seats.

We were quite popular there, because we were a band from the mainland. In Hawaii, a band from the mainland – if you play halfway decent music – you're like a star, you have star status over there. Also, the music in Hawaii is like a month behind.

So you were playing the hits before they were hits?

You got it. We were playing Santana's *Evil Ways*[3] before it got over there. As a matter of fact, we were playing it before Santana put it out because I had heard this other guy named… what was this drummer's name? Willie Bobo. Willie Bobo put it out on one of his albums[4] and I heard it and said "Wow! This is a very good song" and so I had the band learn it and we started playing it.

We were playing it for something like five months and all of a sudden it came out on the radio and everyone says, "Hey, we heard your hit on the radio – although it's by Santana. Who's he?"! We would do that, we would learn all these hit songs because after doing it for a while I was able to tell which ones were going to make it and move right up the charts.

---

2 This was actually the name of the band Brock formed after his first stint with Zappa, in 1976.

3 From their eponymous 1969 debut album. The song was written by Clarence "Sonny" Henry.

4 *Bobo Motion* (1967).

So we would learn the top 15 or 20 songs and we would go to Hawaii and after we'd been there a couple of months, they'd start playing them on the radio. All these people would come running in saying, "We hear your music on the radio!" It was just really funny.

But anyway, during one of the intermissions, Marty Perellis walked up to me and said, "Someone wants to meet you." And I said, "Well, I've only got 15 minutes. Is it important? What's it about – you want to hear songs? Tell me which song you wanna hear and I'll play it for you." And he said, "No, he actually wants to meet you." I said, "Who is it? I only have 15 minutes." He said "It's Frank Zappa." I said, "Okay, who's Frank Zappa?" He said, "You don't know who Frank Zappa is?" and I went, "Well, no. Is he a musician?" "Yes." "Well, what does he play?" "He plays guitar" " Does he record? I've never heard of him.

He doesn't play jazz because I would have heard of him and he doesn't play top 40 because I'm knowledgeable about who plays top 40. So what kind of music does he play? Where is he?" He pointed to him; he was in the back there. My vision was much better then and I said, "He looks like a guy I saw on a poster – a music store in Haight Ashbury – sitting on a toilet flipping the bird. Is that him?" He says, "Well, yeah." I said, "Well what does he want with me?" "Well, he wants to talk to you." And I thought 'Okay, but that's not a very good endorsement – some weird guy sitting on the toilet – wonder what he wants with me?'

That was going to be my next question – you obviously weren't familiar with his music at all.
I wasn't familiar with his work; I'd never even heard his name before. I was just a top 40 musician. So I went back and was introduced to him. He said, "I like the way you play. I like the way you sing."

"I like the way you dance"?
He didn't bring that up then, you know [laughs]. At the time I was playing organ, playing bongos with mallets, saxophone, flute and singing and dancing. That was what I did; a little bit of whatever had to be done to get the song out.

He said, "I like the way you sing and I like the way you play. I'd like you to come to Europe with me next week and do a European tour." I said, "I've got to be honest with you; as I told your road manager, I'm not familiar with your music." He said, "Well, that doesn't matter – I'll come over and teach you everything you need to know on Monday."

"Well...err. Okay, who's in your band?" And he said "George Duke, Jean Luc Ponty[5]..." I said "Stop right there..."

You'd heard of those guys, obviously – from the jazz world?

"...I have all of George Duke's stuff – with Cannonball Adderley. I have a couple of Jean Luc Ponty albums. There's nothing you can teach me in one day that's going to prepare me to play a tour or concert or engagement with George Duke and Jean Luc Ponty; it's not possible. There's no way in the world that I would accept such an offer knowing the calibre of musician that they are. But if they play with you, you must be good. Because they're really good." And he says "Don't worry, we can do it." And I said, "It's not possible. Number one, I have a contract: I'm booked to be here for three months and we've only been here six weeks; we have another six weeks to play." "Well, I'll buy the contract." "That's not the point – you can't buy this contract because it's not a written contract: it's a verbal one between two gentleman, the club owner and myself. He owns a couple of clubs and I go and play them all."

The club was owned by a guy called Claude Hall – he was the first Marlboro man[6]. Dickie Smothers – one of the Smothers Brothers – they owned a couple of clubs and we played their clubs. They paid us quite well. They paid for our transportation – whether by plane or by land. They paid our hotel bills. Because we were quite good – we bought them a lot of revenue. Every time we came to their clubs, they said, "When you're here, this is what we make. When you're not here, this I what we make." So I said "You can't buy the contract, because we have a gentleman's agreement." He says, "I wish you'd reconsider." "Well, I can't because I promised these guys. This is paradise; why would I want to leave here to go and embarrass myself in front of two of my idols? That wouldn't be very smart. No, I'm sorry – I'm going to have to decline your offer. I appreciate it and, because of the personnel in your band, I feel quite honoured for you to even suggest such a thing. But this is my number and I'm not doing anything after October."

---

5 French virtuoso violinist and jazz composer, who worked with Zappa between 1969 and 1973, appearing on the albums *Hot Rats* (1969), *Over-Nite Sensation* (1973), *Apostrophe (')* (1974), and his own *King Kong: Jean-Luc Ponty Plays The Music Of Frank Zappa* (1970). He later worked with the Mahavishnu Orchestra, Stéphane Grappelli and Return To Forever.

6 Actually the third man to be used in the Marlboro Man TV adverts, and the subject of the book *Hazardous To My Health: The Marlboro Man I Knew* by Marcia N. Hill.

This must've been in 1972?

It has to be 1971 or 1972 – the late part of the year, because I started touring with him in late 1972.[7]

He had the accident at the end of 1971, when he was pushed off the stage.

Yeah, 1972. When I saw him, his leg was healed. He was walking okay. Next thing I know, in October, I get a phone call. He says, "Hi, this is Frank Zappa." I said, "Oh, hi. How're you doing? I remember you." He says, "Well, I'm at the airport." I said, "I don't really know what that means." He said "Well, I just got back from Europe. I just got off the plane. I'm at the airport. You told me to call you and I'm calling you." I said, "Well, yeah. But I didn't mean for you to call me at the airport – you could have waited until you got home." He said, "No, it's important. I want you to come down as soon as you can. Can you come down and make a rehearsal next week?" I said, "Sure, I'm not busy right now – I have no more engagements."

So I went down to the audition. He introduced me to everyone: Ruth Underwood[8], Tom Fowler[9] and Bruce Fowler, Jean Luc, George and Ralph Humphrey[10]. He says, "Well, sit down and take a listen." And they played about ten songs without stopping. Seven or ten – I forget how many because I couldn't separate them. I didn't know where one stopped and the next one started because of all the diverse time signatures that he uses in his music. But I knew there were at least seven different songs.

The next thing I knew, they'd finished and he came down and says, "What do you think?" And I'm like "Whoa! How did you do that?" It's quite interesting, you know. Well, he asked me "Do you think you can do it?" I said, "Sure." Because to me it was the same as a rock opera – it had all the characteristics of a Broadway musical, except it was a little weird. A lot of different time signatures and everything. That was the jazz element – you know, with all the jazz musicians, I could understand that. I understood that all of the musicians were from the music conservatory, so that made sense too. I figured I could do this. I said, "This is a real good opportunity for me." He says "Sure, let's do

---

[7] Brock's first gig with The Mothers was actually at the Armadillo World Headquarters in Austin, Texas on 26th October 1973.

[8] Percussionist with Zappa from 1969 to 1976.

[9] Bassist brother of trombonist Bruce, with Zappa from 1973 to 1975.

[10] Drummer with Zappa from 1973 to 1974.

it." Next thing I know, "Here…" I get a big stack of charts "… this is what you'll be singing"!

Presumably he also wanted you as a sax player?
Sax, flute and lead vocalist… as it turned out, more a lead vocalist and front man. I could see when they played these songs they badly needed a front man – someone to explain some of this stuff. Or to at least kind of physically describe what it felt like.

You sounded like you had a ball during you first stint with Frank – with Ruth Underwood, Jeff Simmons[11] and George Duke. What are your fondest memories of those times? It was such a great band.
Jeff came along after the Roxy[12] – that's when I met Jeff Simmons. Before that it was one of the most difficult learning sessions I've ever been involved in, in my life. Because here I am learning this music, memorising this music, reading these charts – because he didn't allow music on stage. Didn't even allow lyric sheets on stage. They had to be memorised. It was a very difficult time for me because… it would have been a lot easier if I had heard his music before, but it was very foreign to me. It was so completely different from any other music I had heard in my life and so I had to empty my memory banks of everything else that I had learned in my life to make room for this collage of really strange bizarre music.

I was raised up with a 1-3-5 chord structure and he was doing 1-2-4. I felt that was kind of strange and I said, "Aren't you making it kinda difficult on yourself? Why are you doing it like this?" I learned later that's his signature – this was basically one of the ways you were able to tell the difference between his music and others. You try to play the chords, you figure 'this isn't it' and then you start to move a couple of notes and it's 'Oh, that's what he's playing. But why?' What sticks in my mind most was learning his music. I had to spend a lot of time before the tour, during the tour, in hotel rooms just day and night. Chester Thompson came in the next day, so him and I were basically on the same page as far as playing Frank's music. He had never played it before either. He would play with people like Webster Lewis[13], who were just basically jazz. But he had also graduated from the Berklee

---

[11] On/off bassist, guitarist and vocalist with Zappa between 1969 and 1974.

[12] Simmons made a guest appearance at one of the December 1973 Roxy concerts, performing *Dummy Up* with Brock.

[13] American jazz and disco keyboard player.

School of Music, so he was quite a good drummer.

But him and I, we were just being introduced to the band at that time so we were collaborating and we were going "Shit! Did you listen to that? Did you look at those charts? This is ridiculous!" That was the hardest part and the most memorable, because when we started the tour, all of the members of the band would request that I be put in a room at the end of the hall – as far away from them as possible.

Why was that?

Because I'm up all night practising! He wouldn't let me play my saxophone and flute on stage until I memorised the parts. I said, "Well, why even bring them?" He says, "No, no, no, no, no. You need to learn it. As you learn them, then you can play them." So I had my saxophone and flute on stage for the first couple of concerts that I didn't even play at all. I just set them up. Frank said, "Set 'em up so that people get used to seeing them."

You talk about learning the music. What about the vocals? There was a lot of improvisation there – songs like _Dummy Up_ and _Room Service_[14].

That came along later. First of all you've got to realise that he was a strong disciplinarian: every note had to be as written and as charted. The intonation had to be absolutely perfect. Fortunately for me, I'd had a lot of experience with light opera. I did light opera for about four or five years – you had to articulate there, you had to be absolutely perfect. I mean with Rodgers and Hammerstein[15], you couldn't sing whatever notes you wanted. _Oklahoma_ had a specific melody line – all those plays, _Oklahoma_, _Carousel_, _Guys & Dolls_, _Damn Yankees_ – all of those had very acute melody lines that had to be adhered to.

So I had the discipline already – except I didn't know the level of the disciplinarian that I was getting involved with. Some of his melodies were very beautiful – for example, _The Idiot Bastard Son_. But I thought it was kind of strange that he would put those words to such a beautiful melody. Then he would tell me the stories about how he created the songs – that they were real-life experiences. I was not getting discouraged, but a little bit frightened about spending my spare time

---

[14] These can be heard on the albums _Roxy & Elsewhere_ (1974) and _You Can't Do That On Stage Anymore Vol. 2 – The Helsinki Concert_ (1988).

[15] The American musical theatre writing team consisting of composer Richard Rodgers and lyricist-dramatist Oscar Hammerstein II.

with this guy – I didn't want to be one of these experiences that he wrote a song about!

You mentioned Marty Perellis – of course he was the subject of quite a few of the improvisations.
Marty was quite a character. He was a very good road manager, but he was quite a character too. He would have to be quite a character and very charismatic to deal with all the personalities that he had to deal with. So, many times he became the brunt of the joke of the day – simply because of some of the things that he would do. You've seen the video, *The Dub Room Special?*[16]

Yeah.
You saw the gorilla that came up behind Chester?

Oh, from the TV show – *A Token Of His Extreme*?
Yeah. When Chester was playing, you saw the gorilla that came up with the clock and a comb? Well that was Marty Perellis in the gorilla outfit. No one knew – even Frank – that he was gonna do that. He would do that impromptu to blow our minds. As you saw, Chester was quite surprised – and the rest of us were too... I looked back, "A gorilla?"... but I got to the point where I was learning to expect just about anything from this organisation.

And the whole thing about the *Room Service* routine, that was all ad-lib – we ad-libbed that every day. There was a basic format: "You call me up and tell me what you want," and we would bounce off of each other. By the time we did that, we had a camaraderie where we would challenge each other without saying, "I'm gonna challenge you." We would just challenge each other. Because he would challenge me to see if I was gonna fuck up. I would challenge him to say, "Okay. Not only am I not gonna fuck up, but I'm gonna throw something different at you every day. Let's see if you can deal with it." We would kind of look at each other out of the corner of our eyes – because we were basically challenging each other.

At that point I was like, "Okay, I've learned your music to the point where you're allowing me to ad-lib now. So I'm gonna show you that you made the right decision when you chose me. Because, yes, I do have these qualities and abilities that you recognise that you have

---

16 A documentary that features two concerts: Zappa's 1981 Halloween show at New York's Palladium; and one from KCET Studios in December 1974 for the TV special *A Token Of His Extreme*.

yourself. I'm not you and you're not me, but I can do this and let's go. Here's another night, this is another show – let's see where we can go." So it wasn't so much a challenging thing as a game that we started to play to see if we could incorporate into the dialogue many of the events that took place the night before.

So the whole idea about me bringing up the dogs... I said, "What about the dogs?" He started to crack up and said; "I didn't tell you about the dogs!" I said, "You didn't have to tell me – I saw them when you registered." All of that was completely ad-libbed, but it was just the truth. It was what happened. "I saw you when you registered. I know those dogs were with someone." "Well, hell - they weren't with me! They were with the guy with the gorilla outfit!" And so he made that quite clear right on tape. I thought that was quite neat.

But we did that a lot. If you listen to different tapes of that performance, you'll see that it was different every time. It was a basic format, but anything that happened to the band the night before that was significant – we would try and throw it into the show someplace. Like George on the Helsinki concert tape was saying something about Ruth having a party in her room with someone. I would say, "Well, George made a tape of it." So Frank would say "Okay, we'll listen to it later!"

Would it be right to say that any songs were written with you in mind? He used to tailor songs to suit the abilities of the musicians, so would you say that your flute was an inspiration for *Dupree's Paradise*?[17]

I don't know if it was or not. I didn't hear it until I came along – that was the first I'd heard of the song. I was just trying to hold up my end. Here comes another song, "Oh, great!"

But the whole Evil Prince[18] thing we developed together. We did that before he did *Thing-Fish*, because he hadn't even met Ike Willis yet. It wasn't even conceivable that here was a character that we could incorporate into an idea that he had that talked like Kingfish from *The Amos 'N' Andy Show*[19]. That was one of Ike's things, he had this deep voice and he used to mimic Kingfish. And Frank, anytime he saw something like that, he'd go "I can use this over here," and would structure something and utilise it to suit the new band's style.

---

[17] From *You Can't Do That On Stage Anymore Vol. 2*.

[18] A character played by Brock that eventually turned up on Zappa's album *Thing-Fish* (1984).

[19] American radio and television sitcom, set in Harlem.

The whole idea of the Evil Prince came just by chance. We were doing a tour with Terry Bozzio, Roy Estrada and Andre Lewis. One of the new songs we started doing was *The Torture Never Stops*, about this little cave where this mad scientist was doing all these nasty things. Now by this time, it was easy for me to elaborate on a concept. I would look at the lyrics and I'd know what he was trying to say. I was spending a lot of time at second-hand clothing stores. So for each song I would get some clothes and develop a character. I would wear these white gymnastic pants with American flag suspenders. With these pants I could put on a jacket and a hat and I'd be a new character. Every jacket was a different colour. So while he was singing, "Flies all green and buzzin', in his dungeon of despair..." I would turn into this person who was a mad scientist that I found out later was called the Evil Prince.

That's what I was doing on stage; he would have a song and I would develop a character to go with the song. He allowed me to do that because he trusted my ability to ad-lib his creations at that time. If you listen to any of the bootleg stuff – either from when George and Ruth were in the band, or the other band with Terry and Roy Estrada – you heard a lot of ad-lib stuff. He started allowing me to do that after I'd learnt all of the music and I didn't have to read the charts anymore and I could play my parts on every song. Sax. Flute. Whatever. I knew the music and he was comfortable with it and then he allowed me to ad-lib. Because that was one of the qualities that he really hired me for. I did a lot of that when he first saw me.

When I put together songs for the bands I was working with, I would extend them because they would be too short for the people who wanted to dance. They were usually only a couple of minutes long. So what I would do was say, "Okay, here's a song by Sly & The Family Stone. But this is what they should have done. They should've just continued on and taken it over here. Because this is what the song really suggests." So the rest of this would be all ad-lib, but it was connected to the original creation. So I guess he must have heard that when he first saw me. He was probably familiar with the material himself because I found out later that he loved rhythm and blues; he was really enthused by Afro-American music.

But anyway, he started allowing me to ad-lib and he would give me sections of a song and he'd just let me go on. But I would taper it because I didn't want him to stop. I didn't overdo it and I kept it within the context of his original – but at the same time, I extended it: "This is fine right here. But if you're gonna have this space here where you're playing this funk vamp, this is what goes here." I used it, because I had to have something to do while I was dancing around all over the place.

So that's how things like *Ruthie Ruthie* came about?
Yeah, all that... *The Velvet Sunrise*...

That was on the Beefheart tour. What are your memories of the Bongo Fury tour?
Van Vliet – whew! Deep. Quite a funny guy. Within his own right, a genius for what he does. I've read some of his lyrics; after you dissect them, it's really saying something quite powerful. He spent a lot of time in the bathroom [laughs]. That's what I remember. He used to come into my room and spent a lot of time in the bathroom. The rest of us were in there talking about whatever and he'd be in the bathroom. He liked to do that. I don't know why.

There are stories about him drawing all the time on that tour – even on stage.
He used to do his drawing. Him and Frank...

...their relationship was a bit strained at that time?
Yes it was. As you can tell by the picture on the cover of the album!

Tell me about your departure from the Mothers – you went off and worked with George Duke?
Well, no – I went home and de-programmed myself from his music first. I spent about six months doing that. To do his music, you can't listen to anything else.

Terry Bozzio said the same thing – that it's pretty much 24 hours a day.
It's all encompassing. You can't hear anything else. Everything else sounds wrong or so different that it just disturbs you. It doesn't allow you to perform other music because it is 24/7 – as Terry says. So I went home and de-programmed myself. I knew I had to do that, because every time I tried to listen to music I just heard his. It's so overwhelming. I did that and I started writing my own music. That was the way I pushed his out and allowed mine to come through.

How would you describe your own music?
My music is happy music. I write about things that you're familiar with, that you would recognise. I write songs about happy situations – very positive. So I allowed that to come through and immediately after I did

that, I went out and got a bunch of musicians together and recorded it. As a matter of fact, six of those songs are gonna be six of the songs I'm gonna release. As we speak, they're being transferred from 8-track to Pro Tools. I'm gonna go into the studio and brush them up a little bit – add a few things here and there – but basically they're almost ready to be released now. It's raw, but it's real. It's really real[20].

So that wasn't the songs George Duke produced?

No, that's another set of songs. After that first band I put together, I reformed Gregarious Movement and we started playing again and that's when George called me and asked me to join his band[21]. The reason I left Frank was because I told him I'd stay with him for about four or five years – no less than four, no more than five – and it ended up about four years and it was time to go. He was having some internal conflict with Herb Cohen[22] – they were getting ready to separate – and it was affecting the band too. So I thought it was a good time to leave.

So you went away and worked with your own band.

Yeah, I started playing with Gregarious Movement again – after I'd recorded my originals and put them away in the vault. Because it wasn't time to release them then. The record companies would never have given me a contract for that music because it wasn't mainstream. You'll hear it; I plan to release it this summer. I'm gonna sell them at concerts and on the Internet.

If it's your music, you're free to do that.

That's the beauty about that. I'm going to copyright it – to protect it – with the Library of Congress. I'm gonna put it out and if you like one song, then I'll be happy. Anyway, George asked me to join his band and I accepted. He had Leon Ndugu Chancler on drums, Sheila E on percussion; Josie James was female lead vocalist, Byron Miller on bass and Charles "Icarus" Johnson on guitar. I thought 'Here's another nice opportunity for me.' I knew I'd already made history with Frank, because by the time I went to that audition, I'd checked him out and I learned he was a genius. I said, "Thank you!" Here's an opportunity for me to get into the music business with someone who's really respected

---

20 These tracks were released later in 2002 on Brock's debut solo album, *Balls*.

21 Between 1976 and 1979, Brock appeared on four albums by Duke: *Liberated Fantasies, Don't Let Go, Follow The Rainbow* and *Master Of The Game*.

22 Zappa's manager from 1965 to 1976, when Zappa claimed Cohen and his brother Mutt were profiting unduly from his earnings.

in the industry – away from the top 40, away from the mainstream. Here's something that has cult status. Most music you like today and it's gone tomorrow. But this kind of stuff will go on forever.

Then I heard about his European connection and how much the people in Europe loved him and I thought 'I've never been to Europe before. This is my destiny.' George asked me to do in his band what I did in Frank's – which was to be the front man, do a lot of dancing around and lead vocals. Which I didn't understand because I thought George had one of the most beautiful voices I'd ever heard in my life – why did he want me to sing lead vocals?

Well, some of the songs you do together – *Village Of The Sun...*
This is true. So you know. He was thinking of the order of what you're saying: creating with his own music the kind of vocal camaraderie that we had developed within Frank's band. So I went 'Okay, I understand that.' The first thing we did was an album. I thought, 'Okay, that's a good way to get started.'

He had me singing most of the songs – which weren't his style. They were his creation, but they weren't for his voice. He has a very pure, natural falsetto. Not many people have that, but George Duke does. I'd give my eyeteeth to have that. If I had his voice too!

So I joined his band, did a few albums, did a few tours. It was destiny, too. That stuff is now coming full circle – now the opportunity is now coming for me to utilise that. What better way to go out to a ready-made audience – people who love George Duke and people who love Frank Zappa – sing the songs that they love and stick mine in the middle. If they like me, then they'll like my music too, I hope.

How did you get back with Frank?
Frank called me in 1983 and he says, "Listen, I'm doing this Broadway play called *Thing-Fish* and I've got a part here that's perfect for you. Would you like to come down and audition for it?" I said, "Sure, why not?"

I went down and said, "What's the part?" He says, "It's called *The Evil Prince*." He told me all about it. I said, "Oh, wait a minute – that's the character that we created when we used to do *The Torture Never Stops*." He said, "That's right. You're perfect for the part." I said, "Okay, well where's the music?" He said, "Well, I haven't written it yet. I was waiting for you to come here."

He described *The Evil Prince* as this part time theatrical critic and mad scientist who was hired by the Government to create this vaccine, this stuff called Galoot Cologna. What it really is, is AIDS.

And this was really before it was full blown.
Yeah. His theory was that the Government hired these scientists to create it to get rid of gay people. The way they wanted to find out if this serum – or whatever it was – worked, was to try it on prisoners in state penitentiaries. If they died, that means they were gay and if they lived they weren't gay but they turned into what they call a Mammy Nun: they've got a head like a potato, a mouth like a duck, feet like a duck and they dressed in nun outfits. They talked like Ike Willis. That was the side effect of the drug – it didn't kill you, but it turned you into a Mammy Nun.

Anyway, this scientist the Government hired, he was called the Evil Prince but he was a mad scientist, a part time theatrical critic and a fake opera singer. He said, "This is the character."

Now Frank knew that I used to work in light opera and you know: light opera/fake opera singer – that kind of goes together. He knows there had been times where I had used my little opera voice [demonstrates]. So he knew I could do this before he called me, but he made it like, "You want to try out for this?" But knowing all the time that he wrote it with me in mind.

So after going through all the stuff together that we would do together in his studio – as far as singing and things like that – he'd send everybody else home and say, "Okay, come on, into my studio to the piano and we're gonna do the song *The Evil Prince*." He says, "Bring your tape recorder," which I always did. I put it on. He says, "Here are the lyrics, now I'm gonna play the notes. I'm creating it right now and I need you to tape it so you can learn it and when you come back I'll have the tracks ready and you can sing on it." So he played one line at a time, then I'd record it. That's how we did the whole song. And it's a very long song.

Have you heard the album *Thing-Fish*?

Of course!
Then you know *The Evil Prince*[23]. But did you hear the one called *Amnerika*?

Yes?
And that one too, the same way.

---

23 On the album, the song was actually part of the track *The 'Torchum' Never Stops*.

I've never heard you sing that. I've seen the lyrics and I've heard someone else sing them, but Frank only ever released Synclavier and orchestral versions[24].

I don't know why he didn't put it on there because it's brilliant[25]. You've got to hear me sing it and then you'll appreciate it more.

So will you be doing that live when you tour?

If I can get a band to learn it [laughs], the music's quite difficult. [To his friend, Cathy:] I played it for you yesterday, remember? This is one thing about me with Frank: I used to tape everything. So actually I'm going to do it on tour with Bogus Pomp[26] and Project Object; I'm going to have them learn it. Because no one knows about it. You've heard the music, but there's no vocal performance. You haven't really heard it until you've heard me sing it. Because we created it together. I mean, I still have the tape and it's funny... it's so funny. I mean him and I are cracking up. I'm laughing and he's laughing because he's putting this melody to those words: "You're crazy!" and he's going, "Yeah. Isn't it cool!"

And it is a beautiful melody.

Oh, it's an incredible melody. I started touring with Project Object and playing with Bogus Pomp and I had them both learn *The Evil Prince* and the people just go crazy – they can't imagine it. Because they never thought they'd ever hear it. So that song in particular from the album *Thing-Fish*... as a matter of fact, no one's doing anything from the album *Thing-Fish* live. There is a live version that I did from that small tour I did with the 1984 band. I did the small tour of America and I sang it then and after he had Ray White sing it. He did all right, you know[27] [laughs].

I was going to ask you about the 1984 tour. As you say, it was a short tour for you.

Yeah, I could only do the short American leg. I couldn't do Europe and the rest of the tour. When we got back together for the *Thing-Fish* album

---

24 On *Civilization Phaze III* (1994), as the backing to *That Evil Prince* on *Thing-Fish*, and as *Amnerika Goes Home* on *Everything Is Healing Nicely* (1999).

25 The track was issued posthumously in 2016 on the album *Frank Zappa For President*. In the same year, Brock recorded and released a new acoustic version of the song, with Mats Öberg on grand piano and harmonica, for an EP called *Let's Have a Good Time* by The Vegetarians.

26 Zappa tribute band based in Tampa Bay, Florida.

27 A live version sung by White can be found on Zappa's 1991 album *You Can't Do That On Stage Anymore Vol. 4*.

and some things for *Them Or Us*, Frank said "Why don't you come and do the tour with us?" I said, "Well I can't do the whole thing, but I'll do what I can."[28]

I don't think he released any recordings from that early part of the tour. He's released lots from the subsequent part and I have to say it's some of my least favourite stuff. So I'd loved to have heard you with them.
He was trying so hard to keep them happy. I was playing flute, alto sax, tenor sax and baritone sax. So I wasn't doing a lot of singing.

And after the 1984 tour, you lived in England for a while?
Yeah, I came over here with my wife and stayed with her for a while. Then I wrote a lot of other songs.

I heard a story that you were training poodles?
No! English Staffordshire pit bull terriers. They all carried two tennis balls in their mouths – which will be the cover of my CD.

So there's that old conceptual continuity thing – dogs figure hugely in Zappa's work.
Yeah. I had raised dogs before I met Frank. German shepherds. I love dogs. I love intelligent animals. I know that animals are more intelligent than most people think they are. I would raise these animals and I would train them and I would give them to my relatives and friends – to protect them and to protect their children. I would raise English Staffordshire pit bull terriers. At that time, pit bulls in the United States were getting a bad rap. So I would raise them with children and cats. Their signature was they would all carry two tennis balls in their mouths. I have video footage of these dogs playing with kids and sleeping with cats.

One day I plan to use that in my videos that I will make. I will use this footage to show people... I was on a mission, I was gonna do a project, I was gonna do a documentary to show people that these dogs – the ones that are bad – it's not the dogs, it's the people that raised them. That's what I was doing then. At the same time, I was writing a bunch of originals – more music. That's what I was doing; I never worked with poodles. I think poodles are stupid [laughs]. No, they're

---

28 Brock was on the tour from 17th July to 1st August. Zappa's explanation for this was, "Chemical alteration is not something that mixes well with precision performance."

not as intelligent as English Staffordshire pit bull terriers.

Okay. So how did you come to link up with Bogus Pomp?
All this time I was writing music and I was waiting for the right time. Because I believe timing is the most important element of anything that has yet to evolve. You must prepare yourself and be ready. But you must wait until the time is right.

Bogus Pomp had this guy looking for me. This girl that I was going with at the time, her sister wanted to find out who I was. She was trying to protect her sister and she wanted to find out who her new boyfriend was. So she went on the Internet. She called her sister and asked, "Do you know who you're going out with?" She said, "Sure. I'm going out with Napoleon." "No, do you know who he is?" "Yeah. He plays in a night club at the weekends…" She says, "Well, no. Not just that. Listen, I'm gonna send you some stuff off the Internet."

Anyway, the guy who was looking for me also searched the Internet all the time and he saw that my girlfriend's sister was trying to find out about me and he called her and got my address. He sent me this long letter. It was so sincere, that I called him. He sent me a CD and a video and said they'd love me to play with them. So I checked them out.

At first I said no, I have to rehearse with someone before I can decide whether I want to play with them or not. Anyway, I figured that with a little coaching from myself – because they have to play the music right – I figured this would be a good opportunity for me to get out there and play this music again. They don't play long tours and I thought it would be quite good.

And then you played with Project Object – and more recently, the ANT-BEE.[29]
Yes, I have a beneficial relationship with Billy James. We both believe in the same things. We believe in destiny. We believe in fate. We believe that fate brought us together for something that's very important for both of our futures. We're very excited about it and he's really helping me a lot. Without him, I wouldn't be here with you.

That's true. So next it's the Grandmothers West. I assume that came about through working with Project Object?
Well Billy put me in touch with Don Preston again.

---

[29] Brock appears on the ANT-BEE's 2011 album *Electronic Church Muzik* singing an *Uncle Meat*-flavoured version Todd Rundgren's *Don't You Ever Learn?*

Of course, you two played together in the Roxy band.

That's right. Anyway, we'll be playing some dates in Germany in the summer. I think all of these things – and the live in Australia album[30], the *Roxy* DVD[31] – are making it the right time for me to get back into music full time. I've looked after myself and my voice is now more disciplined, more mature... just better. I know what works and what doesn't. I have another CD planned with more originals that I recorded with Ed Mann and Peter Wolf. Some of that is pretty wild and probably closer to Frank's music than anything else I've done.

Can I have your final thoughts on Frank.

The last time I spoke to Frank was when I finished the 1984 tour. But we were still friends. I'll never forget creating songs like *Kreegah Bondola*[32] with him – me on alto sax, him on guitar and overdubbing George's vocal on *Village Of The Sun* for the *Roxy & Elsewhere* album. A lot of people don't realise that that's all me, because you can harmonise best with your own voice.

On *Inca Roads* on *One Size Fits All*[33], George sang that solo, but on *The Dub Room Special* video we sang it as a duet. I also remember taking various women through some of the songs for the *Hunchentoot*[34] project. Did he ever release that?

Well, some of it turned up on the *Sleep Dirt*[35] and *Them Or Us*[36] albums, but that's about it. Thana Harris finally did the female vocals.

Well, he had me sing the songs for these women, then we would do them together, then they would sing them on their own – and it was like "Next!" He was such a hard taskmaster[37].

Interview conducted on Monday 29th April 2002.

---

30 The *FZ:OZ* album.

31 A trailer for the proposed Roxy performances DVD was posted at zappa.com in December 2000; *Roxy - The Movie* was finally issued in 2015.

32 This is the piece known by many names - such as *Let's Move To Cleveland* on the Zappa album *Does Humor Belong In Music?* (1986) and *Canard Toujours* on *FZ:OZ*.

33 Released in 1975.

34 A science-fiction musical Zappa wrote in 1972 about a giant spider.

35 Released as an instrumental album in 1979, and then again on CD with vocals by Thana Harris in 1991.

36 Released in 1984.

37 Various ladies auditioned for the part of Drakma. Nigey Lennon was one and she told me: "I remember Napi as a very nice guy. When I auditioned for Drakma, Queen of the Universe, I didn't have a lead sheet to work from so I had to basically do it by ear: a nightmare. Napoleon knew the melody already and stood there and helped me – note by note – when I'd get stuck. He was sweet."

Pauline Butcher with the author.

PAULINE BUTCHER

Pauline Butcher was Zappa's secretary from 1968 to 1972. She was initially hired solely to translate the lyrics for *Absolutely Free* while the Mothers were in London on their first tour of Europe. But Zappa asked her to work for him and she moved from England to Zappa's Log Cabin in the Hollywood Hills where her duties included running the United Mutations fan club.

While in Los Angeles, she had a brief affair with Cal Schenkel and her picture is featured on the *We're Only In It For The Money* album cover.

In 2010, just prior to the publication of Butcher's memoir *Freak Out! My Life With Frank Zappa* (Plexus Books, 2010), I contacted her about the possibility of conducting an interview. She felt it best to wait until after the book was out so, in the meantime, we struck up a friendship. This eventually extended to her guest appearance on a ZappaCast (Episode 4, Part Three) and the penning of an afterword for the paperback version of my first book, *Zappa The Hard Way* (Wymer Publishing, 2011).

I later resurrected the interview idea and this is what transpired.

I know you were keen to get in touch with some of the key players in your book prior to publication. Have you had any interesting comments from any of them since it came out?

I contacted Pamela Zarubica in London when my book idea was a play for BBC Radio 4. She gave me the comments about my role with the GTOs which I use in the book.

Pamela is furious with me because when I approached her, the project was to be a radio play and when I got to Singapore and the plan changed to a book, I didn't notify her as I had not had a reply to an earlier letter. I believe she has written her own memoir yet to be published. Everything else I got from my diaries.

The three living GTOs – Sparkie, Mercy and Pamela – were very supportive while I was writing the book – particularly Sparkie, who looked up photographs for me to use. I saw Gail in Hollywood in 2007 when we had a very pleasant meal together in the Valley with my husband, Peter. She was extremely gracious and showed us around her house which I didn't recognise since Frank built his studio there and Gail had extended the kitchen. She gave me her e-mail address and asked me to keep in touch. I wrote to her saying how much I enjoyed seeing her again. She never replied.

She has publicly complained that I have not had the courtesy to inform her that I was writing the book when I came to Singapore, but I felt no obligation after she failed to reply to my earlier communication.

Of the Mothers Of Invention, Art Tripp[1] has been enormously helpful, sending photographs which I have used and looking over the sections in the book about the Mothers. Jimmy Carl Black was also sweet as he was writing his own book and we exchanged a few e-mails. I spoke to Bunk Gardner on the phone and he was still very bitter about Gail's hostile attitude towards the ex-Mothers Of Invention.

I tried very hard to locate Motorhead because I knew he had lots of photographs of the log cabin which I desperately wanted. I'm hoping someone will be able to locate these from his estate. Ian Underwood[2] has not replied to my e-mail.

What about Ruth – have you been able to get in touch with her?
I tried very hard to find Ruth while I was writing my book but no one seemed to know where she was. Then after the book was published, Mick Ekers[3] told me he'd met with her in LA and Art Tripp too saw her and sent me her address. But because I'm not totally happy about my sections on Ruth in my book, I feel slightly awkward to approach her now.

Yes, your book shows how infatuated she was with Frank. Do you think he played on that – to that extent that he was quite cruel to her? Maybe it was more after your time with them, but Frank did make some disparaging comments from the stage and notably referred to her percussion track on *The Purple Lagoon*[4] as "sort of boring".
Ruth played in Frank's band after I left so I think you need to address

---

[1] Arthur Dyer Tripp III was Zappa's drummer and percussionist from 1968 to 1969. Tripp was later christened Ed Marimba when he joined Captain Beefheart's Magic Band.

[2] Keyboard and windwood player with Zappa from 1967 to 1973, and former husband of Ruth.

[3] Mutual friend and author of the ZFT-sanctioned (but still unpublished) book *Zappa's Gear: The Unique Guitars, Amplifiers, Effect Units, Keyboards And Studio Equipment Of Frank Zappa*.

[4] From Zappa's album *Zappa In New York* (1978).

this question to members of that band. I like the story she tells about how she spent four days at the house before he became finally ill, so any rifts between them, they made up. Shame he didn't do that with some of the other Mothers.

True. Despite being a 'big reader', Gail has said she has no plans to read your book because of something you allegedly said about her mother-in-law's[5] funeral. What's your reaction to that?
Gail has got her wires crossed on this one. I have never commented on her mother-in-law's funeral privately or publicly. I know nothing about it. However, when I did my first radio interview, which happened to be with BBC *Today* programme, Nicola Stanbridge tricked me into answering a question about Frank's funeral. At her first two attempts, I refused to comment. But she insisted:

> *Did you go to his funeral?*
> *No, I didn't. No one went – not his mother, his sister or brothers.*
> *What do you think about that?*
> *I think it was shocking, but you're not going to broadcast this surely?*

You can hear the awkward cut after the word, 'shocking'. Perhaps this is what Gail is referring to and I genuinely regret it. When I came out of the interview, I expressed my dismay at being asked about something which – and I agree with Gail here – is none of my business.

Oh, that's very sad. Now, Frank broke up the Mothers immediately after returning from Ottawa, where you flew out to see him. Do you think things might've turned out differently if you'd succumbed to his advances out there?
This question makes me smile. It's full of innuendoes. There could have been a psychological connection. It is possible, I suppose, that had I succumbed to Frank's advances in Ottawa in 1969 that he might not have felt so miffed towards the band (transference) and may not have broken them up so dramatically the next day.

But supposing I had succumbed and he'd been in a happy frame of mind and not felt the need to tell Jimmy Carl Black over the phone, "By the way, I'm breaking up the band and your pay will stop as of this week," then the Mothers may have had a stay-of-execution for a while, but it would only have been for a while – the end was always in sight.

Remember in June 1968 he told Jerry Hopkins[6] that his ideal was to

---

5 Rose Marie Zappa, née Colimore (1912-2004).

6 American journalist and author Elisha Gerald Hopkins was the Los Angeles correspondent for Rolling Stone magazine from 1967 to 1969.

change his band for each tour. The plan was in his mind, even back then.

There's a scene in your book where Gail's cutting Frank's hair and you ask for a lock as a keepsake. Although Gail giggled at the time, what do you think she really felt about that?
Gail thought I was silly and she probably thought this was another silly gesture on my part. It was February 1970 and during a slightly strained period between us. You really have to ask Gail this question.

Looking back on it now, it does surprise me because at that time I was besotted with Calvin Schenkel, but I do know that I had a strong sense of history so perhaps that was what was in my mind. My biggest regret through the whole experience is that I didn't have my cine camera with me at the Log Cabin to record those strange days.

Yeah, it would be great to have that insight. Don't you have a theory about when and why Frank got his hair cut?
Mutt Cohen[7], a divorce lawyer – and Frank's lawyer – told me that women cut their hair during a divorce and I wondered if Frank's cutting of his hair related to the end of any of his extra-marital relationships or, conversely, the growing of his hair, to contentment in that area. It's no more than a casual hypothesis, as yet not put to the test.

Your book mentions a few of the other women in Frank's life – such as Karen Sperling[8] and Francesca. Did he ever talk to you about any others of any significance – like Lorraine Belcher or Nigey Lennon?
The answer to this question is easy – an emphatic 'no'. I think Frank was very respectful and diplomatic when it came to women in his life.

While researching my book, I asked various band members if Frank ever mentioned the other women on the road and apparently he never did. Although he introduced me to Karen Sperling and encouraged my friendship with her, he never spoke about her to me.

With regard to Francesca, I did not know she was involved with Frank until Gail told me about it and similarly with Lorraine. Nigey Lennon appeared on the scene about the same time that I left California so I didn't know her.

---

[7] Brother of Zappa's manager, Herb Cohen.

[8] Actress/director Sperling is the granddaughter of Harry Warner of Warner Bros. fame. She is referred to as 'Miss Moviola' in Nigey Lennon's autobiography.

Strangely, he was often talking about me to other people and indeed it was through these others that I learned for the most part of Frank's appreciation of me.

I got the impression from your book that you weren't a fan of Frank, the film maker. But you refute that, don't you?
I have never liked *Uncle Meat*. I thought it was nonsense when he was filming it and I still do. *200 Motels* has hit me differently at different times. During filming, I could only shake my head in dismay, but when I saw it in London at the premier, I thought it was fantastic.

Years later, I watched it again with my husband and thought it was rubbish. Then recently, while researching my book, I watched it again and could do nothing but admire the ingenuity, outlandishness, wonderful music and pure spectacle that it is.

In a recent article, you were quoted as saying you thought Frank may have been sexually molested when he went to prison in 1965 – what makes you suspect this?
I'm not sure where you got this quote from.

It was from the December 2012 issue of *Classic Rock* magazine.
Well, it was not my original idea. I hadn't thought of such a thing until I saw it written elsewhere – but where I saw it written, I'm afraid I can't tell you. I possibly repeated it because it does not seem improbable.

In 1968 Frank described those ten days in prison as the worst experience of his life – his hair was long for the day and he may well have grown his moustache (though I don't think it's been documented when the famous moustache was born) and according to reports, forty men were squashed in to a small space. However, in *The Real Frank Zappa Book*, Frank somewhat sanitises the experience and certainly makes no mention of rape.

To my knowledge he never spoke of it to anyone. So I think it's a matter of tracing the person who originally wrote such a charge for further clues.

You mentioned plans to adapt your book into a radio play – any progress on that front?
I was hoping the BBC might do something to commemorate the 20th anniversary of Frank's death in 2013, but that is not going to happen. The good news is that a 45-minute play based on my book may well be on the cards for early 2014. I can't say more than that at present because

it is early days and things, as you know, could well change[9].

Indeed. Someone suggested to me that you should write the definitive biography of the GTOs – what chance?
Zero! Pamela Des Barres is the person to approach about that.

Interview conducted on Thursday 13th December 2012.

---

[9] The play, *Frank Zappa And Me* (adapted from Butcher's book by Matt Broughton), was first broadcast as a BBC Radio 4 'Afternoon Drama' on 6 May 2014.

WARREN

CUCCURULLO

In his teens, Brooklyn-born Warren
Cuccurullo became a devoted Zappa fan.
He appears in the film *Baby Snakes* talking
about how his life at that time revolved around getting "some money to
see Frank in concert as often as possible". In 1978, at the age of twenty-
two, Cuccurullo auditioned for Zappa and the following year toured
and recorded with him.

Zappa said at the time that Cuccurullo was the only guitar player he'd
ever worked with who understood how his music worked: "I can sit
down and play some of that stuff for him and he'll look at my hand and
be able to play it because he understands what it is. It doesn't come out
exactly the same because he plays it cleaner than I do because he picks
every note – I usually slur about 60 per cent of what I'm playing. But
he can comprehend it. I don't think he could read it off a piece of paper,
but he hears it and the way it's supposed to fit inside the bar. He knows
what the joke is, but most people don't."

After leaving Zappa's band, Cuccurullo founded Missing Persons
with Terry Bozzio and his vocalist wife Dale. In 1986, he replaced
Andy Taylor in Duran Duran, becoming a long-term member until
2001.

Along the way, he has recorded a number of varied and interesting
albums, both solo and in collaboration with the likes of Duran
keyboard player Nick Rhodes (*Bored With Prozac And The Internet?* by
TV Mania), violinist L. Shankar (*The Blue*), vocalist Neil Carlill
(*Chicanery*) and sarangi player Ustad Sultan Khan (*The Master*).

In March 1992, I first approached the Capitol/Parlophone press
office about the possibility of interviewing Cuccurullo for *T'Mershi
Duween*. Two years later, he phoned me.

What follows is a transcript of our telephone conversation.

How did you get interested in Zappa and ultimately, come to play with him?

A friend of mine had a copy of *Hot Rats*. At the time I was into Deep Purple and Black Sabbath, but I really liked *Willie The Pimp*; it had a great guitar sound and a great riff.

Then, when I was about 13, I saw him on *The Dick Cavett Show* with the Turtles playing, I think, *Who Are The Brain Police?* with an extended guitar solo. I had started playing the guitar when I was 10 - you know, copying Grand Funk Railroad – and hearing this solo and seeing his fingers move, it got me.

Then I heard the *Fillmore East – June 1971* album, which again had great guitar, plus some funny stuff like *Do You Like My New Car?* By the time of *Over-Nite Sensation*, I was completely into it. I thought, "This is it!" So I went to see him play at Brooklyn College and I couldn't imagine anything else like it in rock; the way he used Ruth Underwood, George Duke, Chester Thompson, Tom Fowler, it was everything I ever wanted.

Then I saw them again at the Forum in 1974 and I started taping the shows.

By 1975 I was going to 14 shows per tour on the East Coast. I followed the band with Terry, Patrick and Eddie in 1976 and I became friendly with Davey Moire[1] – who is now my soundman; we're both from Brooklyn – just before the Halloween shows. One night I was watching over his cases and he came back and said something about, "Well, you know how Frank is." And I said, "No, I don't. I've never met him." And Davey was really surprised and said, "Tomorrow night, come backstage." So I took my girlfriend, Chrissy.

Any connection with the one in *Titties & Beer*[2]?

A lot of people ask that. I don't know. But there are lots of connections to me in *Joe's Garage*. Anyway, I met Frank and he said come up to the sound check and I kind of followed him around. I watched him on some other chat show and afterwards he told me he was putting another band together – the one with the horn section used on the *Zappa In New York* album. That's when our friendship really started to develop. He said he liked my guitar playing, but all his other guitarists

---

[1] Zappa's live recording engineer in the mid to late 1970s, who memorably contributed the high vocals on the studio recordings *Wind Up Workin' In A Gas Station* (on the *Zoot Allures* album, 1976) and *Lemme Take You To The Beach* (*Studio Tan*, 1978).

[2] From the album *Zappa In New York* (1978); Chrissy is the "big-titty girly".

were singers, so I never thought I'd be in his band.

The turning point came when he took me and my friend out to dinner on my birthday. We were in this little place in New York and William Burroughs[3] and Allen Ginsberg[4] were at the next table. Frank introduced us, "This is Malcolm, he's a taxi driver. And this is Warren; he's a guitar player..." And I thought "Fuck!" Two weeks later, he asked me to play on his European tour.

Before you played guitar with him, you told of your encounter with Ms. X on stage at a New York show in 1978 – is that a true story?

Yes. I told him it in Florida and he recorded it. He laughed all the way through. As the shows progressed, he said, "I really want you to do it with us." I changed the name for the show. I think he was testing me to see if I could handle it and I handled it! Later on, in a dressing room, we picked up a couple of guitars and he showed me a riff, I played it and we carried on like that for about twenty minutes. A friend taped this and when Frank heard it he went, "Wow! Do you know this song?" and we continued to jam.

Could you tell me about Al Malkin[5] and The Mongoloid?

Al's a friend – he's also known as Meatball. We used to miss school together, listen to Frank and smoke pot. Frank offered to tape his life story. He was like the Wild Man Fischer[6] of the 1980s.

Do you know what happened to the planned *I Need Your Love* album featuring those tapes of you and Al?

Frank was editing those before his death.[7] I've got another one here called *The Pus Tape*. It's recorded live with Vinnie and Bruce; really weird stuff. Also there's lots of stuff on video.

---

[3] Burroughs (1914-1997) was an American novelist/spoken word performer, and primary figure of the 1950s Beat Generation.

[4] Ginsberg (1926-1997) was an American poet and leading figure of both the Beat Generation and the 1960s counterculture.

[5] Provided the voice for Officer Butzis on Zappa's *Joe's Garage Act I* album and appears in the home videos *Video From Hell* (1987) and *The True Story Of 200 Motels* (1989). Also penned liner notes for the posthumous album, *Carnegie Hall* (2011).

[6] Larry Fischer (1944-2011) was an American 'outsider' songwriter/street performer discovered by Zappa, who produced his *An Evening With Wild Man Fischer* album, released on his Bizarre record label in 1968.

[7] In 2001, Vaultmeister Joe Travers told me the tapes were "completed and sitting on a shelf. I've never heard them. Warren talks about them sometimes. Not too high on the priority list for me right now."

There's a clip of you in *The True Story Of 200 Motels* video with Ike Willis – I think it was recorded during the making of *Joe's Garage*.
Did I look like a punk?

Yeah.
That would be from that time, then.

One obvious question I've got to ask you is why Zappa referred to you as 'Sophia'?
That was because I was always wearing women's clothing.

I thought it was after the actress Sophia Loren – Sophia War-ren.
And she's Italian, too! We both came up with the name. I used to wear glass earrings, tiger coats, big boots, it was my first time in the UK and I went to Kensington Market. I was buying, like, jackets for 50p and I came out wearing everything I bought. I used to go to rehearsals at the Rainbow like that.

Are there any other good studio jams like *While You Were Out* and *Stucco Homes*[8] not yet released? How did those songs come about?
That was originally one piece, but Frank edited it because it had different tonalities. It came about before his studio was built. I was playing along to a live solo of Frank's and he took my track and flew it over a live Vinnie drum track. Then Frank recorded over the top of that with his Acoustic Black Widow guitar. It was unbelievable. He did it in one take! I was there all night watching him put it together and afterwards he gave me the guitar I'd used – as payment. I used that for the next two years with Missing Persons.[9]

Frank did a stint as a DJ on WPIX-FM in November 1979 – have you any idea why he dedicated *The Deathless Horsie* to "the Cuccurullo family"?
Just friendship. I remember one time he came to Canarsie and played in my basement. This was where we used to worship him and suddenly he was there – my friends were just crying. We played *Watermelon In Easter Hay*[10] which, since his death, Duran have been playing; I taught

---

[8] Both included in the 1981 *Shut Up 'N Play Yer Guitar* series of albums.

[9] This was a UK made Vox 'Phantom' guitar with the casing from a Vox wah-wah pedal as the body - described by Zappa as a "fake guitar".

[10] From *Joe's Garage Act II & III* (1979).

the guys it. We'll probably do it at Wembley next week.

I understand you're doing an album of cover versions[11] – is there any chance that it'll include that?
We could do ... *Easter Hay* as a bonus track – I've talked to Gail about it. Either that, or I'd love to do *Willie The Pimp*. We've already done a great version of Iggy Pop's *Success* with Mark Volman and Howard Kaylan and Terry Bozzio – there's going to be some great drummers on it: Tony Thompson[12]. Steve Ferrone...

I assume you were responsible for getting Vinnie to play on the last album[13]?
Yes.

Which Zeppelin song will be on the new one?
Thank You – again, with Terry on drums.

Have you heard Tori Amos'[14] version of that?
I love Tori, she's a real inspiration to me at the moment.

Have you got any good stories about John Smothers you can tell me?
There's loads. The funniest one I remember was when we were at the Hyde Park Hotel with Donovan[15] and his wife and kids. He got some pot out and the kids started helping themselves. Smothers eyes just went really wide because Frank was about to arrive at any minute. So he went and got Gail and ended up throwing them all out of the door saying, "We don't like that kinda stuff." I remember I was playing Donovan's acoustic guitar with the in-laid stars and planets.

The last I heard of John was that he was ill. Do you know how he is?
We played Washington recently, but I couldn't track him down. I don't know what's happened to him.[16]

I've got a couple of questions from a friend here. Did Dale Bozzio ever perform live with Frank?
No.

---

[11] The album *Thank You* by Duran Duran was released in 1995.

[12] Thompson (1954-2003) was an American session drummer, best known as a member of Chic.

[13] Colaiuta plays on the track *Breath After Breath* on Duran Duran's *The Wedding Album* (1993).

[14] American singer-songwriter, pianist and composer.

[15] Donovan Philips Leitch is a Scottish singer, songwriter and guitarist.

[16] In May 2017, it was reported - via Trooper Chuck Ash on Twitter - that Smothers was alive and well and that Moon Zappa had been in contact with him.

The band played Blondie's *Heart Of Glass* during rehearsals in early 1980 – was it ever performed in concert in your time?
No, but I played the Blondie album to death while on the road with Frank.

Okay. Why did you leave the band?
It was the hardest decision of my life. But there were always so many band changes and it got so I wanted a more permanent situation. I had been hanging out with Terry and Dale and we'd made about ten songs together. We thought we had something special and Frank liked it. Then he called up to say he was gearing up for the road again and I said, "I think we're gonna do this band thing." He wished us all the luck in the world. So, with his blessings, we did it.

Did you keep in touch with him up until the time of his death?
Yes.

The BBC made a documentary last year, which shows Bozzio at UMRK[17] with The Chieftains[18] and those throat singers[19] – it didn't look like Frank was participating in that session other than directing things.
No. I think he played with Shankar and those people.

Have you ever been paid for the *Beat The Boots*[20] albums?
The what?

The official bootleg box-sets; they've been a bone of contention with some former band members who haven't been paid any royalties[21].
No. I'm not concerned by any of that.

When I saw Terry a couple of years ago he said he'd work with you and Patrick again anytime, any day: "Perhaps we'll form another band in the future - who knows?" Do you?
We definitely are going to work together again. In fact, I spoke to him

---

[17] The Utility Muffin Research Kitchen was Zappa's home studio.

[18] A traditional Irish band formed in Dublin in November 1962. They recorded tracks at UMRK for their albums *The Celtic Harp: A Tribute To Edward Bunting* (1993) and *The Long Black Veil* (1995).

[19] Huun-Huur-Tu, a music group from the Mongolia-Russia border.

[20] A collection of bootleg recordings of performances by Zappa that were released officially by Rhino Entertainment in 1991 as part of a campaign to stop fans buying illegal recordings of his concerts.

[21] Notably Arthur Barrow, who notes in his book *Of Course I Said Yes!*, "I called the Rhino business office several times but got no response. Finally a secretary called back to tell me I needed to talk to Gail Zappa. I should have dropped the matter then and there, knowing Gail as I did. But no, I decided to call her. What a mistake..."

for about two hours this morning – they've just had that earthquake out there. I'm going to do something alongside my Duran Duran career. There's so little time – Frank proved that: you've got to get stuff out there, make statements. When Terry, Patrick and I get together, there's a kind of magic. With all we know now, it'll be something else.

Steve Vai thanks you on the sleeve of his album *Flex-Able* – have you two ever actually worked together?
No. He's a friend, though.

I read that he recently phoned to compliment you on your work on *The Wedding Album*.
Yes, he loved it. He's a great guy.

What led to your joining Duran Duran?
Well Missing Persons were on the same label and Bozzio and Patrick got to play on some of Andy Taylor's stuff. It was the first time in a while that I had nothing to do so, being a Brooklyn boy, I decided to go for the jugular and I called up the rest of the band. I liked the Arcadia[22] and Power Station[23] outings – stuff like *Election Day*[24] – and I liked the arrangement on *Wild Boys*;[25] I just thought it would be great and I was right. Like them, I was very Bowie influenced.

Have you persuaded the rest of the band to perform naked yet?[26]
No, not yet – but what can you do? Actually, I'm wearing even more on stage these days. Times change.

In 1988, at the time of the Broadway The Hard Way tour, Frank said Thomas Nordegg[27] was unavailable because he was working for you – what was he doing?
He was my guitar technician. Still is. We've been together since about 1980. He still videos a lot of things.

---

[22] Band comprised of Duran Duran members Simon Le Bon (vocals), Nick Rhodes (keyboards) and Roger Taylor (drums).

[23] The supergroup made up of singer Robert Palmer, drummer Tony Thompson, and Duran Duran members John Taylor (bass) and Andy Taylor (guitar).

[24] The first single by Aracadia, released in 1985.

[25] The twelfth single by Duran Duran, released in 1984.

[26] A British tabloid reported that Cuccurullo liked to perform naked in the studio and was encouraging his bandmates to do similar.

[27] Nordegg worked for Zappa between 1977 and 1982, primarily as a guitar tech but he also videotaped over 60 shows (and some offstage antics), earning him the title of "video obsessive" on Zappa's *Video From Hell*.

In a 1990 interview you described yourself as a mini-FZ, in the light of your experiences with Missing Persons and Duran Duran. How come?

I'm becoming a maxi-Frank now! His influence is so strong – I find my capacity for work is endless. I've just organised a 15-piece orchestra for a Duran Duran *Unplugged*[28] show. My experience with Frank is my most valuable asset.

In the same interview you said you had enough material put by for five solo albums, but were committed to Duran for the time being. Is that still the case?

I probably have enough material for about nine albums now! I'm gonna combine careers. I'll be doing this thing with Terry and Patrick... and a mystery vocalist – someone like Julian Lennon. It could be Ahmet!

Have you played with Ahmet or Dweezil?

I've just played on Dweezil's guitar opus, *What The Hell Was I Thinking?*[29] Ahmet and Dweezil are amazing; together they almost equal Frank! No one will ever be quite like him, but they have his musical genius, his humour and they can really play his stuff.

In 1991, you were listed as a 'Guest Artist' in the programme for the *Zappa's Universe* concerts in New York – what happened?

Oh, a problem with transport. It was so unorganised. I would've liked to – I was gonna play *Crew Slut*[30] or *five-five-FIVE*.[31]

I understand you judged the Muffin Men as best Zappa soundalikes in a Cover Contest in Holland a couple of years back?

I don't remember that.

They're a band from Liverpool who play Frank's music – they've got a really good CD just out[32] and are about to tour Europe with Ike Willis.

I haven't seen Ike for ages.

---

[28] This acoustic concert was filmed by MTV on 17 November 1993.

[29] Dweezil started piecing together this still-to-be-released track in the early 1990s. At one point it featured "over thirty guest guitarists on one continuous seventy-five minute piece of music". Other contributors to date include Eddie Van Halen, Brian May, Steve Vai, Angus and Malcolm Young, Yngwie Malmsteen, Albert Lee and Joe Walsh.

[30] From *Joe's Garage Act I* (1979).

[31] From *Shut Up 'N Play Yer Guitar* (1981).

[32] *Say Cheese And Thank You*, released on Muffin Records in 1993, features special guest Jimmy Carl Black.

He made a great solo album, *I Should'a Gone Before I Left*[33].
I've wondered what he's been doing. Mark and Howard were talking to me about doing an album of all Frank's songs that should've been hits – try and get Terry involved, maybe George. I would really like to make one of his songs a big hit.

Mark and Howard remained friendly on and off with Frank over the years, didn't they? At one time they were gonna be on the Broadway The Hard Way tour.
So was I – Frank invited me to join him.

What do you think of Keneally?
I understand he's got a good solo album out[34], but I haven't heard it. Dweezil loves Keneally – he raves about him all the time.

I believe you have your own fan club in the US.
Yeah. It's sort of a Duran spin-off, but it covers my work with Frank and Missing Persons.

Okay, final question: have you ever tried oral sex with a miniature-rubberized homo-replica?[35]
Sort of. I can say that. But it wasn't until this year and it wasn't miniature.

Interview conducted on Friday 21st January 1994.

I remain in touch with Cuccurullo to this day. In 2001, he left Duran Duran to make way for the return of original guitarist Andy Taylor. He initially reformed Missing Persons and continued to work on a number of different projects.

English tone poet Neil Carlill was one of many collaborators. When

---

[33] His first solo album, released on Enigma Records in 1988, features fellow Zappa alumni Ray White and Arthur Barrow.

[34] His first solo album *hat*, released on Immune Records in 1992.

[35] A quote from the track *Sy Borg* on Zappa's *Joe's Garage*. Percussionist Ed Mann told the author, "Frank asked me to teach Warren to do the Sy Borg voice – that took four seconds – and then we recited the Sy Borg Manifesto together, which was a lot of fun, of course. By that time in a Frank production, everything was fun and Frank was making shit up left and right as icing for his sonic comedy-cake."

they unleashed their eponymous debut album together, *Chicanery* – described as 'a surreal and psychotic vision of pop music' – I invited the pair to tell me more.

Neil, tell us a little about your background.
Neil Carlill: Very quiet reserved Englishman from the provinces, always skewed on literature and, later on, music. Got into music via the beat writers and formed a band called Delicatessen; avant-garde Indie Rock. My twisted slightly gothic ways discovered Beefheart and I never looked for anyone else really. *Shiny Beast (Bat Chain Puller)*[36] was my start point but it was the voice and the words. *Lick My Decals Off, Baby*[37] was always my favourite, but I can't stop listening to *Trout Mask Replica*[38] recently. It is unnerving how repeated listens reveal the POP magic revealed in all those twirling guitar lines. And of course Zappa! Zappa! Zappa! (Thanks to my mentor, WC.)

If you were a milkshake, what flavour would you be?
NC: Al Cappuccino.

Warren, what's the ugliest part of Neil's body?
WC: NOT his mind.

When did you two first meet?
WC: I met Neil in London in 1999. I'd seen one of his band's videos on 'the box' and tried to contact him. We met a week later.
NC: Warren was doing TV Mania with Nick Rhodes and he saw a video of Delicatessen and invited me to sing with them. I went round to Warren's house/studio, the only house on the quiet street with blacked out windows with iron grill bars for security. There were usually European girls hanging round outside. It was very rock 'n' roll. Warren was larger than life. I always brought alcohol with me.

You've been working on material together as Chicanery for quite a few years now – when was the album actually recorded?
NC: The bulk of the material was recorded in 2005, in Los Angeles.

You write most of the lyrics – what inspires you?
NC: The Captain, of course. James Joyce[39], the Dadaists, Kurt

---

[36] 1978 album by Captain Beefheart & The Magic Band.

[37] 1970 album by Captain Beefheart & The Magic Band.

[38] 1969 album by Captain Beefheart & His Magic Band, produced by Zappa & released on his Straight record label.

[39] Irish novelist and poet (1882-1941), best known for Ulysses (1922).

Schwitters[40]. I like the concentrated power of the lyric, it should be like hypertext, the confusion of all the doubled up nonsense in the world being expressed through fragments of meaning. Oh and jokes to patch it all up. Art that escapes the mainstream is always appealing.

Warren, you must've had a hand in *Hubert Selby Song* - Selby[41] being a local hero?

WC: The title was my suggestion – he had recently died when we were finishing that track.

Do you normally write music around Neil's lyrics?

WC: With me, Neil has been writing to tracks, or just bits. *I Came Back To You* is a live jam. The four acoustic numbers – *The Midnight Owls*, *I.O.D.*, *Hit The Wall* and *Luminal Dark* – were written on guitar by Neil.

What happened to *His Mind Into Her*?

WC: That track, along with *Cut Me From The Mirror*, were the first things we worked on together in London. In 2004, I used *His Mind...* for the as yet unreleased *N'Liten Up* CD[42] – it is SO that record: Ben Wendel's soprano sax; Chris Golden's fretless bass – it felt a little out of place in this collection.

NC: Yes, it was going to be on *Chicanery* but we went for *Cut Me From The Mirror* as it seemed to fit the mood of the piece better.

Who came up with the name Chicanery?

NC: I think it was a committee decision – me, WC, vino – can't actually remember. I can't believe it's not been used before...to my knowledge.

I used to know a guy who had a band called Chicane, based in Basingstoke. What was working with Terry Bozzio like for you, Neil?

NC: Lovely man, but his drum kit scared me: it was extra-terrestrial. We jammed a little, so it was an experience to hear his energy and creative skills at work. More please!

Tell me about some of the other people on the album – firstly, Simone Sello, who produced the lion's share of the album.

WC: Simone is someone I've been working with on various projects.

---

[40] German artist (1887-1948), most famous for his Merz Pictures collages.

[41] Hubert "Cubby" Selby Jr. (1928-2004) was an American writer, best-known for his novels *Last Exit To Brooklyn* and *Requiem For A Dream*.

[42] This concept album was finally unleashed via Cuccurullo's website as an almost free digital download on 8th December 2015 (Cuccurullo's 59th birthday).

He is a guitarist and a producer/programmer from Rome. He'd been working with Billy Sheehan[43] and a friend of mine suggested him to me. He's excellent and he makes my life a lot easier. We've been working together since 2004.

NC: He really was the glue to many of the pieces – arrangements and sonically. He will be in the band also. The third member of Chicanery.

And Ustad Sultan Khan, the sarangi player?
WC: Sultan Khan and I hooked up in London in 1998; we did a lot of recording at my home studio. He is a genius and a legend. His work on the George Harrison-produced Ravi Shankar's Music Festival From India is magical.

NC: I never met Sultan, but his work is spellbinding, The Tuva throat singer that I always wanted to be.

Any plans to perform Chicanery material live?
NC: Yes, yes with zingy bells on. We're hoping to get Terry Bozzio or Joe Travers[44] and we will be playing in the Fall I sincerely hope.
WC: We'd love to perform this stuff. There is talk of doing some promotional dates...we'll see if that can turn into full fledged touring.

Warren, what did you like about Joe Travers' playing when you first saw him perform with Dweezil – sat next to Frank – in Hollywood?
WC: Joe had the energy and chops of Bozzio and Vinnie and the bang of Bonham. I didn't know what a nice guy he was until after the show.

Neil, ever made love to a vampire with a monkey on your knee?[45]
NC: Oh vampires are so dull these days: they go to high school, for Chrissakes; primp themselves in mirrors; promote celibacy. Shockingly teen and tame. The monkey can stay in the news and I'll nibble the ear of a werewolf.

Please, not Taylor Lautner![46] Where did you find that wonderful album cover photo?
NC: A friend of my wife's family took the picture about 15 years ago, somewhere in Canada. It's very famous in the family circle – such a great image. He very kindly allowed use to use it. His name is Tim

---

[43] American bassist known for his work with Talas, Steve Vai, David Lee Roth, Mr. Big and The Winery Dogs.

[44] Drummer who has worked with Cuccurullo, Z, Zappa Plays Zappa and Mike Keneally and has been the Vaultmeister for the ZFT since 1996.

[45] A reference to a track on *Doc At The Radar Station*, the 1980 album by Captain Beefheart And The Magic Band.

[46] American actor, best known for playing Jacob Black in *The Twilight Saga* film series.

Mahoney and he returned to the house a month later when it was no more.

What's the best smelling hotel you've ever stayed in?
NC: I've never been smelled by a hotel; or the Ramada in Amsterdam at the height of tulip season.

Warren, when I interviewed you way back in 1994, you told me you had enough material for around nine solo albums – the archives should be just about ready to explode now. It must be very frustrating not being able to release stuff quickly – though you did do just that with *O'Bummer (Operation BS)*[47] and you've made demos and other material available via your website. Do you have plans to release material more frequently – eg. for download only, like VaiTunes?
WC: I think once this year is over, the archives are spent as far as I'm concerned: TV Mania, *N'Liten Up* and Chicanery will all be released in 2010; editing is a wonderful thing.

Yes, I noticed *Cut Me From The Mirror* is now half its original length.
WC: Yeah. Theoretical 5 is creating loads of material, so my WC projects are on temporary hold – although I have five or six new things that I've been working on.

Theoretical 5 is the new band with Tommy Mars and Arthur Barrow, plus Andy Kravitz and Larry Klimas. Tell us about your plans.
WC: We love doing these free-form jams. But, we might start a *Fight Club...* or maybe just the senior's branch of the 'He Man Woman Haters' club. Live streaming free-form jams is something Arthur would like to get going.

Sounds great. What about The Composers, with Anthony J. Resta, Eric Alexandrakis and Steve Ferrone?
WC: Steve, Eric, Anthony and me, we'd all worked together in some configuration or another. The musical possibilities are endless and inspiring. These days you have a much better chance of hearing one of your compositions in a movie or a TV show than getting on the traditional radio airwaves.

So how long before the second Chicanery album?
NC: We have four or maybe five songs in development at the moment

---

[47] The track appeared on Cuccurullo's MySpace page in 2009 and features fellow Zappa alumni Tommy Mars on keyboards.

so it will be finished sometime in the Fall, I think, depending on our promotion schedule with the debut.

What do you think of President Obama?

NC: Oh my, oh my – politics and the artist! Hate politicians as a rule, but my household is in love with Obama so I will give him his due. Maybe he needs to stop the bi-partisan chit-chat and convert the liberal agenda he was mandated to do and... oh, there I go: I've said too much already. Yes to Obama. But very little really changes as society crumbles all around us.

WC: Obama is a puppet, probably the most controlled ever. Manchurian is a word that comes to mind, not American. I think my song *O'Bummer* just about sums up my feelings.

Warren, Zappa Records released *Playing In Tongues* – was that a one-off, or is that a question for Gail?

WC: It's not a one-off. Gail would like to reissue my Missing Persons CDs at some point, with added tracks... *Late Nights Early Days* in particular.

How is Sid Arthur[48] as a manager?

WC: Sid didn't really work out as a manager, but he's currently working on a Rodney Dangerfield tribute act where DoUBLEyOuSEe is his acting coach.

Tell me about tap-dancing *The Black Page*.

WC: Not PROPER tap, but I got the beats.

NC: This was in 2006, preparing for Warren's gig at the Viper room. Terry Bozzio was in the band and, as I recall, Warren was tap dancing *The Black Page* for Peter Wolf. He would do a similar thing for the Chicanery track *Midnight Owls*, although it was a percussive performance using his hands on his body as he sang the words. The man performs with his whole being.

Warren, after Duran Duran, you relocated back to the US and (cough) let your hair down a bit. Do you regret any of the naughty-naked-nude snaps, the Rock Rod[49], beating it with your fist on camera...or are you justifiably proud of your bod?

WC: My only regrets are real estate related.

---

[48] Character played by Al Malkin on Cuccurullo's 2009 Playing In Tongues album.

[49] The Rock Rod was a dildo moulded straight from Cuccurullo's cock and balls with a "realistic look and feel", available for purchase in 2001.

What was the name of your first pet, Neil?
NC: Stanley the cat with the shiny belt.

And what colour is your toothbrush, Warren?
WC: Transparent.

Interview conducted on Friday 23rd April 2010.

DR DOT

In an interview that appeared in the 16th March 2003 edition of *The Sunday Times Magazine*, I read the following: "Frank Zappa gave me my nickname...because he referred to me as the doctor. I burped during his sound check and he kept it on his *The Best Band You Never Heard In Your Life* album."

Intrigued, I checked out the website of the shapely 'masseuse to the stars' who uttered these words. There I found pictures aplenty of her hero, Frank – as well as Dweezil, Ahmet, Robert Martin, Mike Keneally, Scott Thunes, Ed Mann, Vinnie Colaiuta, Mr Sting[1] and on and on. So I tracked her down and had a nice little chat with her.

A few months later, she helped me secure tickets to see the Rolling Stones at Twickenham through her friendship with the band's long-time friend and road manager, Alan Dunn.

In 2007, we finally met at Zappanale in Bad Doberan and she proved to be a really lovely lady: very bright and vivacious, with a great bod to boot. Bruce Bickford seemed particularly taken with her, too. For some reason, the other ladies in attendance were a little jealous of all the attention she got.

Now you can share a few moments with Dorothy "Dot" Stein, aka Dr Dot.

Dr Dot with the author at the annual Zappanale Festival.

[1] English musician, singer, songwriter and actor, Gordon Matthew Thomas Sumner CBE.

I read that your forefathers were Swedish gypsy horse thieves that were chased to England and that you have homes in New York... LA... Berlin. So where are you from?
I'm a Mancunian... from Connecticut... just say the East Coast.

And how come Frank recorded you burping?
Well, after a few years going with various bands – at 17, I went on tour with the Grateful Dead, then I was invited on tour with the Rolling Stones – I decided to go to college in New Hampshire. I went to see Frank in Boston and tried to be a normal person; didn't try to meet the band.

But as my girlfriend and me were leaving the show, Scott Thunes knocked on the car window. I thought, "I'm a fucking rock star magnet!" Anyway, he says, "Do you know where the Holiday Inn is? I was signing autographs too long and missed the tour bus." So he got in our car, we went to a club, got some pizza and coke, had a burping contest... and Scott put our names on the guest list for every show!

During the tour, we went to one of the band's sound checks in Portland, Maine. I couldn't believe it, there were only a couple of other fans there. The band was rehearsing Ravel's *Bolero* and suddenly I started burping. Frank stops the band and says, "Who did that?" So I'm like, "Sorry Frank – it was me." And he said, "Come up here, I want to make a sample." I explained that I've got to have coke. So he says, "Somebody get her a Pepsi." I said, "No, it's gotta be Diet Coke." So he says, "Get her a Diet Coke." Eventually I managed three or four burps. He used them throughout the tour[2] whenever he wanted to send up Jim and Tammy Bakker[3].

Where can we hear these on the *The Best Band You Never Heard In Your Life* album?
My burps are best heard in *A Few Moments With Brother A. West*[4]. Have

---

[2] Ed Mann told the author that other burps used on the tour "were done by Eric Bogosian and Frank's nephew from North Carolina, who could mega-burp in a controlled way on command." The nephew is Jade Teta, who is credited with 'Burp Art Performances' on the Zappa album "*Congress Shall Make No Law...*" (2010).

[3] Jim Bakker is an American televangelist and former host, with his then-wife Tammy Faye Bakker, of The PTL Club, an evangelical Christian television programme. In 1987, a sex scandal led to his resignation from the Assemblies of God ministry. Subsequent revelations of accounting fraud brought about his imprisonment and divorce. All of these revelations were mocked by Zappa on his Broadway The Hard Way world tour of 1988.

[4] Andrew West Reid Jr. was invited to perform an evangelical monologue – to 'drive out the demons' and 'create some balance' to proceedings – during the improvised section of *A Pound For A Brown* at the Tower Theatre, Philadelphia on 14th February 1988.

a listen and hear my long ass burps!

Were you massaging at this time?
Yes, but I wasn't professional back then – I didn't have a table. I massaged the whole band – on chairs, on the floor, everywhere.

Frank wouldn't take his shirt off – he couldn't relax, he was a workaholic. I just massaged his hands. Ike Willis wouldn't take his shirt off, either. But Scott was a big massage fan. It sounds kind of surreal now, but at the time it didn't seem that way.

Were you a fan of Frank's before then?
Oh God, yes. My hippie father took me to see him before I could even talk. I don't know how many of my panties are in that quilt! I used to wear a 'Titties N Beer' T-Shirt to school. I was raised on Frank. My mum liked The Beatles, but my dad was really into Frank. Still is. His favourite album is the *Guitar* one, which is my least favourite. Let's face it, that's a guy album.

Well, that's the odd thing – not many girls like Frank at all.
I know. That's what was so great about it. His concerts were all guys, no women and because they like Frank, they're usually very funny. It was paradise for me.

When I lived in Germany, I had all these Frank fans visiting me. They love his music, but they don't really understand the lyrics. I had to translate them and try and explain what they meant.

I was in Berlin the night Frank died and got drunk on cider – I don't usually drink – and ended up singing his songs all night. I came back to the US about a year ago, but I also still somehow live in Berlin; I still have a flat there, all for me. I go back every four months.

But I'm in NYC to pursue a career, in music – no, not really, hee hee – I am aiming for TV, baby! Comedy. And you can bet yer British ass I will be preaching Frank every chance I get, like I have done in Germany for years.

I know Project Object – I massaged the drummer last time they played the BB King Club during intermission. I was surrounded by male Zappa fans and they were questioning my Zappa knowledge.

I was busy blowing them off the map as far as lyric knowledge goes and the drummer came up to me in the middle of all these guys and asked me to massage his hands right then and there.

The guys stood there with their jaws open while I'm massaging

Glenn Leonard[5] – who has carpal tunnel. He wants me to bring my table on 5th April to the BB King Club here in NYC and massage him and maybe Ike and the rest.

I was around 18 or 19 years old and wearing the yellow apron Frank made me wear – when me and about five other Zappa fans danced on stage as the Long Island Dance Ensemble during *Packard Goose*. Wish I could find someone who videotaped that show in March 1988; I would love to see a video of me dancing on stage next to Frank – wearing orange hot mitts and a yellow apron! I have loads of trivial info about Frank. Yesterday I found the apron – which is signed by the whole 1988 band, including Frank and loads of photos from all of his sound checks. As soon as I find a scanner, I will put them up on my site.

You say that you know the Muffin Men?
Yeah, I met them in Berlin when they toured with Ike Willis. They blew everyone away, they were great. I've seen them with Jimmy Carl Black, but I preferred them with Ike.

Tell me about your book.
My book, *Butt-Naked And Backstage: Diary Of The Worlds Greatest Rock And Roll Masseuse*, came out in Germany in 1999. Bruce Willis, with whom I had a brief affair, threatened to sue me for publishing anything about him in the US. I wrote to Gail about it, telling her that I'd written lots of positive things about Frank, but she won't respond to my emails. I don't know why.

She does seem a little, er, overprotective.
Maybe she wants Dweezil to run things[6], I don't know – now, he's a hotty!

Interview conducted on Tuesday 1st April 2003.

---

[5] As well as drumming for Project Object, Leonard also performed with the Grandmothers West and others at Zappanale in 2002. He later formed the west coast Zappa tribute band Pojama People with Ike Willis. Sadly, 'Glennard' passed away in 2013, a month after appearing with Pojama People at that year's Zappanale.

[6] Twelve years later, it transpired that she in fact wanted Ahmet to run things.

ROY ESTRADA

Roy Estrada was born in Santa Ana, California in April 1943. He was a founding member of the Soul Giants, who Zappa took over and renamed The Mothers in 1965.

Estrada played bass with the Mothers until 1969, then co-founded Little Feat with Lowell George, playing on the albums *Little Feat* (1971) and *Sailin' Shoes* (1972). He then joined Captain Beefheart's Magic Band for the *Clear Spot* album (1972), earning the nickname Orejón (or 'big ears').

He rejoined Zappa and toured with the Mothers throughout 1975 and 1976. In 1977, he was a special guest at Zappa's Halloween shows in New York – as can be seen in the film, *Baby Snakes*.

Estrada performed on stage with Zappa more than any other musician, with their last appearance together coming in Los Angeles on 31 December 1977. He continued to record with Zappa in the early 1980s and his voice can be heard on the albums *Ship Arriving Too Late To Save A Drowning Witch* (1982), *The Man From Utopia* (1983), *Them Or Us* (1984) and *Thing-Fish* (1984). He can also be found on the posthumous live releases *FZ:OZ* (2002) and *Road Tapes, Venue #1* (2012).

In 2002, Estrada joined the Grandmothers with Don Preston and Napoleon Murphy Brock (who insisted on rebranding them the 'Grande Mothers') and a year later he reunited with Jimmy Carl Black for the album *Hamburger Midnight* (credited to B.E.P. – Black, Estrada and English guitarist Mick Pini).

I hit upon the idea of setting up an interview with Estrada while chatting with Black before a Muffin Men concert at the Manor, Biggin Hill in November 2002. It helped that I'd just gotten the *Hamburger Midnight* CD from Black, which includes Estrada's email address.

I knew from our earlier discussions at Zappanale that Estrada would be staying in Germany with Black for a couple of weeks in the summer, but I thought they would be taking it easy rather than going into the studio. I'm glad they did; they produced a fine album. Black told me that it was just like old times – as if the intervening 30 odd years since they'd last hung together had evaporated – and they had tremendous fun together, as they always had. When I first introduced myself to Estrada and suggested an interview, he warned, "I have to tell you, I don't like beating around the old bush... I like telling what it is."

Not widely known at this time was the fact that Estrada had been convicted for committing a sex assault on a child in 1977, spending six years in prison.

In 1994, he was again charged with committing a lewd and lascivious act with a child under fourteen.

It was while touring with the Grandmothers that rumours of some past misdeeds started to circulate.

Then at the Zappa Forum on 23rd February 2009, Gail Zappa posted, "Roy has his nerve complaining about FZ in interviews now and if I catch another example I will officially go on record for what he has never taken responsibility for and remind him that we did not report him to the police all those years ago."

Three years later, after pleading guilty to a charge of repeatedly molesting a child under the age of 14, Estrada was imprisoned for 25 years without parole.

He will be ninety-three years old before he is released from prison.

First of all, tell me a little about The Vi-Counts and how Jimmy Carl Black became their drummer.
Jimmy Carl Black was never the Vi-Counts drummer.

Oh?
The Vi-Counts were an 11-piece band that was put together by an early friend and myself, in which I played and managed. I was 17 years old at the time. The band consisted of two trumpets, four saxophones, piano, guitar, bass, drums and a singer. Later, I put together a four-piece group named the Soul Giants. Our Vi-Count drummer did not want to do the club scene, so I was looking for a drummer and Jimmy had an ad at a local music store. He and his family had just moved into the area, from New Mexico. We obtained a gig at a club called The Broadside, where we met Ray Collins and added him to the group – as a singer, of course.

Can you remember your first meeting with Frank?
Our guitar player was being drafted into the armed forces. Ray Collins

said he knew a guitar player that was looking for a group to play with. So, Frank came during a week and sat in with us. At that time, it was like meeting another guitar player, but with original music.

Didn't you first suggest the name 'Muthas'?
After reaching the point of playing mostly original music, Frank asked for suggestions for giving the group a different name. I recall mentioning the name 'The Mothers' – referring to 'motherfuckers'. He said, "No! It will not be accepted." We fiddled around with other names, but later, when he went into Hollywood, he settled on The Mothers. When we signed with MGM, they added 'Of Invention'.

I read in Billy James's book that you have a penchant for dismantling hotel rooms but, unlike Led Zeppelin, you put them back together again afterwards[1]!
When the window air conditioner was not operating, I could not wait for their maintenance person...

Aside from the sex and drugs, what are your fondest memories of those early days?
The fun we had on stage, especially when we made Frank laugh – to the point of falling over. Then his eyes would get glassy and he would go into the realms of uncharted music.

Okay, now tell me about the sex and drugs.
We did not do drugs, for the simple fact of having to play this music. At times, there was no time for extra activities.

What was your reaction when you first heard Arthur Barrow's overdubs on *We're Only In It For The Money* and *Cruising With Ruben & The Jets*?
What can I say; Arthur Barrow is a great bass player.

True. What is your favourite of the early Mothers albums?
One is *Freak Out!*...

Any idea why Frank never released *Oh, In The Sky*?[2]
No!

---

[1] In James's book, *Necessity Is... The Early Years Of Frank Zappa & The Mothers Of Invention*, Bunk Gardner recounts how Estrada's fondness for speed and Coca-Cola meant he never slept: "One night in Toronto, Roy took the air conditioning system in his hotel room completely apart. He then cleaned it and put it back together again."

[2] The song featured a painfully high Estrada falsetto and was performed live a dozen or so times by the Mothers between 1967 and 1969. Estrada performed a version of it with the Grandmothers West at Zappanale in 2002. A recording by the Mothers appeared on Zappa's posthumous album *Road Tapes, Venue #1* in 2012.

You are generally regarded as the funny one; tell us a joke.
You have the Queen – we have our Bush.

Why did you follow Lowell George into Little Feat[3], before Frank disbanded the Mothers?
I quit The Mothers, the last part of 1969. Frank didn't want me to quit. Towards the middle of 1970, I got together with Lowell, Richie and Billy, forming Little Feat.

Why did you then quit Little Feat?
I wanted to get away from the hustle and bustle and pollution of the Los Angeles area. So when Don Van Vliet found out, he asked me to join their group, who lived in Northern California by the ocean and in the Redwoods.

Artie Tripp didn't have many nice things to say about Frank after his stint as a Mother. Did you agree to disagree, or just not talk about it?
Art Tripp's musical ability was not given any appreciation by Frank. The original members were not either, after all the struggles we went through playing Frank's music. We all respected Frank's musical abilities but, evidently, Frank was on his own time frame.

What do you think about *FZ:OZ*[4] being the first release from Vaulternative Records?
We were showcasing some new material; they are showcasing the Vault contents.

What was that band like in 1976 compared to the original Mothers?
The members were all great – they were in a different musical area.

You must be the only person to have performed with Frank in the 60s, 70s and 80s. Did you remain friends up till his death?
Yes! I hoped I could have been with him towards the end.

Does your asthma contribute in any way to your distinctive 'weasel' vocal stylings? And does it limit your number of performances? I

---

[3] George and Estrada met keyboard player Bill Payne when they were both still members of the Mothers: Payne had auditioned for Zappa, but had not joined. The three later formed Little Feat with drummer Richie Hayward from George's previous band, The Factory. Zappa was instrumental in getting the group a contract with Warner Bros. Records.

[4] *FZ:OZ* was recorded live in Australia in January 1976 by the Mothers featuring Zappa (guitar), Brock (tenor sax), André Lewis (keyboards), Estrada (bass) and Bozzio (drums).

guess what I'm trying to say is: why don't you sing more often – I like it?
I get short winded. It's hard to hold long vocal notes with any strength.

How was going into the studio again with Jimmy Carl Black after all these years?
Hamburger Midnight was an all together other reuniting party. For Jimmy and myself, it's been since 1969... no one knows that I had quit The Mothers before Frank disbanded the group. Anyway, we had fun recording this CD. Mick Pini is a great guitar player and thee Indian? Well, need I say more?

What version of the Grandmothers will be playing these gigs next year with the Dresden Philharmonic?
Bunk Gardner, Don Preston, Napoleon Murphy Brock, Ken Rosser, Chris Garcia and myself. The Classic-Jazz division of Warner Bros. Records will be recording the whole crust of the matter[5]. It will be a H-Mungus party!

Interview conducted on Monday 17th November 2002.

---

5 An album titled *A Grandmothers Night At The Gewandhaus,* recorded live in Leipzig, Germany by The Grandmothers and The Chamber Orchestra Of Invention, was released in 2003. A 'bonus track', *Of No Consequence,* penned by Don Preston and recorded at the same concert, can be found on Preston's *Works* album issued in 2007.

Bob and Thana Harris

BOB HARRIS

Bob Harris sang high vocals and played keyboards and trumpet on the road with Zappa between October and December 1980, a tour documented on the albums *Tinsel Town Rebellion* (1981) and *Buffalo* (2007). He also recorded a number of tracks at the UMRK that ended up on the albums *You Are What You Is* (1981), *Ship Arriving Too Late To Save A Drowning Witch* (1982), *The Man From Utopia* (1983), *Them Or Us* (1984) and *Thing-Fish* (1984).

Throughout the 1980s, Harris recorded with guitarist Steve Vai, contributing to his albums *Flex-Able* (1984), *Flex-Able Leftovers* (1984) and *Passion And Warfare* (1990).

In 1986, Harris released his solo album, *The Great Nostalgia* and appeared on the album *Western Vacation* by Western Vacation. Both featured his wife Suzannah (aka Thana) Harris, Tommy Mars, Vai and Vai's Berklee College of Music classmate, Marty Schwartz.

Having contacted Thana earlier in 2000 following publication of her book, *Under The Same Moon: My Life With Frank Zappa, Steve Vai, Bob Harris and A Community Of Other Artistic Souls*, I floated the idea of an interview with her husband. She said to try once he'd done with the latest Axe album.

Axe is a hard rock band that Harris joined in 1997 and has performed with sporadically ever since.

I emailed a bunch of daft questions to Bob and he promised to try and get them answered by Christmas and he did... just.

I met the Harrises at Zappanale in 2002 and two nicer people you couldn't wish to meet. My luggage didn't make it to Germany with me and so I arrived at the festival grounds with very little clothing. Bob metaphorically gave me the shirt off his back (he offered me a pair of his jeans). The couple – plus their darling young son, Nathan – were a big hit with everyone they met that weekend. As well as performing with Thana, Bob also joined the Grandmothers West for their headline set. But this was a little before then.

Tell me about your audition for Frank.

I was finishing up a tour with Warren Zevon[1] and we were back home in LA doing a seven-night stand at the Roxy that became the live album called *Stand In The Fire*[2]. Mark Pinske – a long-time friend, band mate, matchmaker of Suzannah and I and probably the one guy who knows more about Frank than just about anybody[3] – called in the middle of the week and asked if I'd be into coming up to Frank's place to do some falsetto parts that Ike Willis and Ray White weren't comfortable doing – you know, fear of hernia. So I went up there (Thana waited in the car), walked in, Frank stuck out his hand and we shook on it.

Frank had the coolest way of extending his hand for a handshake: just right out there in front – and what's really stuck with me through the years is that it was the same handshake for everyone. How many times have I seen and probably done the same thing where, depending on how well you know someone etc., that it's a different kind of handshake. Frank would engage you from the start; you always started with a clean slate with Frank. He told Mark to play some of a track and told me that he wanted some doo-woppy kind of falsetto stuff in-between the melody. I said, "Okay," then he said, "Okay, there's a mic out there – go do it."

Some people strengthen you, some people the opposite – Frank was a joy from the start. In the short time that it took, he knew when to push, when to lay back and give you a little time to think. Frank was a fun amplifier. So we finished with what I learned during the recording, a song called *Fine Girl*[4] – and that was my audition.

What was the subsequent tour like?

The tour was first class. Great hotels, never a flight before noon, fun gigs, great people. I guess there was other stuff going on, but I didn't care; I was too busy enjoying it and too busy cramming – trying to learn the material, because before working with him I was not very familiar with Frank's music.

What really happened to all those lovely little under-garments donated at the concerts?

They were made into a quilt by a lady in Fort Collins, Colorado, I think

---

[1] American rock singer-songwriter and musician (1947-2003). Zevon's best known compositions include *Werewolves Of London* and *Poor Poor Pitiful Me*.

[2] Recorded at The Roxy Theatre in West Hollywood, California in August 1980.

[3] Pinske was Zappa's recording engineer from 1980 to 1987.

[4] From Zappa's album *Tinsel Town Rebellion* (1981).

– unwashed from their original state.[5] Need I say more?

The 40-odd songs played on the tour included a number of premiere performances, including *Shall We Take Ourselves Seriously?* and *Luigi & The Wise Guys* (then known as *You Look Like A Dork*). Do you know anything about the origin of these tunes? Who worked out the vocal arrangement on the latter?
I don't remember that one much, except that Frank either called the vocal arrangements, or would just say what he wanted and we'd all fill our space.

Did you sing lead on *Luigi* on tour and Roy Estrada in the studio?
I'm sorry, but I can't remember that either.

So who's the best 'boy soprano' – you or Estrada?
Roy, of course.

When did you record in the studio with Frank – both before and after the Fall 1980 tour?
Before and after.

Did he just use you as a vocalist in the studio?
Mostly vocals. I did end up playing trumpet on a couple of things. Pinskie had this habit of telling Frank all the things you could do. That's cool, but I hadn't played trumpet in quite a while and when Frank found out that I played, he asked how long it would take to get my lip in shape – I told him a couple of months minimum and he said, "Good, you've got three weeks."

So three weeks later, I'm doing the part for *Easy Meat*[6]. It's not a very hard part, but it has some sixteenth note concert C scales – elementary stuff – but my first valve kept sticking during those runs and we'd have to retake: very embarrassing. Frank said, "I know there are many difficult things involved in playing a brass instrument, but I didn't think that playing a C major scale was one of them." I switched brands of valve oil.

---

5 During the live track *Panty Rap* on the *Tinsel Town Rebellion* album, Zappa tells the audience, "We are making a quilt... underpants, brassieres, just send 'em up." By the end of the tour, Zappa had accumulated a large collection of unwashed women's undergarments which were passed to the artist Emily Alana James. James then turned them into a playing card inspired quilt, with Zappa as the King of Spades. The quilt has been on display at the Hard Rock Cafe in Biloxi, Mississippi for a number of years.

6 From Zappa's album *Tinsel Town Rebellion* (1981).

Like Thana's contribution to *Sleep Dirt*, did you sing over an old track for *The Planet Of My Dreams*[7] – or were George Duke and Patrick O'Hearn around during your tenure?
I sang over the track. We liked to think of it as Rudy Vallée meets Frankie Valli, by way of Tiny Tim.

Was it a tough decision going to India for eight weeks rather than join Frank for the 1981 tour of Europe?
It was not a tough decision to leave. It felt like it was time to move on and the opportunity to record with Frank was still there.

Is Steve Vai just as enthusiastic about music now as he was when you first met him?
Steve Vai is a true musician. There is no waning of love for music, that would be a waning of life. A waning of love for the music business, now that could or could not be a possibility though.

When did the *Blue Powder*[8] session take place?
Blue Powder was when we lived at Steve's. I think that Suzannah has done a very good job of describing what that was like. Beautiful – both her and the time at Steve and Pia's.

If the Tinsel Town band had been a country, where would it have been?
The Tinsel Town band always had this New York City/Cotton Club vibe to me.

When you played Harry-As-A-Boy on *Thing-Fish*, did you have any idea how the part fitted into the story as a whole and were able to ad-lib, or were you just basically reading lines scripted by Frank?
Harry-As-A-Boy came about by reading lines – it really started with *Teen-age Wind*[9], kind of an offshoot of Howard and Mark on the *Fillmore East – June 1971* record.

Do you recall Thana contributing to *Thing-Fish*?
I thought that Thana did Plastic Rhonda.

I don't think artificial Rhonda got to speak – she had her mouth full.

---

[7] From Zappa's album *Them Or Us* (1984).

[8] From Steve Vai's album *Passion And Warfare* (1980).

[9] From Zappa's album *You Are What You Is* (1981).

Given that it was through him that both you and Thana got to work with Zappa, do you know how Mark Pinske got the 'very chocolate gig' as his sound engineer?

Mark got the gig. I don't know how he got in the door, but I know that he got hired because of his talent, knowledge and gift and work ethic.

If Thana were an ice cream, what flavour would she be?

If Thana were ice cream, she would be an indescribable flavour that would make you gain 10 pounds just thinking about her. Yum.

Has she yet got you to commit your story to tape?

I have not committed anything... to tape.

What sort of music does Axe play?

Axe does hard melodic rock. There's not much of a market for it these days.

What do you and the band hope to achieve?

The band hopes to keep making records, because it's fun making records.

Do you think that getting on your knees in a bathhouse is the way to accelerate your rise to the top of the heap[10]?

It depends on the bathhouse and how foggy it is. What do you think?

What's been added to *The Great Nostalgia*, which you plan to reissue shortly?

I'm adding one or two vocal tracks and one more instrumental. One of the tracks I'm thinking of adding is a cover of Van Morrison's *Into the Mystic*[11].

What was working with the ANT-BEE like[12]?

The ANT-BEE stuff was done through the mail. Billy James is a beautiful soul, gifted musician, great friend and always ready to lend a helping hand.

Are you happy with the way Thana's album turned out?[13]

---

[10] A reference to the track *Harry-As-A-Boy* on *Thing-Fish*.

[11] The album was reissued in 2007 with six extra tracks, including Bob's duet with Thana on *Somewhere Over The Rainbow* live at Zappanale in 2002.

[12] Bob appears on *Pure Electric Honey* (1990) and *Lunar Muzik* (1997).

[13] *Thanatopsis*, released in 2000, features guest performers Steve Vai and Jimmy Carl Black. Bob Harris wrote, arranged and produced the bulk of the album.

I think Thana's record came out great. One always wishes for more time and bigger production budgets in almost every record, but I think there's a vibe there that can't be bought.

Any news on that Rantin & Rayven album?
A Rantin & Rayven project is always in the works – hopefully late 2001.[14]

Interview conducted on Tuesday 19th December 2000.

---

[14] Thana and Bob performed as Ursula Rayven and Irney Rantin on Vai's *Flex-Able* and *Flex-Able Leftovers* albums and ANT-BEE's *Pure Electric Honey* (1990), but to date have not recorded a full album of their own.

THANA HARRIS

S uzannah "Thana" Harris sang lead vocals on the tracks *Flambay*, *Spider Of Destiny* and *Time Is Money* on the 1991 CD version of Zappa's *Sleep Dirt* album. She also provided harmony vocals on *Them Or Us* (1984) and, possibly, on *Thing-Fish* (1984).

Harris and her husband Bob also recorded with guitarist Steve Vai, contributing to his albums *Flex-Able* (1984) and *Flex-Able Leftovers* (1984).

In 1986, Harris appeared on Bob's solo album, *The Great Nostalgia* and *Western Vacation* by Western Vacation. Both featured Tommy Mars and Vai.

In 2000, Harris released her solo album, *Thantopsis* and published her memoirs, *Under The Same Moon: My Life With Frank Zappa, Steve Vai, Bob Harris and A Community Of Other Artistic Souls*.

Prior to her appearance at Zappanale in 2002, I sent Thana a disc of the instrumental renditions of the songs she got to sing on the *Sleep Dirt* CD to help her prepare for the festival. It was very gratifying to then witness her beautiful performances of *Flambay* with Don Preston on piano and *Spider Of Destiny* with Mike Keneally on guitar.

During Thana's solo set, she was also joined by Bob for *Planetary Tango* (from her solo album) and then Jimmy Carl Black for an a cappella cruise through Zappa's *Love Of My Life*.

During Vai's *The Boy/Girl Song*, Bunk Gardner added his horn to Bob's trumpet. For an encore, Bob & Thana sang one of their audition pieces for Frank: *Somewhere Over The Rainbow*. This was truly a spine-tingling moment.

With a deadline to meet, I wrote a fairly flippant review of Thana's book for the *T'Mershi Duween*. I thought I'd try and make amends by conducting an interview with her – but she immediately gave me the following quote on her book, which the fanzine editor (Fred Tomsett) found he still had time to add to my review: *"Sorry it didn't offer you any new insights, although the Sleep Dirt session has never been documented, for those who are interested. The book is the outcome of many motivating factors in my life. It was purely fate that bought me into the sphere of Frank and Steve, not something I actively pursued. The relationship with Steve has been quite strong and lasting for Bob and me, we're so glad. My book was not meant to be a documentary or a journalistic account about Frank and Steve. So I'm grateful to anyone who accepts it for what it is!"*

She followed up with this interview. We of course met at Zappanale and have remained friends to this day: Thana is an incredibly sweet lady.

Tell me a little about the new album – the inspiration for some of the songs, who plays what, etc.

The album didn't fall out of the sky, but it did come together almost out of the blue in a most amazing way. I've been trying to make a record for years and it just wasn't in the cards until this year. My book *Under The Same Moon* threw me into a whole new head space and circumstances in my life changed. Suddenly I had the tools I needed to make this album.

It was more about musicians than money. I asked Bobby Barth, the lead guitar player of Axe, which my husband Bob Harris is lead singer for, if he'd produce a song on the album called *Don't Try To Come Home*. It's a sort of bluesy ballad and I thought it was right up his alley. When I went in to do the vocals and heard the track, I thought, "This is it, I need to get these guys on as many songs as I can." It had such an organic, gutsy live feel. Bobby played guitar on the song and bass player Blake Eberhard and new drummer Christian Teele from Axe were on the track. They were all into it, the connection was strong. Since I felt like it was a great privilege to have Bobby Barth produce and play on one song, it took some courage to email him soon after laying down that lead vocal and asking him if he'd play on another tune.

At the same time, my husband Bob and I were in digital hell with some new equipment in our home studio; Bob finally suggested I just go to the Axe studio – NEH Studios – and record there. We already had some usable tracks, which we transferred. Christian and Blake ended up playing on most of the songs, which Bob produced.

The title song *Thanatopsis* is the tying up of a big loose end in my life, same way my book was. There's a bit of history in how I learned about that word... a high school counsellor I was seeing told me about this poem called *Thanatopsis* written by William Cullen Bryant and although the term means 'view of death', it's not morbid by any means.

His view was that all things die in order to grow and expand and become something better and greater. That's my view as well; that we die and come back to life symbolically, over and over again, in big ways and in small ways and that everything that comes to us in life is simply a chance to improve who we are and why we're here.

Fingers is the song which was recorded at Steve Vai's first home studio in Sylmar, California in 1983. Steve had asked us to sing on *Flex-Able* and then he gave us some time to record a few of our own tunes. He helped produce *Fingers* along with another friend of ours, John Jones, an Australian cat who's the author of some of the Amityville Horror paperback books. Steve was recording everything on his Fostex 8 track.

I'll never forget the night I tracked the lead vocal to *Fingers*, it was magic. We had so much fun. After we were finished, Steve stayed up and put the guitar lead on the song, matching it closely to my vocal. He really showed his professionalism and exquisite taste in the way he played with the vocal.

I wanted to have a duet with Bob on my album, since so many people relate us to *The Boy/Girl Song* on Steve's *Flex-Able*. We decided to do the song *White Bird*, a big hit in the late 60s by a band called It's A Beautiful Day. We've always loved that song, so we did it our own way and it's trippy!

Lastly, besides some other very cool tunes which I won't tell you about here, there's a skit with Jimmy Carl Black[1] – the Indian of the group, that original Frank Zappa band member so many of us love. I never dreamed Jimmy would actually say yeah when I asked him if he'd be on my album. He lives in Germany, so it was a task to get his part edited in with my parts, as we did them separately. It was a cool challenge and I think we pulled it off pretty well! I wanted to deliver something fresh and new to Zappa fans, something off the wall and Bob and I had a lot of fun writing the skit. It precedes a novelty kind of song called the *Cactus Song*.

I feel really happy and gratified with this record. My strength is performing live and I hope that I get to do that if people like *Thanatopsis*. I would love to do a tour in Europe – I spent time there once and fell in love with it.

Are you ever likely to record again with Steve or the ANT-BEE?
I certainly hope so. No plans right now, but everybody knows that I

---

[1] The track *Bart & Claire*.

have no problem asking! If we lived a little closer to Billy James, I think we'd be recording together a lot. Billy's really nice to collaborate with. We actually have Steve on another song, which we recorded in 1996, called *Slow Down*. It's a really cool fast song about living in the fast lane and missing the point of living. It's definitely a Rantin & Rayven tune.

Are there any more gems like *The Boy/Girl Song* and *You Didn't Break It*[2] lurking in the vaults? In your book you mention a song called *Two Jewels*. Will you and Bob do an entire album together – perhaps including another of your 'audition' songs for Frank, *More Today Than Yesterday*?[3]
It's in our plans to do a Rantin & Rayven album, the name we called ourselves when we sang on *Flex-Able*. We have lots of songs, older and newer, too. Besides *Slow Down*, there's *Two Jewels* and some others. We're independent, so it takes longer to complete projects. But we'll get to it.

Reading *Under The Same Moon*, it sounds like you did the *Hunchentoot* science-fiction musical vocals in one day – was anything else recorded that wasn't used? Or were there any songs on the tape that Frank gave you that weren't even attempted?
I'm almost positive I did some background parts for *Thing-Fish*, but I'm not in the credits. I'm not making claims; I'd have to listen to it again to be sure. The tape he gave me only had the songs I had to learn.

Personally, I'd keep quiet about any involvement in that particular album! Now that you've written your story, is Bob going to write about his on the road/in studio experiences with Zappa?
I've asked him about it. That guy is so busy, I think for now he'd rather make music than write, so I told him if he'll put it all on tape I'll put it together for him. We've got so many projects lined up, but who knows?

Sorry for being an 'anorak', but did you know you omitted Bob's contribution to Zappa's *You Can't Do That On Stage Anymore Vol. 6* from the discography at the back of the book?
Are you thinking of Bob Harris No.1[4], who passed away recently? What year was that? My Bob (Harris No.2) started with Frank in 1980.

---

[2] The first track on Vai's album *Flex-Able Leftovers* (1984).

[3] Written by Pat Upton and originally performed by his band, Spiral Starecase, who made it a top ten hit in North America in 1969.

[4] Robert Maurice Harris played keyboards with The Mothers from May to July 1971.

The first disc has six songs featuring Bob No.2 from November-December 1980. What can people find on your website and what goodies can we expect to see on offer in your online boutique?

Besides *Thanatopsis* and my book *Under The Same Moon*, I decided I wanted to have a community where projects by my friends could be featured, some of it being recordings which I've sung on: Zappa's *Sleep Dirt*, *Flex-Able* and *Flex-Able Leftovers* are there. Also, ANT-BEE's two main releases[5] which are really cool and trippy and my friend Greg Russo's books about Zappa and Jethro Tull.[6] I've got Mike Keneally's most recent CD *Nonkertompf.*

The section of the store with stuff from India is because I love India and I have friends who go there and buy lots of stuff right out of the local wholesale markets. I thought it would be fun to have that vibe in my store and share it with people, especially if they can't get it where they live.

Using only five words, describe Steve Vai.
Baba Cool Guy Natural Boy

Mark Pinske?
Can fix anything, anytime, anywhere.

Ike Willis?
At one with Ray White

Ray White?
At one with Ike Willis

Jimmy Carl Black?
"It's me sugar, I'm back!"

Frank Zappa?
Patient, wise, a musical scientist.

Bob Harris?
Pro musician, Master pancake flipper.

Incidentally, how did you meet up with Jimmy Carl Black?
In 1996, we got back in touch with our friend the ANT-BEE, who we

---

5 *My Favorite "Vegetables" & Other Bizarre Muzik* (1994) and *Lunar Muzik* (1997), which both include contributions from Bunk Gardner, Don Preston, Jimmy Carl Black, Roy Estrada and Motorhead Sherwood.

6 *Cosmik Debris: The Collected History & Improvisations Of Frank Zappa* (1998) and *Flying Colours: The Jethro Tull Reference Manual* (2000).

hadn't talked to in a long time (my book – ha ha! – explains the series of events that took us away from people for a few years). We were so happy to hear from him and he told us about Jimmy living in Germany. Bob's band Axe was getting ready to tour in Germany so Bob called JCB up and we talked.

Unfortunately, they couldn't hook up in Germany. We still haven't seen the guy in the flesh, but we hope to this summer while the Grandmothers are on tour.

Anyway, I called Jimmy a few months ago and asked him if he'd record the lines to a skit Bob and I wrote, send it to us and then we'd fly it in with all the rest of the parts, so he could be a guest on my album. He said sure, so that's how that happened. I admire Jimmy; he's a strong soul. I also know he loves spinach salad.

Interview conducted on Thursday 1st June 2000.

MIKE KENEALLY

Mike Keneally played 'stunt' guitar, synth and sang on the road with Zappa between February and June 1988, a tour documented on the albums *Broadway The Hard Way* (1988), *The Best Band You Never Heard In Your Life* (1991) and *Make A Jazz Noise Here* (1991).

His performances from the tour also appear on the albums *You Can't Do That On Stage Anymore Vol. 4* (1991), *You Can't Do That On Stage Anymore Vol. 6* (1992), *Trance-Fusion* (2006) and *Frank Zappa For President* (2016).

He is credited with 'preliminary research' on the posthumous release *Frank Zappa Plays The Music Of Frank Zappa* (1996), provided during his brief time as the Zappa family's first Vaultmeister.

Post-Zappa, Keneally has been steadily amassing a catalogue of tremendous solo albums and collaborated with the likes of guitarist Henry Kaiser (*The Mistakes*, 1995), drummer Marco Minneman (*Evidence Of Humanity*, 2010) and founding member and chief songwriter of XTC andy Partridge (*Wing Beat Fantastic*, 2012).

Keneally performed at Zappanale 13 with Zappa alumni Bob & Thana Harris, Don Preston, Scott Thunes, Ike Willis and Jimmy Carl Black and headlined the festival with a pick-up band the following year (2003).

In 2010, he allowed me to quote extensively from his 1988 tour diaries, as well as adding some contemporary insights, for my *Zappa The Hard Way* book.

He worked with Dweezil & Ahmet Zappa and Joe Travers (Keneally's successor as Vaultmeister) in the band "Z", played guitar all over Napoleon Murphy Brock's *Balls* album, led the rock band during *Zappa's Universe* and has toured with Steve Vai and Joe Satriani in support of their own albums (a number of which he appears on).

When I arranged with Epic Records to interview Steve Vai at the Shepherd's Bush Empire during the UK-leg of the 1997 G3 tour (a regular tour organised by Satriani featuring him alongside two other guitarists – in this instance, Steve Vai, whose band at that time included Keneally and Adrian Legg) it was never made crystal clear to me that I would also get to talk with Keneally. Certainly I had asked about such a possibility, but in all my subsequent dealings with the record company, only Vai's name was ever mentioned. I therefore did not adequately prepare for a chat with the cat in the hat.

What follows is an off-the-cuff chinwag with Keneally after Vai excused himself.

The obvious question – why did you leave "Z"?[1]

It was mainly because, from my perspective, in the last couple of years of the band there were huge periods where there wasn't very much going on. Which was kind of good in a way because that allowed me time to do stuff like *Boil That Dust Speck*[2] and The Mistakes and just whatever projects that I needed to do.

But at the same time, because I was still collecting cheques from them every week whether I worked for them or not, they had to be my main priority. For a while that was okay, but towards the end when there was so little activity it started to feel a little strange.

So I proposed that they take me off a retainer and we work out a schedule whereby for a certain part of the year I would work for them and in a certain part of the year I would do my own projects. Which seemed to me a fairly logical and professional way to go about dealing with the situation. Dweezil was just incensed by the idea that I would try to dictate policy that way and has refused to speak to me ever since.

Dweezil is not exactly prolific – I mean, I think he writes and records a lot, but actual albums coming out, actual tours...

He could easily release four albums right this second of stuff that "Z" recorded. God knows there's still the instrumental album – I don't know whether he's gonna even finish that.[3] But I have a feeling it was headed in a direction where "Z" was about to stop anyway because he had the opportunity to replace Bryan and I – because Bryan Beller left at the same time, just to be with Beer For Dolphins – and he did actually replace us: they did a couple of radio appearances; but since then there's been no real activity on that front.[4]

I'm confident that Dweezil will re-emerge someday, but I have a feeling that me leaving was just a way of hastening the inevitable. That band was gonna end anyway. When I think about "Z", I really think that our legacy, the thing that we really had going for us, was as a live band. In a way, we were never at our peak when we played the

---

[1] Keneally left "Z" following completion of the band's second album, *Music For Pets* (1996). Bassist Bryan Beller also quit to continue working with Keneally and his band Beer For Dolphins. While they are both credited on the album, they are not listed as band members. Keneally and Beller continue to work together to this day.

[2] Keneally's second solo album, released in 1994.

[3] The still unreleased *What The Hell Was I Thinking?*

[4] In 2001, "Z" drummer Joe Travers told me "Dweezil and Ahmet were having 'creative' differences at the time. Tension was apparent. Weird time."

Marquee[5] – there's something weird about the Marquee, the moment we set foot on that stage it was like we weren't allowed to do a really good show.

But we had some unbelievably good live performances. I think the shows in general were a lot more inspired than the albums.[6]

Obviously *The Medley* was a great focal point, I'd love to see that released but I don't think it'll ever happen.[7]
Besides the problems of publishing, I contend that you need to see *The Medley* in order for it to be effective. If you just hear it on a tape, they might as well think that we're editing everything together. But I would be more than happy to re-establish contact with Dweezil. I was a little miffed at the time, but its water under the bridge – I really don't hold anything against him. But I am pretty busy! [laughs]

So Beer For Dolphins is on hold at the present?
Yeah, going with Steve was a pretty difficult decision, because leaving the Zappas was my big independent step out and Beer For Dolphins did a tour of the States in April and May of 1996 which actually went quite well and then I started making plans for the next record and that's when Steve called.

It was not an automatic decision because it was gonna be a lot of touring – and it's ended up being almost twice what was originally planned. So Beer For Dolphins of course has had to take a lengthy hiatus. One thing that was nice was that at the end of last year we did a tour of the States where Beer For Dolphins actually opened for the Vai band. So I'd come out for fifty minutes and play with Beer For Dolphins and then go change my clothes and come back out and play with Steve for two hours – that was a workout.

I read somewhere that before you joined the band Steve – impressed with your work on *Zappa's Universe* – was thinking about asking you.
What happened was while I was on that April/May tour with Beer For Dolphins, I spoke to a friend of Steve's – a guy named Marty Schwartz

---

[5] Dweezil and his band "Z" played two gigs at London's Marquee Club: on 1st May 1991 and 7th July 1993.

[6] Beller later wrote: "Mike, Joe and I often talked about how our experience with "Z" made us feel like we were working with Frank, but a Frank that had been split in two: Dweezil got the serious, workaholic, anti-social, composer/studio-rat side, while Ahmet got the quirky, crazy, obscene, cult-of-personality-fostering outgoing side."

[7] *The Medley* comprised a plethora of popular hits from the 70s, which the band tore through with great aplomb. A version was eventually issued, as *Z 70's Medley NYC 1995*, on the download-only album *Demos And Rarities*, put together as one of the rewards for Dweezil's 2015 crowd funded album *Via Zammata'*.

from Western Vacation – and he said that there was this tour that was being planned and at the time it was just Joe Satriani and Steve and they didn't know who the third guitarist on the bill was gonna be – they wanted it to be Eric Johnson, but there was a question mark over his availability. He also mentioned that Steve was looking for a guy who could play guitar and keyboards in his band. I jokingly said if they let me be the third guy on the bill, I'd play in Steve's band.

I was wondering about the third G. Adrian Legg, for this part of the tour, seems a strange choice – a totally different style from Joe and Steve.

On last year's tour, Adrian was the opening act. The 3 of G3 were considered to be Joe, Steve and Eric. But I like the contrast. Besides, the fact that Adrian is so magnificent, anybody who can appreciate somebody who picks up a guitar – doesn't matter the style – if you like guitar music, you're gonna love Adrian Legg. He's just so fucking good.

Anyway, I jokingly put out this word that if I could be the third guitarist on the bill, then I'd play in Steve's band. Well word comes back that the offer was kind of taken seriously, but they said, "You can't really be the third guy on the bill because we need somebody with more name recognition. But we wouldn't mind having you in Steve's band!" I thought, 'Jeez!' I told Bryan that, he just goes "Fuck! Fuck! Fuck!" Bryan was probably the most difficult part of that equation because it was an incredible leap of faith for him to leave the Zappas in order to go with me.

He went at exactly the same time?

The same day. He was ready to completely throw his lot in with me and did. It was tantamount to betrayal for me to go off with Steve for so long. Obviously we've had many long conversations about it and actually Bryan was in contention for being the bass player in Steve's band. I got him the audition and it was down to between him and Philip Bynoe – who ended up getting the job.[8]

That was a chancy thing, but through these type of tribulations, positive things do result. Bryan's in the midst of writing a book right now – a work of fiction – and I think he's really creatively fired up in a way that he's never been before. It's turned out to be a real revelation

---

[8] Since 1999, Beller has appeared on a number of Vai's albums and finally joined his band for the "Sound Theories" world tour in 2007.

for him that he has this facility as a writer and, no doubt, the experiences of the last year and a half have done a lot to fire that [laughs]. He's a fabulous guy.

I'm just about to complete another Mike Keneally studio album – when I get back from the road. We've got a break in July and I'll be able to finish the record then and of course Bryan plays on that. We're all really, really happy about the way that record's turning out – it's by far the best thing I've ever done.[9]

Have you got a permanent drummer?

Not really. The drummer on the tour that we did in the spring of last year was a guy named Frank Briggs. Then in December of last year, when we were on the road with Steve, Toss Panos was the drummer – which was interesting because Toss actually played with Steve.

That's right, in 1993.[10] I thought Joe Travers had played with Beer For Dolphins?

Yeah, Joe's done gigs with us in Los Angeles. They all play on the new album: Toss is on some tracks; Joe's on some tracks; Frank Briggs is on a couple; I play drums on like four of them; and Mike Mangini, who's now the drummer in the Vai band, is due to play on a track as well. Really the core of Beer For Dolphins at this point is me and Bryan and like a rotating cast of drummers. But one thing that this forced hiatus has led me to believe is that it's time for Beer For Dolphins to evolve as a live act, because all along there's been a disparity between the way the albums sound and the way we play the stuff on stage.

On *Half Alive In Hollywood*[11] we're basically a power trio – just guitar, bass and drums. When you're trying to play stuff from *hat.* and *Boil That Dust Speck* – which are very layered and intricate – we have to just strip it way down, which is definitely a fun approach for me but I also think with this new material I'm writing I really need more musicians.

So when I start up again, it'll probably be a four or five piece band.

I know that XTC have had a big influence on your music, but live you do a cover of Led Zeppelin's *Immigrant Song*[12], you've done some

---

[9] *Sluggo!* by Mike Keneally & Beer For Dolphins was issued later in 1997.

[10] Panos replaced Abe Laboriel Jr. on the Vai tour that promoted the *Sex & Religion* album, the drummer on which was Terry Bozzio.

[11] A double album by Mike Keneally & Beer For Dolphins issued earlier in 1997.

[12] There is a version on the *Half Alive In Hollywood* album.

tracks for Yes[13] and Genesis[14] tribute albums and of course there's *Faithful Axe*[15] on *Boil That Dust Speck*. **Are you also inspired by the music from that era – from the early 70s?**
Well, in the 60s, I was very young – I was born in 1961 – and I pretty much just listened to the Beatles. Then in the early 70s I got a good stereo in my room and I discovered FM radio. As soon as that happened, my world just blew apart.

I remember the day *Tarkus*[16] came out, I thought, "Okay, that'll do!" So I have a real fondness for music of that era. It doesn't all sort of stack up over the years – some of it sounds a lot more dated than others – but even the most 'quaint' of it I still like for nostalgic reasons. There is a lot of music of that era that is really wonderful that I still think has as much integrity now.

I just did a track for a Gentle Giant tribute album[17] – they're a band who I think has really stood the test of time. Dave Gregory from XTC came to see us play two or three nights ago in Birmingham[18], which is where I actually first met him and Andy Partridge nine years ago when we played there with Frank – the night I got this hat.[19]

Have you actually recorded with them – down in Swindon?
Yeah...I haven't actually recorded with them in Swindon, but I've been in Andy's shed and heard demos and stuff.[20]

[Steve Vai reappears]
SV: Sorry. Mike, this lovely young lady would like to give you something.

---

13 Keneally appears on a version of Yes's *Siberian Khatru*, credited to Stanley Snail, on the 1995 compilation album *Tales From Yesterday*, replete with Roger Dean artwork.

14 Keneally appears on a version of Genesis's *Back In N.Y.C.*, credited to Kevin Gilbert, on the 1995 compilation album *Supper's Ready - Another Serving From The Musical Box*, and also recorded his own take on the band's *Time Table* in 1996 which was eventually released in 2005 on the charity compilation album *After the Storm: A Benefit Album for The Survivors of Hurricane Katrina*.

15 On his website, Keneally says of this track: "The lyrics and melody had come to me after lying on the couch one afternoon listening to Jon Anderson's solo album *Olias Of Sunhillow*. I know it sounds like a pisstake, and it's certainly not very reverent, but I do have great respect for the way Anderson used words as sound paintings."

16 Second studio album by English prog rock band Emerson, Lake & Palmer, released in 1971.

17 Keneally contributed his rendition of the band's *No God's A Man* to the album *Giant Tracks: A Tribute To Gentle Giant* (1997).

18 Zappa's last ever UK appearance, on 20th April 1988 at the National Exhibition Centre in Birmingham.

19 Which he sports on the cover of his debut album, *hat.* (1992).

20 As noted earlier, Keneally went on to collaborate with Partridge on the album *Wing Beat Fantastic* (2012). Keneally also got to play with Dave Gregory when the former XTC guitarist joined him on stage as a special guest at Riffs Bar in Swindon on 23rd October 2008; among many other pieces, they performed covers of Zappa's *Sleep Dirt* and *Inca Roads* together.

[The 'lovely young lady' presents Mike with a hat of Dr Seuss-like proportions]

[Mike to the 'lovely young lady']: That is really beautiful. Thank you so much. I'm gonna put this on now. This will definitely make it to the show this evening.

I noticed in the G3 video[21] you're wearing a hat like the one Zappa wore in Frankfurt during *The Yellow Shark* concerts – the jester one.
With the bells? No, I didn't wear one of Frank's hats. [Reaches inside bag] This one?

That's the fellow.
No, I bought this some place where we played in the U.S. There was a big stadium and they were selling hats out in the middle of the parking lot.

So you have a big collection?
Yeah, most of them are...
Lovely young lady: ...from friends [laughs]!
You make an album called *hat.* and it's like opening the floodgates. I probably get a hat a week from somebody.

I didn't bring one. Sorry.
That's alright. I've got my requisite one per day [laughs].

You recorded an album with Shankar – has that ever been released?
No, it hasn't. They've been replacing tracks and doing overdubs and messing about with those tapes for years now.

Have you heard any of his pop records – like the Epidemics records? Shankar is a magnificent violinist and I love it when he concentrates on his violin playing, but when he does pop records, he concentrates more on very straightforward pop songs. So what you might imagine of a collaboration between him and I isn't what this record is. I was nothing more than a session musician playing very simple parts. Maybe it'll come out someday. Maybe my parts will be on there – they could very well have been replaced by now.

Are you keeping up with all the various posthumous Zappa releases?
Yeah, I have them all.

---

[21] *G3: Live in Concert* (1997), on which Keneally sings on a cover of Zappa's *My Guitar Wants to Kill Your Mama.*

...the 'Signature Guitar Compositions' album?[22]

I actually helped to make that one. I'm credited with 'Preliminary Research'. Basically that's the album that I helped them compile, except that they replaced one track: for the unreleased version of *Black Napkins* we had originally chosen the complete *Pink Napkins*[23] – that's actually a twelve minute track. But after I was gone, Dweezil decided that he wanted all the live versions to be the earliest ones they could find. So they went for a different *Black Napkins*.[24]

I was hoping they'd have one with Eddie Jobson.

Oh, with the violin solo?

Yeah, but it lasts about 20 minutes.

Might be a bit much for some.

Interview conducted on Wednesday 4th June 1997.

Following the release of his album *Scambot 2*[25] and the reactivation of his 'classic' Beer For Dolphins trio line-up (with Bryan Beller and Joe Travers), we managed to coerce Keneally into talking with us for Episode 31 of the ZappaCast.

What follows are just my questions from that episode, with Keneally's responses. Yes, I have almost totally edited out my ZappaCast colleagues, Scott Parker (SP), Scott Fischer (SF) and Mick Ekers (ME) – so after reading this, please check out the full podcast.

Like many artists today, Keneally has revisited some of his early albums and remixed and reissued them in expanded form. I started by asking about the very first Beer For Dolphins album.

A few years ago, I'm sure you mentioned that you were gonna do a deluxe edition of *Half Alive In Hollywood*[26] – possibly with *Soap Scum*

---

22 *Frank Zappa Plays The Music Of Frank Zappa - A Memorial Tribute* (1996).

23 Zappa's four and half minute solo from *Black Napkins*, performed at London's Hammersmith Odeon on 17th February 1977 and released on the album *Shut Up 'N Play Yer Guitar Some More* (1981).

24 Recorded on 2nd November 1975 in Ljubljana, Yugoslavia.

25 *Scambot* is scheduled to comprise three albums; the first volume in this trilogy was released in 2009.

26 Released in 1997, the album consisted of one 'Live In A Studio' disc and one 'Live On A Stage'.

Remover[27] on DVD. Is that on the cards?

I don't know. It's something that has come up and it always seems to get shuffled to the background. I mean, how many people buy DVDs anymore, you know? I'm more interested... *Half Alive In Hollywood* is available as a download from my website and we could conceivably make *Soap Scum Remover* a download as well.

With album sales being what they are these days, you have to be really, really selective about what you choose to manufacture – you have to make sure that there's a reason to do it. I know there are people who want those things to be available again and I'm not dismissive of that fact. But we just have to be sensible about it.

Half Alive In Hollywood does have a vibe to it, though. There's something about that record that even though it was cobbled together and disc two is in mono, it's like a little bit strange. But it definitely captures that moment in time really effectively. Toss Panos is the drummer on that album and he's a beast all the way through it. There's ferociousness to that stuff. We were all a lot younger and all a lot hungrier in a way.

But believe me, I take it into account that there's a desire for that stuff. But to me I think maybe a reissue of *The Mistakes*[28] might be a slightly higher priority because that album is so obscure and it's an interesting collection of players, I think more people might get some mileage out of that... but maybe I'm mistaken about that!

So I guess, based on what you say, there are no plans to reissue more of *The Tar Tapes*?[29]

That has not come up in quite a while. I think that, that is another thing where possibly the way to go might be to make them available for download at some point. But, I'll be honest with you, when I hand selected songs from those cassettes to put on those two CD volumes that came out in the 90s – *Tar Tapes 1* and *2*[30] – I quite intentionally left off a lot of songs that frankly embarrassed me.

But it's like a part of my life; I can't make believe it didn't happen,

---

[27] Released in 1996 on VHS, the video featured two live Beer For Dolphins shows, interviews, a guitar lesson, acoustic tunes and some previously unreleased music.

[28] The Mistakes released their eponymous (and only) album in 1995. The band consisted of Keneally, guitarist Henry Kaiser, bassist Andy West and drummer Prairie Prince.

[29] Between 1983 and 1990, Keneally compiled five volumes of live, studio and demo recordings on cassette, which he marketed via mail order.

[30] The Tar Tapes Vol. 1 was released on CD in 1997, and The Tar Tapes Vol. 2 the following year. Both featured selections from the five cassette volumes.

because it did. But I understand emotionally why I haven't been in a hurry to get that stuff out there, because there are certain songs that just make me cringe.

But you've gotta give the people what they want!

People have not exactly been clamouring and beating down my door saying when are you gonna put out *Fashion Poisoning*.[31] But it's something that somebody wants to hear and perhaps one day we'll find a way to make it available.

But at the moment... I worked so long and so hard on *Scambot 2* and *Inkling*,[32] that I have quite intentionally given myself some time off from thinking about putting out albums. I have this big tall stack of albums that I put out in the past 24 years and I don't want to sound like Frank breaking up The Mothers in 1969 and saying I'm going to give the public time to catch up with me... but in a way, there is this huge amount of music that only a select very intelligent group of listeners know about. [laughs]

(Scott Parker): You're giving us way too much credit!
You guys pretty much represent the entire fan base! [laughs]

I've been doing a lot of playing live and just sort of attending to other parts of life. I see myself doing that for the near foreseeable future. So if it's a little while before any sort of albums come out – whether it be new albums or reissues – it's just because I feel the need personally to take a little bit of a breather.

I was gonna ask whether you have ever been in a greater rage since the night *Sofa* from Zappa's Universe was awarded a Grammy... but it may have been just a few weeks ago![33]
Have I been in a similar state of rage? [laughs] I think I've managed through meditation and other practices to not allow myself to become that enraged anymore in recent years, although certainly recent developments in our country here have... I can hardly be blamed! But I've managed not to kick anything.

But maybe that's preferable to being catatonic, so we'll see - I may have to kick something.

---

[31] The original *Tar Tapes Vol. 3* cassette (1986).

[32] A companion album featuring 'more from the *Scambot 2* sessions'.

[33] Before we started the ZappaCast proper, Keneally bemoaned the fact that the US presidential election on 8th November 2016 had been won by Donald Trump.

Scott Fischer knows the story behind that. Do you other guys?
SP: No, actually I don't.

Mike, would you care to relay that?
Well, I don't know. There were certain aspects about Zappa's Universe that troubled me and I don't necessarily feel like I need to rehash.[34] But mainly it became sort of a point of contention between Frank and Gail and PolyGram, who put out the album and the video. So something that was intended to be a tribute and an embracing of Frank, became a thorn in his side. That was a drag to me because obviously I took part in it with the best of intentions – as everyone did.

So I was already feeling a little weird about Zappa's Universe and then it won the Grammy. I should have been happy about that, but for whatever reason I was filled with rage and was in Tower Records in New York City with Joe Travers, with the Grammys playing on an overhead TV and when it was mentioned that it had won the Grammy, Joe said something – it was the wrong thing to say at the wrong time - and I became upset and kicked in a window. [laughs]

So Joe and I went out on the sidewalk and we thought we should go. Then one of the guys who worked in the store came running out and he said, "Did you just do that?" I said, "Yeah." And he said, "Wait here," and goes inside.

So Joe and I look at each other for about 10 seconds and one of us said, "Should we run?" And the other one said, "Yeah!" and we started to run. [laughs]

That's some civil disobedience for ya!

In retrospect, that may have been the defining moment in the bankruptcy of Tower Records.

In the Morgan Ågren[35] documentary,[36] you say that after the Broadway tour, Frank wanted to form a six-piece band comprising himself, you, Ray White, Scott Thunes and Mats[37] & Morgan.
Yeah.

---

[34] On his website, Keneally elucidates: "Steve Vai had re-recorded his guitar part for *Sofa* in the studio. Now, I have no moral compunction regarding adding studio tracks to live tapes, obviously; Frank did it incessantly, and the fact that Steve did the same is no cause for alarm in my book. But the fact that Steve's decision to get his track 'just so' was supposed to be such a huge shameful secret always rubbed me the wrong way, and now that the piece had won a Grammy it suddenly just smelled like a mondo fucking deception."

[35] The drumming half of the Swedish duo Mats & Morgan that joined Zappa on stage in Stockholm in 1988, and were part of the Zappa's Universe 'rock band'.

[36] Morgan Ågren's *Conundrum: A Percussive Misadventure* (2013).

[37] Keyboard player, Mats Öberg.

Did you ever rehearse with Ray?
No. That only went as far as him... after the last show of the 1988 tour, he invited each member of the band in turn to join him in his dressing room and when I came in he said, "Well, that's it. I want to do a six-piece band" and told me who was gonna be in it.

He was very enamoured of Mats & Morgan, after hearing them in Stockholm and he wanted to check my availability. I said, "I'll be there."

But his health took a turn for the worse after that tour and it didn't happen.

But the only time I've even met Ray was at a Zappa Plays Zappa show, when he was in the band. I never actually played with him.

That's a big *"What if...?"* to think about that band. Because he cancelled ten weeks of dates in the US that the 12-piece was booked to do. His idea was that he wanted to do this smaller band, which made a lot of sense financially, because even though most of those shows we did in 1988 were sold out, he still lost a ton of money because the band was so huge. So he was excited, at least momentarily, about this idea of a smaller group. But nothing came of it.

So those last dates could have been fulfilled by a smaller band?
That's what he wanted to do. He said I've got these ten weeks of dates to do and I'd like to try to do them with this smaller group. He told me it was exactly those players. I said, "Okay, I'll wait for the call" and that call never came.

I've asked various band members about those dates and no one knows when or where the gigs were – any venue that was actually booked.
Yeah, we never saw an itinerary. There was never a specific schedule presented for those dates. I just remember hearing that it was ten weeks of further dates in the US, presumably covering the parts of the country that we didn't hit the first time.

To change the subject drastically now: with the recent sad passing of Nigey Lennon, I just wondered what memories you had of recording with her – especially *It's Just A Black Guitar*.[38]
That was a very, very pleasurable recording session. My primary recollection was of her and John Tabacco really having to cajole me

---

[38] From Lennon's album *Reinventing The Wheel* (2000), on which Keneally provides additional guitar.

into doing a Johnny Cash impersonation in the studio![39] [laughs]

It was extremely relaxed – laughing the entire time. I seem to recall there was incense burning in the studio, tapestries on the wall – it felt very much like a hippy environment and I felt very comfortable there.

I was very sad to read about Nigey.

Yep, me too. Now, Francis Dunnery[40] has just completed a tour of fans' houses around Europe. I wondered how likely are you to resume your 'MyKeneally'[41] living room performances with Mr Beller – and when are you coming to play the UK again!?

It's interesting that you should mention Francis Dunnery because we just played a place called Kennett Flash in Pennsylvania and he had been there the night before us. When we came in to set-up, they were playing his show from the night before over the PA and it sounded absolutely unbelievable. He's in incredibly good form these days.

So you're asking about the possibility of doing house concerts in the UK with Bryan Beller? It hasn't come up, but it would be an interesting and relatively cost-conscious way to get over there and do some playing

My door's open.

Thank you very much! Right now I'm talking about doing some stuff... returning to Germany next summer with Jaan Wessman[42] and Schroeder,[43] who I played with earlier this year.

Originally we were Mike Keneally & Friends back in the early aughts and we played at Zappanale and a bunch of places in Germany. Then we didn't play together for like fourteen years or something, then this year we reconvened and I found that I really missed playing with Jaan and Schroeder.

It's a very different vibe to when I play with Bryan and Joe: it's a little mellower, it's a little more hippy-dippy, I guess. It makes me play differently and that's something that intrigues me: different contexts that bring different things out of me. It's also obviously very cost-effective, the fact that they're already in Europe when I come over there.

So when I return to Germany in the summer of next year, I'll be

---

[39] This was for *Mesmerized Cowboy*, the final track on *Reinventing The Wheel*.

[40] An English musician and singer-songwriter who was originally the frontman for eighties prog-pop band It Bites.

[41] In 2009, Keneally and Beller performed live "at the venue of your choice". Interested parties were invited to "set it up, and Mike and Bryan are there!"

[42] Finnish bassist.

[43] German drummer.

doing some more performances with Jaan and Schroeder. But I very dearly want to bring my band, Beer For Dolphins, back over there. If it's possible to do more stuff in the UK – because last time we played there was in 2013, I think, when Godsticks[44] were opening, which I guess was the last time I saw you.[45]

Indeed.
I can't say with absolute certainty when the next time will be, but I will say with certainty that there will be a next time.

SP: Can I have you play in my living room, Mike? I'll just get millionaire money, coz having you on the show is the closest we've come to having The Beatles on! [laughs]

Ah! I have a question: *Rubber Soul* **or** *Revolver?*
Rubber Soul. I have to say specifically, US *Rubber Soul*. Because to me, I think that album is supposed to start with *I've Just Seen A Face*. That's my conditioning.

But I honestly do think that *Rubber Soul* as it got butchered and recontextualised in the US kind of makes more sense as an album, because it's more acoustic. I think that's the thing I find enchanting about that record. It sort of sounds like The Beatles just sitting around on the floor playing acoustic guitars with a pile of really amazing songs.

When I think of *Drive My Car* in that company it feels anachronistic somehow, even though I know that's the way the album was supposed to go and that's the way The Beatles intended it. Even as a huge Beatle fan, I can't ignore my heart when I say that my favourite collection of Beatle music is the US version of *Rubber Soul.*

Any idea why the names Bing Jang and Arkansas were applied to you and Mr Beller?[46]
Those were the names of actual dogs that were in the Zappa house at the time.

I recently asked Dweezil what were the chances of you two working together again. He said, "Probably not anything happening any time

---

44 Four-piece progressive heavy rock band from South Wales.

45 At London's Borderline, on 20th March 2013.

46 On the "Z" album *Music For Pets* (1996), Keneally and Beller are listed as 'sidemen' and depicted in the band photograph as dogs. This was in retribution for what Dweezil saw as Keneally's attempt to "dictate policy" - see interview with Keneally from June 1997.

soon." Do you think it's ever going to happen?
Not if that continues to be his position on the topic!

But this was before he invited Ike Willis to play with him![47]
Well, we are treading onto controversial territory.

Let me just say this as an all-encompassing thing: I love and respect all of the Zappa children and I'm really very sad about what's happening between them.[48]

I worked with Dweezil briefly at the very beginning of Zappa Plays Zappa. He actually asked me to come up to the house to show him some stuff while he was in the early processes of learning things like *Inca Roads* and *The Black Page* and what. He recorded me playing some of that stuff in software that can slow it down and began to practice those songs.

Dweezil's done an incredible job of morphing his guitar technique in a way to be able to execute these things. At that time, Dweezil did say "I'd like to have you as a special guest with Zappa Plays Zappa." And I'm like, "Sure. Give me a call." And I've seen him a bunch of times since, I've gone to a bunch of Zappa Plays Zappa shows and the invitation hasn't been forthcoming.

Whatever his reasons are for that are totally his reasons and I respect them entirely. I'm not in any way trying to talk my way onto that stage. I'm friends with everybody in his band and everything. Things have probably gotten a little more complex given the fact that I'm working so closely with Joe Travers. And Joe is working so closely with Ahmet.

---

[47] In 2011, Willis told a reporter: "I've been getting grief from Gail Zappa from the day I walked in Frank's door. Dweezil and I talked about me doing some gigs with ZPZ, but anything we wanted to do would have to be approved by Gail. Once I got on the phone with her, she cursed me out for five minutes and slammed the phone in my ear. So, basically, nothing has changed in the last thirty-odd years." Since Gail's passing, Willis has performed with Dweezil on several occasions.

[48] After Gail passed away on 7th October 2015, the eldest siblings Dweezil and Moon received a 20% share each of the Zappa Family Trust, while the youngest children, Ahmet and Diva, got 30% each. A few months before she died, Gail also put Ahmet in charge of the daily operations of the family business. A public war of words ensued, with Dweezil writing an open letter to Ahmet stating that "during her tenure as the executor of the ZFT, our mother created a Zappa Plays Zappa merchandise contract with me that she did not honour. She kept 100% of all of the ZPZ tour merch money since day one instead of paying me my portion. I challenged her regarding her actions for a decade. When she passed away the situation was brought to your attention as the new executor of the ZFT and instead of making it right you demanded the same." Since then, Dweezil has accepted an invitation to play at Zappanale in 2017 – an event he had previously said he was "not a fan of". Feeling threatened by the actions of his youngest siblings, he has also changed the name of his band to 'Dweezil Zappa Plays Whatever The F@%k He Wants!' and is seeking legal action to continue "to use ZAPPA as my last name and identify myself that way performing music on stage as well as recordings, teaching music or making public appearances."

So overall it's a very unfortunate political tangled web that has been woven.

I would happily do anything with any of the Zappa kids at any time they wanted to do it and that's my official position on that.

Are you likely to feature in Alex Winter's 'Zappa Movie'? [49]
I have no idea. I haven't been contacted about that. But if elected, I will serve!

Have you ever been approached to play with Banned From Utopia?
I have. I've spoken to Robert [Martin] a couple of times and he's been somewhat diligent about inviting me to play and it has never worked out for any number of reasons. But I love all of those guys too.

That would be a chance to play with Ray White.
That's right.

Any insights into the likelihood of any more material from 1988 being released? Maybe the Madrid concert on DVD?
I don't want to release any information out of school there. That's Joe Travers' territory if he wants to reveal anything about that. But I know that he has enthusiasm about putting out a 1988 release of some kind, which is a very good sign.

I would be delighted to have another look at that material, or have another version of something from that tour for people to check out, because all of those albums that came out then have a very specific mixing style that was in keeping with Frank's proclivities at the time and I would be delighted – given the really stellar sonic quality of things that have been coming out from the ZFT lately – for a newly mixed version.

The guy that Joe has been working with, Craig Adams, on new mixes of things, he's doing such a good job. The stuff just sounds very natural and it really breathes, it's very full and there's nothing missing. I would love for Craig to get his hands on some '88 recordings.

And I definitely would be delighted if the Madrid show got some

---

[49] In March 2016, English-born American actor/film director Alex Winter, best known for his role as Bill S. Preston, Esq. in the Bill & Ted films, launched a Kickstarter crowd-funding campaign to save the vault and make the definitive Zappa documentary film. Later that year, the Zappa house was sold to American singer/songwriter Lady Gaga and the contents of the vault moved to a new location. The Kickstarter exceeded its goal, creating a new record in the documentary category when 8,688 backers pledged $1,126,036. At the time of writing, Winter and his team - in conjunction with Travers and the ZFT - are transferring as much of Zappa's film and audio tape into the digital domain as is practicable.

kind of video release, because I think that was a much better show than Barcelona.[50] That would be sweet, but I don't have any inside information about any kind of release schedule for a Madrid video.

I'd like to ask about your daughter Jesse, who is an occasional guest vocalist on your albums. How old is she and what else does she do – wasn't she a designer or artist or something?
She is trained as an illustrator and animator – she went to San Jose University for a couple of years working on those disciplines.

Right now, she's doing more of a standard type paying gig where she is working for a placement agency – she interviews applicants who are looking for employment. So she's gainfully employed in an honest to God job.

But whenever possible, I love having her sing on my records. She's got such a pure voice. It's always fun to work with her, obviously.

She's doing great, thank you for asking after her.

In 2013, you resumed your 'Mike Types To You' blog on your website… since when, you've done nothing. What the fuck?
It's a combination of being very busy and… I don't want to get too deep into my emotional issues, but just know that they're there! [laughs]

Right! Were you ever formally anointed 'Vaultmeister' by Gail?
Yes, for a few months that was my position there. Then when the great purge occurred, that was the end of that.

I was working in Dweezil's band and I was working in the vault at the same time, so when things went south with "Z" then the Vaultmeister position obviously was also rendered inoperative. I'm just grateful that Joe was there to pick up the slack and to do it in such magnificent fashion.

I know it's unlikely we'll ever see a _Vai Piano Reductions Vol. 2_,[51] but did you ever actually record any more of Steve's songs?
I arranged three of them, of which two of them I was really happy with.

That first record was really, really difficult. It was the hardest album I've ever worked on – with the possible exception of _Scambot 2_, which took a long time.

---

[50] Zappa's show in Barcelona on 17th May 1988 was televised and has been subject to 'grey area' release on DVD.

[51] In 2004, Keneally recorded 11 solo acoustic piano interpretations of Vai songs for the album _Vai Piano Reductions Vol. 1_.

The whole discipline of boiling those songs down to just solo piano and coming up with arrangements that I was happy with and then performances that I was happy with and that Steve then was happy with... because I was recording multiple versions down in San Diego, bringing the tapes up to Steve. Then Steve would transfer them – because we were recording analogue – he would transfer the tapes to digital, then edit together his ideal versions from all the different renditions that I was giving him.

But coming up with the arrangements and doing the performances was like really a sweating blood process for me. I'm really happy with the album, the way it turned out. But it was really not cost-effective. When he proposed a second volume and he gave me his list, it was like a lot of really insane stuff.

The two that I was happy with that I worked on were *Oooo*[52] and *Under It All*.[53] I worked for months on arrangement for those two before I was happy with them. Not only do you have to know the arrangement, you have to be able to execute it!

I never went into the studio with them but you'll find on YouTube renditions of me playing those at a Vai festival from Groningen at De Oosterpoort in 2010. Steve was there premiering some orchestral material and I went and did a performance of the *Piano Reductions* – some stuff from the first album and then the premiere of stuff that was supposed to be *Volume 2*. So if you want to hear what those arrangement sound like, you can find them on YouTube – of *Oooo* and *Under It All* and also I did one for the piece *San Sebastian*[54] but I was never really fully satisfied with that one, I kind of whipped that one out really quickly in order to perform it at the festival.

So I did that and several more years went by and I found that between my own projects and Satriani touring and Dethklok[55] touring and all this stuff, there just wasn't time. It really takes me months of hair tearing out work – which explains my hairline now! – to get those arrangements to a point where I was satisfied. I finally a couple of years ago I said to Steve "You're seriously going to be waiting forever for me to do this."

---

52 From the Vai album *The Ultra Zone* (1999).

53 From the Vai album *Real Illusions: Reflections* (2005).

54 From the Vai album *Flex-Able Leftovers* (1998).

55 Originally a virtual band created by Brendon Small and featured in the Adult Swim animated TV programme *Metalocalypse*. Small then set up a real band in order to perform the band's music in live shows, which features Keneally and Beller.

That doesn't necessarily put the brakes on the idea of a *Piano Reductions Volume 2* because I was contacted by a Japanese pianist – I can't remember her name,[56] but she was magnificent. She sent me a video of her playing some of Steve's stuff. I kinda went 'Hmmm!' and I said, "Steve, do you know about this girl?" And he did know about her and I said, "You know what, there's no rule saying you can't do a volume two with another piano player."

So some day there might be a Volume 2, but it won't be me. Unless I go into a studio, which I might do: I would like to get really nice recordings of at least these two – *Oooo* and *Under It All*, which together are like 18 minutes of music so there's an EP – because I did work very hard on those arrangements. But at least they're out there on YouTube.

Interview conducted on Tuesday 22nd November 2016.

---

56 Probably Miho Arai, who has videos of herself performing piano reductions of *Salamanders In The Sun* and *Whispering A Prayer* on YouTube, the latter of which Vai described as a "beautiful interpretation".

NIGEY LENNON

When Zappa passed away in 1993, one of the few genuinely touching obituaries that appeared in the UK press was written by Nigey Lennon (for *The Independent*; another was that penned by his 'good friend', the Australian-born feminist writer Germaine Greer, in *The Guardian*). Most Zappa fans had not heard of Lennon, despite her claim that she had once been a Mother.

It subsequently transpired that she had been a little more than this and although her onstage appearances with the Mothers were few (she played guitar and sang at three shows in August 1971), her offstage antics with Zappa became the topic of much debate and speculation among the online Zappa community – fuelled by her memoir, *Being Frank: My Time With Frank Zappa* published in 1995.

There remain some who dismiss her claims – which was not helped by the fact that when I interviewed Don Preston in 2001, he told me he didn't remember Lennon.

When I relayed this to Robbie Woliver of the *New York Times*, who was writing an in-depth article on Lennon, she asked me to try and correct this "flat out lie" prior to publication.

I contacted Preston and – armed with some detailed information provided by Lennon – he changed tack, saying, "Of course I remember Nigey very well. Especially the night she was fucking herself with Frank's shoe in Berkeley with Frank, Flo & Eddie and some other girls. But I didn't want that to be in the interview as I respect her very much. (I wasn't there but was in the next room and heard about it the next morning.)"

The shoe story is touched upon in Lennon's book, in which she states "a popular performance routine featured me engaging in simulated erotic acts with [Zappa's left purple suede shoe]: it later became the 'thong rind' in the song *Andy*."

In his 2013 book *Shell Shocked: My Life With The Turtles, Flo And Eddie and Frank Zappa, Etc.*, Howard Kaylan dismisses Lennon as "a now-infamous groupie" and graphically expands upon her hotel room performance, saying "It was intense. Masturbation, insertion, groaning and coming. When she finished, she wiped the sweat from her brow, tossed aside the object of her desire and asked, 'Who's first?' She was obliged by one of [Bill] Graham's roadies, but that's all it took to begin the free-for-all..."

When I alerted Lennon to this passage, she confirmed that "Frank seemed to think it was a milestone in the lives of several band members," adding that Kaylan "seems to want to drag me through the muck... but the fact that he mentions me by name suggests he's bothered by any negative connotations inherent in *Being Frank* and is anxious to diffuse them, even though I never mentioned him by name."

Whatever the truth of all this, it's clear that she did have some sort of meaningful relationship with Zappa and it's certainly true that she was a very accomplished musician and writer (as well as *Being Frank*, she published a number of other books including *Sagebrush Bohemian: Mark Twain In California* (1982) and *Alfred Jarry: The Man With The Axe* (1984)).

When I first interviewed Lennon in 2000, she was on the verge of unleashing her first album, *Reinventing The Wheel*. We quickly became friends after that and met a couple of years later at Zappanale 13 (a gig I had some part in helping her secure).

She contributed her unique take on Zappa's *The Idiot Bastard Son* to the *20 Extraordinary Renditions* CD I compiled for Cordelia Records in 2008 and allowed us to use her Zappa-approved master *Opus One*, recorded in 1970 and based on Ian Underwood's improvised piano introduction to *Little House I Used To Live In*, for the subsequent *21 Burnt Weeny Sandwiches* album (released in 2010).

My photo of *Nelson's Ship In A Bottle* atop the fourth plinth in London's Trafalgar Square was to have been the cover of her never completed album of sea shanties and adorned her Twitter page.

I interviewed her again in 2013 with Scott Parker for the ZappaCast (The Frank Zappa Podcast), ostensibly to promote the issue of *Reinventing The Wheel Reinvented[1]* and was very saddened to learn of her sudden passing on 14th November 2016 due to complications from the radiation therapy she received for cancer in 1998.

---

[1] When asked by Peter Van Laarhoven of the United Mutations website if the experience had been fun, she replied, "It was a blast! How could I not enjoy sitting down with a vodka-and-black cherry cocktail and three certifiable lunatics like John Tabacco, Scott Parker, and Andrew Greenaway and free associating for an hour and a half while they laughed at all my jokes?"

She was always very sweet and incredibly funny and I will miss her a lot.

Will your 'super-bitchen debut album' include some of the material mentioned in your book, like *Opus One*, *Statement Of Earnings*, *Moto Guzzi* (featuring Don Preston), *Heavy Lip Action*[2], *Ruin*[3], *Chicken Fried Sex*, *Marimba Green*[4], *Jupiter's Basement*, the trumpet fanfare from Stravinsky's *Agon*[5]...?!

Unfortunately, tape stock is prone to severe degeneration over a 28-year period, especially when it's kept in uncontrolled conditions (stored in the original cardboard boxes in dusty garages, mouldy basements, smoky back rooms, etc.).

The material mentioned above was recorded on 7 1/12- and 15-i.p.s. stereo tapes which were found to be in poor-to-unspeakable condition when I dragged them out and examined them a couple of years ago. I had thought I'd be re-arranging and performing a lot of the *Nigey Lennon's Greatest Hits* material on *Reinventing The Wheel* – until I listened to the original demos. That was a humbling experience. I was struck rather forcibly by the fact that time marches on. Musical styles mutate, sometimes radically. Technology takes giant steps forward. Things that once seemed awesome can begin to sound – well, you get the idea.

So, the only material from that era that made the final cut on the album was *It Must Be a Cigar* and *Yer Wife Don't Like Me*. However, at least 80% of the tracks on *Reinventing The Wheel* have a direct connection to the period during which I knew Frank and the entire project is linked to him through the participation of Candy Zappa, Mike Keneally and Urban Gwerder.[6]

So what's to happen to the recordings of some of those songs that you made for your demo all those years ago?

The tapes themselves will be re-packed, hopefully a bit more carefully than formerly and when I move to New York in a couple of weeks I'll

---

[2] Inspired by "the multiplicity of labial torments stoically endured by Earle Dumler", the Grand Wazoo's oboist.

[3] Described as "a mutant blues number designed to be apocalyptically howled by Captain Beefheart."

[4] With a solo written for marimbist Ruth Underwood.

[5] A part Zappa had Lennon play at one of the shows she performed with The Mothers. In her book she says, "he made a big deal out of stopping right at that point, then grandiosely announced to the audience that I was going to perform the trumpet fanfare from *Agon* on the guitar unaccompanied and totally amaze them. I was thrown into total confusion; I'd never thought I'd be doing it in public. Naturally, I fucked it up. Frank thought it was so hilarious he stood there and made me play it again."

[6] Swiss artist, writer and publicist.

take them to Sound Archeology Mastering on Long Island, where my collaborator John Tabacco may or may not be able to bridge the gap between technology and miracles. If they can be saved, I might release some of the stuff one of these years.

However, you maybe shouldn't hold your breath.

Tell me more about the album. I have a tape featuring *Jihad!*, *Messin' In The Kitchen* and your reggae version of *Any Way The Wind Blows*. Are they gonna be included?

All three are on *Reinventing The Wheel*, albeit in new and improved form. The tape you mention is probably a second- or third-generation dub of three demos I made for Reinhard Preuss at Muffin Records in 1998. Muffin, which unfortunately went out of business last year, was originally going to release *Reinventing The Wheel*.

Frank's sister Candy Zappa sings on *Any Way The Wind Blows* which of course was written by Frank. She has been singing that song since she was a teenager and has some great vocal harmonies for it.

Other tracks of possible interest to Zappaphiles are: *It's Just A Black Guitar*, on which Mike Keneally plays about twenty hilariously clichéd wank-'n'-spew guitar parts; *It Must Be A Cigar*, an instrumental which is a stylistic cross between *It Must Be A Camel*[7] and *Twenty Small Cigars*[8]; *Yer Wife Don't Like Me*, which Candy also sings: and *Mesmerized Cowboy*, which features lyrics by Urban Gwerder, Swiss eccentric and publisher of the Zappa 'zine *Hot Raz Times* during the 1970s.

Mike Keneally contributes some guitar parts throughout the CD and does vocals on *The Pirates Of Old Northport* and *Mesmerized Cowboy*.

David Walley[9] provides the "last laugh" on *Messin' In The Kitchen*, which Candy also sings.

How on earth did you manage to get Candy Zappa and Mike Keneally involved?

Candy lives in the LA area and one day in 1996 she called to say she had read *Being Frank* and wanted to meet me. We subsequently hooked up, I heard some demos she had made when she lived in Las Vegas and we became friendly. She will be performing live with me, John Tabacco and Victoria Berding next year.

---

[7] From Zappa's album *Hot Rats* (1969).

[8] From Zappa's album *Chunga's Revenge* (1970).

[9] Walley (1945-2006) was a critic, cultural historian, freelance editor and author of the first Zappa biography, *No Commercial Potential: The Saga of Frank Zappa* (1972).

John Tabacco, my collaborator on *Reinventing The Wheel*, was a big fan of Mike Keneally and wanted to have him play on something. It just so happened that I mentioned that fact on the phone to my friend David Walley, who the next night went to a Keneally/Beer for Dolphins gig somewhere in New Hampshire and in his inimitable fashion, walked up and asked Mike if he'd play on my CD.

Anyway, Mike and I exchanged a few e-mails and he finally drove to LA from San Diego to play on the CD. He seemed to enjoy himself, although I think he'd expected that he'd just breeze in and nail everything in half an hour. John had written out a bunch of parts for him on *Just A Black Guitar* – 'tuplets with controlled feedback but specific pitches, places where there were highly structured rhythmic breakdown 'events' (we called them 'singularities') – in sum, a bunch of diabolical things that would give a lot of players the heebie jeebies.

The *Black Guitar* parts were supposed to sound like a weekend warrior-type guitarist going bonkers in a Sam Ash store, but they were actually technically demanding. If they hadn't been, I would have played them. Mike, of course, got through everything okay, then at the end I asked him to go back and play those feedback 'tuplets again, this time over a bolero beat!

After that, we asked him to do a couple of vocal parts, both of which were off the wall. On *Mesmerized Cowboy* I asked him to use the 'Johnny Cash" voice he did on Frank's 1988 tour – you know, the *Ring Of Fire*[10] shtick. He said he hadn't done that voice since the tour and was kind of reluctant to do it again, probably for sentimental reasons. But to my ear, he almost does it – it sounds a bit more like John Wayne than Johnny Cash, maybe. He was a good sport, I must say.

In your book, you don't dwell too much on the specifics of your 'optional recreational activities' with Frank, but you do refer to him as a degenerate – care to elaborate now?
There was a TV documentary done on Frank for, I think, the Arts & Entertainment network here in the U.S. It was shot during the last few months of his life and it ended with a great valedictory scene. You see Frank sitting in his work chair at UMRK and he looks spectral, skinny, gray-haired, very tired and his voice is barely audible – but there's a wicked gleam in his eye as he whispers, "I'm unrepentant."

Frank's energy was perverse. He loved being 'bad' – and doing

---

[10] On Zappa's album *The Best Band You Never Heard In Your Life* (1991).

whatever he wasn't supposed to be doing. In a very real sense, he turned the polarity of negative energy around and it kept him going, gave him a sense of purpose in life.

He was a Catholic, what can I say?

Gail has said that she won't read *Being Frank*. If the purple sock were on the other foot, do you think you could say the same?
Hard to say. I can't imagine being in that position.

She says she anticipated books like yours and she's sure other people are thinking of doing them – "but it doesn't necessarily imply there was an ongoing relationship". Obviously there was. She appears a few times in the book, so must've known of your existence. Can you give any more details about any encounters with Gail?
I avoided her. It was the right thing to do under the circumstances, don't you think?

I do. You obviously feel you deserved a credit on *Over-Nite Sensation* - can you be more specific about your contribution? Is that you on the extended version of *Dinah Moe-Humm* on *Have I Offended Someone?*
If you mean the vocal on *Dinah-Moe Humm*, the moaning and groaning stuff, I believe that's Bianca Thornton.[11]

I contributed the following to the tracks on *Over-Nite Sensation*: keyboard and rhythm guitar parts on *Dirty Love*; guitar on *Camarillo Brillo*; back-up vocals on *Dirty Love*, which were later re-recorded by Tina Turner; back-up vocals on *Camarillo Brillo*, which were not used; and a few VSO'd vocals on *Camarillo Brillo*, which are audible.

These tracks were recorded at Whitney Studios in Glendale. On *Camarillo Brillo*, Frank basically came into the studio with some lyrics and a simple chordal riff – V, IV, I, etc. It was late at night and the band had gone home, so he asked me to sit down at the piano and play some chords to help him flesh out the song – he was basically a one-fingered keyboard player. I ended up adding a minor-chord change and fleshing out the voicings and suggesting a rhythm guitar part, which he then asked me to play on his guitar. He had tape rolling during both the piano and guitar parts and later he copied the parts exactly.

I also recorded three back-up vocals, which were nice, although I didn't expect him to keep them because the pitches weren't great.

---

[11] As noted elsewhere, Thornton worked with Zappa in 1976. The backing vocals on *Dinah Moe-Humm* – both on *Over-Nite Sensation* (1973) and the reconstructed & remixed version on *Have I Offended Someone?* (1997) – are performed by Tina Turner, Debbie Wilson & Lynn Sims of The Ikettes.

On *Dirty Love* he had a series of basic instrumental tracks and the lead vocal up on the board, including a harpsichord part by George Duke, which he said he didn't like the tonality of. Duke's keyboards were set up in the studio and I sat at the clavinet and played another part. As far as I can tell, that's the same part that was released on the album.

I'm also fairly sure my rhythm guitar part on *Dirty Love* is intact, although it's extremely low in the mix.

I've already explained in *Being Frank* about the back-up vocals on *Dirty Love*. I came up with the parts and recorded them, but they sounded so white-bread that Frank and I were rolling on the floor laughing. A little later when Frank was doing sessions at Bolic Studios in Inglewood, which was Ike Turner's studio, he got Tina Turner and a couple of the Ikettes to re-record them.

I think it would have been appropriate under the circumstances for Frank to have given me a credit, even if it was just a 'thanks to'. It really used to bug me, though I think I've gotten over it. Hell, it was a long time ago.

Apart from the 'thong rind' in *Andy*,[12] what other references to your relationship are there in Zappa's work?
The song *Muffin Man*[13] seemed to refer to what he believed was a relationship I was having with Ray "muffins...pumpkins...vegetables, etc." Collins.

While he was recording *Apostrophe (')*[14], he called me and asked if I could ask Ray to contact him about doing some vocals. Ray was out of work at the time and was living in a fleabag hotel, the St. Moritz, which was next door to Frank's office and rehearsal complex on Sunset Boulevard. Frank apparently didn't want to call, or have someone 'official' call Ray at the St. Moritz. I told him I thought that was kind of cowardly and he got pissed off and the next thing I knew he'd recorded Muffin Man – "girl, you thought he was a man, but he was a muffin."[15]

---

[12] From the Zappa album *One Size Fits All* (1975).

[13] From the Zappa/Beefheart/Mothers album *Bongo Fury* (1975).

[14] Zappa album released in 1974.

[15] Collins sang back-up vocals on *Don't Eat The Yellow Snow* & *Nanook Rubs It* on the *Apostrophe (')* album.

Since completing the book, have you had any further encounters with Ray Collins, either of the Underwoods, or Captain Beefheart?
No. I've been through some major changes in the past few years. My marriage ended, I subsequently got into a great relationship, I had some serious health problems, I met John Tabacco and I've been spending more and more time on the East Coast. Frank and the people I met through him and Los Angeles, have begun to take on an increasingly 'historical' aspect for me.

In an interview you did with Bob Dobbs[16] in 1995, he said he'd talked to Frank through a medium and had a message for you. So, did he like the book?
I don't remember what Bob's medium said on that score, but Candy Zappa has a psychic friend who claims to have contacted Frank and she claimed he was still fond of me, for what it's worth. He didn't specifically mention the book, though.

Interview conducted on Thursday 15th June 2000.

---

[16] A fascinating individual who the author has met on a number of occasions. As well as talking to the deceased Zappa, Dobbs claims to have been born in 1922, met Hitler, befriended Captain Beefheart in the fifties and participated in the cover-up of the true facts of JFK's assassination. Dobbs is now a member of a "weird cult-type thing" that broadcasts on Radio iON and travels the world lecturing on the life and work of Wyndham Lewis and Marshall McLuhan.

MARTIN LICKERT

When bassist Jeff Simmons quit the Mothers just prior to filming *200 Motels* at Pinewood Studios in early 1971, the first candidate to replace him was actor Wilfrid Brambell (1912-1985), best known for his role in the British television series *Steptoe And Son*. He had also played Paul McCartney's grandfather in The Beatles' film *A Hard Day's Night*.

Brambell rehearsed with the band for about a week, then decided he couldn't handle it anymore. When Ringo Starr's assistant Martin Lickert walked into the dressing room, the band thought he might be good for the part of 'Jeff'.

In the home video *The True Story Of 200 Motels*, Zappa says of Lickert, "He took the script and he read it and he sounded good and then we found out that he was a bass player. I think he's good for the part... quite professional on screen and as a bass player he's not astonishing, but he can make the parts."

That was the start of Lickert's brief time as a Mother.

As well as his supporting role in *200 Motels*, Lickert also makes a cameo appearance in Genesis drummer/vocalist Phil Collins' autobiography *Not Dead Yet* (2016).

He later became a bookmaker, a horse race owner and finally, a barrister. He died suddenly, in his late 50s, in March 2006.

In 1993, after appearances on Danny Baker's BBC Radio 5 show and *After All* TV programme, I arranged an interview with him in the heart of London's legal district, the Temple.

I played him some of the dialogue portions from Zappa's audio documentary of the 'vaudeville' band, *Playground Psychotics* (1992), as I took up my spot on the bench.

I notice the accent's changed a bit since then. Where do you originate from?
The West Midlands – which is a bit different from that accent.

So what were you doing before you came down to seek your fame and fortune in London?
I always wanted to be a rock musician and to that end I had a couple of groups in the West Midlands. Interestingly enough, the first group we ever got together had Bob Plant of Led Zeppelin singing – and he's still as bloody tight as he was then!

He went off with various groups and the rest of us sunk away. He obviously had star potential. We used to jam at a pub called the Seven Stars near Stourbridge Junction. One night we had Stan Webb from Chicken Shack, Chris Wood from Traffic – who's regrettably died since – we had a future all-star band. But I won't say I was very good at it.

I had a succession of no-hope day jobs. Then I came down to London in 1969 with 19 shillings and 6 pence in my pocket. I eventually got a job as an office cleaner. On the first day I was cleaning brass railings in Regent Street and the second day they sent me to get the marks off the walls at the Apple Building.[1]

Someone said, "Do you want a job as an office boy?" An office boy then was getting eight quid and I was getting ten quid for cleaning dirty marks, so I thought this was a huge drop in wages. But clearly there was more potential than polishing buildings. So that's what I did. I started work as an office boy for Apple.

They had quite a few employees around that time, didn't they?
This was their place at Savile Row – I wasn't around in the Baker Street days, where I think they were lucky to have any fixtures and fittings. Anyway, I did that for nine months and then Ringo's driver, a chap called Alan Hagan, lost his licence.

Do you remember those stubs – you're probably too young to remember; instead of those zig-zag lines, there were these stubs – he parked across those. What we call a 'totter'. So that was the end of him. Ringo put me on three months' trial and that was it. It was great, a lovely job – great chap. Took me to America – I'd never been out of the country before.

Can you tell me your version of how you came to be in *200 Motels*?
It's exactly that. I said I went out for some cigarettes, but I seem to remember it was tissues from Uxbridge because Ringo had a terrible cold.

---

[1] 3 Savile Row, the Headquarters of the Beatles' Apple Corps Ltd. and home to the Apple Studio.

So had you been around much before then and met the band?
Oh yeah, because I had to take Ringo to the rehearsals at Pinewood, which is where it went on. Bloody good. Ringo very kindly said, "Alright, I'll get Mal Evans[2] to drive". He's dead now, too. So Mal drove for Ringo and I stayed with the Mothers at some... poor hotel!

Zappa was presumably in a different hotel?
No, he was staying at a house in Holland Park with Janet, Lucy[3] and Gail.

Had you heard much of his stuff before then?
No, I thought he was weird. But he was absolutely straight; it immediately struck me how conservative he was – you know, nothing like Jim Black!

I was fortunate enough to meet Black recently.
Did he tap you up for a tenner?

No, but the editor of *T'Mershi Duween* bought him a beer. Did you get to meet Jeff Simmons before he quit?
No, I don't know anything about Jeff Simmons other than I was glad he left – purely for selfish reasons.

Did you actually play and record the stuff live at Pinewood?
We played and recorded it live, but whoever was doing the mixing and whoever was doing the sound job clearly wasn't listening very closely to the bass parts. So I think Frank in fact re-recorded and overdubbed most of it. For someone of my limited ability, some of the stuff on that album is pretty difficult.

***The True Story Of 200 Motels* video shows you playing a six-string acoustic on the song *Mystery Roach* – was that just a posed shot?**
In fact, I play six-string better than I play bass.

There's also a scene with you playing bass in a corridor with Ian Underwood.
That would be us rehearsing then. If it hadn't been for Ian, my limited

---

[2] Malcolm Frederick Evans (1935-1976) was road manager, assistant, and friend of the Beatles.

[3] Janet-Neville Ferguson (aka Gabby Furggy) and Miss Lucy Offerall, who played groupies in *200 Motels*. Ferguson was married to Zappa's technician Paul Hof (one of the faces of the two headed roadie on the cover of *Over-Nite Sensation*) and sings on the albums *Burnt Weeny Sandwich* (1970), *Waka/Jawaka* (1972) and *The Grand Wazoo* (1972). Miss Lucy was a member of the a cappella girl group The GTOs, and also appeared in Zappa's films *Uncle Meat* and *Video From Hell*. She passed away in 1991 having contracted AIDS.

abilities would have come to the surface a lot quicker than when they got back to America and listened to the master!

Do you still play music at all?

I've got a Fender six-string at home. In fact my daughter, who's six, she got the guitar out about three nights ago – she's started taking piano lessons – she said, *"Do you still play this, dad?"* And that was the first time I'd picked it up for two years, I should think. But, yeah, I enjoy it.

At the time of making the film there apparently was some bad feeling between the director, Tony Palmer and Zappa. Was that evident at all?

Not to me. I don't think I was close enough to the nub of things to be let in on that. So any screaming and shouting certainly went on behind closed doors.

He threatened to erase the master tapes at one point.

Maybe it would have been better if he had of done!

Have you watched it lately?

It was on telly – I didn't watch it. But someone here – who shall remain nameless – her boyfriend works for Sky and she mentioned to him that I was in chambers and he said, "Oh, I'll get him a copy." So he got me one, courtesy of Sky. Then when I did Danny Baker, he gave me one – I'm not sure if I was supposed to have walked off with that.

He said he'd recorded *Slade In Flame*[4] over the top!

Well, I've yet to see if he has.

Presumably you've not had any contact with Zappa or the Mothers since then?

About a year afterwards, I had some contact with Frank. He wanted to know of a decent restaurant. In London, there are many – or were many. There used to be one called Keats in Hampstead, quite cheap. I said, "Well, Ringo goes there sometimes and he seems to like it." So he said, "Okay, well lets all go out for dinner." I think Keats, up until the time that it closed, used to send him menus across the Atlantic to try and encourage him to come back. Obviously they'd make a decent bundle if he goes there with over nine people. But I've had no contact after that and I understand Frank's ill?

---

4 The 1975 film starring UK rock band Slade - unlike *200 Motels*, it has been described as 'the *Citizen Kane* of rock musicals'.

Yes, quite seriously ill.

I didn't know anything about that until somebody told me. I don't read the music press and the only place I would have picked it up off would have been the news.

The *Daily Express* said he had six months to live two years ago.

Well, I'm glad they got that wrong!

He's got prostate cancer, which has spread to his bones.

Oh shit. Does that stop you playing then?

Well I don't think he's picked up the guitar for a long time; he tends to record exclusively on the Synclavier now.[5] Did you continue to work with Ringo after the film?

I did. I was going to go back with the Mothers, but I really wasn't good enough – no, I shouldn't say that: they discovered that I wasn't really good enough. I'd already said to Ringo I'm gonna go back because they'd said, "Do you want to play?" And then I had to ask Ringo if I could go back to work with him.

But it wasn't the same – I would have left at the drop of a Fender, as it were. I went back to work with Ringo for about three months and it didn't work out, so that was that.[6]

So how did your subsequent career start?

I then worked for CBS as a promotion man in 1973. I got out of London in the mid-1970s. I eventually bought a bookmakers shop – I was a bookie for a bit. But again, my bookmaking abilities were about as good as my bass playing.

I came back down here at the end of 1981. My wife I met through my cousin's husband, who was a pupil barrister at the time. So was she. They said, "Why don't you read for the bar?" I said, "Christ, the last time I did anything like that was in 1964!"

I got a place at South Bank Polytechnic, did a law degree there from 1982 to 1985. Then in 1985/86 I did my bar exams and that was it. I was called to the bar in 1986.

So that's what I've been doing ever since. I'm glad to say that it seems my abilities in this respect are a lot better than bass playing or bookmaking.

---

5 One month after this interview, Zappa passed away.'

6 Jimmy Carl Black suggested that Lickert began acting like a rock star after *200 Motels* and trashed Starr's London flat.

Finally, have you got any good stories about the Mothers, Ringo, Keith Moon – anything that happened during the making of *200 Motels*?

Well, I'll tell you one. Lucy Offerall had got the hots for me. One night we'd all been down in the bar of the hotel and as usual, with Keith around, everyone was pissed out of their brains and I sort of lumbered up to my bedroom at about 10 O'clock and passed out. I was on the second floor. Lucy said, "Oh Keith, I want to get into Martin's bedroom". He went, "Don't worry, my dear, I'll get you in."

Apparently it was pissing down with rain outside, he climbs out onto the window ledge, creeps along, smashes my window, gets in, opens the door. I woke up absolutely covered in glass and Lucy!

It was just a good, fun time. You know, Ringo was extremely good... letting me off for that time.

We shouldn't call him Ringo anymore – he likes to be called Richard Starkey now he's in his fifties and a grandad.

Really? Oh, good.

You were also gonna play at the Albert Hall?

That's right.

I've got a picture of you standing outside with a kipper tie and your wide lapels.

Someone sent me that picture. Yeah, we were all gonna play. But that bunch of buggers at the Royal Philharmonic, after they'd grabbed the money for *200 Motels* – I perhaps shouldn't say this: let's say that after they'd done the film, they didn't want to demean themselves in public. It was the lyrics that caused the trouble.[7]

So you didn't end up in court defending Zappa a few years later!

No, no. He's what I would call a very clean living, drug-free man. He used to take great exception to those members of the group that used drugs.

Yes, they've been the downfall of many members over the years.

That's right. He used to go mad if they would sneak off for a joint or

---

[7] In his book *Shell Shocked*, Howard Kaylan suggests that plans for the Royal Philharmonic and the Mothers to perform the score from *200 Motels* in a sold-out show at London's Royal Albert Hall was all an elaborate publicity stunt on Herb Cohen's part. The performance was banned by the Hall as "the programme content was not agreeable to us". In 1975, Zappa and Cohen unsuccessfully tried to sue the Crown for breach of contract at the Old Bailey.

whatever. I think he could stand Jimmy's drinking – if you can stand Jim, you'd better stand his drinking!

Interview conducted on Friday 5th November 1993.

ROBERT MARTIN

Robert 'Bobby' Martin sang and played keyboards, sax and French horn for Zappa between September 1981 and June 1988.

Before then, Martin was a big part of the 'Philly sound': his French horn can be heard on a number of major hits from the 1970s, including *Didn't I (Blow Your Mind This Time)* by The Delfonics, *Betcha By Golly, Wow* and *I'm Stone In Love With You* by The Stylistics, *Me And Mrs. Jones* by Billy Paul, *Back Stabbers* and *Love Train* by The O'Jays and *If You Don't Know Me By Now* by Harold Melvin & The Blue Notes.

Martin says of this period, "It was an amazing experience, cutting my studio teeth at the level of one gold record after another, back in the day when we had 30 people all moving air in the same room at the same time. Great players, great songs and great arrangements by Gamble, Huff[1] and Bell.[2]"

In the 1990s, Martin enjoyed a five-year relationship with the actress Cybill Shepherd and became the musical director of her successful CBS sitcom, *Cybill*.

In 2000, he made a guest appearance on *The Persuasions Sing Zappa - Frankly A Cappella*, along with Bruce Fowler and Mike Keneally.

Today, Martin is the musical director of the reformed Banned From Utopia, featuring Ray White and Albert Wing.

I first made contact with him in 2008 when a friend brought his *Look Great Naked At Any Age* website to my attention. He readily agreed to answer my questions – and also to be put in touch with the Arf Society regarding appearing at a future Zappanale, which he first did the following year.

It took several months to get this interview together, but it was worth the wait.

---

[1] Kenneth Gamble and Leon A. Huff were the creative team behind the Philadelphia International Records label.

[2] Thom Bell was Martin's fellow in-house arranger at Philadelphia International.

Tell me about your earliest musical experiences.
The first piece of music I remember identifying and asking for was Stravinsky's *Firebird*. I was 2½ years old. It's such visual music and I had vivid images in my imagination about what the sounds suggested.

My parents were both opera singers and growing up in the 1950s in Philadelphia, I was exposed to an amazing variety of music. My parents were into all kinds of music and there was always something playing on the old RCA Victrola.

My grandmother worked at RCA in Trenton, New Jersey and I still have quite a collection of 78 RPM records. I was watching *American Bandstand* before Dick Clark was on.[3] The original host was Bob Horn. Rock and roll grew up in Philadelphia as the nation tuned into the phenomenon and I grew up right along with it.

There was an active jazz scene and John Coltrane[4] spent quite a bit of time there to study with a teacher named Dennis Sandoli.[5]

The Philadelphia Orchestra has always been one of the best in the world and I remember outdoor summer concerts at the Robin Hood Dell Theater. Years later, when I went to the Curtis Institute, I would study with many of the first chair players that I admired so much as a boy.

Music always made perfect sense to me. We had an old Lester spinet piano when I was growing up and I taught myself to play all the music I was hearing as soon as I was big enough to reach up and touch the keys.

From a very early age, I recognised both chord progressions and melodies and was able to play them back after one hearing.

You say you're self-taught, but didn't you have some formal musical training: you can read music, right?
As I mentioned, I began playing piano as soon as I could reach up and touch the keys, even before I could see them. By the time I began to take lessons at age eight, I already knew how to play blues and compose strictly by ear. I took lessons for a short time and learned to read music, but preferred what I was able to learn on my own and quit the lessons.

I had no formal lessons on French horn until I'd already been playing

---

[3] *American Bandstand* was a music-performance TV show which aired in various versions from 1952 to 1989. It was hosted by Dick Clark from 1956 until its final season.

[4] John William Coltrane (1926-1967), also known as "Trane", was an American jazz saxophonist and composer who helped pioneer the use of modes in jazz and was at the forefront of free jazz.

[5] Dennis Sandole (né Dionigi Sandoli, 1913-2000) was an American jazz guitarist, composer, and music educator from Philadelphia.

for ten years, then plunged into intensive classical studies at the Curtis Institute of Music in Philadelphia.[6]

I'm entirely self-taught on saxophone and vocals.

Okay. How did you get to work with Frank?

There are so many horror stories about top-notch musicians crumbling at a Zappa audition, but my audition was a blast!

Zappa's guitar tech for the 1981 tour, Dave Robb, used to work for Orleans when I was in that band in the late 1970s. Dave called me and said Frank needed one more musician for the tour and told me to come down the next day.

I realised there was no way to prepare for a Zappa audition in less than twenty-four hours, so I decided not to try to prepare at all and just go down and do what I do.

He had me sight-read various keyboard parts and whenever something was technically beyond me, I would just play the right hand.

So he could tell I was able to follow the crazy polyrhythms and metric modulations.

Then he had me transpose keyboard parts on tenor sax and French horn. Being a classically trained horn player, transposition is a way of life, so it was no big deal, but certainly not easy to transpose Zappa melodies on sight!

He had me sight-read *The Black Page* on tenor sax from a keyboard part. The beginning of the melody moves fairly slowly, so that was no problem, but when it got to the fast sixteenth notes, I would just play the first note of each group through that section in order to stay on top of it.

Then he said, "Well, you can obviously read and play. I understand you sing really high and strong. Let me hear you sing something. What do you know?" I hadn't prepared anything, so I just said, "I don't know, *Auld Lang Syne?*" So Frank turned to the band and said, "*Auld Lang Syne*, key of A."

Back then, I had a pretty bizarre range and could sing a high "G" an octave and a half above middle "C" with no problem in natural voice, no falsetto. So I sang the tune an octave higher than anyone expected, in natural voice. Frank literally sat there with his mouth open and I knew I was in.

---

6 When Martin sings a 'a big ol' cadenza' during the song *Planet Of The Baritone Women* on the *Broadway The Hard Way* album, Zappa butts in with: "Robert Martin from Philadelphia, Curtis Institute graduate, 1971. Let's hear it for him!"

I did every tour from then on. I didn't have to audition for anything after that, since most people in the business know that if you can handle Frank's music, you can handle anything.

I was asked to join Bette Midler's[7] band strictly on reputation and things just went on from there. I spent most of the 1980s touring the world with major stars.[8]

What do you remember of the MTV performance in 1981?[9]

That was my first Zappa tour – I still had a moustache! I just watched some footage from that show and the energy was amazing. It's great to see Frank when he was young and healthy.

As I recall, at one point, the audience was passing a rubber raft around over their heads. It was a wild night, Halloween in New York City: killer band, amazing music – great to have been a part of it with Frank, Tommy Mars, Steve Vai and all the rest.

Which was your favourite tour with Frank?

1988, hands down. The band was flat out amazing and I was the primary keyboard player for the first time. We had a superb five-piece horn section, so I didn't get to play sax and very little French horn. But it was such a blast to hear those guys play! We did some really elaborate re-arrangements of old material and a lot of free-form blowing as well.

And your memories of the 1988 band's demise?

Not a happy subject and not an easy one to talk about, since it turned out to be not just the demise of the 1988 band, but the demise of Zappa tours as such.

Essentially, the feeling of camaraderie within the band disintegrated due to what I would describe as poor social skills on the part of one band member in particular. He was a colleague, a friend and an intelligent and gifted musician, so I don't choose to name names here. I had a better relationship with him than most of the rest of the band, partially because he respected my heavy classical background.

When personal differences within the band began to affect what was happening with the music onstage, we all knew something had to change. A rift developed in the band and there was a move to try to

---

[7] American singer, songwriter, actress and comedian. Midler has won three Grammy Awards, four Golden Globes, three Emmy Awards and a Tony Award. She has sold over 35 million records worldwide.

[8] Martin has worked with the likes of Prince, The Moody Blues, Lyle Lovett, Gladys Knight, Glenn Frey, Michael Bolton, David Sanborn, The Stylistics, The O'Jays, Sheila E and The Blues Brothers.

[9] Released on DVD as *The Torture Never Stops* in 2008.

convince Frank to make a personnel change.

I was actually surprised that Frank seemed more intent on maintaining control of the individual band members than he was with fixing what had become an obvious musical problem. He wasn't going to let the band force his hand on making a change, even though the music was suffering and he cancelled the remainder of the tour.

Needless to say, we were all disappointed, since the band was just so ridiculously good.[10]

You referred to when Frank was 'young and healthy'. Were there any signs of his ill health in 1988?
None that I was aware of, or anyone else to the best of my knowledge.

When did you last speak to Frank?
Frank became much more social towards the end and had many eclectic gatherings of very diverse people at his house on Friday evenings. The last one was only a few weeks before he died.

You've made one solo album – what does it sound like?
I landed a deal with MCA in 1982 and had in mind to do a record that would be kind of like Ray Charles[11] meets Steely Dan,[12] because that's the way I write, or one of the ways. But my producer and manager and the label had a very different idea of what they wanted. The result was a compromise that didn't really please either me or them.

It didn't matter, though, because a few weeks after it was released, MCA was bought by a large conglomerate and virtually everyone at the label was replaced.

Me and the new regime didn't really connect and we just said goodbye to each other and that was it.

Any plans for any more?
Frankly, it's not a burning desire at this point, but it might become one. Of course, with the technology today, I don't need a label's money to do it.

When and why did you decide you preferred being called 'Robert' over 'Bobby'?
I honestly never liked 'Bobby', it sounded like a baseball player. Not

---

[10] Martin talked to me some more about the tour, for my *Zappa The Hard Way* book.

[11] Ray Charles Robinson (1930-2004) was an American singer, songwriter, musician and composer who pioneered the genre of soul music during the 1950s.

[12] American jazz rock band whose music also blends elements of funk, R&B, and pop.

that that's bad and I thought about being one professionally. But I turned 40 in 1988 and decided it was time to go by the 'grown-up' name my parents gave me and I asked Frank to start introducing me as 'Robert'. He was totally cool about it.

Are you happy to talk about your time with Cybill Shepherd – as her musical director?
Cybill is more talented as a singer than most people give her credit for. She was understandably nervous about covering an Aretha Franklin tune for an episode of her TV show, but we worked together on it quite a bit and she pulled it off really well.

She's incredibly focused and has a remarkable work ethic. We played cabarets in NYC, London and LA, sometimes with a quartet and sometimes as a duo with bass and drum tracks that I pre-recorded.

She was great with an audience and always gave an engaging, entertaining performance.

We were together for nearly five years and there was a lot more good than bad.

You've played with a lot of 'names' – Prince, McCartney, Midler, The Moody Blues. Tell me about some of your favourite sessions.
One of my favourite experiences, other than every concert with Frank, was the 1993 Earth Day performance at the Hollywood Bowl with Paul McCartney.

I was there singing backgrounds for Kenny Loggins and before Paul went on, he brought everyone together backstage and said, "I want everyone to join me to sing Hey Jude at the end of my show."

When it was over, Paul turned around, looked across the stage directly at me and came over and shook my hand, before going on to greet everyone else. He didn't know me, it just worked out that way.

There's a video of the performance on YouTube, but it cuts off before the end. Anybody out there have a photo?

What are your recollections of The Persuasions' *Frankly A Capella* sessions?
It was fun, it was quick, they liked me, I liked them, not much else to report.

Aside from the Banned From Utopia, have you worked with any other Zappa alumni since?
No, just Banned From Utopia. I did a performance with the Belgian Radio Symphony Orchestra in 1994 called *The Purple Cucumber*,

featuring music by a number of European composers in the style of Zappa. But I was the only Zappa alumni involved.[13]

I'll be performing at the 20th Zappanale in Germany this August with some other alumni.

How did you become involved in *The Purple Cucumber*[14] project?
They called me, I said yes. It had a bit of an academic overtone, but it was fun. I think the orchestra members truly enjoyed it.

What are the chances of you being a Zappa Plays Zappa special guest at some point?
I have no idea, but I'd be happy to do it.

Tell me about your *Look Great Naked At Any Age* venture – how did that all start?
It started years ago, when I was touring all over the world with Frank and various other artists. I've always been an athlete and I wanted to stay in kick-butt shape, but most of the time all I had out there was me and my hotel room. So I created a system of bodyweight exercises for myself and fine-tuned it over the years to be more and more efficient and effective.

People have always asked me how I kept it together, when a lot of the people I used to tour with are either dead or not doing so well. So I decided to put it all on DVDs and make it available for everybody. I also recently posted a series of ten videos on my blog to give people a very complete crash course in getting yourself into great shape fast – including one where I nail a rock solid handstand at the age of 60.

Interview conducted on Friday 22nd May 2009.

---

[13] The 'rock band' included former Muffin Men Andy Jacobson (keyboards), Andy Treacey (drums) and Jake Newman (bass).

[14] The project was the brainchild of Belgian radio producer, Zjakki Willems.

ESSRA MOHAWK

Essra Mohawk is better known to Zappa fans as Sandy Hurvitz. During her brief tenure with The Mothers at New York's Garrick Theater in 1967, she was introduced as Uncle Meat.

Zappa was to have produced her first album, *Sandy's Album is Here at Last!* (released on his Bizarre label in 1968), but delegated the task to Ian Underwood.

Her voice can be heard on the track *N. Double A, AA* from the Zappa album *Lumpy Money* (2009).

As well as performing with The Mothers, Mohawk has worked with Gary Lucas, Jerry Garcia,[1] John Mellencamp, Carole King, Kool & the Gang, Al Jarreau,[2] Bob Weir and Keb Mo.

She has released a dozen or so albums over the course of her long career and has had her songs successfully covered by the likes of Cyndi Lauper (*Change Of Heart*, 1986), Tina Turner (*Stronger Than The Wind*, the b-side of *I Don't Wanna Lose You* in 1989) and country singer Lorrie Morgan (*Hand Over Your Heart*, 1991).

Ahead of her first ever European tour, which included an appearance at Zappanale, she found time to chat with me.

How and where did you first meet Zappa?
I was visiting New York with two friends from LA that I had met in Philly when they came to see Cal Schenkel. We were walking down Bleeker Street in the Village when we saw Frank coming our way. He was headed towards the Garrick Theater, where he and the Mothers were playing every night. The LA girls yelled out, "Ben Frank's! Cantors!", two popular hangs in LA that Frank was familiar with, so he let us all in for free and that's how we met!

---

[1] Jerome John Garcia (1942-1995), American singer-songwriter and guitarist best known for his work with the band the Grateful Dead.

[2] Alwin Lopez Jarreau (1940-2017), a seven-time Grammy Award winning American singer and musician.

What attracted you to Frank?

His music, his performance, his band, his whole deal! I loved *Freak Out!* the first time I heard it and I was blown away after hearing the Mothers live in New York a year before meeting Frank and being asked to join the band!

What are your memories of that period – the individual Mothers?

I'll start with Ray Collins, the smooth lead voice of the Mothers. His demeanour and spirit were as gentle as that velvety voice. He came up with the name 'Uncle Meat' at one of our rehearsals, telling Frank that he thought it was a great name for a rock star. Frank immediately spun around and pointing at me, proclaimed, "You're Uncle Meat!"

Bunky Gardner was the gentleman of the band. His hair and beard distinctive and well-groomed. His playing was perfection. He was extremely talented like the rest of the band, but not as crazy! A Taurus like myself, he was down to earth but never down and dirty. Bunk always seemed to have it together. He was the most refined member of the Mothers. A kind and friendly man. I can't remember him ever losing his cool.

Jimmy Carl Black was also down to earth while at the same time stretching up to the moon! He was bigger than life. A great performer, full of fun and mischief!

When I first joined the band, he handed me a fat joint to give Frank – knowing Frank didn't smoke pot and would freak out at the sight of a joint! "Tell him it's from the guys!" he said and I, unsuspecting, complied. After Frank screamed for me to take the unlit joint away, I did so running back into Jimmy who was having a good laugh with the other guys over the prank!

I loved Jimmy. He was one of a kind! I last saw him in 2000 when The Grandmothers came to Tennessee. Half of the band stayed at my house here in Nashville while they readied themselves for their US tour. There's a great photo of me and Jimmy taken in Memphis! It's hard to believe that he's no longer with us. It's a huge loss.

Billy Mundi used to call me 'Peanut'. He was a kind friend and we remain friends to this day. He has been through a lot with his health for years due to advanced diabetes. He's had heart attacks and amputations, facing it all with courage and a smile (and his loyal wife and caregiver, Patti).

It was over Billy's playing that Frank and I disagreed the first day we started tracking my album with the Mothers. Billy really started to cook during the ride out, after the charts that Frank had written ended. So I asked Frank very respectfully if we could record it again with Billy playing like that from the top so that the track would cook right away rather than having to wait till the end of the song.

Frank's response was less than supportive. Let's just say the session ended badly. I ended up walking out. I was an inexperienced youth of 19 and many years away from learning patience, tolerance and restraint.

By the way, the song we began recording was the one we performed every night at the Garrick: *Archgodliness Of Purpleful Magic*. I can still remember Frank's guitar line, which I'll be teaching to Sandro for Zappanale where the song will be heard as close as possible to how the Mothers played it, for the first time since 1968!

It was quite an honour to have my song included in the Mothers' set.

The only other song in the set not written by Frank, was a beautiful instrumental called *Epistle To Thomas* composed by Don Preston in memory of his son who had died as an infant. The piece was progressive and celestial, slow and exquisite. Of all the songs performed nightly by the Mothers, it was my favourite! Don Preston is a unique and sensitive musician.

I'd love to hear *Epistle To Thomas*!
I truly wish I could hear it again. It was so incredibly beautiful.[3]

And Sandro? You mean former Grandmother Sandro Oliva? He'll be playing with you at Zappanale?
Yes, that very Sandro! He is a great guy and a great musician; I call him the Italian Frank Zappa!

Getting back to Billy, several years ago he visited me here in Nashville. I took him to a studio where he could produce a singer he was working with. While we were at that studio, something very mystical happened: as we sat on the couch during someone else's session, suddenly – in the middle of the song they were recording – the two horn players began jamming, transforming the music into exactly how the Mothers sounded when they improvised at the Garrick Theater in 1967!

Billy and I looked at each other in amazement. We both recognised and knew what we were hearing. It was as if the spirit of Frank had

---

3 Don Preston told me: "The name of the song Essra was speaking of is the first song I ever wrote, called *Aegospotomas* – named after a Greek river. It's on the CD called *Retrospective on Crossfire*." A version with Bunk Gardner appears on Preston's *Vile Foamy Ectoplasm*, also available from *Crossfire* (www.crossfirepublications.com)

taken over the room. We marvel about it to this day. It was so beautiful. Transcendent and orgasmic! It was nothing short of the unique sound of Frank Zappa and the original Mothers of Invention.

So it felt like my heart was being ripped out when the people whose session it was erased over it and in its place recorded a very bland and unmemorable horn line. There was nothing we could do. It wasn't our session.

Billy and I both agreed that special moment of music existed briefly just for us, commemorating our reunion after over three decades since we had played together in the Mothers! We almost got to be in another band together – Rhinoceros[4] – but that's another story.

Roy Estrada used to close his eyes while he played his bass on stage with the Mothers. Every now and then he'd open his eyes, look around confused and ask, "What show is this?"

I was never sure if he was kidding or he actually was playing in his sleep. He never missed a note so my guess is he was awake!

Meanwhile, after all these years, I will be seeing him again at Rochefort-en-Accords where we may get the chance to play together again for the first time since 1968! Thinking about the possibility of us jamming together at Rochefort brought tears to my eyes. If it happens, I hope someone videos it. Music history in the making![5]

The Mother I've had the most contact with over the years is Don Preston and, even though we haven't been in touch lately, I consider him a close and lifelong friend. I hear he's in Europe playing with Roy.

It's because Don didn't feel well when the new keyboard arrived that Frank asked me to play it for him so he could hear how it sounded. The only music I knew how to play was my own. As I began playing, I started to sing along. That's all Frank had to hear. He instantly recruited me for the Mothers!

I know you're unhappy with *Sandy's Album*... can you tell me a little about the recording of that and what led to Frank 'sabotaging' production?

Not long after I walked out of that first session, Frank delegated the production to the newest member of the Mothers, Ian Underwood. In Ian, Frank found an obedient soldier, albeit not the most inspired

---

[4] Rhinoceros was a rock band 'manufactured' by Elektra Records in 1967. They made three albums before disbanding in 1970.

[5] Estrada did not make it to the festival: he was incarcerated at the time, awaiting trial on a charge of child molestation.

musician.

In all of my over 40 years of recording experience, I've never witnessed a more inept or insensitive 'producer'. Ian was good at only one thing: wasting studio time. He actually erased one of my best vocals for no rational reason. I was with a friend who witnessed it and was shocked when Ian gave the lamest reason I ever heard. He said he couldn't mix it which, of course, is absurd as it wasn't a mixing session. We were recording my vocals.

He would spend days putting down his own horn parts and then erasing them over and over! Not a single note of his noodling – thank goodness! – ever ended up on the album.

Production ended before the album was even close to being finished. A raw demo, it was released after I left Zappa, the Mothers and New York for LA and a deal with Reprise being offered to me by Mo Ostin,[6] with David Geffen[7] offering to help. My second album was finished to my satisfaction and released on Reprise in 1970.[8]

Ultimately, I forgave Ian. He was young and didn't know any better. I ran into him years later in LA. He seemed surprised and appreciated that I treated him kindly and forgave him for screwing up my first album all those years ago.

It still has merit, even though it's so bare bones, as it shows the songs I wrote and my voice and piano playing at 19 and 20.

Tell me about the track *Bizarre Beginnings* on your *Revelations Of The Secret Diva* album.[9]

Frank was demoing a bunch of my songs in a row to consider for the album and we were just finishing up recording *Woman* (which appears on the album) when I got silly during the ride out. So Frank joined in with his, "Bo, bo, bo!" and kissed me three times at the end, in time to the music. It was the beginning of our romance.

When and why did you move out of Frank's orbit

Things deteriorated between us at about the same rate the album progressed. I guess it all came to a head one day when Frank dropped by uninvited and physically forced me out of my own session.

---

[6] American record executive who has worked for several major companies.

[7] American business magnate, producer, film studio executive and philanthropist, who co-founded Asylum Records and DreamWorks SKG.

[8] *Primordial Lovers*, the first release under the name Essra Mohawk.

[9] Released in 2007.

The details of this event and much of what I've shared with you, are in my book – a continual work in progress that I hope to finish and release before too long.

At any rate, before I left Bizarre, I ran into Mo Ostin who was then vice-president of Reprise (he went on to become president). Upon hearing me sing at Steve Paul's Scene in Manhattan, he approached me and asked me to come to Reprise which ultimately resulted in the recording and release of *Primordial Lovers*.[10]

Did you have any subsequent contact with FZ?

On two occasions. Once, years later, when I was staying with my mom in Philadelphia – Frank used to introduce me on stage as "that strange little person from Philadelphia" – the phone rang. Mom picked it up and came to get me, telling me Frank Zappa was on the phone. He called to let me know, "We're doing more music and less bullshit these days."

I was amazed – and continue to be – that he carried my words with him for years, as I used to tell him how much more incredible his music was than the low-brow humour. I enjoyed a lot of the humour too, just not when it made fun of someone – though no one ever seemed to mind; guess I was overly sensitive when I was 19.

It meant a lot to me that Frank felt compelled to call me and tell me that. I didn't realise that my thoughts were so important to him until that phone call.

I was equally surprised to learn that after I left the Mothers, he later instructed his vocalists to sing jamming and jumping octaves like I had done. I just developed my vocal jam style from improvising with sax players while in the Mothers. It's what came out naturally.

Apparently Frank liked that sound enough to incorporate it in the band later with other vocalists. If that is indeed the case, I am honoured. Frank Zappa and the Mothers of Invention certainly had an influence on me!

Frank and I ran into each other one last time, also in Philadelphia. This time in the mid-1980s. We both had been invited to the Chestnut Cabaret for a special Halloween show being put on by Stella, Philly's late night horror movie hostess – in the same vein as Elvira.

When we spotted each other at the event, we were drawn together like magnets and had ourselves a good long hug. Any negativity that

---

[10] Released in 1970 and produced by Essra's then-husband, Frazier Mohawk (1941-2012).

might've existed years before that moment was banished forever, replaced by the deeper reality of the love and respect we had for each other.

I am certain that we would've worked together again had he not fallen ill soon after our final embrace.

Sorry, but getting back to Sandro: how did you two hook-up – I assume it stems from the Grandmothers staying with you in Nashville 11 years ago?

Yep. You are correct in your assumption. We stayed in touch always hoping I could get over there and we could play together. After several failed attempts, it finally came together for us this year!

So how do you feel about the 'hit' interpretations of *Change Of Heart* and *Stronger Than The Wind*?

I think they both did a great job. Especially Cyndi who released *Change Of Heart* as a single that went to Number Three! That was a dynamic recording!

Tina did a beautiful job on *Stronger Than The Wind* too. It was recorded in London to the tune of $50,000. A lush recording, but it was dropped from *Foreign Affair* after it was originally going to be the statement song of the album. It finally became the b-side on three different singles; one in England; one in Germany; and it was the b-side of *Look Me In The Heart* in the US, which is what led me to nickname it, 'Stronger Than The A-Side'!

Both singers stayed pretty true to the way I sang the songs on the original demos. I'm very happy with both of their versions.

Years later I sat down at the piano and re-wrote *Change Of Heart*, transforming it from an up-tempo 80s pop song to an R&B ballad. The new version is on my *Essie Mae Hawk Meets The KillerGrooveBand* CD.[11]

How did the Beefheart cover come about?

In 2005, I was asked by Philadelphia producer Mike Villers to sing on a track for a special compilation CD of Philly women singing Captain Beefheart entitled, *Mama Kangaroos*. Mike sent me a fantastic track of *Party Of Special Things To Do*,[12] recorded by EDO, an incredible Philly band!

I overdubbed my vocal and all of the backgrounds here in Nashville.

---

[11] Released in 1999.

[12] A song that first appeared on the Captain Beefheart And His Magic Band album *Bluejeans And Moonbeams* in 1974. It was also covered by Detroit garage rock band the White Stripes in 2000.

I'm very proud of the results!

Rightly so! Any chance we'll hear you and Gary Lucas play *The Devil's Gotta Move Along*[13] **at Zappanale?**
You betcha! Gary and I were just talkin' about it on the phone and on his Facebook page! We're both looking forward to it!

What else can we expect to hear in Germany?
We'll be playing songs from every decade of my career, including songs from my first album when I was signed to Frank and Herb Cohen.

By the way, I continued to work with Herbie until right before he died in 2010. We worked together to have that album reissued last year by Collectors Choice Music. He was a pleasure to work with.

We'll also be performing songs from my second LP, *Primordial Lovers*, my 80s LP, *E-Turn* and songs from my more recent CDs – *Essie Mae Hawk Meets The KillerGrooveBand*, *Love Is Still The Answer* and *Revelations Of The Secret Diva* – plus a song from *You're Not Alone*.[14]

Along with my own music, we'll be doing a couple of songs from the Mothers and a Captain Beefheart song.

Interview conducted on Monday 27th June 2011.

A few months after we finished our first interview, I met Mohawk at Zappanale.

On the final day of the festival, I was summoned by her and Bob Dobbs (BD) to take part in a further interview backstage with the pair.

What follows are some choice excerpts from our lengthy chat - transcribed some six years later, with much help from Mohawk. *(Thanks, Essie!)*

I didn't realise that you introduced Cal Schenkel to Frank.
Yeah, I was in college with Cal at the Philadelphia College of Art, where I had a scholarship and he didn't! [laughs] He was a sloppy artist and I could draw exactly what I saw. I did boardwalk portraits on Million Dollar Pier in Atlantic City when I was 17... oh, 16 actually, because at the same time I was doing that my first record[15] came out

---

[13] From the Mohawk album *Love Is Still The Answer* (2006).

[14] Released in 2003.

[15] *The Boy With The Way*, released under the name of Jamie Carter on Liberty Records in 1964.

and the manager came and said, "We have to go do this record hop."

(Bob Dobbs): You were born in 1948 on 23rd April, Shakespeare's birthday. So 17 in 1965 and Frank is just getting out of prison.
That's why he was so afraid, I am told, of being around drugs or anything. I didn't know that until much later.

(Bob Dobbs): That saved him from the draft. See, it was a good thing that he had that on his record!
I just wrote a song called *What You Don't Know Can Hurt You.*

One of the lines in it is, "But even hindsight isn't always 20/20."

You look back and you go, "What was that? What happened?"

I still don't know and most of the people involved are dead – I can't ask them!

Anyway, Cal and I met and we were college sweethearts. Somebody put us together and we hung out.

I was a virgin and he was inexperienced. He said before me, he'd only been with two women. So he didn't know what to do and I didn't know what to do. We lived together, but we couldn't make love – at least not till later. I have a great story about that, but it's going to be in my book! [laughs]

We only had six weeks before he talked me into quitting college.

(Bob Dobbs): Why did you like him?
I really loved Cal. We enjoyed each other's company. Well, young love: I don't think I've ever had enduring love.

Really?
Well, here I am alone! How enduring is that. But I love my music.

Cal was a crazy man. He left me. He took my money and went to LA without me.

In 1966, he came back to Philly and we were together again. He brought back *Freak Out!* and turned me on to that album. Later when these two girls – friends of Cal's from LA – came to visit him, they took me with them to New York.

And that's when we met Frank. In 1967.

I had seen him the year before. I dropped acid and saw The Mothers at the Balloon Farm – also in New York.

Anyway, a year later, the girls yelled "Ben Frank's! Cantors!" at him and he comes up and talks to all of us. He didn't know till later that I wasn't from LA; I didn't yell out anything. We were all let in for free, because they were from LA and mentioned his hang-outs.

I don't recall the details, but I hung out with Frank for enough days... I don't know where I stayed, I don't really remember anything. Except that one day he asked me to play the electric piano, because he knew I could play.

Having heard me play, he immediately asked me to join the band. He said, "How would you like to be a Mother?" And I said, "Sure." It sounded great to me.

It was a lot of fun.

So I stayed in New York, these two girls went back to LA and I ended up in The Mothers!

Did you find him very charismatic?
Absolutely. He was very charismatic.

(Bob Dobbs): Including sexually attractive?
Attractive. You have to understand, I was 19 and fresh out of virginity when I met Frank – I wasn't very sexual. I was more sexy than sexual. Guys would I'm sure think sexual thoughts around me. But I was more romantic than sexual at that stage.

I didn't really get sexual until I hit forty. Then I hit it like most women: I had my couple of hot years when any man around me was in danger! [laughs]

I'm really glad now it's all over with. I can concentrate on getting things done without the hormones leading me around by the nose. [laughs]

Oh, I remember! We all stayed at the hotel.

He woke every day and said, "Another day, another dollar!" First words he said every morning. And I'm sure he did until the day he died. [laughs]

So we're talking 1967?
Ah-hum.

He was with Gail... he was married?[16]
No! He wasn't married! I told him to get married! He told me that he had some girlfriend in California and had knocked her up. He asked me what he should do.

This was months after we had been living together and the first I heard of Gail's existence.

---

[16] Zappa met Sloatman in 1966. She was heavily pregnant when they married in New York on 21st September 1967. Moon was born one week later.

BD: [to AG:] Because he's kinda with Sandy.

EM: Yeah. I think he really loved me.

Frank asked me to take a walk with him in the Village. He had something he wanted to talk to me about. We came to a little tunnel and leaned against the wall. That's when he told me about this other girl that he had knocked up. I asked if he loved her and he said, "Well, Gail's a convenience." He asked me what he should do.

And I said, "Well, if you think you can be happy and live with her for the rest of your life, then you should marry her."

Then he brought her to New York and, little by little, he started treating me incorrectly.

(Bob Dobbs): But you could've stayed, you removed yourself. He didn't kick you out – you left!

I purposely arranged things for Gail's comfort.

(Bob Dobbs): And you moved in with the secretary?

No, no one had a secretary. I moved in with Monica Boscia,[17] the receptionist at Apostolic, the studio where we recorded. The world's first 12 track studio as I recall. They had a 4-track machine and an 8-track machine hooked up together.

Meanwhile, I started calling Frank 'Papa Zappa'. I made that up to create a different relationship – for Gail's sake... and his.

I felt it was a good thing, for him to have a family. After all, I wasn't about to have children. I was only 19.

I was trying to do the right thing and forty years later, I'm alive, I'm healthy – and still singing at the top of my game.

(Bob Dobbs): So you move out.

Yeah, but afterwards he took me along to a gig, I think in Boston. We flew somewhere.

(Bob Dobbs): And Gail was in New York?

Yeah. He had me stay in his room at the hotel, wherever it was – the town we were playing in. I didn't know this, but he registered us as 'Mr and Mrs Zappa'.

Apparently, all the bills came in to Gail. So she sees this and she went crazy. I was just so innocent, you know? Whatever. Take me along!

---

[17] Her voice can be heard on the Zappa albums *Lumpy Gravy* (1968), *Frank Zappa Meets The Mothers Of Prevention* (1985) and *Civilization Phaze III* (1994).

(Bob Dobbs): Did you sleep together?
Probably.

Your real name was Sandra Elayne Hurvitz? How did you become Essra Mohawk?
Well you see, I lived with Frank until Gail came into the picture. Monica and I got to be friends while I was recording and I ended up being her roommate. She called everyone by their initials. So her boyfriend Jerry she called 'Jay'. I was 'Ess'. So because we were close buddies, I became 'Essie'. I thought, 'Well, if Sandy stands for Sandra, then Essie stands for Essra'. So I became Essra and not long after that I moved to California and no one knew me. Then this couple – Jud and Jenny, who I went out to California with – convinced me to use that name from then on. They said, "We're just going to help you to enforce your new name." So they introduced me to everyone as Essra and it became my name. My mother, my brother – everybody calls me Essra. It's been my name a lot longer than Sandy, which only lasted 19 years.

By the time I was 20, my name was Essra Hurvitz, until I married Frazier Mohawk a year and a half later and my last name changed to Mohawk.

(Bob Dobbs): So you're working with The Mothers and then Frank asked you to do an album or you asked him to do an album for yourself?
He asked me to sign to him as an artist, then we started work on the album. I was the first artist he signed to Bizarre. It wasn't a label yet, just a production company.

(Bob Dobbs): And that was at Apostolic – and Frank wanted to direct it, kinda control how you did it?
No! We never got that far. We were doing the first track, it was wonderful. Just like when we performed it every night at the Garrick. I just respectfully suggested that we do it over with Billy Mundi playing like he did at the ride out – he played this great groove at the end and until then it was like marching band music because Billy had to follow the chart. But once the chart ended, Billy really got into a great groove. Frank wasn't big on the groove thing. My music required a groove. Why do you have to wait until the song is over for it to cook? Let's let Billy cook from the top. He says, "Who's producing this album anyway?"

What I should have said was, "You are. That's why I'm asking you this question!" But I didn't have that sense – I was a kid. He humiliated me and I was too sensitive. I just walked out and said, "I guess you're not!"

That was it. Suddenly I'm stuck in the studio with Ian Underling. [laughs]

There's this part in *Love Is What I Found* where I did this move at the control board, I knew how to turn the pan pot into this special effect and then back at the correct point in the song. It was a very precise move. After I did it, they went, "Oh, look how she did that – by accident."

Either it was because I was young, or I was a female, or whatever it was that kept me from getting the proper respect for what I was capable of. It doesn't matter how young I was, I still had the ear for music.

Then I walked into the studio one day and they told me it was over, they had all gone to Europe. Nobody had told me they were leaving. This was 1968. I've read that I went with them. Honey, I didn't. Instead I went west with Jud and Jenny.

(Bob Dobbs): No, they took Pam Zarubica.
That's entirely different. Pamela was Suzy Creamcheese! She was a groupie, not a band member. She was almost always in the audience for many of our shows. I tried to be friendly with her but she was a nasty piece of work, I mean she had a really negative attitude towards me. Maybe she was jealous because I was in the band and also Frank's girlfriend. You'd have to ask her.

(Bob Dobbs): So tell us how... you're with Frank, you're being distanced from your own album and it doesn't end. Frank has this argument with you: the final argument.
No, I was never distanced from my own album. Nothing could ever do that! Once Ian took over, Frank was gonna stay away completely from my sessions.

After Ian erased one of my best vocals, I was afraid to leave him alone in the control room. So Frank comes in one day and he asked me to leave. I just sat there – I wasn't going to leave, I was trying to protect my music. He said, "Aren't you gonna leave?" So I said, "No, I'm not gonna!"

He then pulled me out of my chair, twisted my arm behind my back and shoved me down the stairs, which is part of how I got out of the contract. Everyone at the studio saw and they were ready to be my witnesses, if necessary. The whole studio was on my side.

What possessed him to do that?

Because I defied him – I wouldn't leave my session.

BD: He was called a control freak back then, which is undeniable – one saw it occasionally and this is an example.

Just seems a bit extreme.

I mean it was a bit extreme.

BD: [laughs] He also was a great guy!

EM: I loved him, you know? We got over that, I forgave him. I've had fights with my brother and I still love him. So Frank was like early family for me – music family.

(Bob Dobbs): And you thought that would all disappear, you thought you'd get the album done?

Yeah, but they cleared out – they went to Europe. They released the album without my permission, unfinished. I was not happy. Though there is a nice picture of me on the back cover that Cal took!

Where was Cal at this point?

I don't know.

(Bob Dobbs): Well Cal was doing the albums, so he was in LA?

At one point, when everything was still good, Frank was doing everything himself and was ready to delegate. He says he needs a guy for his art department. I said, "I know just the guy!" So I went to Philly and I helped put together the right portfolio with stuff of Cal's that I knew Frank would like. Then I took that to New York and showed it to Frank and Frank said, "Yep, go get him. Just bring him here." I went to Philly and Cal and I came back to New York together. I brought Cal to Frank!

So what was the status of your relationships with Cal and Frank at that point?

I was with Frank and Cal was totally cool about it. You know, it was the sixties. Everyone was cool with stuff. If he wasn't, if it bothered him, he didn't say because Cal was passive.

I read a thing on his website at one point and he totally got it wrong. I called him and said, "What is wrong with you? How could you forget that I got you this gig?"

He remembered once I reminded him and corrected it. We're still good friends.

Interview conducted on Sunday 21st August 2011.

KENT NAGANO

Kent Nagano first worked with Zappa in January 1983, when he conducted the London Symphony Orchestra for a concert at the Barbican Centre and recordings at Twickenham Film Studios that resulted in the albums *London Symphony Orchestra Vol. I* (1983) and *London Symphony Orchestra Vol. II* (1987).

The following year, he conducted the Berkeley Symphony Orchestra during "A Zappa Affair" at the Zellerbach Auditorium, a performance which also featured life-size puppets.

With these two orchestras, Nagano conducted the world premiere performances of a number of Zappa's orchestral works, including *Bob In Dacron*, *Sad Jane*, *Mo 'N Herb's Vacation* and *Sinister Footwear*.

Since working with Zappa, Nagano's career has skyrocketed. He was music director of the Opéra de Lyon (1988–1998), principal conductor of the Hallé Orchestra in Manchester (1992-1999), principal conductor and artistic director of the Deutsches Symphonie-Orchester Berlin (2000-2006) and music director of the Bavarian State Opera (2006-2013).

In 2006, he also became the music director of the Orchestre Symphonique de Montréal. Since 2015, Nagano has been the general music director of the Hamburg State Opera.

Back in 1990, all it took was a casual remark by the editor of *T'Mershi Duween*, a couple of phone calls and four days later I was nervously sitting in the Queen Elizabeth Hall on London's South Bank watching Kent Nagano rehearse the London Sinfonietta, a borrowed Dictaphone in my hand.

Nagano was taking the relaxed nine-piece ensemble through Pierre Boulez's[1] *Mémoriale* in readiness for a concert that evening

---

[1] French composer/conductor (1925-2016) who is listed in the liner notes of the *Freak Out!* album as one of those who "contributed materially in many ways to make our music what it is." In 1984, Boulez conducted the Ensemble InterContemporain's performances of Zappa's *The Perfect Stranger*, *Naval Aviation In Art?* and *Dupree's Paradise* that appeared on the album *Boulez Conducts Zappa: The Perfect Stranger* (1984).).

commemorating Japanese composer Toru Takemitsu's 60th birthday.[2]

The rehearsals over, I was ushered into the Green Room for the first of this book's interviews to chat with the man about his stick wiggling exploits for Zappa.

Firstly, I'd like to ask you how you met and became involved with Frank Zappa.
I was visiting IRCAM[3] in Paris – some of my friends worked there under the patronage of Pierre Boulez – and I saw the list of the various pieces that were to be performed in the future. Included on that list were some pieces by Frank Zappa. Now, being a Californian and Frank Zappa comes from California too...

You're actually based out in America, aren't you?
I live in San Francisco. Of course, for us Frank Zappa is someone that everyone knows – regardless of whether you're involved in popular music or not, everyone knows Frank Zappa – he's one of the most well known people over there.

I was really surprised and I said, "Why are you doing Frank Zappa's music?" My friend said, "Well, it seems he's written a number of serious compositions and he wanted the Ensemble to perform it and Pierre Boulez has agreed to conduct it."

So the next time Frank Zappa toured through the Bay area – the San Francisco area – I contacted his manager.

Bennett Glotzer?
Yes and asked him to request that he send me some scores. Then I got a message that Frank Zappa wanted to meet me during the intermission of one of his concerts.

Was that about 1981 or 1982?
Yes, somewhere around then. It was the first time in my life that I'd been to a rock concert.

It was a phenomenal experience; it was packed, completely sold out, millions of fans, everyone just incredibly excited and enthusiastic.

I remember meeting Frank Zappa and his entourage and meeting his bodyguard.

---

[2] Takemitsu passed away six years later while undergoing treatment for bladder cancer.

[3] Institut de Recherche et Coordination Acoustique/Musique, a French institute for science about music and sound and avant garde electro-acoustical art music. It is situated next to the Pompidou Centre.

John Smothers?
Yes, who scared the hell out of me!

Anyway, he showed me these scores – which he allowed me to keep – and they were indeed extraordinary. Extraordinary quality, very surprising that anybody could write something so original, much less someone who wasn't known in the classical music field.

So I asked Frank if I could perform some of the pieces in California because they looked really interesting. So that was fine.

I received a telephone call out of the blue many months later – because I never heard anything from Frank for a long time; he'd said he wanted to think about it because he had, had a few performances of his music done recently that were so poorly prepared he was really choosing much more carefully the groups that he would allow to perform his music. He didn't want his music to be massacred, which is very easy to do; it's such difficult music.

This is something that has come up in interviews throughout his career – that he's unhappy with the performances.
He's absolutely right. People don't treat them seriously and if it's not treated seriously it doesn't give an accurate reading of what the piece is.

So he was considering whether or not he would let me perform the music with my orchestra for several months. I never got a positive or a negative answer from him. But what I did receive about four months later was a telephone call asking if I'd be interested in recording a couple of albums of his music with the London Symphony.

Had you worked with them before?
No, in fact I had never really worked with any, what I would call, strong world-class orchestra before.

Just the Berkeley Symphony Orchestra?
Yes, they were a small Symphony… they were not really a full big-time orchestra. Now they are, but at the time they weren't full time.

So, of course, I was delighted. It was much more than 'would I be interested'; I considered it a privilege, a real honour to be able to work with someone like Frank.

We did some initial rehearsals together at his home in Los Angeles and there I realised that it was indeed going to be an extremely exciting project.

From my knowledge of his music and his incredible musicianship, I knew that for him it was just as important to have music performed as close to perfection as possible as it was for me. That's one reason why I got my reputation - both negatively and positively - because I rehearse until it's really very, very accurate.

I think he was unhappy with the amount of time the LSO rehearsed – he quoted 38 days, which to me sounds an extraordinary amount of time.
It was a phenomenal amount of time for the London Symphony. But in all fairness, the writing is extremely difficult – it's very, very difficult – and that was such a gruelling and intense period.

I think it's fair to say that the London Symphony, when they heard they were doing Frank Zappa's music, had no idea what that really meant in terms of the complexity. But I will say that they were really quite exceptional; they worked so hard and I really fell in love with the orchestra – just as a group.[4]

As they did with you – didn't they hang a sign on your podium?
Yes [laughs]! They hung a sign on my podium, which they had torn off of one of the electrical transformers, which said "DANGER – LIVE CONDUCTOR". I still have that plaque.

But they really gave 100% and they appreciated Frank's music. At the end they gave an ovation that was for Frank and for his music. It was wonderful.

At the time, I think Frank was quite happy too, but subsequently he's made a few comments about their performance at the Barbican. There's a huge bar at the back and he was unhappy with the second half of the show – he thought they had been drinking too much.
Um...well, I don't know. I wasn't aware of any of that.[5]

Also, on the last recording session, the trumpet section was late back, necessitating 50 edits in six and a half minutes of music. I certainly could not pick up any errors from what I've heard on the

---

[4] Ed Mann was involved in the recordings and told the author "The orchestra was NOT used to playing music that was so difficult and that required homework – and there was some grumbling which of course made Frank irate because he was, after all, paying them. It did feel strange at first playing some of the band music with the LSO (like *Strictly Genteel*) – we were all used to it being so BIG. But what a great orchestra, and in the end I think that Frank was happy too."

[5] In *The Real Frank Zappa Book* (1990), Zappa says, "One unique facility offered by the Barbican is the stand-up bar backstage – for the use of the orchestra members. It is well stocked and very efficient. They can pour a whole orchestra's worth of booze in nanoseconds. During the break between pieces, the LSO left the stage and availed itself of this convenience. When it returned to play the next piece, many members were roasted – and so was my music."

recording on *London Symphony Orchestra Vol. II*!
Well, that's because Frank is such a superb editor. In fact, I've even entertained thoughts of doing a classical record with him in the recording truck – because he's an incredible, incredible musician.

Do you actually compose yourself?
I have written, but I'm not an active composer. I've studied composition.

But in all fairness to the orchestra, the music is humanly very, very difficult. When you're doing two – sometimes three – sessions a day, it's pretty hard to keep your chops going.

Do you know if there were any pieces recorded by the London Symphony Orchestra that have yet to be released?[6]
By Frank?

By Frank, yes.
I think we have some parts of some pieces. The idea was to get as many pieces as we possibly could as close to perfection as we could, to see if we might be able to get something like that.

I think there are seven pieces that have been released now. It's all going to come out on CD soon, that's his next hope – to remix it.[7]
Well, for me, it's phenomenal music. I just did a re-performance of some of his pieces in Lyon.[8]

I've been sent a review of that, but it's in French and I can't translate it! Somebody who did said that you were the Musical Director of the Orchestra de Lyon.
Yes, I am indeed.

I assumed that perhaps you lived there, but you say not. You're based in San Francisco.
I divide my time between Lyon and San Francisco.

That was with a ballet performance as well?
That's right.

---

[6] I had seen mention of a piece played by the LSO named *WOooOl*. It later transpired that this was Zappa's alternative title for the 2nd and 3rd movements of *Mo 'N Herb's Vacation*.

[7] In 1986, Ryko issued a CD comprising *Sad Jane*, *Mo 'N Herb's Vacation* and *Bogus Pomp*. The complete LSO sessions were however extensively remixed and remastered to Zappa's approval in 1993, and reissued across two discs in 1995.

[8] Dancing Zappa took place at the Auditorium Maurice Ravel in Lyon in September 1990. Nagano conducted L'Orchestre de l'Opéra de Lyon for performances of *The Perfect Stranger*, *Strictly Genteel* and *Bogus Pomp*.

Did you actually record *Sinister Footwear*? I heard that was due to be recorded and the Ballet was going to tour with the tape.

That's what we wanted to do. When I requested a number of rehearsals, that wasn't so much of a problem – that's why I felt so enthusiastic that we could finally get it because there, since I'm Musical Director, I can book as many rehearsals as I feel necessary. The problem came with the fact that there were a number of instruments that we didn't normally carry in the orchestra – like bass flute, alto flute, contrabass clarinet, things like that – and the enormous expense of hiring all the extras, we would have had to hire something like 35 extras and that's when it became fiscally impossible.

So you didn't do any recordings of the performances?

Unfortunately, we didn't. I was really sad about that actually, because *Sinister Footwear* for me is... that's a great piece.

The only orchestral works I know really are Zappa's and those by people that have inspired him – like Webern[9] and Varèse.[10] That I find is one of the more accessible pieces.

Sinister Footwear to me is one of the best pieces that he's written and it doesn't exist in a recording.

I've heard a tape of it from the June 1984 performance at the Zellerbach Auditorium...[11]

That was us, yeah...

...with the marionettes!

And that gives a loose idea, but its not... it really needs a studio recording.

There are also some 'rock band' versions of that, or extracts from it.[12]

Yeah, but it should be done with an orchestra.

---

[9] Anton Webern (1883-1945) was an Austrian composer/conductor, and exponent of the twelve-tone technique – a method of musical composition that ensures all 12 notes of the chromatic scale are sounded as often as one another in a piece of music.

[10] Edgard Victor Achille Charles Varèse (1883-1965) was a French-born composer who spent the greater part of his career in the United States. His music had a profound affect on the teenage Zappa.

[11] This recording was released on Zappa Records on *Beat The Boots III* (Disc Three) in 2009.

[12] For example: *Sinister Footwear II* on *Them Or Us* (1984); *Sinister Footwear 2nd Movement* on *Make A Jazz Noise Here* (1991); *Theme From The 3rd Movement of Sinister Footwear* on *You Are What You Is* (1981); and *Variations On Sinister #3* on *Guitar* (1988).

Is it within your power to commission a piece by Zappa so that he can write for the instruments that are readily available to you?
Yeah, it is possible. At this point Frank doesn't seem to be interested in writing for human orchestras.

He's playing with the Synclavier down in the basement.
And he's been frustrated in a sense; the way that his mind works – it's such a sophisticated, complex mind that his impatience when people can't go at the same pace gets him down sometimes. I think he has been frustrated that musicians just don't… yeah, we don't care enough really, we don't care to the point where we will practice until it's perfect. I mean most of us don't. For me, it makes a big difference, but the real constraints of the economic realities of a symphony orchestra do place economic limits on how much time you can place…

Have you read *The Real Frank Zappa Book*?
I've seen the book but I haven't had a chance to read it yet.

It goes into great detail about the complexities of organising a performance of one of his pieces and the phenomenal cost of it all.
Phenomenal cost. You know, when Frank does his rock music, it's no less complicated. But they rehearse until its perfect and then they go out on the road. Which means if it takes two months of rehearsal, it's two months of rehearsal.

In the symphonic world, the financial realities just don't make that possible right now. It is frustrating for someone who's written music that he knows is totally playable, given enough rehearsal time.

I totally understand his point… he's right, in fact.

He's been writing orchestral pieces for a long time, but it seems the rock world is where he finances it. I think in the future we'll see him going off into more orchestral works and hiding away with the Synclavier. He's always talking about giving up touring – he's said that many times. Have you any idea what his plans are? Has he any collaborations lined up with you in the future?
No, not for the moment.

But you do hope to get together again sometime?
Well, every time I'm in Los Angeles, I go and visit the Zappa family. I have enormous, enormous respect for Frank. For several reasons: one, because he's a great composer; and two, because he gave me my first chance.

People don't realise that he recognised... he made telephone calls and he did investigations of what my reputation was – but someone has to give a young conductor their first chance. Frank gave me my first chance and I'll always be grateful to Frank for that.

He pays tribute to you as well; he thinks you are a world-class conductor and he thinks you can do things that conductors who have been working for 50 years can't do.
Really? I didn't realise that.

Thinks you're "fantastic", he said.
When you stop and think about it, someone in his position could have hired anybody that he wanted and the fact that he gave me a chance... I never ever will forget that. Because I have a career now. Had to start some place.

So the LSO was really the big break for you?
Well, it was one of the breaks. It certainly was the first time that I got to work with a superior orchestra.

Do you know how Boulez feels about Zappa's music? I get the impression from what I've seen that he doesn't take it altogether seriously – possibly because of Zappa's 'rock' background.[13]
I don't have that impression. I find that he finds it fascinating

I know they seem to be friendly – they did an interview together last year.[14]
I think that he is fascinated by his music.

Okay. Thanks very much. That's great.
You're welcome.

Interview conducted on Friday 23rd November 1990.

---

[13] In 1987, Boulez was confusingly quoted in the French newspaper Libération saying, "I reserve judgement about all the qualities of Zappa's music."

[14] On 23rd May 1989, the Los Angeles Philharmonic and the UCLA Music Department presented *An Evening With Pierre Boulez And Frank Zappa*, in conversation at the University's Schoenberg Hall.

LISA POPEIL

I n 1981, Lisa Popeil unsuccessfully auditioned for Zappa but ended up providing 'dramatic soprano' for him during a concert at the Santa Monica Civic Auditorium on 11th December that year.

Excerpts from her guest spot appear on *Teen-age Prostitute* (from *Ship Arriving Too Late To Save A Drowning Witch*, 1982) and *Lisa's Life Story* (on *You Can't Do That On Stage Anymore Vol. 6*, 1992).

Bassist Scott Thunes believes Zappa hired him because he wanted to see how he and Popeil would interact: "She jumped on my back and let me ride her around inside the studio within a few minutes of our meeting. Frank saw chemistry and was happy," Thunes told me.

While Popeil does not recall this incident, she does admit, "I was a pretty free spirit in those days, so I wouldn't put it past myself!"

Over the years, Popeil has provided backing vocals on a number of "Weird Al" Yankovic recordings, including his 1984 *In 3-D* album on the song *Mr. Popeil*, which pays homage to her father, the inventor of the Ronco Chop-O-Matic hand food processor. The song is a parody of The B-52s' *Rock Lobster*.

Throughout the 1990s, Popeil taught pop and classical voice classes at the College of the Canyons in Santa Clarita, California.

In October 2016, Popeil made a one-off appearance singing *Teen-age Prostitute* with Banned From Utopia at a ZappaUnion concert in Oslo, Norway.

In the course of writing my *Zappa The Hard Way* book in 2010, I had occasion to throw some questions Popeil's way. She very kindly told me some more about her brief stint with Frank...

My time in the band began surprisingly since I had come to the audition merely to give moral support to my boyfriend at the time, Chris Armstrong, an avid Zappa fan and talented drummer.

I do remember what I was wearing and it was definitely not dressed-to-impress: red gym shorts and a silly white t-shirt with tiny red hearts on it.

I came to the studio with no acquaintance with Frank's music and was acting mostly as a 'roadie' for Chris. When I saw sheet music lying around, I took a glance and hummed through it. It seemed purposefully difficult but I got a kick out of trying to get the rhythms.

Tommy Mars caught me glancing at the music and suggested that I audition for Frank. After several terrified auditionees were summarily dismissed from the studio after failing to meet Frank's expectations and definitely after Chris' audition was also not up to 'snuff', I had every intention of helping him pack up and head home. But Tommy approached me again and was quite insistent that I audition.

Not one to say no, I sat at the piano while Frank placed music in front of me, testing my musicianship, playing and singing. I remember auditioning for quite a long time, perhaps 45 minutes, turning around occasionally to observe an ever-growing group of guys behind me looking stunned, as though they were thinking "Who is this girl?"

When the audition was over, Frank pulled me aside and gave me a stack of music to memorise and said to come back in several days and play for him again.

Well, that was my first real challenge as I had developed my ability to read music but not my ability to memorise it! I did my best to learn it and came back for my second audition. The singing went well and it was obvious that Frank enjoyed my over-the-top operatic renditions, basically opera with boozy jazz styling. Then I was informed that I would be put on a trial period which eventually lasted three weeks.

There's much to tell about those three weeks, which overall I found quite harrowing. My background was classical and pop piano but I was expected to play primitive synthesizers and learn four hours of almost unplayable music and then be able to play it in any style and in any key. That was quite beyond my experience.

All the while, though, Frank was very supportive – even warm – towards me and I gave the process everything I had, even to the point of swollen hands from practicing.

At the end of three weeks, Frank called to let me know that my trial period was over and I agreed that it wasn't working out. I had not come to the situation as an experienced player; I had just gotten my Master's Degree in Classical Voice and had fallen into the situation.

He was kind when breaking the news to me and although I was of course disappointed, I was also very relieved. Going on a 60-city tour with 40 guys and one girl – me – was a daunting thought to say the least!

I did hear later through the grapevine that if Frank had not been able to find a replacement, he was planning to call me back. But he found Bobby Martin, an extremely skilled and experienced performing musician.

The one thing I think I brought to the picture, besides being female, was that I was funny – I really knew how to crack up Frank. I was later thrilled to receive his phone call and invitation to perform live with the band in December of 1981.

The lyric idea in *Lisa's Life Story* was to make it seem as though Frank was the 'perfect hunk', but then at the end, throwing in the zinger *"I like them tall...and BLOND!"* to deflate the build-up.

Interview conducted on Saturday 29th May 2010.

DON PRESTON

O nly Roy Estrada performed on stage with Zappa more times than Preston, with their last appearance together coming at the Notre Dame University in Indiana on The Mothers' 10th Anniversary Tour in May 1974.

While Preston was keyboard player for the original Mothers from 1967, he was also the musical director for American avant-garde vocalist Meredith Monk and started performing electronic music.

Preston has recorded numerous experimental albums, scored more than twenty feature films (including parts of the soundtrack for Francis Ford Coppola's *Apocalypse Now*), played with the likes of legendary clarinet player and composer John Carter and is recognised for his pioneering use of synthesizers.

He co-founded the Grandmothers in 1980, with whom he still performs to this day and periodically performs in a duo with Bunk Gardner as The Don & Bunk Show.

In 2001, Billy James told me that Preston had a new album coming out and suggested I might like to contact him for an interview. I wasted no time...

Tell me about *Transformation*, the new album from your jazz trio.
The trio consists of myself on piano, Joel Hamilton on bass and Alex Cline on drums. The material is: two songs by Carla Bley; two songs by John Carter; one song by Zappa[1]; one song by Cole Porter; and three songs by me – one of which is in the sonata form and is actually six songs.

The other musicians are fantastic and there is a harmonious blend to the entire CD.

---

[1] *The Eric Dolphy Memorial Barbeque*, which first appeared on the Mothers' album *Weasels Ripped My Flesh* (1970).

You mentioned you were also working on an album of archival material: any plans for a CD release of *Eye Of Agamoto* or *I Can't Breathe*?[2]

No plans, but not out of the question.

After the break-up of the original Mothers, how did you personally feel about being selected to go back and join the Flo & Eddie line-up?

I was living in New York and working with Gil Evans.[3] I got a call from Zappa saying the band would be in New York and would I like to come down and sit in. I did and after the concert Mark and Howard told me that they were having trouble with the keyboard player and would I consider joining the group.

I had a tour in Europe with Gil, but after that I was free. My feeling was that I knew this band would never replace the original band. To me I was just joining a different band with no comparison. The fact that the band had the same name and same leader didn't occur to me.

Tell me a little about the Montreux Casino fire.[4]

That incident was very strange to me. First of all, the tour schedule was printed on a box of matches! Second, on the day before the fire in the middle of my solo on *King Kong*, someone ran out on the stage and issued a fire warning.

On the next night, in the middle of my solo on *King Kong*, someone threw a firecracker up to the ceiling – which was covered with dry palm leaves and started the fire.

While that was happening, Zappa's sewer backed up in his LA home and the entire basement studio was flooded with piss and shit.

Do you remember Nigey Lennon? In her book *Being Frank* she says you played an improvised synthesizer section on a song of hers called *Moto Guzzi*; do you recall this, or her presence on the tour?

I don't remember.

---

[2] Both are pieces composed by Preston. The former was played a few times by The Mothers circa. 1968-69, and both were regularly performed by the original Grandmothers in 1981. The songs were included on *Grandmothers*, an anthology of previously unreleased recordings by ex-members of the Mothers in 1981, but mysteriously excluded when a revised and expanded version of the album was issued on CD in 1993. They subsequently re-appeared on the Preston album *Retrospective* in 2009.

[3] Ian Ernest Gilmore "Gil" Evans (1912-1988) was a Canadian jazz pianist, arranger, composer and bandleader, best known for his collaborations with Miles Davis.

[4] This happened at a Mothers' concert in Switzerland on 4th December 1971 and was the inspiration for Deep Purple's classic song, *Smoke On The Water* (1972).

You mean you don't remember recording, or touring with Nigey? I thought she was you and your wife Tina's rent paying roommate in Echo Park for several months in 1972 – and remained friends with you right up until she left for Europe.
Of course I remember Nigey very well and I respect her very much.

Okay, thanks for clearing that up. What were the subsequent *Waka/Jawaka* and *The Grand Wazoo* recording sessions like?[5]
Nothing unusual. I was in the studio by myself with Zappa and the engineers in the control room. I laid down my tracks and went home.

And your recollections of the 10th Anniversary tour?
I mostly remember how great the band was and getting to know George Duke, who was an exceptional musician.

Who was the best: the Roxy, Vaudeville, or original Mothers?
My heart says the original band, but my mind says the 1988 band.

'The Best Band You Were Never In', then! I have just been reading Greg Russo's excellent book, *Cosmik Debris: The Collected History & Improvisations Of Frank Zappa*, which implies that you hooked up with Frank in 1981 to record a track called *On The Throne Of Saturn* for the *Music From The 21st Century* compilation.
Completely wrong. The Mothers were recording *Burnt Weeny Sandwich* and I had all my gongs set up. I arrived at the studio first and Zappa suggested that we record some free improvisation with the gongs. So he engineered and I played. That is all Zappa had to do with that piece.

Another error to do with that piece is the name. I originally called it *The Thrones Of Saturn*, based on the book *The Inner Realities Of Evolution* by Rudolf Steiner. In the book he describes beings that live on Saturn called Thrones. That track is available on the CD *Io Landscapes*[6] which is mostly electronic – or 'music concrete' – in style.

Most of the material on *Thrones* was done with a large modular Moog.

Thanks for clearing that up, too! So when and why did you finally fall out with Frank?
You know, I really don't know. Probably when I formed the first

---

[5] Preston plays piano and Mini Moog on the title tracks of both 1972 Zappa albums.

[6] Released in 2001. The track is named Loki.

Grandmothers. I got a call from Frank saying, "Get rid of the doll."[7]

Can you tell me how the pseudonyms 'Dom DeWild' and 'Biff Debris' came about?
My ex-wife's name was DeWild before we married and I used it on occasion. Biff Debris was a product of Frank, used in the movie *Uncle Meat*, which was supposed to be loosely based on the movie *John And Mary*[8] with Dustin Hoffman and Mia Farrow.

When did you last cry and why?
Day before yesterday, when I watched *Galaxy Quest*.[9]

What's that sample at the start of the track *Moon Unit* on your album *Vile Foamy Ectoplasm*?[10]
It's not a sample; it's a modular Moog where three voices are tracking one keypress. Sawtooth waveforms going through a low-pass filter.

Right. What have you got in your pockets right now?
I don't have any pockets.

What magic tricks did you perform with the Muffin Men in the summer of 1993?[11]
I made two cans become magnetic and I made my leg disappear.

And your pockets too, presumably? Are the Grandmothers going to tour again?
We will do some limited touring this summer. Roy Estrada and Billy Mundi will be joining the band.

Jimmy talked to me about how the Grandmothers were recording a new studio album of all original material – will it include *New Age Mumbo Jumbo*[12] and *The Great Generic Side Show*?[13] Tell me more.
No plans as of now.[14]

---

[7] For the early Grandmothers shows in Europe, Preston made a huge doll bearing Zappa's face. This would be used in a "skit where it looked like we were giving birth to this doll head"...up until that phone call.

[8] A 1969 American romantic drama, directed by Peter Yates.

[9] A 1999 American comedy sci-fi film, directed by Dean Parisot.

[10] Originally released in 1993.

[11] The Grandmothers played nine double shows with the Muffin Men that year.

[12] A Preston composition that first appeared on the album *Necessity Is...* by The Don & Bunk Show in 2000.

[13] To the best of the author's knowledge, this track has still to appear anywhere. When I asked Preston about it in 2017, he said "I'm lucky if I can remember my name. I have no idea what that was."

[14] It is now evident that, following a lengthy tour of the US by The Grandmothers in 2000, Black and Preston had become estranged at this point: Black was excluded from the next line-up of the Grandmothers and, as noted in my interviews with him, felt sidelined by Preston at their last ever appearance together at Zappanale in 2002.

Shame. What about a re-recording of *I've Fallen And I Can't Get Up*?
No comment.[15]

Thought not. How's The Don & Bunk Show album coming along?
It's coming along great.[16] Right now we're working on *The Little House I Used To Live In*.[17]

What are your plans for the future?
I am starting a musical series here in Los Angeles at The Downtown Playhouse to promote new music and avant-garde jazz with artists like Bobby Bradford[18] and Vinny Golia.[19] I want to do a recording with a group I formed last year called The Akashic Ensemble, with Alex Cline and Nels Cline. I also want to tour with The Don And Bunk Show – possibly doing our lecture *The Evolution Of Frank Zappa's Music*.

Okay. So what was Zappa really like?[20]
Ask Gail.

Interview conducted on Sunday 18th February 2001.

———————————

I have continued to correspond with Preston on and off over the years since our first interview. Here's one exchange that may be of interest.

Were you aware of FZ's brief tenure as a beat poet? In April 1959, he submitted a poem (entitled *LA Night Piece*) to Grover Haynes of the Three Penny Press, using the pseudonym Vincent Beldon. Does any of this mean anything to you? I don't think you'd met Frank then, so possibly not.
I remember about 1967 Zappa recited a poem very much like Beefheart. It was very good, but I never heard it again.

Interview conducted on Saturday 25th June 2011.

———————————

15 This is a track by Roland St. Germain from the 'Austin' Grandmothers album *Dreams On Long Play* (1993). When Preston returned to the band from 'temporary retirement', the two did not get along and St. Germain ended up getting fired by fax.

16 *Joined At The Hip* by The Don & Bunk Show was released in 2002.

17 A track first released on *Burnt Weeny Sandwich* (1970).

18 American jazz trumpeter, bandleader and composer, noted for his work with Ornette Coleman.

19 American composer and multi-instrumentalist, specializing in woodwind instruments.

20 Preston wrote a song called *The Eternal Question* (on *Vile Foamy Ectoplasm*, 1993) which he hoped would put a stop to Zappa fans asking this!

CRAIG 'TWISTER' STEWARD

Craig "Twister" Steward plays harmonica on the Zappa albums *Joe's Garage Acts I, II & III* (1979), *You Are What You Is* (1981) and *The Man From Utopia* (1983). He also guested on stage with Zappa a couple of times in the early 1980s.

When I learned that he was scheduled to join ZAPPATiKA[1] on stage for their *Joe's Garage*-heavy set at Zappanale in July 2015, I was impressed by the stellarity of that year's line-up: also set to perform was Ike Willis, Denny Walley, Napoleon Murphy Brock, Tom Fowler, Robert Martin, Albert Wing, Ed Mann, Ray White, Candy Zappa, Mats Öberg & Morgan Ågren and Jeff Hollie.[2]

Out of the blue, Steward sent me a message asking if I'd be there too. The answer was, "Of course! How about an interview to celebrate?"

After our online chat, we met very briefly at Zappanale and then hooked up a few days later when Steward travelled from Amsterdam to London. We spent a lovely afternoon together, culminating in me watching him jam with my friends in the Spanner Jazz Punks on stage at the Gunners Pub in Highbury.

We have remained friends since.

I understand you first auditioned for Frank's Roxy band in 1973? How did that come about?
Frank played a concert in Wichita around 1972-73. He went to a few popular clubs that played good cover tunes and asked if anyone knew of a club playing more progressive music. I was sitting in with guitarist

---

[1] Netherlands-based band that has been performing Zappa tribute shows since 2008.

[2] Close friend of Ike Willis who played tenor sax on the track *Joe's Garage*.

David Carie, a long time best friend, whose group called Bliss was more what Frank was looking for. Bliss played early George Benson,[3]other jazz, Mahavishnu, etcetera. The club was called Caesar's Palace.

Tony Duran, guitarist of Ruben And The Jets[4] and drummer Jim Gordon[5] had gotten to this club and were sitting in playing a shuffle in the key of A. I only had one harmonica with me, a key of D, which is used most often in the key of A in what is called second position.

After we finished, Frank stood up from a table and yelled out my name, "Craig!" I went over and he was with a girl my older brother Marty used to date called Glenda. Frank stuck out his hand, which I promptly shook. He asked if I would go up and sit in on a slow blues with him. It was a lot of fun.

After we played, he asked me if I would come out to LA and audition. Later on, many Zappa players shared that they never knew of Frank sitting in like that.

Yeah, that was pretty rare. It wasn't until *Joe's Garage* that you got to play and record with Frank. What happened?
Well, on the third day of my audition for the Roxy band, Frank called me over and asked what I thought. I told Frank I thought I should go home!

He swayed back a bit and said he had never heard anyone say that before. He said, "I agree with you, but don't consider this a failure. Just go home and improve to where you can understand better what I need you to play."

I said, "Frank, it is no failure to me. It isn't every day a tree trimmer gets to jam with you, Ponty, George Duke and company!"

I had only been playing harmonica five years and I could only play blues and, as Frank shared, blues in a unique way. I went home and practiced and played with a guy named Donn Salyer who really helped mentor me.

I called Frank and shared that I was now ready and he flew me and

---

[3] American guitarist and singer-songwriter whose breakthrough pop album, *Give Me The Night* (1980), was produced by the legendary Quincy Jones.

[4] Los Angeles-based rock band whose first album, *For Real!* (1973), was produced by Zappa. Slide guitarist Tony Duran (1945-2011) toured with Zappa in 1972 and appears on the albums *Waka/Jawaka* (1972), *The Grand Wazoo* (1972), *Apostrophe (')* (1974), *Joe's Domage* (2004), *Imaginary Diseases* (2006), *Wazoo* (2007), *One Shot Deal* (2008), *The Crux Of The Biscuit* (2016) and *Little Dots* (2016).

[5] American session drummer who was part of the supergroup Derek And The Dominos with Eric Clapton. Gordon toured with Zappa at the same time as Duran, and appears on many of the same albums – though only on the title track of *Apostrophe* in Zappa's lifetime. Gordon is currently in prison for murdering his mother in 1983.

my wife out to LA, all expenses paid. Frank also asked me at the end of that audition how much I made a day trimming trees. I said, "$50." He told his assistant Steve to cut me a check for $150.

Did Frank explain the story of *Joe's Garage* to you? He claimed to have dashed it off over one weekend.
Frank never discussed this with me.

You next appeared on the track *Harder Than Your Husband* from the *You Are What You Is* album. Did you get to meet Jimmy Carl Black?
You know it is a shame as I never got to meet Jimmy. At least we got to record together.

He was a great character, for sure. That album was the first recorded at the UMRK – how did that differ from working at Village Recorders?
Well they are two different exotic animals. Village has all of that awesome heritage and how can you beat recording in Frank's home studio?

You know Village was so defining in that it was my first really big time recording session. I had done some recording in Wichita with some really fine musicians, but not internationally famous and rock royalty like Frank.

One awesome guitarist I played with in Wichita is Dawayne Bailey.[6] He recorded and played lead guitar with Bob Seger and later in the 1990s played lead guitar with Chicago. It is too bad Dawayne could not have been backed to do his own thing as he is in the upper ranks of electric guitar, like Steve Vai; sings like a combination of Stevie Wonder and Paul McCartney; writes original compositions - oh ya and plays decent piano!

Dawayne and I had a group called Further And Suns, which was Blues Traveler twelve years before, but with Dawayne on guitar we were more like a Mahavishnu version. Big words I know, but I may not live a lot more years and this is just simply the truth.

I tried to get the Hohner harmonica company to use me in their promotion and I put together a little video[7] featuring Further And Suns on Steff Signer's *I'm Alive* album – with me on harp on *Stars Fell Into Joe's Heart* and Billy Cobham on drums. Steff is known by many as the

---

6 As noted elsewhere, Bailey also co-wrote a number of songs with Jimmy Carl Black.
7 On YouTube at https://youtu.be/wZY8Dj640rM

Zappa of Europe. I wanted Hohner to share the historical truth about the first modern harmonica speed players, but they just blew me off!

Thank goodness for Zappanale and the artists I will be featured with so that I can share the music I have been blessed with! Especially Jeff Hollie!

Around the time of *You Are What You Is*, you also made guest appearances on stage with Frank: first, in 1980.
I contacted Frank when he came to Wichita for his concert there. Earlier that week I had been recognised by the board of the Wichita Jazz Festival as the New Aspiring Artist in Wichita. When I asked them if I could play, they said that I had not submitted a tape according to their process. I asked them why the *Joe's Garage* album I had recently recorded on wasn't sufficient and that I would think that a local player who had just recorded with Zappa would be joyfully showcased, but they blew me off.

I shared this with Frank, so when he introduced me to my home town audience, he stated this: "The Wichita Jazz Festival won't let Twister play, I think that stinks so we are going to feature him here with us tonight!"

Typical Frank Zappa, a phenomenal artist who would go to bat for a tree trimmer who was on the correct side of an ethic!

You again appeared during the show at which Nicolas Slonimsky also famously guested – in Santa Monica in 1981.
Well! Frank introduced me and let me solo for several minutes, then motions me back to trade licks, back and forth and motions me back again to do it all over again! Ha! Frank I think played some of the very best guitar I ever heard him play, He was hot! This was the finest night in my career!

It is on YouTube somewhere but you have to locate our playing in the timeline of the entire performance. A couple weeks later, Frank shared with me how much he enjoyed our playing and that my playing was outstanding.

Wow, whether I was or not, how sweet to hear that from the master!

Frank once described you as *"the Al Di Meola[8] of the harmonica"* - high praise.
I am just glad that someone else said that and not me! Ha! In that same

---

[8] American jazz fusion and Latin jazz guitarist.

quote, Frank also compared my playing to Coltrane!

Please let me elaborate on how touching it is to have Coltrane's name mentioned. Black musicians have been the majority of influence on my playing. From my friend Willie Dixon[9] and the Chicago blues artists, Ray Charles, Little Walter,[10] my late great friend, Jay McShann[11] – who discovered Charlie Parker and gave him his first job – to Jimi Hendrix, along with many others have been such an inspiration!

Of course that is the most flattering compliment I have ever received, except from my wife Vic! I hope who ever reads this book understands that I am just a person who was found by the harmonica and that I believe God blessed me with the ability to make some folks enjoy what I share.

One cannot take credit for a gift, it comes from a higher source!

You also played on *Cocaine Decisions* on *The Man From Utopia*. Did you have any influence over the tracks you played on, or did Zappa just know when he needed you?
The only influence I ever had with Frank was that he decided that what I played was suited to whatever composition I was blessed to perform on!

Aside from what we know, did you play on any other tracks – that maybe never got used?
On a visit to Frank's house one day with Jeff Hollie, Frank played us a completed version of *Bamboozled By Love* with an outstanding guitar solo he had played. He had me play a solo on *Bamboozled...* and thought what I had played was, in his words, "an amazing moment in innovation." Or something like that.

He never used my solo on a recording. Ask Jeff Hollie about it and get his take.

Tell us about your friendship with Jean-Luc Ponty.
Well I want everyone to know that Jean-Luc Ponty is as nice of a man as he is a player!

On my original audition with Frank, I approached the rehearsal

---

[9] William James Dixon (1915-1992) was an American blues musician, record producer and the composer of songs such as *I Just Want to Make Love to You*, *Little Red Rooster* and *Spoonful*. He also played upright bass on many of Chuck Berry's biggest hits.

[10] Marion Walter Jacobs (1930-1968) was an American blues musician whose revolutionary approach to the harmonica earned him comparisons to seminal artists like Django Reinhardt and Charlie Parker.

[11] James Columbus McShann (1916-2006) was an American jazz pianist and bandleader.

studio and heard this Hendrix sounding electric violin – what in the world! I had never heard of Jean-Luc.

I went up to him, as he was on stage all by himself practicing, as the other artists had no yet arrived. I told him I loved what he was playing and that it was amazing! He answered very thankfully with a heavy French accent. I spoke a little of my basic broken French to him and I think he was touched by my effort.

When the whole band got there for rehearsal, Frank had me come up to the stage and had a mic and a basic amp for me to play through. We played *King Kong* and I followed Ponty's solo. I did a pretty good job without my own rig and Frank was pleased.

After practice or a break, Jean-Luc invited me to go to a cafe for a sandwich together. From that day on we have shared emails of life and family – not in-depth, but friendly and cordial.

In the last couple of years I haven't been able to contact him, but Jamie Glaser, his guitarist and I email a bit and I hope when I get to Europe perhaps Jamie can let Jean-Luc know how much I would like to see him again.

You know Jean-Luc and Jon Anderson of Yes are presently putting together a new CD with Jamie playing guitar? Should be great!

Yes, I helped 'kick-start' that project.[12] Did you strike up any friendships with any other of Frank's musicians?
Of course Ike Willis and I shared good times together from the original *Joe's Garage* days and Jeff Hollie has been one of my few lifetime friends; as I shared earlier, Jeff is the one responsible for me playing Zappanale.

Jeff was doing an interview about Zappanale and he shared with the promoters that they needed to get the harmonica player over for the festival. They kinda said, "Is he still alive!?" Ha! Jeff kinda shared, "alive and wailin'!"

I am married now thirty-seven years to my only wife Vickie. Jeff and I lived in the LA area near one another for twenty years. We did a few things together musically but were never able to sustain anything in LA. This Zappanale show is a crowning glory to our determination to play together in a meaningful way again.

We hope much more will result from Zappanale, to return again in

---

[12] *Better Late Than Never* by the Anderson Ponty Band was released in 2015. It is essentially a live recording made in 2014 before Glaser joined the band, but he overdubbed all of the original guitar parts now present on the album.

2016 and as many times as they will have us and to work together in Amsterdam with our own music and groups. Of course wherever that then might take us in Europe and elsewhere.

The other great friendship I have shared is with Vinnie Colaiuta. He also lived near me in the LA area. He has recorded on some of my original music. I recorded a tribute to Jimi Hendrix on *Spanish Castle Magic* – Jeff on vocal, Vinnie drums and me on bass and guitar.[13]

Vinnie and I have not been in touch for a year or so as he is soooooo justifiably famous and busy! I love Vinnie and I know he loves me; we shared some wonderful times together in our formative years!

Yes, Vinnie is amazing! Tell us some more about your other line of work - I believe you even trimmed the Zappa's trees?

What an honour. Yes, on several occasions!

I have been in the tree care industry about exactly as long as I have played harp. I started in Wichita with the city where I learned my high climbing skills with rope and saddle and then employed those skills for twenty years in the LA area.

I was the City Arborist in La Cañada Flintridge through a private company called West Coast Arborists. I was also the Consulting Arborist for the gorgeous Descanso Gardens in La Cañada.

When Vickie and I returned to the Wichita area, I was employed as the City Arborist for Wichita for almost ten years. I shot a little homemade video and provided narration and original music about Descanso Gardens.[14]

Now, your thoughts on the Zappa family...

Gail was always an equal partner with Frank, as I say it! She was very influential and active in all of what Frank did!

I remember Dweezil practicing the riff on *Smoke On The Water* in his bedroom as the sounds of his guitar drifted out of his window. He must have been in his early to mid-teens.

I pruned some of Moon's trees at a home she was living in – in Laurel Canyon, I think was the area.

My fondest memory of Frank was one Christmas Eve night in his studio. Frank was sitting on the coach in the studio with Gail by his side and Ahmet and Diva on each knee. Frank Zappa the husband, father

---

13 On YouTube at https://youtu.be/YxBl9IZ2uak
14 On YouTube at https://youtu.be/S4mzbd6Vkfk

and friend to a harmonica player he never ever needed to hire!

Have you had any contact with the family since Frank's passing?
I have spoken with Gail on a few occasions. As far as the kids, no I have had no contact.

When did you last speak with Frank?
About a year before his passing. I remember sharing that I was going to pursue my own original music and how thankful I was for all of the doors he was directly responsible for opening.

Most of the opportunities I have been able to enjoy came about because Frank Zappa believed in me.

Can we expect you to 'sit-in' with anyone other than ZAPPATiKA at Zappanale?
As I shared before, Jeff Hollie is responsible for me performing at Zappanale.

The generosity of Ike Willis to share the stage with me and the hard work of promoter Hank Woods for facilitating my travel and accommodations and of course the fantastic provision of the Zappanale promoters to allow me the honour of standing on their stage!

Most of all I am more than looking forward to hugging each *Joe's Garage* artist and providing the best I can give for a powerful concert! Whatever happens on top of that is what is acceptable to the *Joe's Garage* artists and powers that be.

Finally, how did you come by the nickname 'Twister'!?
I love the questions you have posed! Great job!

In 1971 I had been out of the US Army about a year. I left the Army giving them a two week notice, as I morally could not agree with the Vietnam policy and the draft that victimised the poor, minorities and illiterate.

I finally, after accepting to face a five year prison sentence and $10,000 fine, received a letter from Senator Bob Dole of Kansas approving a General Discharge Under Honourable Conditions based on a lengthy letter I had sent him.

The contents of that letter maybe I can share at another date.

It was important for me to try and see how other countries in the world lived and thought. I got together some funds painting a house with a friend and flew over to Luxembourg. I then hitch-hiked over to Amsterdam, where I stayed at a Christian Youth Hostel and made friends with about twenty young men and women who were mostly from Canada, Europe and England and a couple from Egypt and Morocco.

Mohammed from Morocco was one of my best friends. I became very close with an English mate named Dave Adams. All of these twenty some folks had never met anyone from Kansas before.

Dave started calling me 'Twister' – after Kansas tornadoes, not Chubby Checker – because of my Kansas ties and the huff and puff required to blow the harmonica.

Of the twenty some, I have only been able to stay in touch with Dave Adams who is going to meet me in Amsterdam and is going to try and make the Zappanale festival.

Is that cool or what? Forty-four years later, we will see one another again!

Interview conducted on Tuesday 2nd June 2015.

SCOTT THUNES

Scott Thunes started playing bass for Zappa in 1981 and was appointed Clonemeister for the 1984 and 1988 tours. He can be seen in the *Dub Room Special!* (1982), *Does Humor Belong In Music?* (1985), *Video From Hell* (1987) and *The Torture Never Stops* (2008) home videos and heard on numerous albums – including *Ship Arriving Too Late To Save A Drowning Witch* (1982), *The Man From Utopia* (1983), *Them Or Us* (1984), *Thing-Fish* (1984), *Frank Zappa Meets The Mothers Of Prevention* (1985), *Broadway The Hard Way* (1988), *The Best Band You Never Heard In Your Life* (1991) and *Make A Jazz Noise Here* (1991).

Thunes also played with and recorded for Dweezil from 1986 to 1993, on his albums *Havin' A Bad Day* (1986, produced by Frank), *My Guitar Wants To Kill Your Mama* (1988), *Confessions* (1991) and *Shampoohorn* (1993, credited to the band "Z").

In December 1991, Thunes was part of the 'rock group' for the *Zappa's Universe* series of concerts at The Ritz in New York, alongside Mike Keneally, Mats Öberg and Morgan Ågren.

Following brief stints with Steve Vai (on the tour supporting his *Sex & Religion* album), the punk band Fear and The Waterboys, Thunes quit the music business, saying that after Zappa, it had been "one unappreciating employer after another," and worked with a software company for a number of years.

In 2002, he performed with The Lewinskys (his sister Stacy's band) at Zappanale and he has been the special guest of Zappa Plays Zappa a number of times, even playing the whole of its February 2012 US tour (from which Dweezil's *F.O.H. III - Out Of Obscurity* album is culled).

In 2009, Thunes assisted the author greatly with his *Zappa The Hard Way* book, which provides a far better understanding of his part in the demise of Zappa's 1988 band (it wasn't his fault!) During *An Audience With Scott Thunes & Jeff Simmons*, part of a celebration of Zappa's 70th birthday at London's Roundhouse in 2010, Thunes proudly displayed his copy of the book on the table next to him.

In 2011, Thunes became a member of Californian band The Mother Hips.

In October 2013, Thunes was part of the rock band that performed *200 Motels – The Suites* in LA and London (for the London performance, he additionally played the part of 'Jeff'). A recording of the US production (which featured the Los Angeles Philharmonic) became Official Release No.101,[1] and was issued one month after Gail Zappa passed away.

In May 2017, Thunes left the Mother Hips and was appointed 'ScoreMeister' (curator of Zappa's written music) by the ZFT.

A chance meeting with his actress/singer sister before Zappa Plays Zappa's first ever UK show at London's Royal Albert Hall in 2006 led to me first contacting Thunes.

Would he be interested in being interviewed? "Sure thing. I got no problems with the historicals. Lay them on me. But I hope you don't mind if I lie my ass off," was his response.

This was just before I flew off to Zappanale 17 and I wanted to delay things. But Thunes said, "Gimme something before you go." So I quickly rattled off a bunch of questions, fully expecting to see his reply on my return – but no, his response was immediate: full of wit, sarcasm and hilarity. He dismissed some of my more inane questions, pointing me in the direction of Thomas Wictor's excellent book *In Cold Sweat: Interviews With Really Scary Musicians*.[2] (In the flesh, Thunes is far from scary: warm, sexy, engaging, instantly likeable... the bastard!)

---

[1] An album entirely "envisioned by Gail Zappa and Kurt Morgan". Morgan, who used to "lay down the grooves night after night" for Hilary Duff (aka Lizzie McGuire), is currently ZPZ's bass player and was the ZFT's 'ScoreMeister' from 2010 to 2016.

[2] Published in 2004, the other interviewees are Gene Simmons of Kiss, Peter Hook of New Order and Jerry Casale of Devo.

Of course, I wanted to take it further and on my return from Germany, I did. And he came through in spades.

Do you have fond memories of *Zappa's Universe*?

Wow. That's interesting. I've never been asked that before. Um, yes and of course, no.

The 'yes' is big. Orchestra. Real musicians. Late-night partying with Virgil Blackwell[3] that sticks with me to this very day. Being treated like a valued resource by people with far more talent than I will ever have. Have I sucked up enough to orchestral musicians yet? No? Well, I haven't gotten started yet. That girl with the backless suit...

The 'no' is pretty big, too. I had recently written my only composition, a *Duo For Violin And Cello* that pretty much rocked. I'd brought copies of it for possible classical-musician-performance and I was quite excited. There was a cute blonde violinist who was excited to look at it/perform it, as she'd just started a duo and needed material. I gave her the score.

Later that night, the actual first violinist – a distinguished African-American gentleman who I regret to not remember the name of[4] – asked me if I'd let him have a copy of the score as well and I demurred, saying that I was giving 'first performance' rights to the person who'd asked first.

Fucking bitch never got back in touch with me and therefore I dropped the chance to have at least one more person look at my music before I lost part of the original score and can't recreate it because it was in an ancient Macintosh program format. Nobody uses it anymore and I can't make more copies and that piece is lost to history because of my short-sightedness. So, that's bad.

Also, I lost the keys to the apartment of the really nice lady who was allowing us to stay at her place.

Also, I had a crush on the daughter of the conductor[5] and she was really nice and she blew me off.

Also and this should sit higher on the list, but it's been dealt

---

3 The Orchestra Of Our Time's clarinettist.

4 Sanford Allen, the husband of Indian-born actress, food and travel writer and TV personality, Madhur Jaffrey.

5 Joel Thome, both conductor and artistic director of the Orchestra Of Our Time.

with already (during my first years on the Internet, I had a nice back-and-forth with the subject of this story), but one of my favourite moments in rock and a showpiece for me at the concert was ruined by the keyboard player[6] who forgot to switch the sound on the Mini Moog synthesizer (that I used for the bass part on *Sofa No.1*) from the lead sound he was using on the previous song back to a useful bass tone.

I stood there like a chump on the floor riser in front of hundreds of paying customers for thirty seconds or so twiddling knobs like an amateur as I realized in horror that I was not going to be able to play the Minimoog as I'd done on every single performance of that song since I'd been playing with Frank (not that I'd ever played it before working with him) and I was going to have to jump back on the stage and grab my bass guitar and play it on that, learning the fingerings on the fly and attempting to grab the correct attitude out of the ether while alternately squinting my eyes in furious fuming and glaring at the offending keyboard player who was watching aloft from the wings.

I ruined his evening by giving him a load of shit in front of his parents after the concert (I apologise!).

Other than that: bonus!

You describe yourself as an ex-musician: when was your last gig?

I played several casual gigs this year: last week, I played a wedding with a guitarist friend of mine. We drove about a hundred miles to play a gig overlooking 4,000 acres of Northern Sonoma County hills at some defunct ranch for some rich cats. I played an hour and got paid $225. My friend told me I was getting paid for the drive, not the playing.

Before that, I played about a month ago with some people from my daughter's school who have a bluegrass band. We played at a place 40 miles north of my house at an Irish pub, where there were three regulars at the bar. I made $14, but my family was in attendance for the first set and I got to play a friend's upright

---

[6] Marc Ziegenhagen, who attended Berklee with Joe Travers and later played in Mike Keneally's *Beer For Dolphins*, playing on the albums *Dancing* (2000) and *Live At Mama Kin* (2013).

bass, so that's a plus.

Four months or so back, I played with the above-mentioned guitarist for a medical convention's End-of-the-Convention Party at AT&T Park in San Francisco (used to be PacBell Park, the Giant's baseball team plays there; it's rad). I made a nice chunk of money and wore my suit, played some jazz, some Brazilian music and some surf tunes for three hours, sitting in a metal chair on the VIP level where my friends who have season tickets and worship the Giants have never been. I felt guilty for not giving a shit. There were fireworks.

Think you'll ever play professionally again – what would it take to get you out of your self-imposed exile?

Since we've recently experienced my wife getting a raise and our car payments ending, we've been doing pretty well. I don't think there'd be anything that could get me to leave my family for several months at a time. I mean, really: how the fuck is a family supposed to function without one of the members of the Parent Class MIA for long periods of time? I love her too much to leave her or my children for more than a couple of days anyway. She's always asking me if I need a rest, would I like to go have a beer with the boys, get out of the house for a bit and I always say no. Well, most of the time.

Alternately, the question is kinda loaded. I was never exiled, self-imposed or not. The only reason I was in music is the same reason most musicians are in music: I needed money and I could make some plying my trade, or whoring myself out, whichever you prefer (for those musicians of the world that 'need' to make music, please disregard the previous sentence and remain 'needy'; us listeners thank you).

Once I was unable to make money – for whatever reason – I quit trying to make more money at it.

Are you still composing?

Nope. I haven't really touched pen to paper since the debacle with the *Duo For Violin And Cello*. My musical self-directed adventures are limited to a project I'm thinking of where I'll post songs to one of my web pages that have a limitation of one hour spent on

GarageBand.[7]

That is to say, I'll spend an hour on GarageBand and whatever I end up with, I'll post. An entire album of simple things that just pop out of my fingers and head is I think a worthy exercise.

Other than that, I'm hoping to put something together with my family. My son plays drums (he's almost five) and my daughter sings something scarily good. I still have plans to teach my wife the bass (it doesn't take much to be a bass player in a rock band, that we all know) and I'll play guitar or keys or accordion.

But the most important thing is, I'll finally be in a band with some friends instead of an orchestral hired-hand like every other band I've ever been in, professionally-speaking.

When I spoke with Ed Mann, he said he finally was able to appreciate your "unique sense of humour"... and "would welcome the opportunity to play with [you] anytime." What are the chances?
Well, pretty damn high, considering. I mean, playing with Ed wouldn't even remotely 'bring up' any bad feelings from him specifically, if that's what you mean. Ed and I are thoroughly reconciled.

If someone has a huge talent, do you think it's kind of a waste not exploiting it to its full potential, or is it just a sad fact of life that unless someone else spots it and thinks they can make some money from it, it will remain hidden away – therefore being happy and contented is really far more important?
It's a waste, sure, but name me one thing about this life that isn't tainted with some kind of delightful horribleness. The fact that an artist, or a creative person in any way can be thwarted and have their talents either disregarded or ruined by the system of the world is small potatoes compared to the pressing problems that face humanity. Namely, the boy band factory and the company

---

[7] A line of digital audio workstations for macOS and iOS that allows users to create music.

that produces those plastic six-pack holders (hi, uncle Bob![8])

Was it your idea to bung a bit of Bartók into *Packard Goose* on the 88 tour?
Nope. Frank's. He asked me to orchestrate it – and the Stravinsky[9] – for the band. He tweezed it a bit, so it's not 'reeeely' all mine, but I take credit for it because he stole credit for the music for *Promiscuous*, as bad as it is.

Comparing the two versions of *The Deathless Horsie* on *Shut Up 'N Play Yer Guitar Some More* (1981) and *You Can't Do That On Stage Anymore Vol. 1* (1988), did you have an influence on the variations apparent in the latter over the original more laid back recording?
I have no idea what you're talking about. Seriously. I have never heard those two versions back-to-back nor have I ever compared any two performances of mine from live tapes or records or what-have-you. Any influence I may have imparted to that type of improvised music of Frank's was purely coincidental and no meaning should be impugned.

Your audition piece for Frank was *Mo N Herb's Vacation* – did you ever record that (or *Mo's Vacation*) for him?
Nope. We were going to do a rock-band/orchestral concert in Poland that would have contained that piece, among others, while in rehearsal for the 1982 tour, but it never materialized. All the pieces I worked on during my audition phase were looked at for possible performance but the project was scrapped.

I recorded three songs with Frank in the studio: *Cocaine Decisions*,[10] *Valley Girl*,[11] and *Be In My Video*.[12] Every other single

---

[8] In 2017, I belatedly asked Thunes about uncle Bob. His response: "Bob Hall was my uncle. He had a brother whose name escapes me and I can't believe I haven't thought of him in years, but this brother worked for the company that made those things. I have a photograph of me with him when I was around ten. First, last and only time I ever saw him. No, I didn't expect Uncle Bob to read this interview. He was dead at the time."

[9] *The Royal March* From *"L'Histoire Du Soldat"*, played before 'the Bartók' during *Packard Goose* in 1988. On the *Make A Jazz Noise Here* album, these two pieces were edited out sandwiched between *City Of Tiny Lights* and *Sinister Footwear 2nd mvt.*

[10] From the album *The Man From Utopia* (1983).

[11] From the album *Ship Arriving Too Late To Save A Drowning Witch* (1982).

[12] From the album *Them Or Us* (1984).

piece of bass performance came from live recordings, either raw or tweezed/massaged in the studio.

What do you know about the song *Solitude*[13] that Frank wrote for Gail?

I'm sorry you brought that up. Sadness.

I recorded many, many tapes during the rehearsal phase of 1981. Most of these are lost from lendings or movings. The tape that contained the sole performance of that song was given to Steve Vai as a Zappa-Band-Member to Zappa-Band-Member Temporary InterLibrary Loan.

Fucker lost it. I would appreciate it if he'd send that baby home to me. Other than that, it was an incredible song and I was looking mighty forward to performing it for the rest of my time with Frank. 'Twas not to be. Damn.

Arthur Barrow was still Clonemeister after you joined Frank. Did he give you any particular advice that stuck with you as regards playing bass for Frank?

Nope. In one ear and out the other was all the information I received from old Arty. He wasn't very one-to-one, if that's what you mean. He was nice enough during the initial putting-together-of-the-band and all, but he and I are not what you'd call compatible.

I do recall one item though. We were a Nike endorsement band for the Eighties and we'd have to go to Santa Monica to get shoes at the Public Interface where we'd be given two pairs of shoes for each tour. Once, during the 1982 rehearsals, Arty came with us to get his shoes and I arrived wearing my Converse High Tops. When they only gave me one pair in revenge for wearing another brand's shoes, Arty was there at Nike's defence, asking me why I thought they should honour their end of the bargain if I wasn't honouring mine. Nice guy!

What can you tell me about the session with Lisa Popeil?

You mean the original meeting? Or the week she was a fully-

---

[13] A never released/recorded 'love' song written by Zappa for his wife in the 1970s.

fledged member of the ensemble before Frank had to fire her because it was painfully obvious that she was unable to deal with the real-music elements (ie. non-classical) of a rock-band's particulars?

Or the time we were in the bathroom together, making out? I don't recall much about that particular time, so I was glad she mentioned it in song.

I fondly recall her soft smooth skin and her bounteous breasts and her obvious sexual passion, but I'm a gentleman and she's a lady and we don't talk about such things.

Also, I can't mention what Frank told me about her without her permission, so that will probably stay hidden until after her death. I love her. She's a sweetie.

Do you think you've mellowed to the point where you wouldn't now put on headphones and do a crossword puzzle on stage during a drum/guitar duet?[14]
I deny categorically your definition. It was stage-craft, improvised around the idea of a non-rock situation where all elements of stage-craft are considered equal.

It wasn't until after the tour ended that I ever heard anything at all about that particular element of the 'show'. My understanding of our situation was that rock posturing is stupid and bands that participate in such behaviour are pathetically under-brained and deserve ridicule.

You're talking about the European Dweezil tour of 1993 where I was already quite bent out of shape for having to deal with the idiocy of one of my band members on a daily basis and was in no mood to be told what to do, what to think, or anything at all other than "You're great. I like what you do with my songs and have for almost eight years and I won't let the simple complication of not having had the good fortune to tour with our first choice for that position (due to medical issues), so if there's any bad blood about this, I'll just jettison the offending party."

---

[14] Thunes reveals this scene – which took place during a "Z" gig in France in 1993 – in Wictor's book *In Cold Sweat*. Three weeks after the tour, Thunes says Dweezil phoned him to say he needed "somebody nicer in the band" and fired him.

Instead, I was ejected – thank you, Lord! – rather than the truly 'difficult' member (the person who was new, who was not part of the 'original crew', who was not of a sufficiently intelligent nature and therefore didn't 'fit in' as I saw it[15]). I found that our original conception of the band – that we were the 'Anti-Rock' band and our job was to show up rock stage conventions (rock 'face', stances, attitudes and positions, grimaces, head-banging, hair-throwing) for the farce that they were – changed during our time on the road and so my previously non-offensive, part-of-the-proceedings "schtick" stuck out like a sore thumb due to a conflict with Dweezil's apparent search for 'seriousness'.

Never in a million years could I have imagined that he would have switched over to a place in his mind where what we had all previously imagined and unwritteningly decided was thrown away to make way for his 'music' and that the proper stance for listening was pure concentration.

I did what I did because I thought it was funny, not because I thought it would hurt him.

Story of my life, apparently.

The story about sticking you cock in Bruce Fowler's face to shut him up – true or false?[16]
Super-duper true. Double true, dat.

On a scale of one to 26, just how scary do you think you are?
One.

Did your brother Derek ever try again to get into Frank's band after you'd joined?[17]
Nope. He concentrated on parking cars (like I had) and composition (like I wished I had). Then he got in a very bad motorcycle accident that eventually killed him (complications from AIDS).

---

[15] This was drummer Joe Travers, who Thunes described in Wictor's book as "a classic bonehead."

[16] This too is detailed in Wictor's book.

[17] It was through his brother's failed audition that Thunes learned Zappa was looking for a new bass player.

You said the Vai tour was "hellish" – what was so bad about it?

Pass. I am keeping these things to myself. He's a nice guy, I've heard. I have no urge to dispel that myth.

Is Tommy Mars really an alien?[18]

Huh? He's a nice guy. I love him. Wished things went better between us, but personalities are what they are.[19]

Musically, he's the most advanced individual I've ever had the pleasure of playing with. I wish him double-happiness for the rest of his life.

What memories do you have of Napoleon Murphy Brock on the 1984 tour?

He was great. I loved the way he stayed in bed 'til it was time to leave for our first gig in San Diego[20] – a three-hour drive away – without even remotely getting his room ready to leave.

We out-of-towners – me, Ray White, Napi – were put up at a residency apartment in the San Fernando Valley. Kitchen – utensils and plates – that type of thing. We were there for about three month's worth of rehearsals and so we were very much 'living' there.

Napi's room was a fucking mess. We were due to leave at – oh, say, noon – and I went to go get him and, bless his heart, he was lying there asleep or something. I went in to wrangle him and it was obvious that he wasn't planning on driving with us in the van, but intended to use his own very large old-school boat of an American car to drive himself. Mistake number one.

He very seriously completely missed the entire first sound check. This is a serious no-no and I only did it once in the seven years I played with Frank and that was for a pretty serious reason – I'd lost my passport – and Frank had even threatened to fine me for it. I told him to go ahead, I couldn't help it. So whatever, dood. He didn't.

---

18 Steve Vai's affectionate description due to the keyboard player's 'otherworldly' abilities.

19 Mars was to have been part of the 1988 band, but walked out of rehearsals claiming he'd been bullied by Thunes.

20 The first gig after leaving LA.

So for Napi to whip that out at the beginning of the tour was pretty righteous.

The next two weeks were repeats of this type of thing. After a while, Frank just figured he was too high to proceed. I have no idea if drugs were involved – I'm just guessing – but you'd have to have a serious priority-issue if you thought that what you were doing was more important than what Frank needed you to do.

I wish he'd stayed.

Do you think Frank put out too much stuff from the 1984 tour – for example, on the *You Can't Do That On Stage Anymore* series – simply because it was well recorded?
Frank liked clean sounds, tight bands and no mistakes. I don't really care for that stuff all that much so I am not really able to gauge his recordings using those criteria.

I liked the dangerous elements of the 1988 tour, where one didn't know if one was going to hear a gigantic fucking-up right after a righteous exaltedness or what.

You're featured playing with Terry Bozzio on *Rhythmatist* on Dweezil's new album[21] – I assume that is an old "Z" outtake?
Yep. I had to look it up on the Dweezil website to find explanations of what they were.

Actually, they're not 'outtakes' as much as 'end of tape' takes. We always filled out the last couple of minutes of tape with random 'grooves' or 'jams' or 'hate filled diatribes'.

Since I got paid $300/week, I never knew what was going to end up on an album unless I had to do overdubs (because we'd sometimes record up to twenty songs a day, my memory of any particular surrounding recordings with the Dweez are utterly devoid of content). I didn't even remember doing 'end of tape' takes with Terry. Cool!

I think we sound like *Red*-era King Crimson.

When I interviewed Joe Travers about your departure from Z, he said you had problems with him. "He has problems with

---

[21] *Go With What You Know* (2006).

a lot of people. He had been working with Dweezil for a long time. It just ran its course pretty much. You should ask Scott."
So?

Sounds pretty damn good to me. Good on ya, mate! Okay, whatever.

I offered to perform fisticuffs upon Joe's person for throwing drumsticks into the audience after telling him repeatedly that this was not a good thing as people have a propensity to throw things back.

Sure, a Joe Travers drumstick is something that most people would fetish like a... well, a fetish. But, like they say in *Men In Black*[22]: "A person is smart, but people are dumb." Throw something broken with splinters sticking out of it into a post-rock concert crowd and you'll watch me cower in abject fear.

Joe not only couldn't 'get' it, but argued with me all the way down the stairs into the backstage area. Mike Keneally was with me so he'll corroborate. I kept on Joe until I was nearly apoplectic. He never backed down, bless his pointed little heart, but it just inflamed me all the more.

I apologised, but I got no joy back. He said: "I accept your apology, but I'll never forgive you." Whoa. Cut off, dood.

When I got home from auditioning with the Waterboys in New York after the tour was over, I got a call from Dweezil, firing me. He said he needed 'nice' people in his band because he couldn't afford to have separate rooms for each of his band members (even though he flew First Class all the time and stayed in Four Star hotels wherever we went).

You see, we alternated sharing rooms and, after the argument with Joe,[23] we got to stay by ourselves (something band-leaders should take into account when booking tours). Sure, most bands use a single van as their hotel, but how many Zappa-quality musicians would do a van tour of the US?

Oh yeah, that's right: Me.

---

[22] 1997 American science fiction action comedy film directed by Barry Sonnenfeld and starring Tommy Lee Jones and Will Smith.

[23] Travers would continue to work with Dweezil up until 2013 (when he left Zappa Plays Zappa), and has been Vaultmeister for the ZFT since 1996.

It was great to go back to having separate rooms for the remainder of the tour, but it wasn't enough to resolve my issues with Joe.

How would you rate Dweezil as a musician/composer? Were song ideas with "Z" greatly influenced by you and/or Keneally?

I absolutely loved playing with Dweezil specifically because of his thoroughly fecund musical imagination. For a year and a half, Josh Freese[24] and I (hi, Josh - how's the Eternal Tour going?[25]) would rehearse the shit out of Dweezil's bedroom noodlings and turn them into nuggets of pure golden ambrosia.

Those few months really were part of the reason I remained mostly unfazed by my lack of financial success and Other-Than-Zappa musical possibilities, keeping me happily sucking at the teat (or, more to the point, shooting up the China White) of the Zappa Family instead of getting off my ass and getting a job, as they say.

I really shoulda, coulda been a contender if it weren't for them Damn Zappas and their Damn Music (this is a joke).

Ahmet seems very unlike Dweezil; extroverted and extremely funny. I imagine you two got on like a house on fire? Miss him?

I love Ahmet to death. He was very much a Zappa the entire time I knew him, so he was funny yet distant. He wanted nothing more than to have fun and laugh with his older brother, but other humans amused him at times.

He and I shared hardly anything in common but we respected each other. The one time I tried to turn him on to some art was

---

[24] American drummer who played on Dweezil's *Confessions* album and was replaced by Travers in "Z". Freese has played with many bands since, most notably Nine Inch Nails, A Perfect Circle, Guns N' Roses and Devo.

[25] Over ten years later, I also asked Thunes about this - was it the name of a Nine Inch Nails tour? His response: "That may very well have been during his NIN time of employment, but no, the tour wasn't called anything and I only meant as per the fact that I never saw him and he was always - more than any other of my friends - on the fucking road non-stop. He's finally made a decision to play pretty much only with Sublime With Rome and Sting. With the former, the tours are short and he makes 'more than he's ever made before' and with Sting, well, you play with Sting when he fucking asks, don't you? But it's also quite sporadic, as you can imagine."

going up to his bedroom and trying to play him *Plan 9 From Outer Space*.[26]

He got bored rather quickly. But he was in his early teens so I couldn't have expected too much... he was addicted to comics right then.

Do you have any contact with the Zappas these days?

Not really. A couple of years back, I got a phone call from Gail (my phone number hasn't changed since I moved up from LA eleven years ago) asking me if I'd like to be involved in Zappaween. I said yes and got a phone call directly from the biggest music promoter in New York, Ron Delsener. Pretty dramatic.

A contract was sent a few weeks later with terms that confused me, so I got in touch with Steve Vai to ask him if he had the same terms. He did, but he felt that it would have been okay with him if the terms were changed on my account, seeing as I didn't have millions of dollars in the bank and I lived hand-to-mouth at the time.

After that particular conversation, without hearing anything from Gail about anything, I read in the alt.fan.frank-zappa newsgroup that the gig had been cancelled. Gail never called me back.

I went to see Zappa Plays Zappa last month and had a nice conversation with everybody there, including Dweezil (he was about to have a baby[27]); Gail (like I'd never left her house, old friends); Joe Travers (told him good tourist destinations for him and his girlfriend – yes, we were on good terms); Steve Vai (he wanted me to know that he'd finally become a fan of the music of Gustav Mahler, twenty-five years after I tried to turn him and everybody else on the 1981 tour on to him); Terry Bozzio (who – not having ever particularly gotten along with him [understatement for dramatic purposes] I was not expecting to even make eye contact with, let alone have him come up and grab

---

[26] A 1956 independently made American black-and-white science fiction-horror film written, produced, directed and edited by Ed Wood, and dubbed the "worst movie ever made" in 1980 in the Medved brothers' book *The Golden Turkey Awards*.

[27] Zola Frank Zappa was borne by Dweezil's fashion stylist then-wife, Lauren Knudsen, in July 2006.

my arms in your standard male side hug, like in a photograph you'd take with a fan – was smiling and goofy and made a comment to the assembled hero-worshipping band members [who probably thought there would be a fight] that made light of our previous meeting; I appreciated this); and Warren DeMartini, the ex-guitarist from RATT, an old friend.

Did you enjoy the show?

I did! They – the musicians on hire – comported themselves admirably. Had to take a couple of pee breaks so I unfortunately missed the drum solo section and one other part that I can't remember. Other than that, they rocked the world.

Do you still have any contact with Mike Keneally or Ike Willis?

Strangely enough, Mike never calls when he comes up to Northern California and plays with whoever he plays with, but I enjoyed our time together in Germany for Zappanale 13.

I tried to get up to see him the last time he was here, but there was a mismanagement of time on my part and I missed him.

Ike? Uh, no. I'm not interested too much in communicating with him. I'm still recuperating from having spent six or eight months of my life in close proximity to him back in 1988 (he still owes me $95).

But more importantly, I have hard feelings concerning an interview he did with JamBands.com where he thoroughly put the blame of the entire 1988 debacle on my shoulders, completely destroying – for the audience of that interview and any and all future historians who might read the damn thing – any semblance of a balanced viewpoint concerning the proceedings of that time.

The main impetus for me to get 'online' back in 1997 was to battle the conception of the times: that I was at fault, that I was a bad bass player, that I ruined the tour and even worse, Frank's music with... well, with myself.

I'd spent the better part of a year writing my Once-Asked-Questions on Geoscott.com (you can find them on the Wayback Machine, a part of Alexa.com's web history function) and going on the above-mentioned newsgroup to rehabilitate my history. Ike comes along and without even attempting to communicate with me, like Ed Mann did (Ed, being the original instigator of a large percentage of the negativity surrounding 'me' during the 1988 tour, has since not only apologised to me – and would also apologise to Frank were he alive – but has gone on to be one of my more trusted and simpatico cyber-buddies) lays the entire negativity of the tour on my doorstep, as if he'd never talked to any single member of the touring ensemble after the tour was over to find out the truth, but only read some blatherings on some chat room wall about what happened.

I'm happy for him and glad that he's got a career singing music, but I've only seen him at the Zappanale – where, yes, I was gracious and reasonable to him.

I was told that he moved to my locale and I was shocked and dismayed. I am under the impression that he leaves disasters in his wake so I thought that his injection into my area would be a 'bad thing' but it seems that he's already left without any damage to me, my family, my reputation, or my friends' businesses.

I wish him luck in all his endeavours.

How did the invitation to play at Zappanale 13 come about?
My sister Stacy met the guy who puts it on. He asked her what I was doing and she had a brainstorm that we should perform live on stage for the very first time in our forties after never having any previous artistic combinatorality.

I jumped at the chance.

Of course, free airfare, a week in Germany with some Euros in my pocket, time spent with Stacy and my niece Isabella and a thousand Euros helped me to agree to leave my 'self-imposed exile' from music.

You seem a very happy and contented family guy. Do you ever worry about the time when your kids are less dependant on you?
Absolutely. I know it's kinda creepy – hopefully she'll remember this in her future, with fondness – but I tell my daughter to never leave me and to not grow up and all that jazz.

They are seriously the most adorable things on planet earth and I'll miss them horribly when they go (even though I'm sure I'll be as ready to see them ejected from the pod as they'll be to be ejected) but when you think about it, my daughter at age six is one third of the way to college. One third! It's disgusting to contemplate so I reject the notion that they'll leave me.

Ever dream about spoons?
Not recently. But I do dream about Frank and that's far more disturbing. I dream about being on tour with him and it's always great. I'm always excited to be about to play and it's mostly backstage stuff at outdoor concerts, as that was my favourite place to be while on tour. Grass, tents, amphitheatres, all the people, the girls, the beer and sky and the sound of PAs pumping out pre-concert music or the music of others.

These are what make up the majority of my pleasant memories of touring so they find themselves inside my dreams of Frank.

What do you miss most about him?
His voice. Talking to him. Listening to him pontificate about every little thing on the planet that not only was interesting to him but to whoever asked him a question. He was the most generous genius I'd ever met, who'd give any moron the time of day and would explain in gracious languor and excruciating detail elements of an idea, thought, situation or position to anybody who asked. If he had the time. On tour buses, he had time.

How would you like to be remembered?
As a good father, a good husband and a good bass player.

My sense of humour, my giant wangus and my attention to the clitoris. For my bottomless ability to drink beer without becoming an asshole, my fantastic driving skills and my *Duo For Violin And Cello*.

For my children who shall go on to amazing things and have my name associated with them in its correct role as footnote to their greatness (as Beethoven's and Mozart's fathers were footnotes to theirs).

For being Frank's longest-concurrently-tenured musician.

For having that fist fight in Wales during the Vai tour with that guy who crashed the backstage area drunk and waved that chicken wing at this cute vegetarian girl who I was not hitting on but I felt protective of.

For the Young Republicans.

For my string bass part on the Waterboys' *Love And Death*.[28]

For having played string bass in a staged performance of Stravinsky's *L'Histoire Du Soldat* in San Anselmo – my crush, Sarah Fairchild, in attendance.

For being even remotely associated with Derek Thunes' music by conducting the only performance of his *Fantasy For Electric Violin And Jazz Band* at the age of 17.

For not being the reason many people were unable to attend any concerts by the 1988 Frank Zappa band. Wasn't my fault, people! Impetus or no!

Interview conducted on Tuesday 8th August 2006.

I have continued to correspond with Thunes since our first interview and more so since his invaluable help on *Zappa The Hard Way*.

I got an excuse to chat with him some more when he was drafted into Zappa Plays Zappa by Dweezil for their US tour of February 2012. Scott Parker was interviewing Dweezil himself for Episode 6 of the ZappaCast, so I asked Thunes to talk about his involvement in the tour and much more besides.

Can you give us your thoughts on Zappa Plays Zappa.
My thoughts on Zappa Plays Zappa? Hmmm.

At this point, all I'm doing is working on the songs – I've got a list of the songs here, there's about twenty-three of them. I have made charts for all of the sixties stuff, that I have been listening to

---

[28] From the album *Dream Harder* (1993), with words written by the Irish poet W. B. Yeats (1865–1939).

my entire life but never actually had to play. Most of the stuff I have played with Frank during the '88 tour, but there's a bunch of stuff from *Freak Out!* that I've never played. Even though one of the first albums that I ever bought was *We're Only In It For The Money*, I have never actually had to play *Mother People*, or *Flower Punk* obviously – nobody ever plays *Flower Punk*.

The Muffin Men did!

It's really nice to have a chance to delve deep into these songs and I've always loved Roy Estrada merely because he was in the band, but I never actually realised how good he was and what magic he brought to the simple parts. I always considered him 'the first bass player', so I never really cared whether or not he was good, but the fact is he is a perfect foil for these songs – his tone, I love listening to him play. It's absolutely hilarious delving deep into the songs and finding the magic in his playing.

I was listening to *Lumpy Money* earlier today and the instrumental versions of the earlier songs are really interesting. Like you say, when you first listen to some of that stuff you don't really appreciate quite how much is going on.

Yeah, we don't actually get that much instrumental work. Frank likes to put crap on top of things. So as soon as you get into something that feels really good, he either switches gears on you or puts a snork in. Or, like he does in *The Idiot Bastard Son*, he does a bunch of crazy hippies talking nonsense in the studio. Which is really great when you're a twelve year old kid and you've been listening to pop music and you don't know what music is. To hear sound being used musically – I played it for the kids in the car this morning and tried to blow their minds, but it's not having the same effect that it did on me for some reason.

So what instruments do you play, Scott – apart from bass, obviously. You can write music, you can read music. But do you actually play other instruments?

I have been playing the guitar for quite some time. When I moved to New York after the 1984 tour, I moved in with my girlfriend, I brought a guitar with me and I had to do a lot of four-track recording for myself. I brought this guitar that I had bought a long time ago along with me. I think of myself as a bass player who plays a guitar. But with GarageBand and with the effects that are built in, anybody can sound like any guitarist they want. I'm a really good GarageBand guitar player. I consider myself a guitarist, without portfolio.

I played guitar in a punk band a long time ago. I love playing the guitar. I love bending notes. I love distorted, crunchy rock guitar. But I don't have a chance to play with anybody. Nobody will hire me as a guitar player. I can't play those normal guitar riffs that everybody plays.

I play piano. I sit around and I play my Brahms. I play my Bartók. I try and go through as much as I can. I'm a really crappy good pianist, or a really good crappy pianist. I'm about the same level on the guitar and the piano. I really enjoy playing them both.

If you tell me to play something, I could probably get it down but I wouldn't call myself a guitar player or keyboard player. But I have done both in the studio and I really enjoy it a lot.

So when did you get the call from Dweezil to join the West Coast tour?

I was at my final dress rehearsal for *The Nutcracker*[29] that was done by my son's ballet school. For the past five years, I have been in the production on stage being what they call a party parent. I was hanging around in the back room, getting dressed – there was about eight of us, all getting dressed and ready to put on our finery to get on stage. I was telling two of the people my musical life story. I was basically telling them how I had worked with Frank, how I had worked with Dweezil, how I'd just gotten fired by Dweezil and the phone rang and it said blocked call. I said to them, "I bet this is Dweezil." I answered the phone and it was Dweezil!

Very, very odd. Wasn't expecting... except that I kind of was expecting to hear from him because I had just played with Mike

---

[29] A two-act ballet, with a score by Pyotr Ilyich Tchaikovsky (1840–1893).

Keneally in San Diego, I had invited him to sit in with my band The Mother Hips. We played down at his local club that he has been playing at since he was a kid – the Belly Up. He jammed with us. We had a wonderful time. He really played well. I got him to come up to play on even more songs, coz I really loved what he was doing, he really enjoyed what he was doing. He had a great time and backstage at one point he told me that Pete was probably not going to be in ZPZ much longer. So I hoped that I would get a call from Dweezil, but I didn't expect it. So the fact that it happened within a month was strange, odd and fun.

The conversation was awesome. He sounded exactly the same as he did when he called me to fire me. He had the same hesitant, kind of 'I'm adorable, I really don't know how to have this particular conversation with you' kind of effect. It was very disarming and very charming. It was really fun to talk with him. It was the longest conversation I've had with him in years.

He explained a bunch of the band politics. I explained what my situation was: my band was going on hiatus for two months, I had an empty spot. I would love to do it, thank you very much. It was awesome.

It's interesting, because we interviewed Dweezil for the ZappaCast last week and I interviewed him in 1991 and when I listen to both recordings he doesn't seem to have changed at all.
No. He may be 42, but he still seems like the 12 year old kid he was when I met him.

It's interesting that you say Mike Keneally was in the know, because I'm never quite sure what the relationship is between Dweezil and Mike these days. Because they fell out years ago...
Mike knows everybody. Mike is the nicest guy on the face of the planet. He's the best musician, blah-blah-blah. Everybody knows him. Everybody loves him and everybody wants a piece of him. But he just as much gets a piece of everybody else, just by being open like that.

He is best friends with Joe Travers. Joe Travers is his drummer.

Joe Travers is Keneally's bass player, Bryan Beller's drummer. It's not even incestuous. When Mike Keneally and Bryan Beller got fired, Joe Travers didn't. Joe Travers was employed by the family, so there was no reason to get rid of him.

So there's never been a separation – there's a direct connection between Mike Keneally and anything that happens up at the Zappa house. Even though there's a wall there. He's on the other side of the wall.

I can talk to Gail whenever I want. But there's no reason to, so I don't. But he talks to Joe probably ten times a day.

When we spoke to Dweezil for the ZappaCast, he was saying he was a bit disillusioned with the alumni. But he said that he was looking forward to you joining them because of your enthusiasm.
Really? Well, that's nice to know! Every once in a while, you stand on stage – and I did this a lot in 1988 – and you say, "What's my job? My job is to play the bass." I've never wanted to just play the bass. So there's a disconnect between what I expect from myself, what I offer to people and what they accept from me. Quite often, that disconnect is terminal. Sometimes it's funny.

I'm having the same problem with my current band, The Mother Hips. I have to decide whether I'm going to act like the employee that I still am – because I'm still not a member of the band, I'm still a salaried employee. I have to decide how much I'm going to give. I get on stage and then I forget that I ever had a conversation with myself and Scott Thunes does what he has to do. I think that's probably the best thing for everybody, because it's nice when I shut up.

Did you know Eric Buxton[30] before the '88 tour?
No. Only from the tour. He was part of the gang and that was really awesome. Power to him. But I was busy with Dot.[31] Most of the time. As much as I possibly could be.

---

[30] Zappa fan who followed the 1988 band around the East Coast and was invited on stage to perform the *Twilight Zone* soliloquy that appears in *Jesus Thinks You're A Jerk* on Zappa's *Broadway The Hard Way* album.

[31] Dorothy Stein (aka Dr Dot).

Were you involved in a documentary about Jaco Pastorius?[32]
Yes. I have not heard anything officially since then. Strangely enough, Robert Trujillo,[33] who is spearheading the project, he and his wife[34] are building a house in Los Angeles. But he still comes up here to rehearse with Metallica and he was with his trainer running in a hilly area that my wife likes to go and run at. So they met each other in a parking lot and he had told her that the footage he got from me was absolutely superb, he's extremely pleased I don't want to say anything more about how gushingly awesome he thought it was, but he was very, very pleased and as far as I know it's still moving on.[35] I'm sure he's very busy with Metallica, so the director's probably doing what he needs to do and hopefully we'll see something soon.[36]

I wanted to play the bass around that time, too. I was listening to Jaco and Stanley Clarke[37] and all those people. But I got frustrated because I couldn't play like them overnight, so I gave up.
The way to do it is to not try and copy those assholes.

[laughs] **Yeah, I guess so.**
That's the way you do it. You just do what you do and go "Oh wow! That's really awesome."

But I never perfected *Donna Lee*. We all thumbed our way through it. The idea of trying it was fun. But virtually the only other thing of Jaco's that I've tried to play was – I don't think it was *Teen Town*,[38] but *Punk Jazz*[39] maybe. Whatever. It was one

---

[32] John Francis Anthony Pastorius III (1951-1987) was an American jazz musician, composer, big band leader and electric bass player, best known for his work with Weather Report from 1976 to 1981.

[33] An American musician and songwriter best known as the bass guitarist of the heavy metal band Metallica.

[34] Chloé Trujillo, and artist, singer, designer and magic maker. She and her husband recorded a version of *The Torture Never Stops* for download-only *The Frank Zappa AAA·FNRAA·AA Birthday Bundle* album (2010).

[35] Thunes' contribution appears during the end credits of the documentary, in the chapter on the DVD titled *Outtakes & Short Stories*.

[36] *Jaco* was released in 2014, following a successful PledgeMusic crowdfunding campaign.

[37] American jazz musician and composer known for his innovative and influential work on double bass and electric bass.

[38] A Pastorius composition from the Weather Report album *Heavy Weather* (1977).

[39] A Pastorius composition from the Weather Report album *Mr. Gone* (1978).

other piece of his that I tried to play and I still to this day cannot play it. I don't kick myself for it. But it does help me to realise what my strengths are. One of them was to not ever be a Jaco clone. That actually is a very nice thing to know.

A friend of mine, Mick Ekers, he's writing a book about Zappa's gear. He's friendly with Thomas Nordegg and he managed to get himself an invite to the house to photograph Frank's surviving equipment.
That is awesome. The only piece of equipment that I care about is the Minimoog that I used to play with Frank. I'm sure it's gone. I'm sure she got rid of it. But that was, out of all the things there, that was the only thing I cared about. I really would have loved to get my hands on that. Or his Bösendorfer. I asked her to give me the Bösendorfer at least ten times, but she keeps on saying "No!"

I wonder why?!
Yeah, Unbelievable.[40]

Any tales to relay about any of Frank's gear?
I don't have much in the way of stories or anecdotes. I only know that it was really nice to have that, because I always wanted a Minimoog, then when Frank said, "I want you to play it," it was a wonderful day. I never really was able to spend time learning the sound-making process: I got Tommy Mars to give me a nice big fat bass tone and that was the one I lived with. I was never really a sophisticated Minimoog player. I did enjoy my time with it.

But other than that, the only other real piece of equipment of Frank's that took mind share was Tommy Mars' Yamaha synthesizer. That was my least favourite instrument that was ever created. I really have always hated what that sound did to Frank's music. Because Tommy was an organist and he did this thing with it that I read a quote about Keith Emerson,[41] where the synthesizer for him was just always a super-charged organ.

---

[40] Zappa's 1979 Bösendorfer 290 Imperial Concert Grand Piano in Ebony Gloss Polish sold for $115,200 at an auction of Property From The Estate Of Frank & Gail Zappa in Los Angeles on 4th November 2016.

[41] Keith Noel Emerson (1944-2016) was an English composer/keyboard player and founding member of the progressive rock supergroup Emerson, Lake & Palmer.

That's kinda the same thing I always got from Tommy Mars with this Yamaha keyboard. It was one of the first multi-phonic synthesizers that you could play more than one note on and it had this blast patch that you know he used on everything. I just really hate that sound. Hate it, hate it, hate it. It really infested and infused that period for me. I could never understand why such a wonderful musician would love to make that sound on purpose and do it all the time on every song.

But that's just me.

Interview conducted on Wednesday 25th January 2012.

Thunes' emails are invariably hilarious and I keep urging him to write his own book.

Here's an exchange that may be of interest, which he kindly allowed me to use in the liner notes for *On Broadway: Covers Of Invention*, an album I curated for Cordelia Records in 2013.

One thing my book doesn't properly address is why the hell Frank chose to play so many cover tunes in 1988.[42] Any thoughts?

My thoughts on 1988, as you know, are very few and quite scattered, not to mention mostly missing. But if you were to ask me now, after having read your book, I would say that Ed Mann might have had a good point if he were to answer that Frank was 'tired' and 'sick with butt-cancer' and that it was pure laziness that allowed him to add songs he didn't write.

Others might say that he knew he was dying and he wanted to

---

[42] On the tour, Zappa had the band regularly perform Ravel's *Bolero*, Led Zeppelin's *Stairway To Heaven* and The Beatles' *I Am The Walrus*, as well as lyrically 'fucked with' versions of Lennon and McCartney's *Lucy In The Sky With Diamonds*, *Norwegian Wood* and *Strawberry Fields Forever*. The resultant CDs from the tour add a 'Reader's Digest' classical medley of Wagner's *Lohengrin*, Bizet's *Habanera* and Tchaikovsky's *1812 Overture*, *Bacon Fat* (Williams/Brown), *Stolen Moments* (Nelson), *I Left My Heart In San Francisco* (Cory/Cross), the *Royal March* from Stravinsky's *L'Histoire Du Soldat*, the theme from Bartók's *Piano Concerto No.3*, *Murder By Numbers* (Sting/Summers), *Purple Haze* (Hendrix), *Sunshine Of Your Love* (Brown/Bruce/Clapton), *Ring Of Fire* (Kilgore/Carter), *When Irish Eyes Are Smiling* (Ball/Graff/Olcott) and the themes from *Bonanza* (Livingston/Evans), *The Untouchables* (Riddle) and *The Godfather Part II* (Rota).

get to the songs he loved so well and for so long. But that would mean we would all have to put his earlier comments loathing the Beatles into sharp relief and take his word as bullshit of the highest order. So let's not go there.

My feeling, on the other hand, also holds no secrets. If I were to look deep into myself and ask myself a question, that question would be 'why aren't I getting even more sex from my lovely wife, seeing as how she seems to come every time we get nekkid and my penis is no slouch in the size department'. But you don't care about that particular answer any more than anybody else would, so let's not go there, either.

But you want to know if I have any thoughts on the cover-song issue. I don't. I truly believe the 'unexamined life is worth living', so I have unexamined that particular area of my life even less than many other equally-unimportant areas.

But let me say this, with the power of hindsight so very much in abundance everywhere but in my musical life: Frank loved to be the contrarian. Even more than I.

My guess would be that, like many evenings, he took his own advice to us, "Anything, anywhere, at any time..."[43] or whatever it was and applied it to a full tour.

He already played *Whipping Post*[44] as a set/show ender enough times to show that at least in that way, he saw no difference in something to present to his audiences between a song he wrote and another's composition.

But I also think that he, in a queer sort of way, maybe wanted to show how his band might have 'been the best' by tackling other's works and 'making them his own' to the detriment of the originals.

Of course, that begs the question of why he would even try to make an improvement on the Allman Brothers' version. None could be made, to my knowledge. We know he liked Duane,[45] so

---

43 'Anything Anytime Anyplace For No Reason At All'.

44 'Song originally written by Gregg Allman (1947–2017) for the Allman Brothers Band. A version recorded by Zappa first appeared on the album *Them Or Us* (1984), and became a regular Zappa show-closer in the 1980s.

45 When Zappa performed *Whipping Post* in Atlanta on 25th November 1984, he dedicated it to Duane Allman (1946-1971). His solo from that performance was subsequently issued on the album *Guitar* (1988), titled *For Duane*.

that dog don't hunt.

I guess, once again, you're on your own. Please let me know what you find.

Do you know any of the cancelled dates/venues on the 1988 tour? Were you ever provided with an intended itinerary?
No itinerary was ever presented. I always thought he was lying just to make us feel worser. Not me! I didn't do nothin'![46]

Interview conducted on Saturday 14th July 2012.

---

[46] This final exchange actually took place via email on 11th August 2015.

THE

TORNADOES

The Tornadoes were a moderately successful surf band from Redlands, California. They temporarily changed their name to The Hollywood Tornadoes in 1962 when the English group, the Tornados, topped the charts on both sides of the Atlantic with the Joe Meek written and produced single, *Telstar*.

Between December 1962 and June 1963, The Tornadoes' recorded ten songs[1] at Paul Buff's Pal Studios in Cucamonga. All of these were engineered – and, in the case of *Moon Dawg*, unofficially produced – by Zappa. Officially, these songs were all produced by Buff's associate, Dave Aerni[2]. Eight of them appeared on the band's first long player, *Bustin' Surfboards*, released in July 1963.

In the late 1960s, the Tornadoes disbanded to pursue other careers. But in 1993 their debut album was reissued by Sundazed Records and the original members reunited to play a large surfing reunion concert in Huntington Beach with Jan & Dean,[3] Dick Dale,[4] The Safaris and The Kingsmen.[5]

In 1994, the title track from their first album was included in the Quentin Tarantino film *Pulp Fiction*, renewing interest in the band.

---

[1] *Moon Dawg, The Inebriated Surfer, Shootin' Beavers, The Swag, Raw-Hide, Malagueña (Dark Eyes), The Tornado, Bumble Bee Stomp, Vaquero* and *Johnny B. Goode.*

[2] During his involvement at Pal Studios, David Lee Aerni also co-wrote the song *Love Of My Life* with Zappa, which later appeared on The Mothers' *Cruising With Ruben & The Jets* album.

[3] American rock duo consisting of William Jan Berry (1941-2004) and Dean Ormsby Torrence (b. 1940). Their most successful song, *Surf City*, topped the US charts in 1963.

[4] Richard Anthony Monsour is an American guitarist, known as 'The King of the Surf Guitar'. His 1962 version of *Misirlou* plays during the opening credits of the film *Pulp Fiction*.

[5] Portand based 1960s garage rock band best known for their 1963 recording of Richard Berry's *Louie Louie.*

A few years later, they recorded and released an album of mostly new and original material titled *Bustin' Surfboards '98*.

In 2003, the Tornadoes performed at Zappanale, where their set included a cover of Zappa's *Grunion Run*. Then in 2005 – partly at the author's behest – they recorded their version of another Pal-era song, *The Cruncher*, which was the b-side of the single *Heavies* by The Rotations. While Zappa had no involvement in the recording of either song, he did sample the a-side at the start of *Nasal Retentive Calliope Music* on The Mothers' *We're Only In It For The Money* album.

The Tornadoes' versions of *The Cruncher* and *Grunion Run* are included on the 2005 compilation album *Now And Then*, issued by Greg Russo's Crossfire Publications. The CD mixes Pal Studio material with other more recent studio recordings and live performances from the band's Zappanale set.

Following my peripheral involvement in that CD, I thought it would be good to get the band to say a few words about themselves and their time working with Zappa.

I spoke with bassist Gerald Sanders, his brother and lead guitarist Norm "Roly" Sanders, their cousin and rhythm guitarist Jesse "The Hookman" Sanders, original saxophonist George "Wild Man Saxon" White, current saxophonist Joel Willenbring and the CD's compiler, Greg Russo.

I first read about your involvement with Zappa in Greg's excellent book, *Cosmik Debris*. Until then, I knew nothing – and *Pulp Fiction* was already my favourite film! How did you find out that Tarantino wanted to use *Bustin' Surfboards* on the soundtrack?
Gerald Sanders (GS): I received a call one morning from Karyn Rachtman, music supervisor for *Pulp Fiction*. She said that Quentin Tarantino wanted to use *Bustin' Surfboards* in his new film. I thought, "Oh, another 'straight to video' film!"

She said he had, had our album from the 1960s and liked our music and that the music came first and then the screenplay. It wasn't until a few months later that I noticed that *Pulp Fiction* had won the Palme d'Or at the Cannes Film Festival. I then began to follow the film with great interest!

I was told that Quentin makes cassettes of his favourite music and then writes a story line around it. He was obviously a big fan of surf music.

Tell me a little about how and why The Tornadoes came together, to play the sort of music you play.
Norm "Roly" Sanders (NS): I think The Tornadoes came about out of necessity. We all had very limited funds for recreation. Getting together to play our music was a natural thing to do. It was great fun and free of cost.

Our group truly was family. Not only the three blood relatives Gerald, Roly and Jesse, but Leonard,[6] George and later Joel

---

[6] The Tornadoes' original drummer, Leonard Delaney, who sadly passed away in 2014 from complications of Alzheimer's disease.

dovetailed perfectly into our "family."

Our early repertoire was probably split equally between vocals and instrumentals. Gerald would show up with the vocals he wanted to sing. Since I wasn't much of a singer, my efforts were spent playing along and learning songs by The Ventures,[7] Duane Eddy,[8] Johnny Cash,[9] and such.

Jesse "The Hookman" Sanders (JS): Because of the influence our parents had on us in their love of music and how that was such a bonding agent in our family, it just felt natural and still does; I never gave it much thought. Hell, I guess I just thought everybody did what we were doing!

As to the music, there was influence from groups like The Ventures, Link Wray and a lot of others. But there was that foundation of country I feel has always been there; you know the ol' saying: "you can take the boy out of the country..."

GS: The three Sanders band members come from musical families. All our parents played guitar and my dad played mandolin also. They all sang as well and, in fact, our mothers had a professional trio that sang on the radio in the 1930s in Birmingham, Alabama called The Flagpole Mountain Gang.

After we moved to Southern California in 1957, Jesse met Leonard Delaney in the Redlands High School band – they were both drummers. Jesse and Roly were playing guitar also. Their mothers taught them. I was more interested in singing like Elvis.[10]

Leonard had his own set of drums at home, so Jesse invited him to come and play with him and Roly. I didn't yet play bass, so I would just sing Elvis, Rick Nelson and Fats Domino[11] tunes with

---

[7] American instrumental rock band who achieved worldwide recognition with their version of *Walk, Don't Run* in 1960.

[8] American guitarist known as 'The Titan of Twang'. His hit records include *Rebel Rouser* (1958) and *Peter Gunn* (1959).

[9] J. R. Cash (1932-2003) was an American singer-songwriter, widely regarded as one of the most influential musicians of the 20th century. One of his signature songs, *Ring Of Fire*, was performed by Zappa in 1988.

[10] Elvis Aaron Presley (1935-1977) was an American singer, regarded as one of the most significant cultural icons of the 20th century, known as the 'King of Rock and Roll'.

[11] Antoine Domino, Jr. is an American pianist and singer-songwriter of French Creole descent. His many hit records include *Blueberry Hill* and *Walking To New Orleans*.

them. I didn't hang out with them because I was older, so they got together by themselves sometimes and learned some instrumentals by Duane Eddy, Link Wray,[12] The Fireballs[13] and later on, The Ventures, et al.

When we finally got together as a band and were playing small dances, our repertoire consisted of Top 40 tunes, oldies and instrumentals – all covers. I heard about this band on Balboa Island that was drawing a lot of people at The Rendezvous Ballroom and I went to check it out.

Of course, it was Dick Dale and he just blew me away. I told the guys we needed to do some surf music, so we got to thinking along those lines.

And how quickly did Gerald learn to play bass?
JS: Gerald's ability to master the bass was amazingly quick, as he had little desire to play it at first – after all, he was the lead vocalist and that in itself was enough to keep him busy.

As we ventured out and heard more 'live' bands, we began hearing music with a bottom end sound that was missing in our group and we realized it was the sound of bass that was missing.

Once we decided that's what the group needed to round out our sound, Gerald mastered it very nicely.

How did you meet Dave Aerni?
NS: I'll let Gerald answer, as he will be more accurate than I could be. The truth is, I was so young; I really was along for the ride at that point. Hanging around with the older guys was a great source for good music, laughs and beer (for the underage consumer)!
GS: Dave Aerni was a dance organizer for The Inland Empire and had hosted such bands as The Bel-Airs,[14] Dick Dale, The Ventures, The Marketts[15] and many others. He had heard about the 15 year-

---

[12] Fred Lincoln Wray, Jr. (1929-2005), was an American rock and roll guitarist, best known for his 1958 instrumental hit *Rumble* - also used in *Pulp Fiction*.

[13] American rock and roll group, particularly popular at the end of the 1950s and in the early 1960s. They originally performed *Vaquero*, which the Tornadoes later covered.

[14] Influential surf rock band from LA, best known for their 1961 hit *Mr. Moto*.

[15] American instrumental pop group, best known for their 1963 million-seller *Out Of Limits*.

old guitar phenom named Roly in Redlands and came to one of our dances to check us out. He liked us and basically became our manager. He booked us at his and George Taunton's dances as well as other gigs. He knew some of the local DJs and got us some gigs that got us radio exposure, but no pay.

Had you met Paul Buff or Frank before Dave Aerni took you to Pal Studios?

GS: We never met Paul Buff or Frank until Pal. I don't recall having met any of the other Mothers, but that doesn't mean I didn't; we met tons of folks back then that I don't recall. We didn't meet Frank or Paul Buff until late in 1962.

What were those Pal Studio sessions like?

GS: The Pal sessions were fun, relaxed, high-energy sessions, with an informal – some may say messy! – atmosphere.

William Locy's studio – our previous studio – was friendly, but more formal and uptight. The engineer there was an older gentleman who seemed like your Sunday school teacher. The band members were separated from each other with movable partitions and I played the bass and sang in the control room separated from the other band members.

Pal, on the other hand, had us set up like we were on stage and we all played together. That made an enormous difference in the energy and feel we generated! Paul and FZ were young and made you feel as if you were more a part of the process.

JS: Pal Studios was very relaxed compared to Locy. I felt more like we were just at home jamming, with no pressure to get it perfect.

How did your invitation to play at Zappanale come about?

Greg Russo is totally responsible for getting us invited to Zappanale. I'll let him relate his story to you.

Greg Russo (GR): After the 14th Zappanale in 2003, I was thinking one day that The Tornadoes would be perfect to play at the next one. I was expecting people to say, "The Tornadoes - who? What do they have to do with Frank Zappa?"

Well, I thought that this sort of ignorance had to come to an end! Since they recorded ten tracks with FZ engineering – and I have to add that it was his first engineering job at Pal Studios – The Tornadoes are as much a part of Zappa's history as anything else that he was more known for. Quite simply, Frank Zappa learned how to be a recording engineer by working with The Tornadoes.

Zappa fans know that all aspects of his work in a recording studio were just as important as the material itself. For example, think of how *We're Only In It For The Money* would have sounded if someone else edited it! This point was very clear to me, so I e-mailed Gerald and told him to contact Wolfhard Kutz of The Arf Society to express their availability for Zappanale 15.

I gave Wolfhard background on The Tornadoes and mentioned how important they were to Frank's development as a recording artist and musician. Soon after, they were offered a slot at Zappanale in July 2004.

Between late 1962 and the middle part of 1963, The Tornadoes listened to FZ's thoughts about recording their material and between all of them, The Tornadoes came out of Pal Studios with a series of recordings that they remain very proud of.

A perfect example of this is *Moon Dawg*, on which FZ asked Gerald Sanders and his late buddy, Jack Sessums, to bark like dogs. The sound that Frank got on that track cannot be duplicated.

Another example was the exciting first take of *Shootin' Beavers*. When The Tornadoes re-cut *Shootin' Beavers* at William Locy Studios months later, none of the excitement that FZ recorded on the original version was present.

Without question, Zappa captured the essence of The Tornadoes at Pal and, because of this, The Tornadoes have the right to appear at any Zappanale held in the future!

Did you hear the calls there for you, Norm?
NS: I did hear the 'crazy man' yelling "Roly, Roly!" It really gave me a warm feeling inside. What a wonderful memory our week in Germany will always be.

Well, that soldier was me! In his liner notes, Greg mentions that you played the festival with borrowed, unruly guitars

that refused to stay in tune.
NS: I had some serious tuning issues with my guitar. The kind gentleman who loaned it to me uses very light gauge strings. I tend to really stretch and bend the notes I play, so I pulled the strings out of tune several times. If you listen closely, you will hear me trying to re-tune as we play some of the songs.

Oh well, it was great fun.

Having played Bad Doberan, is there a chance we'll see you in Europe again?
JS: We had such a great time in Germany, it was truly an experience that none of us will forget. If given the opportunity, I'm sure we would do it again. Almost every time the group gets together, the subject of our Germany trip is brought up and we re-live it again in 'remember when's'.
Joel Willenbring: The trip to Europe was a great party for us. We hope to do it again sometime.

Gerald, tell me a little about The Gross Prophet, the band you were in, in the 1970s. What sort of music did you play?
GS: The Gross Prophet was the band I started when Roly got married, started a family and moved to San Diego in 1969 to study aviation and ultimately become an airline pilot.

My best friend Jack Sessums, a lead guitarist, left his band – The Never So Few – and we joined up with Roy Parker on B3 organ and Carl Hubert on drums to form The Gross Prophet. We played night clubs for about five or six years and then started to play private events: weddings, festivals, shows, conventions, parties, class reunions – you name it, we played it. We were the most popular band in the Inland Empire for years. We did Top 40 covers; Hendrix, Beatles, Stones, Elvis, Creedence Clearwater Revival,[16] etc.

In 1985, Jack had to leave the band because his movie special effects company was becoming too demanding. He did TV shows like *The Dukes of Hazzard*, *Airwolf*, *Knight Rider* and others. His

---

[16] American rock band who performed at 1969's famed Woodstock Festival and, after four years of chart-topping success, disbanded acrimoniously in late 1972.

movies included: *Speed, Broken Arrow, La Bamba* and *Tough Guys*. He also did videos for people like Neil Young.

When Jack left, Mike Gooch (E.B.) took over as lead guitar and played with the Prophet until 1994 when George White and I left to re-join all the original Tornadoes for a big surf concert in Huntington Beach with Jan & Dean, Dick Dale, The Chantays[17] and The Kingsmen.

I forgot to mention that George White, original sax for The Tornadoes, played with The Gross Prophet for many years.

JS: The Gross Prophet did mostly vocals, with a few instrumentals in the mix once in a while – after all, The Beatles had already come through and ruined it for all the surf groups! The Prophet was a group with a very wide range of sounds; we did country, oldies and a lot of current songs that were popular in that era.

The Gross Prophet was a group that had sounds that were and still are, very much in demand for nightclubs. With Gerald's wide range of vocal abilities, we could do just about any song we wanted.

George, having been with The Gross Prophet and in and out of the Tornadoes on and off over a number of years, you obviously remain very close to the guys to this day.
George "Wild Man Saxon" White (GW): We were more than a band, we were the Five Musketeers - like, "one for all and all for one." It should be noted that from my perspective, we were the progenitors of punk rock. Our audiences were rowdy and boisterous and so were we. We were definitely not 'girly men'.

Gerald Sanders has always been and will always be, one of my very best friends. We were all like family back in the day and had many an exciting adventure together. Gerald and I, in particular, got into a lot of fun mischief.

Tell us a little about some of that mischief!
GW: Well, there was the time we all got into Jack Sessums old Hudson or Packard or something, we had all had too much

---

[17] American surf rock band from Orange County, known for the hit instrumental *Pipeline* (1963).

alcohol, we decided it would be fun to put a couple of us in the trunk – I believe it was myself and a friend of mine named Bub Salticof in the trunk – and cruise the local burger bar hangout.

When we arrived at the burger bar, Jack backed into a spot in front of the windows, someone got out and opened the trunk and there was Bub and I, bent over with our asses bared and equipment hanging down. This was followed by much horror and consternation by the employees and patrons and much merriment and laughs by all of us. Someone hurriedly shut the trunk and we sped off into a night of much frivolity but, much to our dismay, someone called the local gendarmes and we were stopped and taken in to the local constabulary where we were grilled about our mischievous deed.

Very fortunately for us, the detective doing the interrogation was none other than Jesse Sanders' brother, Jerry. It was explained to us that we could be considered sexual offenders and we would have to register as such in each new town we entered.

Wouldn't that have been the berries! *"Tornadoes arrive in town tonight, playing at your local Armory. Parents, keep your children home: they are known to be sexual offenders."*

My everlasting thanks to Jerry Sanders.

And what about how you were auditioned and initiated into the Tornadoes?

GW: Ah! The infamous Tornadoes audition story. To preface, I had a band called Little George And The Crescendoes. This was the summer of 1962, around the first of July. Being a sax player, the band was a rhythm and blues band. I was an avid surfer and liked surf music, but it wasn't the music I wanted to play. I had another sax player in my band also.

Anyway, we had a gig to play at the Ontario National Guard Armory, it was an entirely surf music gig featuring Dick Dale And The Del Tones, The Ventures, The Bel-Airs, The Tornadoes and Little George And The Crescendoes.

Why my band was put on the bill is something I'll never know. My band was the opening act, so we played and then stuck around to hear some of the other bands. I believe The Tornadoes were next up on the bill and I liked their sound. I think it was Gerald – could have been all the guys - came up to myself and the other sax player in my band and asked us if we would be interested in auditioning for their band. We thought things over and said, "What the heck, why not?"

The next week, we drove to Redlands to audition for the Tornadoes. It was like a phantasmagorical experience. After the initial amenities had been dispensed with, all the guys never looked us in the eyes again until after the audition.

Now, you have to understand, this lasted a couple of hours. They stared at our genital area the whole time, sometimes pointing at one or the other of us, muttering things like, "I bet he's a good suckie," and other such off-colour remarks.

Well, it finally came time for a break, so me and the other sax player went outside, to get away from their incessant stare of our genital area. The other sax player was really freaked out by their behaviour and wanted to get out of there pronto. As for myself, I tried to tell him they couldn't really be 'for real.' I think he must have led a very sheltered life as he was scared to death. I thought it must be some bizarre auditioning ritual they went through, as I could tell it was all in fun. But it sure was unnerving.

I guess the guys made up their minds as to who could handle their particular brand of humour and who couldn't, as they chose me to be in their band.

I don't think I ever spoke to the other sax player again after driving him home. This was the beginning of a friendship that lasts to this day. They were really a great bunch of guys and I might add, so were their parents and families. I spent more time at their houses than I did my own for several years.

Do you have any memories of Frank Zappa from that time?
GW: There was a club named The Broadside in my home town of Pomona, CA. Sometimes after a Tornadoes' gig I would drop by The Broadside and catch the last couple of sets. There was an awesome trio that played there called the Mothers.[18] I couldn't

---

[18] This would have been around 1965, when the three musicians - Zappa, Black and Estrada - were aided and abetted by local lad/vocalist, Ray Collins.

believe the musical expertise I was hearing and all this from a trio.

I stopped by there every chance I got just to hear them. Little did I know that the leader of this band was the same guy who engineered our cuts at Paul Buff's studio a few months earlier, Frank Zappa. I was a big fan of Frank's.

I heard him at UCLA's Pauley Pavilion with the Los Angeles Philharmonic Orchestra with Zubin Mehta conducting.[19] By this time they were called the Mothers of Invention. The Philharmonic had an inch thick score on their stands and the Mothers didn't have anything except Frank leading them through it all, with his jumps and kicks. It was an awe inspiring performance by some of the best musicians I've ever heard and a man who was definitely before his time.

Greg, your involvement with the band seems like a labour of love for you. Tell me a little about how you discovered the band and aside from putting the CDs together and writing *Bottom Feeder*, what else did you do on these compilations?
GR: During the six-month process of updating *Cosmik Debris*, I found out that the Sundazed label released two CDs by The Tornadoes. When I looked at the label's site, I discovered that The Tornadoes recorded at Pal with Frank engineering. It turned out to be Zappa's first engineering gig.

My first response was, "How the hell did everyone – including me – miss out on this?" These CDs came out in 1993 and 1999 and it was the first time that The Tornadoes mentioned recording with FZ.

In the booklet for the second CD (*Beyond The Surf*), Gerald's fax number was included. I sent Gerald a fax and I soon got a call from him!

After getting original copies of every Tornadoes release, it was clear from listening to both CDs that all of the recordings were transferred from either records or acetates and the sound was really lacking.

---

[19] On 15th May 1970, when excerpts from *200 Motels* were performed by a reunited Mothers & Orchestra, as part of Contempo 70.

So, after I recorded *Bottom Feeder* with The Tornadoes, I mentioned to Gerald that I could put together something that was more to everyone's liking.

While at Gerald's house, he gave me a cassette of five unreleased cover versions that the band did in 1995. I figured that these tracks could be combined with some older stuff and some Zappanale tracks, along with *Bottom Feeder* and your excellent suggestion (*The Cruncher*) for a really definitive Tornadoes CD.

The covers were included on the side of the cassette called "*Now*", with the other side consisting of 1960s tracks called "*Then*". I used this approach for the CD *Now And Then* and kept refining it along the way.

I assembled and laid out the CD booklet, wrote the notes and selected from a wealth of photos in Gerald's collection. No one else has researched The Tornadoes to this extent. The band's history had to be given more than the typical superficial CD treatment. The Tornadoes mean a lot of different things to different people. I wanted to make sure all of their abilities and accomplishments were presented fairly and equally.

Surf purists will probably not like the more recent stuff, but more recent fans might prefer the fresher tracks. There's something here for every type of music fan, who The Tornadoes actually appeal to. They don't play favourites with fans – if you enjoy any type of music they do, you're part of the family. The Tornadoes love being appreciated for their surf-oriented material, but they equally enjoy performing other people's songs as well. After all, at this late date, who would have figured that they would still be playing? That speaks volumes and no surf-only fanatic can stop that!

Joel, tell me a little about The Lively Ones – and how you wound up joining the Tornadoes.
JW: I was asked by Gerald to play a New Year's gig in Death Valley for 2000. After that gig they asked me to stay on permanently, which I did as saxophonist and back-up singer. I love being a member of The Tornadoes. All of the guys are like brothers to me and we all get along very well. I was one of the original members

of The Lively Ones who also had a song, *Surf Rider*, in the *Pulp Fiction* movie. I also worked with many well-known singers and musicians as a sideman. In addition to the saxophone, I also play a little piano, guitar, trumpet and banjo.

The Lively Ones were the remnants of a band called The Surfmen around the time of Dick Dale. We got Jim Masoner to play lead and I played sax. The rest of the guys were from the old group. We made about four albums and some singles around that time and played with bands like The Beach Boys,[20] Chantays, Tornadoes, Jan & Dean, Lou Rawls,[21] Glen Campbell,[22] Ann-Margret,[23] and others during that period. We were a very good surf band and got the ear of Gene Weed, who was a jockey on KFWB (at that time, the radio station was a music station). Gene got us going and helped us through the beginning years with venues and concerts.

There are many books written which include information about us during the early years and our dealings with Del-Fi Records, which in my opinion held us back from doing great. It is amazing, I get emails asking all kinds of questions about The Lively Ones; I guess we are some kind of classic big guys in the surf music area.

We were all surprised when we showed up in *Pulp Fiction*. Most of the guys were not playing anymore. I was still working with bands and so was Jim Masoner when the *Pulp Fiction* thing arrived. I understand Ron Griffith also did some music stuff after The Lively Ones.

What else have you been up to lately?
JW: I recently recorded some stuff with The Dynotones on their *The Dynotones Beach Party A Go-Go*[24] CD. This is Tim Fitzpatrick's

---

[20] American rock band formed in Hawthorne, California in 1961, famed for their 'California Sound' and distinct vocal harmonies.

[21] Louis Allen Rawls (1933-2006) was an American recording artist, best known for his song *You'll Never Find Another Love Like Mine*.

[22] American rock and country music singer, guitarist, songwriter, television host and occasional actor. He is best known for a series of hits in the 1960s and 1970s, including *By The Time I Get To Phoenix*, *Wichita Lineman*, *Galveston* and *Rhinestone Cowboy*. Was briefly a touring member of The Beach Boys.

[23] Swedish-American actress, singer, and dancer. As an actress, she is best known for her roles in *Viva Las Vegas* (1964), *The Cincinnati Kid* (1965) and *Tommy* (1975).

[23] Released in 2006.

new band (Tim was the drummer for The Lively Ones). They are all very nice guys and it was a pleasure working with them.

Jim Masoner and I are beginning a new CD project that will include all new songs written by Jim and me. We don't have a backer yet, but we hope someone will pick it up. It may take some time before it is complete.

I was thrilled when you guys played *Grunion Run* at Zappanale, but gutted that you ran out of time to play *The Cruncher*. When Greg told me you'd rehearsed *Now & Then*, I was naturally dead chuffed. It's a great way to end an excellent CD.
GS: We changed *The Cruncher* quite a bit. No waves: been there, done that. No piano: Roly did that part on the guitar. The original had no bass, but we added a rudimentary bass part – so as not to be intrusive. Joel does his own sax part, but he does a great job. Bottom line: it is still *The Cruncher*, but it's our *Cruncher*!

Greg, you had plans for the group to record some other Cucamonga-era stuff – like *The World's Greatest Sinner*?
GR: I wanted the band to record some other early FZ or Ray Collins songs, like *Jessie Lee* and *Deseri*[25] – basically, all the early Donna/Original Sound singles that Frank or Ray wrote. Roly's unavailability at the time put that idea on hold but, yes, I'd like The Tornadoes to record some other tunes.
NS: Andrew, if your travels ever bring you to California, please call us. We will personally perform *The Cruncher* and *Grunion Run* for you!

Roly! Roly!
GS: Yes, if ever you get a chance to come to Southern California you'll have five mates to show you around. Hopefully, it would be in the summer when most of our gigs and other concerts take place.

Interview conducted on Saturday 31st December 2005.

---

[25] Both songs were originally produced by Buff in 1963: the former was released as the b-side to *Mr. Clean* by Mr. Clean, which would later appear on Zappa's posthumous release, *Joe's Xmasage* (2005); the latter was re-recorded by the Mothers (as *Deseri*) for the *Cruising With Ruben & The Jets* album.

STEVE VAI

Steve Vai was initially employed by Zappa in 1978 to transcribe his recordings – "everything from lead sheets to orchestral scores." Some of these would be published in *The Frank Zappa Guitar Book* in 1982, by which time Zappa had recruited Vai as his stunt guitarist.

Vai can be seen, inter alia, in the *The Torture Never Stops* (2008) home video and heard on the albums *Tinsel Town Rebellion* (1981), *You Are What You Is* (1981), *Ship Arriving Too Late To Save A Drowning Witch* (1982), *The Man From Utopia* (1983), *Them Or Us* (1984), *Thing-Fish* (1984), *Frank Zappa Meets The Mothers Of Prevention* (1985) and more.

He released his debut album, *Flex-Able*, in 1984 after which he toured and recorded with Alcatrazz, David Lee Roth and Whitesnake – all the while carving out a hugely successful solo career.

Vai's cover of Zappa's *Sofa* from the *Zappa's Universe* album won a Grammy Award for best rock instrumental performance in 1994.

In 2006, he was of one of the three 'sternly accomplished special guests' on Dweezil Zappa's first Zappa Plays Zappa tour. In 2009, ZPZ and Vai won the best rock instrumental performance Grammy for their live rendition of Zappa's *Peaches En Regalia*.

He regularly performs with his former guitar tutor, Joe Satriani, as part of the G3 concert tours. It was when G3 played London's Shepherd's Bush Empire on 4th June 1997 that Vai took time out from talking to various muso mags to shoot the breeze with me. At that time, Mike Keneally (MK) was in his band and he too joined us on the fat floating sofa in Vai's dressing room.

While waiting to meet the pair, I got to tell Satriani who Frankie Howerd and Tony Hancock were (their photos hang by the backstage door). Then, midway through the actual interview, Queen guitarist Brian May walked in and had to be ushered away by Vai.

All in all, a surreal experience for this author!

Most of us are aware of how you came to work with Frank, so I'll by-pass all that. Tell me about the song *Solitude*, which you performed for Gail at the *Zappa's Universe* rehearsals.
How do you know about that?

I... er, have a tape of it.
Jeezus, how did that get out?
Mike Keneally: [laughs] You can't stop it!
SV: It was a song that we rehearsed in the 1980 band. Frank had written it before then, but we had rehearsed it in an attempt to persuade Frank to play it – which you really can't do.

It wasn't a typical Zappa song.
It was the least typical Zappa song I ever heard. When I asked him if it was written for Gail, he said "No." But I know it was because Gail told me it was. Obviously it's written for her!

It wasn't actually recorded – just rehearsed?
Well I have heard a tape, I believe, of tracks for that song with the David Logeman[1] band – for the *You Are What You Is* album. We rehearsed it. Frank came in, as he does sometimes if he's in a certain mood – he just started chopping songs from the list. We learned a hundred songs and that was one that got chopped.

But I remember Arthur Barrow had a cassette of it from rehearsal and years later I wanted to record it. I wanted to do something with it but Gail's very sensitive about that song. It's a very special song for her and rightly so.

---

[1] Zappa's drummer between March and July 1980, while Vinnie Colaiuta was otherwise engaged.

Did you sing it at that time?

Yeah, I did. I got the tape from Arthur. I believe it was Arthur – it was either Arthur or Scott Thunes. I think it was maybe Scott Thunes. I can't even remember now!

Then I learned it and I did a little version of it for Gail at the sound check for *Zappa's Universe*. I totally blew it. I remember she just sat there with her hand over her mouth. But I talked to her about that song.

So probably it'll never see the light of day officially?

Well there were other people that wanted to record it. But I think Gail wants Dweezil to record it first.

Are you still in touch with the family?

Occasionally. I was talking to Gail a few months ago before the G3 tour because we were gonna do *My Guitar Wants To Kill Your Mama* and I kind of wanted her blessing and I got it.

MK: Did you ever tell her I was singing on it?

SV: No [laughs] - why, you think she'd say don't play it? I don't think so.

[To Mike] I take it from that, that you're not so well in with the family these days?

MK: As far as I know they don't wish to speak to me. I've talked to Ahmet a few times; he's totally cool with me. But I think it's Dweezil in particular who doesn't really want to know about me.

That's a shame.

[To Steve] **You did a concert at the Eastman Concert Hall in New York with Joel Thome and a 60-piece orchestra last year[2] – how did that go?**

Well, the thing at *Zappa's Universe* went kinda good...

...you got a Grammy, didn't you?

We got a Grammy for the performance of *Sofa*. It was a nice arrangement by Mike and Scott. So Joel and I talked about doing something else together.

---

2 The Eastman School Orchestra, 28th September 1996.

Was it your own material that you played?

Yes, what we did then was my material. We did a couple of Frank's songs and we did a piece by Joel.

Did it include *Rescue Me Or Bury Me?*[3]

No.

Oh, I really like that song.

Thanks. But it was a nice event. It was really hard to get it together. I worked really hard for a couple of years just getting the orchestrations together. The logistics of putting together an orchestra show are pretty staggering.

I understand there's another one coming up in Israel?

There was, but it turned into a big disaster.[4]

But you've actually written a long orchestral piece?

Well the thing is, it's an avenue that I can walk down one of these days. I have all this material from the past that I've orchestrated – just pieces of music like *For The Love Of God*,[5] a couple of new things – but what I'd like to do is create a new piece for orchestra and rock band and have it performed. But you're talking five months of undisturbed writing and then $200,000 to record it.[6]

Are you two going to record together – you've obviously done the G3 stuff live, but are there plans to work in the studio?

MK: Yeah, I'm sure.

SV: Yeah, I really hope so. We just did a Christmas song for a record that's coming out on Epic.[7] Mike played piano on that – it's beautiful.[8]

---

[3] From the Vai album *Sex & Religion*, 1993.

[4] A concert went ahead in Jerusalem on 12th June 1997, but featured the Banned From Utopia performing Zappa material with the Shalom BSAL orchestra conducted by Thome.

[5] The seventh song from his album *Passion And Warfare* (1990).

[6] Between mid-2004 and 2005, Vai collaborated with the Netherlands Metropole Orchestra, performing compositions, old and new. These are captured on the *Sound Theories Vol. I & II* double-live CD and *Visual Sound Theories* DVD, both released in 2007.

[7] Between 1996 and 2001, Keneally toured and recorded extensively with Vai, appearing on his albums *Flex-Able Leftovers* (1998), *The Ultra Zone* (1999), *The 7th Song* (2000), *Alive In An Ultra World* (2001) and *The Elusive Light and Sound, Vol. 1* (2002). In 2012 he was part of both the Vai and Satriani bands for a G3 tour of New Zealand and Australia.

Is it something you've written yourself?

It's this record I'm trying to put together with Epic. It's all instrumental guitar. It has different players – Joe Satriani is on a track.[9]

Something like Dweezil's *What The Hell Was I Thinking?*

SV: Yeah.

MK: But that's all one song – this is a collection of different Christmas tunes.

SV: And we did *Christmas Time Is Here*, which is that Charlie Brown... [to Mike] who wrote that again?

MK: Vince Guaraldi[10] - it's a beautiful song.

SV: It came out really good.

MK: We were actually playing it live on the tour that we did at the end of last year.

Do you have any plans to work with Terry Bozzio again?

Well, nothing in the near future. But I have tapes of Terry.

From the Vai band project?

Right before that, when Terry and I started hanging out.

A friend of mine owned a studio he was turning into a video-editing facility and he gutted it so it was like this 20,000 square foot room that had three floors in it. We set up Terry's drums – he was wired for 48 track SSL – and I recorded three hours of Terry Bozzio improvising.

It's some of the most wonderful stuff and I hope to take that one of these days and orchestrate around it.

Tommy Mars – still a friend?

Yeah. Mars, he's an alien [laughs]. There's few people that are as musical as he is.

He's appeared on some of your solo stuff.[11]

Yeah, but you can't get Tommy Mars to come in and do little

---

9 *Silent Night/Holy Night Jam.*

10 The song was written by both Lee Mendelson and Guaraldi for the 1965 TV special *A Charlie Brown Christmas.*

11 Mars appears on the Vai albums *Flex-Able* (1984), *Alien Love Secrets* (1995), *Flex-Able Leftovers* (1998) and *Modern Primitive* (2016).

plinky piano stuff. He's like a wild cat. You've got to put spurs on and ride that bucking bronco!

He of course has been involved with the Banned From Utopia.
MK: I think they actually ended up doing this thing Steve was gonna do in Israel.
SV: Yeah.

Do you know what happened to Scott Thunes after the 1993 tour? I saw him on *Top Of The Pops* with the Waterboys, then he seems to have disappeared.
MK: If you can find a back issue – from about four months ago – of an American magazine called *Bass Player*, there's a fairly lengthy interview with him called 'Requiem For A Heavyweight'. It's basically his farewell to the music business. He has decided it's caused him enough pain and he's done now. So he's just gotten re-married and he just wants to be a househusband. The last couple of times I've seen him he seemed to be happier and more content than I've ever known him to be.

[To Steve:] Your time with Whitesnake – is that something you look back on fondly?
Well, when I was doing it I was enjoying it but afterwards it got kind of weird because I just started reading funny things in the press. Some of the guys were saying stuff.

Anyone in particular?
I don't want to get into that. It was good when I was doing it because touring with a big rock arena band, you get treated like a king, first class everything, I made a ton of dough and I got to go on stage every night and act like a lunatic.

And you also did some of your own songs.
Yeah, my solo section was a good opportunity for me to promote *Passion And Warfare*. But afterwards, because the record didn't sell 14 million like the previous one,[12] some people were a little

---

12 *1987, which featured Aynsley Dunbar on drums.*

upset about that. I have nothing bad to say about that. David Coverdale's a total gentleman; we always got along real well.

I think he's gone back to the bluesier stuff now.
Well, he's making a blues record but, contrary to popular belief, that Whitesnake record that I did was the furthest thing from the blues [laughs]. [13]

Are you still friendly with Laurel Fishman?[14]
Oh yeah – she's my best friend. She writes for a lot of magazines. She's one of the best editors I've ever worked with.[15]

Did you record an interview with her – or was it Frank – about the time of *Stevie's Spanking*? There was talk of a lengthy tape.
I think Frank talked to her about that.

On *Sex & Religion*, Ahmet Zappa provided backing vocals – on just one track?
Yeah. There was another called *Manic Panic*, but it didn't make it to the record.

But the best stuff I got of Ahmet is where he's standing in the studio just talking [laughs]. He's possessed, that guy. He's really funny - totally out there.
MK: [laughs] He's actually writing songs and rehearsing with a band apart from Dweezil now. He'll get into a rehearsal studio every couple of months and work up a new batch of tunes. I've

---

[13] Dutch guitarist Adrian Vandenberg sustained a serious wrist injury prior to the recording of Whitesnake's *Slip Of The Tongue* album, for which he had co-written all of the songs with the band's founder and vocalist, David Coverdale. Coverdale brought in Vai to record all of the guitar parts, which Vandenberg felt inappropriate, believing a bluesy rather than flamboyant approach would have suited the album better. In 1990, the band toured with both Vandenberg and Vai in the line-up, after which Coverdale temporarily disbanded Whitesnake. All parties expressed some reservations about the album and tour, but Coverdale reappraised that chapter of Whitesnake when preparing the release of the '20th Anniversary Edition' of the album (2009) and the *Live At Donington 1990* CD/DVD (2011).

[14] According to Zappa, Fishman won a radio station contest in the early 1970s by describing how since hearing the song *Call Any Vegetable*, she had started using them "internally". When she showed up to meet Zappa, Fishman brought along a perfectly spherical ball of her own faeces in a mason jar. Some ten years later, Vai spent an evening with Fishman in a hotel room – an encounter Zappa describes in detail in the song *Stevie's Spanking* from the album *Them Or Us* (1984). Her voice can be heard on Vai's albums *Flex-Able* and *Real Illusions – Reflections* (2005).

[15] Fishman specializes in entertainment media and reports regularly for GRAMMY.com.

heard tapes of them and they're good. Ahmet has tremendous potential as a front man.[16]

Yes, I was really impressed when I saw him with Dweezil at the Marquee in 1991, the first time he toured.
MK: He just keeps getting better. He's taking a more serious attitude towards singing and the lyrics. He's got a lot on his mind. As he gets older he starts to have more serious thoughts and the lyrics have really evolved from there.

[To Steve:] **I was surprised to hear *Bangkok*[17] on the *Fire Garden* album[18] – I never had you down as an Abba fan. How come you chose that?**
Oh, that's a long story. I have a stack of music: when I was on tour I would just write whenever I had an idea and I threw it in a pile. Then I would get my engineers – when they weren't doing anything – to type them into the computer so I could hear them.

That's how I discovered a lot of the songs that I have recorded – from these pieces of scrap paper.

So I listened to one of the tapes and I heard that melody [sings] and I thought "That's kind of nice, I could make a song out of that". I saw the manuscript and it had my name on it: it said *Taurus Bulba*. I remembered writing a song called *Taurus Bulba*; the melody was so familiar.

So I recorded this whole thing and I sent it to my manager and her boyfriend listened to it and said, "Yeah, that's Bangkok." She calls me up and she goes, "Is this Bangkok from *Chess*?" I said, "I've never heard any of that – that's crazy. No, it's just like a Russian folk dance."

So she played it for me over the phone and I almost died. I thought I was in a dream – how did those guys get my music?

Then I realised what had happened: years ago, when I was with David Lee Roth, he gave me this tape – didn't tell me what it was

---

[16] Ahmet played with the Idiot Sevilles and Leather Dynamite; the latter released a filthily funny album titled *Testicular Manslaughter* (2002), the cover of which bears a picture of sister Moon with a ballbag chin.

[17] A song from the musical *Chess*, written by Benny Andersson, Björn Ulvaeus and Tim Rice.

[18] Released in 1996.

– and said, "Transcribe this. Let's learn it and play it in the band between set changes."

So I transcribed it and we only did it a few times. Then I took the music and threw it in my pile. I didn't know the name of it or anything. So ten years later when I dug it out and listened to it, I couldn't remember that was the event so I thought I wrote it. It's a great melody – I thought it was too good to be mine!

A few years ago you mentioned you were going to remix and add some more 'leftovers' to the *Flex-Able* album.
Yes, that's my next project. I want to release a box that has: *Flex-Able* remastered; *Flex-Able Leftovers*, with some tunes from the *Passion And Warfare* days; a remastering and licensing of the Alcatraz record; a disc that I want to put together of all the film cues that I've done...[19]

...from *Crossroads, Bill & Ted's Bogus Journey*...?
Yeah and a bonus disc that's sort of like Frank's *Lumpy Gravy* album, all this talking and funny things.[20]
MK: Most of which was recorded on the bus last night [laughs]!
SV: Yeah, when these guys got back in a drunken rage. Oh! Everybody: Mike Keneally. Wow! [laughs] Poor guy!

So, do you have a backlog of 'leftovers'?
I've got a real, real lot of stuff. The fact is I just used to record, never thought I'd ever release it or that anyone would ever want to hear it.

Being signed to Epic Records, is that a problem – you can't release as much as you'd like?
No, it's not that. I just don't have the time. The time to record it and finish it.[21] I'm touring so much and I have a family. No, with

---

[19] In 2001, Vai produced *The Secret Jewel Box* containing the CDs: *The Elusive Light And Sound; Alcatrazz: Disturbing the Peace;* and *Archives Vol. 2: Original Recordings Of Frank Zappa.* The box will house a total of 10 CDs (or eleven, if you count the interview disc hidden in its base): at the time of writing, Vai has yet to issue the final few: *Alcatrazz: Panic Jungle (Live In Japan)* and *Hot Chunks.*

[20] This will be *Hot Chunks,* which purports to be the Box's most unusual component – a potpourri of music interspersed with conversations, source music and weird scenes from touring.

[21] As well as slowly filling up *The Secret Jewel Box,* Vai has now started issuing archival material via his download-only Vai-Tunes series.

Epic I can record anything I want.

You mention your family – are your sons Julian and Fire going to record any more songs with you?[22]
We're gonna find out, huh? I still have a lot of them on tape.

So, after the band project, the half instrumental/half song oriented _Fire Garden_, G3, the orchestral collaborations – what direction is Steve Vai heading off into next?
For my next proper studio record I want to really focus on the guitar and make it a guitar record. It'll have vocals, but I want to try to sit back and think where will the guitar go from here – what's the next evolutionary stage? I'm not talking about in the mundane pop world of the guitar. You know, a real development of the guitar. I want to try to saturate my consciousness in that frame of mind and see where that takes me and try to make it a reality.

I don't know if it'll be the be-all and end-all, but it should be fun to listen to. It'll be fun to play![23]

Where did the sample at the start of _Kill The Guy With The Ball_[24] come from?
That's not a sample! It's a guitar going through a DSP 4000, an Eventide piece of gear. It's a vocal filter that I constructed. What it does is, you hit a note and it makes it go "Ai-yeh, ai-yeh, ai-yeh." On top of that I have the whammy pedal, which takes the pitch and throws it around in octaves: "Ai-yeh, ai-yee, ai-yeh, AI-YEE, ai-yeh." So that's with one foot and with the other I'm using the wah-wah. Then you've got "Ai-yaw, wah-yee, ai-yeh, wah-yeh." And then when I've got the whammy bar and I'm foxing with the notes: "Ai-yaw, ah-rai-uh, wuh-yehh-urr-yeh." That's how I did it!

Interview conducted on Wednesday 4th June 1997.

---

[22] Julian provides baby vocals on _Alien Love Secrets_ (1995) and spoken vocals on _Fire Garden_; Fire provides spoken vocals on _Real Illusions: Reflections_ (2005) and was his father's personal tour assistant on 2015's The Story of Light World Tour.

[23] His next album, _The Ultra Zone_ (1999), was indeed largely instrumental and featured a homage to legendary guitarist Stevie Ray Vaughan (_Jibboom_) as well as Vai's former mentor, Zappa (_Frank_). It would be six years before he released another studio album of original material.

[24] From _Alien Love Secrets_.

MARK VOLMAN

Mark 'Flo' Volman was part of the Mothers – with his partner from The Turtles, Howard 'Eddie' Kaylan – from June 1970 to December 1971. Together they can be heard singing on the albums *Chunga's Revenge* (1970), *Fillmore East— June 1971* (1971), *200 Motels* (1971), *Just Another Band From L.A.* (1972), *Playground Psychotics* (1992), *Carnegie Hall* (2011), *Road Tapes, Venue #3* (2016) and three volumes of the *You Can't Do That On Stage Anymore* series.

They also starred in the film of *200 Motels*, for which they are credited with providing 'Special Material'.

While they remained friends with Zappa and were special guests at some later shows, it wasn't until 1987 that they planned to tour together again. In the event, this didn't pan out. But in his final year, Zappa released the audio documentary *Playground Psychotics*, which collects together in-concert and off stage recordings from a period he clearly relished.

For many teenagers in early 1970s, their first encounter with Zappa came around the brief but incredibly eventful Flo & Eddie era, with the *Fillmore East—June 1971* album in particular holding a special place in their hearts.

In 2005, I contacted both Volman and Kaylan about their planned participation in Dweezil's first Zappa Plays Zappa tour. They were both very discrete and said they'd be happy to subject themselves to some questioning should the tour come off.

Of course, it didn't – at least, not with them involved. So the following year, when my dear friend Billy 'ANT-BEE' James and his Glass Onyon PR company started doing some promotional work for Volman and his Ask Professor Flo website, the idea of an interview was revived.

Since then, the pair have performed one concert with Dweezil and ZPZ – at the Bearsville Theater in Woodstock NY in 2011. In 2016, when asked by *Downbeat* magazine if there was anyone they still hoped to tour with, Volman said, "We've had some discussions with Dweezil in the past and one of the things we felt would be fun to do would be a tour with him where we sing the music of the era that we were with Frank... I feel somewhere along the way we can maybe find a way to do a worldwide tour before it's too late."

That same year, Kaylan told me "Mark went through radiation and chemo and is now cancer free." When I asked if he would now be interested in taking part in an interview for this book, his reply was, "Sorry. I don't talk about the Zappas anymore."

Kaylan has though published his own insightful book – *Shell Shocked: My Life With The Turtles, Flo And Eddie and Frank Zappa, Etc.* (2013) – and provided some very helpful input to my *Zappa The Hard Way* book about the abortive 1987 rehearsals.

But that is Eddie.

This was Flo.

Why did you go back to the 'mainstream' after the Mothers – the Care Bears, etcetera?[1]

We went back to what came naturally. It was a challenge to get back to the mainstream, as you call it. We went back to making Flo & Eddie music and *The Care Bears* paid a lot of bills. We loved it.

In an interview a few years ago, you said you didn't know what had become of Martin Lickert after *200 Motels*. Do you now know that he became a Barrister and racehorse owner, but sadly passed away earlier this year?

No. I'm sorry to hear that.

Any particular fond memories of Martin?

Not really. I never met him before we started working on *200*

---

[1] In the 1980s, Volman and Kaylan provided music for US TV successes *Strawberry Shortcake* and *The Care Bears*.

Motels and he really fell out of my life four weeks later when the movie ended. He was in the right place at the right time. Jeff Simmons quit and we needed someone to step in and Martin fit the bill.

I still can't believe how much material he learned in that short amount of time. He even played the bass on stage.

Frank overdubbed himself playing bass when we got back to Los Angeles.

Did you remain friends with Frank up until his death?
Yes I did. He and I always were friends.

Was there any animosity after the accident and the end of that particular Mothers of Invention?
Not for me. We all just moved on to new things. It ended very abruptly but we had no time to sit around and wonder what to do. We just moved on.

At the Zappa Forum, you recently commented that Frank should have said more in *The Real Frank Zappa Book* about touring with the Vaudeville line-up. Aside from the Montreux Casino fire and the Rainbow Theatre,[2] what's to tell?
Not interested in dishing dirt about that era. It was great fun and incredibly rewarding, working within the Mothers. Great musicians and great music.

What do you think of the *Playground Psychotics*?
That is one of my favourite projects we did in that particular group. I think if you look at it as a sociology case study of alcohol and drug induced humans in an environment that emphasises rape and pillaging, you can enjoy it.

It really captured the group as we were on tour. I do think that we got so used to Frank having a tape recorder running all the time that we actually not only performed for those moments but enjoyed it as well.

Many of the routines people might have enjoyed during the

---

[2] On 10th December 1971, Zappa was pushed from the stage of London's Rainbow Theatre by an irate fan; he was knocked unconscious and broke a leg.

Mothers/Flo & Eddie years were created just the way that tape sounds; the groupies, *Magdalena*[3] and many of the others.

Do you know the nature of Frank's negative run-ins with Aynsley Dunbar?

I didn't know they ever had any negative run-ins. That is news to me.

Oh. It may have been Howard who mentioned that. Did you ever speak with Jeff Simmons after he quit? Frank obviously did!

Just saw him this past Summer. He looks great and still is one of the funniest people I have ever known. He hasn't ever changed as far as I can see and we spoke at length about the great time we all had.

What was working with Marc Bolan[4] like?

Marc was a great guy. He was always someone to have a good time with.

We loved Marc and making those records with him and Tony[5] were some of the best records we ever sang on. He had a vision and I was happy to be able to help him pull it off. I think he will grow better with age.

I wish I had received all of the Gold and Silver records we sang on. It would have filled up a room; *Electric Warrior*,[6] *The Slider*,[7] *Bang A Gong*,[8] *Jeepster*,[9] *Hot Love*,[10] *New York City*,[11] *Metal Guru*[12] and all the others... great stuff, all written with the same three chords.

---

[3] From the album *Just Another Band From L.A.*

[4] Marc Bolan (1947-1977) was an English singer-songwriter, guitarist and poet, best known as the lead singer of the glam rock band T. Rex.

[5] Tony Visconti, an American record producer, musician and singer, who worked extensively in the 1970s with both T. Rex and David Bowie

[6] T. Rex album released in 1971. Reached No.1 in the UK chart.

[7] T. Rex album released in 1972. Reached No.4 .

[8] T. Rex single, released as *Get It On* in the UK. Reached No.1 in the UK chart in 1971

[9] T. Rex single, released in 1971. Reached No.2.

[10] T. Rex single, released in 1971. Reached No.1.

[11] T. Rex single released in 1975. Reached No.15.

[12] T. Rex single released in 1972. Reached No.1.

And Springsteen?[13]

Bruce was hard to get to know. Bruce was another one of those artists who had a vision and an image he wanted to convey. I always thought Bruce was one of the smartest people I ever sang with. He was bigger than life and he was very generous with us the way he handled us with him in the studio and on tour.

We did about eighteen live shows with the E Street Band and we always felt like one of the group. Jon[14] was a great partner for Bruce and he was also very respectful of Flo & Eddie.

I think Steve[15] was the really talented member of that whole project we worked on with them and he really brought the sound of Bruce and The Turtles together. I love the record. It may be one of The Turtles best singles!

The 1987 Broadway The Hard Way rehearsals – what exactly happened?

It was really sad. It was all about money. Frank wanted us to get paid very close to nothing. He had brought together all of these great musicians and when the concept of money came up he had a figure in his head which was a figure from 1972. We wanted 1987 money; Frank was paying 1972 money. It was an easy decision to make. We left the project and never looked back.[16]

Tell me about Zappa Plays Zappa!

What about it? I did not see it.

Flo & Eddie were advertised as special guests and tickets were sold for concerts that were either postponed or cancelled.

We had a deal between us and the management company. When

---

[13] Bruce Springsteen – nicknamed 'The Boss' – is an American singer-songwriter, best known for his work with the E Street Band. Flo & Eddie sang harmony vocals on *Hungry Heart* (1980) – from his album, *The River* (1980) – which was Springsteen's first top ten single in the US.

[14] Jon Landau, co-producer of all of Springsteen's studio records from *Born To Run* (1975) through to *Human Touch* and *Lucky Town* (both 1992).

[15] Steven Van Zandt, guitarist with the E Street Band, who co-produced *The River*. His protest song *Sun City* (1985), performed by Artists United Against Apartheid, played a part in the broad international effort to overthrow the system of institutionalised racial segregation and discrimination in South Africa in 1991.

[16] Regarding the brief rehearsals with Flo & Eddie, Ed Mann told the author, "I think the most fun they had was on the first day - remembering old routines a capella over the mic with Frank. That was cool to behold. They were just cracking each other up and it was always so great to see Frank laugh like that."

they cancelled the first tour of Europe, they came back about six months later and forgot we had worked out a deal. They offered us another deal.

I feel like the management company represented themselves poorly and we did not want to be involved with them. I also felt that when Ahmet chose to not go along with the group and the tour, the music we would have liked to have been around to sing was not going to be a part of the final choices. It happened just that way in my eyes.

I was glad it worked for Dweezil. I think he is a great guitar player and what I heard was nothing but positive things about the tour... okay, maybe a couple of negative things, but mostly good things. I hope we can do something with Dweezil someday, doing the music we did with his dad.

What's the aim of Ask Professor Flo?
After teaching at universities for 10 years I thought about a way that I could continue to work with the thousands of students I had and how I could pass on information to others who might need help.

The Turtles was a sad story not unlike many artists from our era that sent us spinning out of control in a flurry of bad business choices. I had no mentors, no consultants and certainly no books to offer me insights into the spiral onto which I had just embarked... a spiral through seven managers in the first five years and worse yet, I had signed 100% of my song-writing publishing away before I had even written my first song.

The music business has changed dramatically since that first contract was signed in 1965 as a member of The Turtles, but many things still remain the same.

The incredible amount of stories I have personally heard, telling of lost careers and lost human beings, could fill a very large book. For every successful story, there are many more reflecting the outcomes of battered lives left to fade away in the wake of misguided musical choices and decisions.

Today, musicians, artists and songwriters still sign agreements they do not completely understand and the results of that turn their dream of success into a battle of survival, not just as a musician, but as a battle for life.

Record companies, for the most part, still function as a small cog in the much larger wheel of the corporate structure and the musicians, artists and songwriters are the oil that greases the cog in the wheel.

Many, I should say most artists, have no idea of a long-range plan for survival and the idea of having a plan for a career is so far away from their reality that most will find themselves signing one bad deal after another... over and over again.

The promise for success lays a foundation for those bad choices and bad decisions just as it did for me over forty years ago and continues for others today.

I hope that Professor Flo can help those who might have the dream but not the knowledge.

What's so special about your relationship with Howard? Very few partnerships last as long in the music business. Is it because you're not brothers?
I guess! I have never really stopped and tried to guess why we would be able to stand each other. I think we are both respectful of each other's opinions when it comes to our business. He allows me to hang myself and then rescues me and I think I do the same thing for him.

We never really have fought over decisions for the group. If either one of us really did not want to do something, the other person just always backed down.

We have really experienced so much together. I like hanging out with Howard when we are on the road. We both like vinyl records, good wine, skirt steak and looking at beautiful woman.

Howard recently made a solo album[17] and film.[18] Do you have any similar plans?
No plans but, well... I don't know. I'll never say never. I have

---

[17] *Dust Bunnies*, released in 2006.

[18] *My Dinner With Jimi* (2003), written by Kaylan about events in 1967 when The Turtles met The Beatles, and Kaylan had dinner with Jimi Hendrix in London.

written or co-written about twenty-five new songs and I do sing around town here in Nashville with great friends and great musicians like Bill Lloyd (Foster & Lloyd), Steve Allen (20/20), Garry Tallent (E Street Band), Steve Eby, drummer Craig Krampf, Chuck Mead (BR549) and many others.

We have a group of us in Nashville that I have been singing with this past year called The Long Players. We play entire albums of groups from beginning to end and great singers from town come out and sing. Walter Egan, Beth Nielsen Chapman, Mark Hudson and so many more I'm leaving out. After paying for the wine, we donate the money to charities and it is really fun.

In the past we have done Beatles, Elvis Costello, The Pretenders, The Kinks, The Cars and many others. I am new to the group but they seem to like me being involved.

I also do some singing for a project created by the Vanderbilt Universities First Amendment Centre. The show features songs from the last four or five decades that have been banned from the radio. Again, the players are just outstanding and the singing of Don Henry, Jonell Mosser and all of the others is incredible. I love being in a city that revolves around music so much. Everyone is very encouraging and even though I am not ready yet to do any original music, I also have no idea what I would sound like, so...

I guess that is one of the reasons I wouldn't say no as a firm answer, but I also know it would be strictly a personal thing.

Whatever happened to Jim Pons?[19]

Jim has had such a blessed life. After the Flo & Eddie records – he did the first two Flo & Eddie records[20] with us after Frank was pushed off the stage at the Rainbow. He then had a chance to leave music and take a job with the New York Jets football team as the head of the film department.

He retired after twenty-five years with a nice NFL pension and

---

[19] Former bass guitarist and singer for The Leaves, The Turtles and The Mothers. Pons has now published his memoirs, *Hard Core Love: Sex, Football, And Rock And Roll In The Kingdom Of God* (Waterfront Digital Press, 2017), which give a behind the scenes glimpse of his years with Zappa.

[20] *The Phlorescent Leech & Eddie* (1972) and *Flo & Eddie* (1973), which also feature contributions from Jeff Simmons (as co-writer of the song *Nikki Hoi*), Don Preston and Aynsley Dunbar.

he drove a limousine for a while. He retired from that and he and his wife Pat, who was in paediatrics, began working towards a dream they had which was creating a centre in Long Island dedicated to parents with children who have autism.

Jim and Pat were two parents who needed the help and so a centre was started called The David Centre. It was named after their son David and it became a successful endeavour.

After wearing himself out with that, they retired to Florida where he now works part-time with the Jacksonville Jaguars and plays in a bluegrass band called Deep Creek Blue Grass Band.

Jim and Pat and the boys were just here at our house for a three day visit on their way to North Carolina for some bluegrass shows.

I love Jim and Pat and they bring a lot of love in to our house when they are here.

What are the chances of The Turtles featuring Flo & Eddie touring the UK?

We are still playing and have done some shows about five years ago in Germany. We are not the standard oldies show. We have our own band so we don't play in front of guys in black outfits who work in the studios for a living.

We don't just sing our hits – we do some Turtles, some Flo & Eddie music and we have recently added some of the music we sang with Frank – and our show is expensive to bring overseas.

It would be fun, but nobody ever calls us.

Interview conducted on Saturday 28th October 2006.

CHAD WACKERMAN

Chad Wackerman started playing drums for Zappa in 1981. He can be seen in the *Dub Room Special!* (1982), *Does Humor Belong In Music?* (1985), *Video From Hell* (1987) and *The Torture Never Stops* (2008) home videos and heard on numerous albums – including *Ship Arriving Too Late To Save A Drowning Witch* (1982), *The Man From Utopia* (1983), *London Symphony Orchestra Vol. I* (1983), *Them Or Us* (1984), *Thing-Fish* (1984), *Frank Zappa Meets The Mothers Of Prevention* (1985), *London Symphony Orchestra Vol. II* (1987), *Broadway The Hard Way* (1988), *The Best Band You Never Heard In Your Life* (1991), *Make A Jazz Noise Here* (1991) and the 1985 remixes of *We're Only In It For The Money* and *Cruising With Ruben & The Jets.*

Wackerman also plays alongside Scott Thunes on Dweezil's debut album (produced by his father), *Havin' A Bad Day* (1986).

Since 1991, Wackerman has released five solo jazz fusion albums and regularly toured and recorded with Allan Holdsworth.[1] He has also performed with James Taylor and Banned From Utopia.

Between 2000 and 2005, he played a series of all-percussion concerts with fellow Zappa drummer Terry Bozzio, billed as D2. The pair also appear in the DrumChannel.com DVD *The Drummers Of Frank Zappa* (2009), together with Chester Thompson, Ralph Humphrey and Ruth Underwood.

The Chad Wackerman Trio headlined Zappanale in 2007 and released a live-in-the-studio DVD, *Hits*, in 2010.

---

[1] Holdsworth (1946-2017) was a British guitarist and composer who played with a variety of artists, including Bill Bruford, Soft Machine, Jean-Luc Ponty, Gong, U.K. and Level 42 and released twelve studio albums as a solo artist. Zappa often praised Holdsworth in interviews, citing him as one of his favourite guitarists.

Just prior to his appearance at Zappanale, a tour with Holdsworth and American jazz pianist Alan Pasqua brought Wackerman to London's Queen Elizabeth Hall. I approached him about the possibility of an interview and he was happy to oblige – I couldn't believe how amazingly youthful he still looks.

I have met him a couple of times since and he really is an incredibly nice man. Indeed, it's difficult to comprehend how he could have fallen out so badly with Scott Thunes during the 1988 tour.

Despite asking him to contribute to my *Zappa The Hard Way* book, he has maintained a dignified silence on the subject.

Wackerman met his wife, professional actress and singer Naomi Star, while on tour with the rock band Men At Work down under in 1985. They lived together in Australia for ten years, but relocated to California in 2005. Star sadly lost a two and half year battle with cancer in 2015.

How did you get to audition for Zappa?
I heard about Frank auditioning drummers in 1981. I first thought that it would be pointless, that I wouldn't get the gig. It wasn't until I spoke with Jim Cox[2] who said I had to go and audition, because I'd get a funny story out of it. I thought it over and realised that I had nothing to lose.

I called Frank and spoke to him, telling him that I was a drummer who lived in LA and was interested in auditioning for the band. He said, "Do you read?" I told him I did. Then he said, "Are you a good reader or are you a phenomenal reader?"

Not knowing quite what to say, I told him I had experience in percussion ensemble music, big band, session work, etcetera, but I hadn't seen his notation, although the reputation of his music was that it was complicated stuff.

He gave me his address and asked if I could be there in an hour. I packed up my drums and drove up to Frank's house. I was let in the gate and the first person I saw and met was Steve Vai. Steve

---

[2] Keyboard player who appears on Wackerman's albums *Forty Reasons* (1991), *The View* (1993), *Scream* (2000) and *Dreams Nightmares And Improvisations* (2012).

introduced me to the other core members of that tour – Ed Mann and Tommy Mars. I heard a couple of quick drum auditions and then it was my turn.

The pieces he auditioned on were *Alien Orifice*,[3] *Drowning Witch* (the classical interlude part),[4] *Mo 'N Herb's Vacation*[5] (which is arguably the most difficult drum part of his compositions).

After somehow getting through the music, the next stage of the audition was playing in odd time signatures. We played in 21/16 and 19/8. The other guys in the band were extremely solid on this stuff and we played these grooves for a long period of time. Frank then had me play in just about every style imaginable; heavy metal, swing, funk, New Orleans style rock (he called it a Delta groove), a Weather Report-type feel, Latin styles, swing reggae, straight reggae, ska, punk... then it was combining an odd time and a ska feel or a reggae feel... after this, Frank put on his guitar and played various rock feels, solos, riffs and we began to improvise off of certain feels. This ended day one of my audition.

Frank had me return for the next two days for more playing – I got to take home some of the music and we basically just did lots and lots of playing.

At the end of the third day, I went home and got a call that night from Frank saying that he just had a meeting with the band and they had decided to offer me the gig. This meant three months of rehearsal, five to six days a week, eight hours a day. Frank had about eighty songs that we were to memorise and arrangements changed regularly. The tour was three months in the US and Europe. He then asked me if I was interested in the gig! I answered yes, of course.

I was to go to his house the next morning to pick up a stack of music and entire albums to start memorising, as rehearsals started in two weeks. He then said that I got the gig because he liked my feel.

---

[3] From the album *Frank Zappa Meets The Mothers Of Prevention* (1985).

[4] From the album *Ship Arriving Too Late To Save A Drowning Witch* (1982).

[5] From the album *London Symphony Orchestra Vol. I* (1983).

What were you doing prior to that – playing with the Bill Watrous band?

Yes, Bill's Refuge West big band, small group and touring with singer Leslie Uggams.

What sort of music was that?

Bill Watrous is a famous jazz trombone player. He has a beautiful French horn type of sound and ridiculous facility. I played in his big band which, at that time, played originals and some arrangements of Chick Corea[6] tunes.

Leslie Uggams is a singer and a Tony award winning Broadway actress.[7] She toured with a rhythm section and picked up the rest of the big band in each city. This was my first road gig.

Can you describe your first tour experience with Frank?

My first tour was especially exciting. I remember that our first show was at a University in Santa Barbara, California.[8] I was very nervous, but Frank was so relaxed on stage, it really put me at ease. He was such a great leader.

By the third week on the road we were playing at the Palladium in NYC during Halloween and being recorded by MTV.[9] We had rehearsed for three months before this so the band was very tight. It was such a change for me going from being a local LA drummer to getting to play with Frank. I'll never forget what Frank did for me.

Did you work with Arthur, or separately when recording the new drum parts for *We're Only In It For The Money* and *Cruising With Ruben & The Jets*?

Separately. Also, on *Ruben & The Jets*, Jay Anderson[10] overdubbed acoustic bass after I had done the drum tracks.

You were also called in to overdub tracks from the *Studio*

---

[6] Armando Anthony Corea is an American jazz fusion keyboard player and composer.

[7] She is perhaps best known for portraying Kizzy Reynolds in the US TV mini-series *Roots* (1977).

[8] On 27th September 1981.

[9] Released on DVD as *The Torture Never Stops* in 2008.

[10] A jazz bassist/composer who has also done numerous jingles and non-jazz recordings with people like David Bowie, Tom Waits and Chaka Khan.

Tan,[11] *Sleep Dirt*[12] **and** *You Can't Do That On Stage Anymore Vol. 2*[13] **albums; did Frank have a programme of studio work for you, or did he just randomly call you in?**

Those overdub sessions were all done in one period. Frank told me he had always dreamed of redoing the drums on those early records – to get a modern, more hi-fi drum sound.

At first, I felt like we should not be messing with these classic recordings. But then I realised: The originals still exist. The engineers transferred the original master tapes to a new digital tape, so the masters are intact.

If I passed on doing the recording, I would disappoint Frank and he'd hire another drummer to do it. And... Frank was the composer and producer on those recordings and it was what he wanted to do.

Anything still unreleased?

I haven't yet heard the version of *Mo 'N Herb's Vacation* that I recorded in the studio. I had overdubbed to a recording of a small wind ensemble that David Ocker[14] put together for Frank. The recording is a very tight version of *Mo 'N Herb's*. This was done before the London Symphony Orchestra recording.

Did you ever play *Mo's Vacation* – the rock band version of *Mo 'N Herb's Vacation*?

I am on the LSO recording and no we never performed it live with the rock band. I did a studio recording for Frank.

Do you regret the electronic drums on the 1984 tour?

No, not at all. It was Frank's idea to use them at the time. We experimented and came up with a hybrid kit of a DW kick and snare, real Paiste cymbals and 11 electronic pads. The unit at the

---

[11] Wackerman plays on an Excerpt from "*Revised Music for Guitar and Low-Budget Orchestra*" on the cassette-only album *The Guitar World According To Frank Zappa* (1987).

[12] Wackerman plays on three tracks on the 1991 CD reissue of this album.

[13] Although Chester Thompson plays drums on this live album, it is widely believed that a more modern drum sound can be heard throughout. When I pressed Wackerman on this in 2017, he said "I don't know. You should try the engineer who worked on it I guess." While Mike Keneally has stated that there is "a triggered sample of Chad's bass drum throughout the Helsinki album", engineer Bob Stone has dismissed this as a fallacy.

[14] A copyist, computer programmer and clarinettist that worked for Zappa between 1977 and 1984.

time was a modified Simmons SDS7. I had four digital samples on chips per pad, plus a basic analogue synth section per pad and 16 setups programmed for the show.

I did enjoy the melodic possibilities when I would solo. I still enjoy playing melodically on the drum kit, but now I do it all on an acoustic set.

What was working on young Dweezil's first album like?
It was fun. Dweezil played great and he was young too, maybe 18 I'm guessing. Steve Vai was his teacher and Scott Thunes helped him arrange his tunes, so they had it all planned out arrangement wise before I even heard the music. A good time was had.

How did you hook up with Allan Holdsworth?
In 1982, through my old friend and drummer buddy John Ferraro. John played in a band with Ernie Balls'[15] sons, Sterling, Dave and Sherwood. Dave used to cycle with Allan, so John auditioned, then John called me and said to give Allan a call and brought over the *I.O.U.* record.[16]

I auditioned shortly after. Allan had met Frank as well and Frank also mentioned that he thought I'd be a good choice in Allan's band. Allan was Frank's favourite guitarist.

You originally made a guest appearance with the Band From Utopia, then subsequently played on the whole Banned album... any more plans to record or tour with any of those guys?
The Fowler Brothers got a call from a festival in Stuttgart to play a set of Zappa music. This became the Banned From Utopia. I was called at the last minute to be a guest, so I played a couple of tunes with them at the festival.[17]

We then went into the studio and recorded various Zappa tunes and originals over a five year period and the result was the CD, *So*

---

[15] Roland Sherwood Ball (1930-2004) was an American entrepreneur, musician, and innovator, widely acclaimed as a revolutionary in the development of guitar-related products, such as "Slinky" strings.

[16] Holdsworth's second studio album, released in 1982.

[17] Drummer Jay Dittamo (who also auditioned for Zappa in 1981) played the bulk of the set at the Jazz Open Festival in 1994, with Wackerman taking over for the encores.

Yuh Don't Like Modern Art.

So, do you think you'll work with Banned From Utopia or the Fowlers again?

I sure hope so. They are such wonderful players. Bruce and Walt are very busy orchestrating music for film, so Banned From Utopia has been put on hold.[18]

Tell me about your work with Ed Mann on his solo CDs.

Ed and I connected from the first tour that I did with Frank. Ed is also a drummer and I found his influences very interesting – he was into all sorts of ethnic music and various urban dance styles. Ed got a record deal with the German art label, CMP Records. I played on two of Ed's CD's: *Get Up*[19] and *Perfect World*.[20]

Would you say you were influenced by Ed's writing or the recordings you did with him?

I really like Ed's compositions and really enjoyed playing on his solo CDs, but I wouldn't say that I was trying to copy his writing style. I think the similarity is a sonic one because Daryl Pratt plays vibraphone on *Scream* and *Legs Eleven*.[21]

CMP also released some of your solo albums – do you have any deal or plans for more solo records?

I have four solo project CDs: *Forty Reasons*; *The View*; *Scream*; and *Legs Eleven*. I've recorded a live performance of my band in Sydney – I need to mix and master it before putting it out.

I also am working on a wild studio CD with Allan Holdsworth and Jimmy Johnson – all trio stuff.[22]

And what about the Bozzio duo tours – obviously Terry's a good friend; any more plans to work together?

We are looking at possibilities now, but nothing is confirmed.

---

[18] Wackerman did return to the Robert Martin-led BFU in 2014, in which Tom Fowler was the only one of the brothers still involved.

[19] Released in 1988.

[20] Released in 1990.

[21] Released in 2004.

[22] Wackerman's fifth solo album was 2012's *Dreams Nightmares And Improvisations*; as well as Holdsworth and bassist Johnson, it also features keyboard player Jimmy Cox.

Japan is interested, as is the US. I love to play with Terry in duet format. We have a very strong musical connection.

What was working with Barbra Streisand like – did that effect your playing at all?

It was actually really fun. She was very serious about the gig. We rehearsed in a recording studio in LA. It was also a small eight-piece band, so it was nice to work in that environment. More connection than with a large orchestra.

It was one live show, which was made into an HBO special, Video/DVD and CD.[23]

We rehearsed for a week and played one gig, so I can't say that it affected my playing. It was at a very professional level and she sounded amazing.

What was the move to Australia all about?

My wife is Australian and when we had our first child we were looking at options – living outside of Los Angeles. Sydney looked like a great option because it's a great place to raise a child; it's a beautiful city, very cosmopolitan.

What was it like getting back together with Keneally for guest appearances recently?

How do you know this? It was great. I did two gigs with Mike. One with his band at the Baked Potato club in LA,[24] and one gig in San Diego[25] with Doug Lunn[26] – the second gig was completely improvised music. We had a great time.

Your brothers, John and Brooks, are also drummers – all taught by your father?

My father started us, but after a while we all took lessons from

---

[23] *One Voice* (1987), which includes renditions of *Happy Days Are Here Again* and *America The Beautiful*, songs would that feature on Zappa's Broadway The Hard Way tour in 1988.

[24] On 30th December 2005, where they performed a diverse mix of originals and compositions by the likes of John Coltrane, Neil Young, Thelonius Monk, Stevie Wonder and Zappa - including *The Black Page*.

[25] At Dizzy's on 7th September 2006.

[26] Multi-instrumentalist/composer (1954-2017) who specialised on the 5-string fretless electric bass. As well as being a part of the Chad Wackerman Trio, Lunn also worked with a number of other Zappa alums, including Mike Keneally, Chester Thompson, Vinnie Colaiuta, Terry Bozzio, L. Shankar, Warren Cuccurullo and Eddie Jobson.

Murray Spivack[27] and Chuck Flores.[28] Murray also happened to be the recording engineer on *200 Motels*, as well as *The Sound Of Music*,[29] *Hello, Dolly!*,[30] etc.

Murray was the first person who made me aware of Frank, when I was 13 years old.

Murray is someone I've heard you talk about a lot – he was obviously very influential and someone you hold in very high regard. Can you tell me what was his major contribution to your style of playing?
In fact, Murray did not believe in teaching style. It was extremely focused on hand technique and reading. The grip, rudimental strokes and the patterns he showed me did affect my playing and sound. The up and down stroke exercises – similar to the Moeller technique[31] – I use all over the kit for accents strokes.

During your master class at the Queen Elizabeth Hall, I asked you about your opportunities and interest in non-Western music. You told us about odd time signatures and made it sound very easy – "Think only in 2 and 3, etc." Could you run that by me again?
Any odd time signature has combinations of 2 and 3 counts – for example, if you play in 5/8, then you can count it in 2/8 plus 3/8, or reverse it – 3/8 plus 2/8. The composition determines the 2 and 3 counts. The first counts (the 1s) are accented and these accents define the groove.

If you think in that way, it's easy to understand: 2+3+2+3+3 would be called 13/8, but since you know where the accents fall, you can make it groove. You can write a sticking pattern for a 2 count, then one for a 3 count and connect them together.

Bass drum plays the accents of all the downbeats. From there

---

[27] Spivack (1903-1994) was a Russian-born American sound engineer and drum teacher best known as the sound designer for the film *King Kong* (1933).

[28] Flores (1935-2016) was one of a relatively small number of drummers associated with West Coast jazz who was actually from the West Coast.

[29] A 1965 American musical drama starring Julie Andrews and Christopher Plummer.

[30] A 1969 American romantic comedy musical film directed by Gene Kelly, and starring Barbra Streisand.

[31] Named for drummer Sanford A. Moeller (1886-1960), who documented the way of playing snare drum by the army during the American Civil War.

you can edit notes out, experiment with half time, etc... it's endless.

The goal is to make music out of it, not to make it sound difficult.

You make it look easy, too. I read on one fan site that you guested on the Zappa Plays Zappa tour towards the end of last year, but I have not seen that mentioned anywhere else. Is that right or wrong?
All rumours, I'm afraid. I think Terry might be a guest artist on some shows. They got us mixed up. You can't believe everything you read on the net.

This is true. So what are you going to play for us at Zappanale, Chad?
We've been rehearsing for it with my new trio; Doug Lunn and Mike Miller.[32] So far we are playing my music and some of Mike's. We have been re-arranging tunes because my previous band was a quartet. It's already sounding amazing and we are thrilled to be a part of the festival.

After the Holdsworth tour and Zappanale, what does the future hold?
This year is full of touring with the Allan Holdsworth trio, with Jimmy Johnson on bass. The Pasqua / Holdsworth / Haslip[33] / Wackerman group is putting out a live DVD on Altitude Digital.[34] It's in HD surround sound and really captures some wonderful performances of the band.

I also need to finish up my live band CD from Sydney and the studio trio CD with Allan and Jimmy.

Would you like to say anything about Kurt McGettrick?[35]
I was shocked to hear the news that Kurt had passed away. I had

---

[32] Los Angeles-based guitarist who has also played with Zappa drummers Vinnie Colaiuta and Ralph Humphrey. He is also a former member of both Banned From Utopia and The Grandmothers.

[33] Jimmy Haslip, an American bass player and record producer who was a founding member of the jazz fusion group the Yellowjackets.

[34] *Live At Yoshi's* (2008). They also issued a live album, *Blues For Tony* (2010): both releases were a tribute to former Lifetime drummer Tony Williams, who died of a heart attack on 23rd February 1997.

[35] A member of Zappa's horn section on the 1988 tour, who died on 6th May 2007.

such a great time working with him. We got to stretch and improvise together quite a lot on the Banned From Utopia tour of the US some years ago. He played with a huge sound and was very interesting rhythmically as an improviser. Because of the way he played when he improvised, he left space and enjoyed lots of interaction. He was a monster of the baritone sax and all the low woodwinds.

I'll miss him and his music.

Finally, do you know any of the cancelled dates on the 1988 Broadway The Hard Way tour? Were you ever provided with an intended itinerary?
I'll save you some time on researching this. Nothing was booked beyond the dates that we played. It was an idea to possibly add more, so nothing was cancelled.[36]

Interview conducted on Saturday 26th May 2007.

---

[36] This exchange actually took place via email on 11th August 2015.

DENNY WALLEY

Denny Walley spent his childhood in New York City before his family moved to Lancaster, California in 1955, where he met the teenage Zappa.

In 1972, he played guitar and sang with Geronimo Black alongside former Mothers Jimmy Carl Black and Bunk Gardner.

Walley played slide guitar for Zappa in 1975 and then again from 1978 to 1980. In between times, he joined Captain Beefheart's Magic Band and played on the Zappa-financed *Bat Chain Puller* album, finally released by the ZFT in 2012. Beefheart gave him the nicknames 'Feelers Reebo' and 'Walla Walla'.

Walley can be heard on a number of Zappa albums, including *Bongo Fury* (1975), *Joe's Garage* (1979), *Tinsel Town Rebellion* (1981), *You Are What You Is* (1981), *Halloween* (2003), *Joe's Camouflage* (2014) and *Chicago '78* (2016).

He released his one and only solo album, *Spare Parts*, in 1997, which he recorded in Sweden with Morgan Ågren and Mats Öberg. It includes a number of blues songs written by the likes of Muddy Waters, Elmore James and Willie Dixon, plus two penned by Zappa (*Suicide Chump* and *Bamboozled By Love*).

For eleven years, from 2003, Walley toured regularly with the reformed Magic Band, featuring bassist Rockette Morton and drummer/vocalist John 'Drumbo' French.

Today, he regularly tours Europe as special guest of the Muffin Men and also sits in with Dweezil and his band when the opportunity arises.

The following is an interview I conducted with Walley ahead of his headline performance at Zappanale 19 in August 2008.

Tell me about your earliest musical experiences.

At age seven I was with my parents visiting friends. They had a small 12 bass accordion in the basement and I asked if I could try it. They agreed and left me to toy with it. It took me about an hour to figure out how to play a couple of simple melodies using both the keyboard and bass buttons. I decided that I liked the sound and smell of it and my parents agreed to pay for instructions and a rental accordion to practice on. I played it for about five years.

Around 12, my parents moved from New York to Lancaster California. We lived in a new housing development called Tamarack Fair and by coincidence, the Zappa family lived in the same development. I became best friends with Frank's younger brother, Bobby.

The first time I ever heard the blues was in Bobby and Frank's bedroom and I was hooked.

That's when the accordion went under the bed never to be seen again... until *Harry Irene*, for *Bat Chain Puller*.[1]

I didn't realise that was you!

Only the guys in the band and Gail Zappa, knew about it. The accordion that I used on that session belonged to Gail's father. It was in a pink road case!

I wanted so bad to be a part of that music. The closest I could hope to get to it would be to get a guitar and try and play along with the records.

The first time I ever heard a live band was in an assembly at Antelope Valley Joint Union High School (AVJUHS). The band was The Blackouts: Frank Zappa on drums; Terry Wimberly on piano; Fred Salizar on baritone sax; Fred's brother Wally on guitar; and three soulful vocalists, Henry Strawberry, Chuck Spencer and a third singer whose name I don't recall at the moment but I will get it from my yearbook.[2]

At the time that was the first mixed band I or anyone else had ever seen. From that time on I knew exactly what I wanted to do

---

[1] Recorded in 1976.

[2] I reminded Walley about this when he played Festival Moo-ah with the Muffin Men in April 2017; he said he would check his yearbook soon!

in my life.

A few years later, my father got transferred back to New York and I lost track with all of my old friends. In New York I met some other guys that felt the way I did and we formed a trio. We called ourselves The Detours. We played together for about nine years and played all over the country.

We were a blues band at heart, but we had to learn a lot of the current songs in order to get gigs. We would play two or three of the current hits then would launch into our 'blues bag', which usually got us fired before the night was over!

We played just about every club in Greenwich Village and all over Long Island, as well as some gigs in Vegas, California and the usual assortment of 'buckets of blood'.

We had a manager who somehow managed to get us signed with Atlantic Records. Tom Dowd[3] and Arif Mardin[4] produced two of our (only) singles that were released on the ATCO label,[5] but nothing ever came of it. The timing was not good for us as Atlantic had just signed The Rascals and Cream and we were toast. About the only claim to fame we had was that we played the Copacabana Lounge in New York seven nights a week for twenty-seven weeks: a record that still stands.

So how did you then hook up with Geronimo Black?

I moved back to California in 1969 with a promise that I would have a chance to audition for Canned Heat,[6] as the guitar player had quit or was fired.[7] Not true.

So I crashed with my parents for a few days and then met some musicians that had a huge place in Laurel Canyon and invited me

---

[3] Thomas John Dowd (1925-2002) was an American recording engineer and producer for Atlantic Records, credited with innovating the multitrack recording method.

[4] Mardin (1932-2006) was a Turkish-American music producer, who worked with hundreds of artists across many different styles of music, including artists such as the Bee Gees, Aretha Franklin, Bette Midler, Chaka Khan, and Phil Collins.

[5] Most notably, *Who Do You Love* b/w *Peace Of Mind* (1966).

[6] American rock band formed in Los Angeles in 1965.

[7] Henry Vestine (1944-1997) was Canned Heat's guitarist in 1969, and he did briefly quit then and missed out playing with the band at the Woodstock festival (Harvey Mandel was his temporary replacement there). Vestine had previously been hired by Zappa for the original Mothers in late October 1965, but left before the recording of *Freak Out!*

to crash there. It was fantastic. The best place to find out about work was at the Musicians' Union in Hollywood. There was a guy named Frank Sorkin that worked there that everyone knew as 'Scooby', He was 'the man' for all the rock musicians. This guy knew everybody that was anybody and got me hooked up with all kinds of work.

My first gig was with a soul band called The Real Thing. We played together for about three years. We were part of Bill Cosby's[8] road band called – are you ready? – Bradford Bunions Funeral Marching Audience Band! Stu Gardner was the band leader and has gone on to do a lot of great things. The bass player from The Detours – Tom Leavey, who was also my best friend from back in NY – moved out to LA and got a gig playing with Jimmy Carl Black. I was doing a lot of work as a studio musician but wasn't all that happy. I wanted to play live gigs with crazy people.

Tom said that the guitar player in Geronimo Black was leaving and I should audition. I did and got the gig. Playing in that band was without question the most fun of any of the bands I have ever played with. We did everything to excess and most of the time we did all of those things at the same time.

Someday I will have to put it down on paper.

You played tambourine on *Motorhead's Bumble Bee*[9] – any recollections of that particular session?
While Geronimo Black was recording our album at Sound City with engineer Keith Olsen,[10] Jim Sherwood dropped by and we were all pretty wasted and decided to do a little impromptu thing with him. Keith set up a boom mike out in the studio and we all continued to drink and mess around and *Motorhead's Bumble Bee* was the result.

It was never intended to be used for anything other than our

---

8 American stand-up comedian and actor.

9 One of the songs included on Grandmothers, the anthology of previously unreleased recordings by former Mothers issued by Rhino Records in 1981.

10 Grammy-winning record producer and sound engineer who has worked with Fleetwood Mac, Ozzy Osbourne, Grateful Dead, Santana, Foreigner and Emerson, Lake & Palmer.

own amusement, but later on Andy Cahan put it on one of the Grandmothers' albums.[11]

How did you wind up working with Frank?

While living in California - I had re-connected with Jim 'Motorhead' Sherwood whom I had also gone to school with back in Lancaster at AVJUHS. He told me that Frank was looking for a slide guitar player and told him about me. Frank said for me come on down the following day.

I loaded up my gear and went into Hollywood to Frank's rehearsal space and set up my rig. The band at that time was Terry Bozzio (drums), Tom Fowler (bass), George Duke (keyboards), Napoleon Murphy Brock (horns & vocals) and of course Frank.

The first song I was asked to play on was *Advance Romance*.[12] It was in the key of G, which was perfect for me as my guitar was already tuned to an open G, plus it is basically a blues. I was nervous as hell, but as soon as we started playing I was totally relaxed. At the end of the song, Frank said, "Anyone with the balls to play those low notes has got the job." He told his then road manager Marty Perellis, "Sign him up."

That was it, I was in!

What was the Bongo Fury tour like?

The band had been rehearsing for about a week or so before Frank brought Don in to start doing his parts. I had seen Don with The Magic Band a couple of times before this, but hadn't had a chance to talk with him.

I knew Don from back in Lancaster when we went to the same school (AVJUHS). He was just amazing. His vocals and harp playing were chilling. He was pure genius. He said twenty brilliant things a day. He was also a handful for Frank's people to try and control. They were very structured and Don didn't work like that. Let's just say that he kept it interesting.

The bottom line is that Beefheart is an amazing talent and

---

[11] The aforementioned compilation was reissued on CD with extra tracks in 1993 as *A Mother Of An Anthology*.

[12] First released on the Zappa/Beefheart/Mothers album *Bongo Fury* in 1975.

added a tremendous amount of excitement to every show. I learned so much from that tour. I owe everything that has come to me in music to Frank Zappa and Don Van Vliet.

So how well did you know Don back in Lancaster?

I didn't know him personally but used to see him quite a bit cruising Lancaster Boulevard in his Powder Blue '51 Olds. He was definitely cool!

When did you join Captain Beefheart & The Magic Band?

After the Bongo Fury tour, Frank suggested that I play with Don as we got on really great and it would put Don back on the road and in the studio.

The new Magic Band was Elliot 'Winged Eel Fingerling' Ingber[13] on guitar, John 'Drumbo' French on drums, Jeff Morris Tepper on guitar, Bruce 'Fossil' Fowler on air bass and me on slide guitar. That was the most challenging music I have ever had to learn to play.

Frank's music was written out and at least you had a clue as to the format, but Don's had to be learned by listening to the recordings over and over again, trying to hear your part through all the other shit going on. Don would whistle a part for you to play, or give you a verbal description of the emotion he was trying to capture. It was a fantastic experience.

I have to say that without John French to help me find some of the more obscure passages on guitar, I don't think I would have ever figured out some of that stuff.

Can you explain your 'Feelers Rebo' stage name?

After being on the tour for a while, I guess Don thought it was about time for me to be officially ordained with my own unique name. I never asked for one or even thought about it.

One night we were doing a show in Vancouver BC and as he was introducing the members of the band he said, "And on slide guitar, Denny Walley from Walla Walla Washington with all those Ds & Ws." After the show I said, "What the fuck? I'd rather not be

---

[13] Ingber was in the original Mothers and appears on *Freak Out!*

announced than to be called that! Please come up with something else." Not long after that he started calling me 'Feelers Rebo'. Don't ask why – I have no idea!

So why did you leave The Magic Band?
I had been with Don and The Magic Band for a couple of tours and was really over the amount of time that we would spend at rehearsals (6-12 hours) and only get to play around 2-4 hours. The rest of the time was spent with Don talking, drawing and going out for tea. All of this was great fun, but I just wanted to play and get the fuck out of that metal storage locker that we used for a rehearsal space.

Whenever it got to be really ridiculous, I would just leave. I was the only married member of the band with a child and had other obligations. Just before we were getting ready to start rehearsals for the next tour, I got a phone call from one of the members of the band. He said and I quote. "You have made your bed, now you can sleep in it."

Basically, I was fired by one of Don's sidemen. In today's world that would be the equivalent of being fired by e-mail. For the record, Don and I remained friends and I played a few guest spots with him as well. We still kept in touch with each other for years after that. The last time I heard from him was 1990. I miss him and his wife Jan a lot.

Tell me about the unreleased track *Hobo-ism* – do you think any of the studio material you did with the Captain will ever be released?
This track was recorded at my house in North Hollywood. It was done on a Sony cassette player. It was one of those stream of consciousness things. Just 1, 2, 3, go! This was around the same time that we were in the studio recording *Bat Chain Puller*.

When we finished recording *Bat Chain Puller*, Don asked for me to play the cassette for recording engineer, Kerry McNabb.[14] Kerry suggested that I let him put it on the ½" reel along with the

---

[13] Zappa's recording engineer between 1972 and 1977.

Bat Chain Puller album as a safety.

What a mistake that was. When the tape was handed over to Virgin Records, someone from within the company ran off a copy of the tape for themselves. The result was that all of the material was bootlegged.

Don and I own the copyright to *Hobo-ism*. Don is registered as writer and I am registered as composer and producer. As a gift, Don gave me a pen and ink drawing of a Hobo that would have been perfect for use as the artwork had we decided to release it as a single, but the project never materialized.

I recently met with someone who is interested in packaging and releasing this and some other interesting items. So the true recording may yet see the light of day.[15]

In his liner notes to *The Torture Never Stops* DVD, Scott Thunes mentions that Frank told him not to worry about remembering his lyrics – as, "Denny Walley always forgot them." Did this result in any interesting changed lyrics, or just general amusement?

I don't know why, but it was a pretty good bet that I would fuck up the lyrics about 30% of the time. The songs that were most in danger of getting fucked up were *Tryin' To Grow A Chin* and *City Of Tiny Lites*. Whenever you hear Frank start singing, *"...Maddie told Hattie"* (from Sam The Sham & The Pharaohs' 1965 song, *Wooly Bully*),[16] that was the signal that I had just fucked up the lyrics. I would scramble for some new never before heard lyrics of my own design to try and fill the void.

The results were mixed.

Tell me about your solo *Who Do/Tiny Tattoo* single.[17]

Frank took a break from touring and I decided that I should try and do something on my own. Most of the guys in Frank's band –

---

[15] For reasons unknown, the ZFT issued an alternate version of *Hobo-ism* on the *Bat Chain Puller* CD, which understandably upset Walley. Although it features him, he is not happy with his playing nor with Van Vliet's reading of the lyrics. The 'correct' take was later used when the album was issued for download via iTunes.

[16] An example of this appears during a rendition of *Tryin' To Grow A Chin* on the album *You Can't Do That On Stage Anymore Vol. 1*, recorded in London in 1979.

[17] Issued by Glider Records in 1982.

Tommy Mars, Ed Mann, Vinnie Colaiuta, Ike Willis – were in town and available.

As Arthur Barrow wasn't available, I asked Reggie McBride to play bass and Chet McCrackin from the Doobie Brothers as second drummer. I asked them to back me on a couple of tunes. We did a few rehearsals and went into Sound City studio.

It came out pretty good but really nothing special. I shopped it around and managed to get some air play but it eventually died a slow death.

I recently discovered about twenty copies with covers in a box of stuff that I had put away in a closet. Garage sale bait?

Are you happy to relay the true story behind *Jumbo Go Away*?[18]
It's hard to explain this without sounding pompous or rude, so I will just say that while in Detroit waiting with Frank for the hotel elevator to arrive to take us to our rooms, the lady in question appeared again! She had followed us/me for the last week to every gig, hotel, restaurant...

Having tried on more than one occasion to let her know that we were not going to become husband and wife, I finally just said, "Jumbo, go away."

The following day at sound check, Frank handed me a song he had written the night before and wanted me to sing. It was *Jumbo*!

How did you and Janet "the Planet"[19] first get together?
We first met in 1978. We were playing in New York at The Palladium, doing our annual Halloween shows. Frank filmed *Baby Snakes* the year before and Janet had no idea that she was included in the final film. When Frank saw her, he said "I'm so glad to see you here; you were so fantastic in my new movie!"

She was brought backstage and that is when I first met her. We started dating in April of 1987 and were married in August of 1989.

---

[18] From the Zappa album *You Are What You Is* (1981).

[19] Janet can be seen during the Audience Participation/The Dance Contest segment of *Baby Snakes*, when Zappa calls upon her to "administer discipline to a couple of members of the audience."

Which was your favourite tour with Zappa and why?
This is a tough one to call. The 1975 Bongo Fury tour with Terry, George, Napi, Tom, Don and Frank was a whirlwind. It was the first time I had ever played to such huge audiences. I had to work like hell to keep up with all of the material that was developing on a daily basis. My music reading skills were nowhere near that of the other members.

That tour was great, but my all time favourite would have to be the 1978/79 European/North America tour: getting to play with Vinnie Colaiuta, Tommy Mars, Ed Mann, Arthur Barrow, Peter Wolf, Ike Willis and Frank every day! There is no way to describe the absolute euphoria of being in the middle of all of that magic. I get chills just talking about it. I know that everyone that caught that tour will back me up on this.

I was there at the Hammersmith Odeon and I concur! Any idea why you weren't credited on the *Thing-Fish*[20] album?
I wasn't aware that I was on this album until someone brought it to my attention. I think the only cuts that I appear on are *The Meek Shall Inherit Nothing* and possibly *The 'Torchum' Never Stops*. But I will have to listen to it to be sure.

In any event, I am sure that it was just an oversight as Frank has always been fair in all of the business dealings that I have been involved in.

When was the last time you spoke with Frank?
I had been in touch with Frank and Gail on a fairly regular basis and was out to see them earlier that year. I got a call from Gail telling me that if I wanted to see Frank that I should come soon. I knew what that meant and was on a plane to LA the next day.

That was 14th November 1993. Frank died on 4th December 1993, less than three weeks after my visit.

We all still cry.

---

[20] Released in 1984. Walley is just one of a number of uncredited performers on this album.

You've made one solo album – *Spare Parts*. How did that happen?

In 1991, I was invited to play at *Zappa's Universe* at the Ritz in NYC, a concert celebrating Frank's music. While there, I had a chance to hear and meet Mats Öberg and Morgan Ågren – two of the most talented and beautiful people I had ever met. We became fast friends and agreed that we should find a way to play together in the future.

Fast-forward to 1995. I got a call from Erik Palm (project manager/producer at Botnia Musik in Sweden) who at the time was in charge of booking talent for the Umeå Jazz Festival and was close friends with Mats and Morgan. Erik was also a great fan of Beefheart's and wanted to put something together to make more people aware of Don's art and music. This was just the perfect excuse for us to finally play together again.

The band was to be Morgan Ågren (drums), Mats Öberg (keyboards), Jimmy Ågren (guitar), Rolf Hedquist (bass), me (slide guitar) and the fabulous Freddie Wadling[21] (vocals). We did a gig in Umeå and two sold out shows at Club Fasching in Stockholm that were both filmed and recorded. We are thinking now about re-issuing the CD titled *The Music of Captain Beefheart LIVE*.[22]

Fast-forward one more time to 1997. I had been speaking with Morgan about getting together to play again and he contacted Erik Palm, who invited us to put something together under my name and he would book us for the 1997 Umeå Jazz Festival as well as some club dates. Great!

At the end of this little mini-tour, brothers Morgan and Jimmy suggested that I record some of the material that we had been playing in our shows. They had a little studio in their parents' home in Umeå. We recorded ten tunes on the first day. The following day we recorded the vocals and I discovered that their sauna had a great natural reverb if you put a mike in the metal

---

[21] Berndt Arvid Freddie Wadling (1951-2016) was a Swedish singer and actor born in Gothenburg, whose 30+ year musical career extended from punk to classical ballads.

[22] The album was originally released in 1996. Footage from the shows appears on the Morgan Ågren video *Live In Magic*.

heater box. Total time for the entire project, eighteen hours. Morgan recorded it all on ADAT and did the mastering at his studio in Stockholm. We had no major distribution but thanks to UAE Records and Per Wikström, we had limited distribution throughout Sweden and parts of Europe.

Although receiving some great initial reviews, it just kind of went away. We are currently planning a re-issue later this year which will also be made available online.

What do you think of Mike Keneally, with whom you duetted on *Sleep Dirt* at the Umeå festival in 2003?
I think Mike Keneally's musical talents are breathtaking and he is an amazing person. I love him.

What are the chances of you being a Zappa Plays Zappa special guest at some point?
When ZPZ played The Tabernacle in Atlanta on 12th December 2006, I was asked to play with them on one song.

Oh, that's right – you played *Advance Romance*.
I just saw them again a few months ago when they played at The Variety Theater here in Atlanta and they really sounded great.

How did the Magic Band reunion come about?
In 2001, John French (Drumbo) was approached by Paul Smith at the suggestion of BBC Producer Elaine Shepherd to see if there was any possibility of the Magic Band re-forming for a couple of dates. One was to be in Los Angeles and the other in England. John had already enlisted Mark Boston (Rockette Morton), Bill Harkleroad (Zoot Horn Rollo) and had tried to interest Jeff Cotton (Antennae Jimmy Siemmens), but he wasn't interested so they called me as I had played in The Magic Band with John and was familiar with most of the material.

I flew out to Lancaster for a couple days rehearsal to see if this could work. We had all agreed beforehand on 3–4 songs that we would use as a trial balloon: *Steal Softly Thru Snow, Moonlight On Vermont, My Human Gets Me Blues*[23] and one other tune that slips

---

[23] All from the Zappa-produced *Trout Mask Replica* (1969).

my mind.

I have to admit that I was not as prepared as I should have been. I had just recovered from a bad case of bronchitis that had me hospitalised and on my ass for three weeks, so I was not 100%. Zoot was great. It was the first time I had met him and we hit it off pretty good. Besides music, we both had a love of beer!

We all decided that this combination of players could work. So we let Paul Smith know that we had a band and to start finalising the business end of it and set up some real dates.

Long story short, ten months passed with no solid deal and Zoot passed on it. That was really a drag. Without Bill in the mix it didn't look good. By this time we were so wired to play that we decided that there had to be a way to salvage this opportunity. A year later, in August 2002, along came Barry Hogan of All Tomorrow's Parties and made us a much better offer with a signed contract for three concerts: Camber Sands ATP, Shepherds Bush Empire and the Long Beach California All Tomorrow's Parties concert at the Queen Mary Ship.

We made one last attempt to entice Zoot to join us as we now had a contract, but he had made his mind up not to be involved. John French was the one that made this all happen. The one thing that John insisted on (and we all agreed on) was that whoever we got to play would have to be a former member of The Magic Band. After running a few different scenarios, we pretty much agreed that it would have to be a guitar player as most of the material that we wanted to do required two guitars.

Gary Lucas's name was brought up. Gary had been Don's manager, had played on stage with The Magic Band and appeared as a guest on the album *Doc At The Radar Station*.[24] Plus he was a great guitarist.

Any chance the reformed Magic Band will play together again?

"Never Say Never!"[25]

---

[24] Released in 1980.

[25] In 2006, John French issued a statement saying, "we decided to no longer pursue the Magic Band reunion project." However, the band resumed activities in 2009, with Eric Klerks replacing Gray Lucas.

I understand you recently ran a film scenery workshop?
I was a 1/3 partner/owner of a scenery shop here in Atlanta called MDM Scenery Works.[26] I resigned after 3-4 years as it took so much of my time and didn't allow for me to do anything else.

Final thoughts?
I'm so happy that Frank's music is still being studied and celebrated all over the world.

I'm absolutely certain that Frank would be pleased to know that this is happening. My chops are up as I have never stopped playing or singing since leaving Frank and Don. I love to play and am still as passionate about it as when I first started.

Interview conducted on Thursday 31st July 2008.

---

[26] The company made the giant pumpkin that appears in the Rob Zombie film *Halloween II* (2009).

Ike WIllis at the annual Zappanale Festival with a tired author.

IKE WILLIS

I ke Willis provided 'bionic baritone' and rhythm guitar for Zappa from 1978 until the ill-fated 1988 world tour. He can be seen in the *Does Humor Belong In Music?* (1985) home video and heard on numerous Zappa albums – including *Joe's Garage* (1979) as the voice of Joe, *Tinsel Town Rebellion* (1981), *You Are What You Is* (1981), Sh*ip Arriving Too Late To Save A Drowning Witch* (1982), *The Man From Utopia* (1983), *Them Or Us* (1984), *Thing-Fish* (1984) as the titular character, *Frank Zappa Meets The Mothers Of Prevention* (1985), *Does Humor Belong In Music?* (1986), *Broadway The Hard Way* (1988), *The Best Band You Never Heard In Your Life* (1991), *Make A Jazz Noise Here* (1991), *Buffalo* (2007), *The Lumpy Money Project/Object* (2009) and *Chicago '78* (2016).

Willis claims he was the last band member to be with Zappa who, the week before he died, told him to keep his music alive.

And that's what he's been doing ever since, performing around the globe with cover bands such as the Muffin Men (UK), Project Object (USA), Ossi Duri (Italy), The Central Scrutinizer Band (Brazil) and ZAPPATiKA (based in Amsterdam, with whom Willis headlined Festival Moo-ah in 2015).

He was also a member of the original Band From Utopia and more recently has performed with Dweezil and his band.

Willis has released two solo albums – *Should a Gone Before I Left* (1988), which features contributions from Ray White and Arthur Barrow and *Dirty Pictures* (1998) – and regularly performs at Zappanale.

It was backstage at Zappanale 20, while Terry Bozzio played his solo drum set finale, that I interviewed Willis for my *Zappa The*

Hard Way book. He also had time to answer a few 'off-topic' questions.

When did you know you were in on the 1988 tour – Mike Keneally's diaries[1] imply that, while you were around for rehearsals in 1987, it wasn't clear that you were to be part of the touring band?

No, not to me.

You knew you were in the band?

Yeah, Frank always called me and said, "Okay, rehearsals start on such and such a date..." No, no, I knew when rehearsals were starting. Mike didn't know.

He said you were there, but..

I'm always there, but I never hang around. When Frank says be there, I'm there. He didn't allow hanging around, it was time to go to work and I was there.

You've got to remember that by the time Keneally came in, there were two different bands: there was me, Flo & Eddie, Ed Mann and Tommy Mars. And Chad Wackerman and Frank and Ray White. Then, a couple of days later, there was no Tommy, no Flo & Eddie. And then there was Keneally and Scott Thunes and Chad, Ray and me and Frank. Within a week, there was two different bands. Rehearsals started on 2nd October 1987.

Good memory!

It was my job to remember! That was my job in Frank's band – to remember everything. That was my job.

There are various theories as to why Flo & Eddie left.

Well, that movie came out called *Making Mr. Right*[2] with John Malkovich and *Happy Together*[3] became a mega hit again. So Flo

---

[1] Zappa's newly hired stunt guitarist kept an audio journal during most of the Broadway The Hard Way tour that included set lists, backstage goings-on and many personal observations. He very kindly allowed the author to quote freely from them in *Zappa The Hard Way*.

[2] 1987 sci-fi/comedy film directed by Susan Seidelman.

[3] A huge hit for The Turtles in 1967. The song was also covered by the Mothers on the *Fillmore East—June 1971* album.

& Eddie had to go take care of those commitments, etcetera, etcetera. I don't know what else, but I know that was a big, big factor.

What happened to Ray White?
Ray disappeared.

Do you know the story behind that?
No, not really. I don't know what happened because I didn't see him again for ten years – until he popped up at my door and there he was.

I heard that his house was burgled.
That part I know about, because Ray and I... we're each other's son's Godfathers. So somebody broke into his house, where they were living in San Francisco. They'd been living there for like twenty-some odd years and then in 1987 things started getting really, really bad. So he was having some troubles there and he came to stay with me.

But then one day he left my house and I didn't see him again for ten years.

It's funny, because I always thought of you and Ray as, like, brothers. Scott and Chad too!
Well, Ray and I, we're the 'Othello Brothers'. That's us!

When did you first notice something happening between Scott and Chad?
About halfway through the Broadway The Hard Way rehearsals. Things were just getting...

Well, I know that Scott is a strange character
To say the very least. Very understated andy, I like that.

Funny as hell, but I'm not sure people always understand his humour.
Scott is wildly, wildly talented – I mean, one of the most amazing musicians I've ever seen. But there's this... it's just Scott.

But they'd been playing together for six years, hanging out..
Sure, sure.

...and then suddenly, it just stopped. Scott can't pinpoint any particular incident.
No, there was no specific incident: it just built up over time. It was Scott's way of dealing with people.

He was still quite young at the time
They were both very young.[4] Scott didn't get along with the horn section... the Fowlers and stuff like that.

According to Scott, "I hate horns, blah, blah, blah." He was the Clonemeister at the time, so that was another thing.

Because Ed Mann used to be the Clonemeister...
Ed was my Clonemeister, when I came in, in 1978, then Artie[5] was the Clonemeister after that and then on my last tour, Scott was the Clonemeister.

But after things started getting really tense between Scott and Chad, Frank tried to split it up between me and Scott: he said, "Okay, you let Scott handle the notes and you conduct the band."

So for the last month of rehearsals, I was conducting the band and Scott was handling the dots on the page.

So you were kind of a mediator?
My job was to sit on Scott and make sure nobody killed him. [laughs] It's true! Frank said, "Just make sure they don't kill him."

I really didn't get that impression from what I've read and heard: Zappa seemed almost unaware of what was going on.
No, no, no. Frank knew what was going on. At all times.

Actually, there was one incident during rehearsal where Scott just pissed off Bruce Fowler and everybody in the horn section. I said, "Okay, everybody stop. Go to lunch." The phone rang and it was Frank calling from the house saying, "What's going on down there?"

He wasn't even there! He knew what was going on. I have no idea how, because this had just happened, like, less than a minute after I'd said, "Lunch! Everybody take a break; Scott, go over

---

4 Thunes and Wackerman were both born in 1960.

5 Arthur Barrow.

there."

The phone rang and it was our sound mixer, Harry Andronis,[6] saying, "Ike, it's Frank – he wants to talk to you." And Frank said, "What's going on. Talk to me. What the hell is happening down there?"

Less than a minute. He was never aloof. He knew exactly what was going on. He was kept abreast of everything. I don't know how he did it [laughs]... but he did it. Trust me.

Mike Keneally (in his tour diaries) and Scott (in Wictor's book) talk about you running up and down the bus, talking to everyone – you and Albert Wing, very upbeat, very chatty.

Is that the sort of character you recognise? Is that you?
Well, I talk to everybody. The thing is... Albert and I, we'd been together... at that point, I'd been with the Fowler Brothers' band almost as long as I'd been in the Zappa band.

So Albert and I were good friends. That's just us.

The crucial thing here is that there were two buses: the smoking bus and the non-smoking bus.
Yeah, there was the guys-who-loved-to-hang-out-with-Frank bus and there was the older guys: which was us. The salty old veterans' bus. At that point, that was like my tenth year in the band.

Talking about Albert – do you recall his 'pretend' marriage?
No?

He got married at some point, in a hotel. With Bruce Fowler presiding
No! When was this?

On the '88 tour... this lady, Randee Pollock, was following the band around...
Oh yeah, Randee! Yeah, yeah, yeah! I remember her, she followed us. My God, that's right. But I don't remember the fake wedding. Her, I remember.

---

[6] Andronis (1956-2010) was Zappa's house mix engineer from 1988 to 1992.

I'm not sure how many people witnessed it.
Maybe it was in Amsterdam. I seem to remember some sort of...

No, it was just before the US leg ended, because Frank mentioned on stage that Albert wasn't available anymore, "He's married now..."
I do remember her.

She was just like a hanger-on?
Oh yeah, definitely – definitely hanging on there. Wow!

So, anyway, there were intimations of some problems during rehearsals. But talking to Scott, he seems to think it was all manageable.
Well of course he did! Ha, ha, ha!

Until... in Springfield, there was this showdown – an unusual band meeting?
That was in Portland, Maine. I remember quite well. Chad said something to somebody in the crew and Scott made one of his offside comments to Chad and Chad said, "That's it. I've had it."

And of course, within minutes, Frank knew about it and called us to his dressing room for a meeting and said, "Hey, I'm not gonna put up with this. I don't like rocking the boat. This is a very expensive tour, a very long tour..."

We know about the East Coast tour and then Europe... were there actually dates booked for the West Coast?
Yeah, yeah, yeah. At the end of the Europe tour, we were gonna come home, break for a couple of weeks and then start rehearsals for the Fall leg and we were booked until New Year's of the next year. Then it all got called off

Were you ever provided with any intended itinerary?
Unfortunately, no – Frank hadn't given them to me yet.[7]

I know Frank talked about possible dates in Israel and elsewhere.

---

[7] This exchange actually took place via email on 11th August 2015.

Yeah, yeah. We had a whole schedule. Frank always told me, "Okay, this is what the schedule is: we're gonna be in blah-blah..."

I'm not gonna say he always called me first, but I was always one of the first he called.

Scott says he was usually one of the last to know, because he lived a long way away.
Yeah, he's from San Francisco. But Frank would always call me and say, "Okay, rehearsals start on this day." Alright?

Okay. Once the problem had been aired, then suddenly things started happening. Like Scott's laminate – his backstage pass – got defaced. Do you know who did that?
Oh, the guys in the crew. That's what I'm saying: he pissed off all of the guys in the crew; he pissed off the horn section. He doesn't play well with others, let's put it that way. Or, he didn't play well with others. So the guys in the crew would find ways to upset him.

So it wasn't anyone from the band, not the horn players?
No, no, no.

It was the road crew?
Yeah. It wasn't anything specific. He rubbed everybody up the wrong way. I was the only one he really got along with and I wouldn't take sides – I'd just say, "Don't do this, man. Don't do it."

Scott says that after the showdown, only you, Robert Martin, Albert Wing and – obviously – Mike Keneally, came up to him and said, "We didn't know anything about this. We don't agree with what was said."
Well, the thing is...I agreed and I told Scott, "You've got to stop doing this, man. You've gotta stop; you're pissing too many people off. Stop!"

And like I said, Frank told me to sit on him and make sure they don't kill him. Those were his words: "Please, try your best."

And on that day in Portland, Maine he got away from me for about five minutes, said something to one of the guys in the crew, set them off. Set Chad off and that's when we had the big meeting.

It seemed like throughout that tour, you and Frank always got along and had fun on stage. I'm thinking of the Barcelona show, with you and Frank arm in arm singing *Find Her Finer*.[8]

Oh God, oh God. Yeah. We had so much fun.

Any particularly fond memories from that whole tour?

Oh, just too many. We just had so much fun. On any given day, it would be whatever was the in-joke of the day... whatever happened to... at any point in time... it would become part of the show.

I'd be at my mic, singing, playing, trying to do my job and Frank would slide over to me and suddenly he's right there and in the middle of a verse, he'd say something and I'm on the floor. Then, of course, now I've got to get him back. We could go on like that all night long – all night long this is going on. As the 1988 tour progressed, it would get more and more like that.

That was the hardest tour. That was the hardest I ever worked on any tour. We worked and worked and worked. See, that's the thing: in 1978, at that point, Frank gave me a lot of room, a lot of leeway.

He seemed to give Scott a lot of room, as well.

Yes, he did. It's like I say: Scott is a wildly, wildly incredible musician. But, of course, consider the rest of the band: we've got the Fowler brothers. We've got Albert, we've got Paul Carman[9] and Kurt McGettrick, Bobby and Ed and Chad. And Mike. Everybody's just a phenomenal musician. So it was quite a great time.

One final question: who is Greg Bolognese?

Greg Bolognese? Of course! He's one of my oldest friends – from Long Island, New York. I've known Bolognese since he was a teenager.

Because he came onstage a couple of times in 1988 – he sung

---

8 First released on Zappa's album *Zoot Allures* (1976).

9 Alto, soprano and baritone saxophonist.

on *Crew Slut* and did a voter registration thing.
I've known Greggie since he was...

Frank described him as a friend of his, too.
Oh yeah. He used to come to the shows before I joined the band.
He was in his teens – he was like 13, 14, 15 years old. I met him
when he was 15 or 16. He always used to come to the shows.

The New York gang. They always bought the same seats. Front
row. Same guys, every tour since 1978, since I was in the band.
Every time we go to New York, same seats, same guys. Bolognese
was right in the middle. I've known those guys forever. They're
still there: Stevie, Eugene, Bolognese, the LaMastro brothers, Jack
Conklin... all those guys, when I'm there with Project Object –
whenever I'm in New York with anybody – those guys are there,
man.

Some of them have moved out to Florida: Stevie lives in Florida;
Eugene moved to Florida. Colin LaMastro moved Upstate, but I
see him when I'm in Upstate New York.

Greggie still lives on Long Island. Conklin still lives in
Manhattan. Joey Psychotic, he died of a liver ailment about five
years ago.

The boys, you know? They're very, very loyal.

**If we have a little more time, are you happy to talk about
other things? Your solo material?**
The Ike Willis Project is actually about to be up and running. In
about three weeks, I've got to go back up North, to the North
West, with Pojama People – Glenn Leonard, our old drummer.

And his wife, Alli?[10]
And Alli, yeah. So we're gonna hit the North West and Northern
California in between that, I may be doing some preliminary gigs
in the Bay Area – Santa Cruz, Eureka, stuff like that – with The Ike
Willis Project. I reformed the Ike Willis Band when I was living in
the Bay Area.

---

[10] Alli Bach, percussionist/vocalist for Pojama People.

Are these the guys that played on your solo albums?

No, not at all. But they are gonna be playing the stuff from my solo albums. Then I'm gonna start working – finally, if I have the time, I'll start on my new album.

So you have the songs written?

Oh, I'm three albums behind! I've got at least three albums worth of material.

It's really frustrating: as much as we love to see you playing the Zappa stuff, we'd like to hear some of your solo material performed live.

Yeah, yeah, yeah. Imagine how I feel! I've got three albums worth of material that I haven't even been able to record because of touring and stuff like that and getting resettled in LA.

So you moved out of Portland?

I lived in Portland. Then the Bay Area for two years. For the last three years, Denise[11] and I have been in LA. Now we're actually moving into our permanent place and I'm gonna start working on the new album as soon as I get home.

I'd like to ask you about Jeff Hollie.

Jeff Hollie!

A couple of years ago, we met him in Holland.

You met him?

Yeah, he played with Cuccurullo Brillo Brullo,[12] and they introduced him as this guy who played tenor sax with Frank.

He's the 'Jeff' on *Joe's Garage*.

He plays on your first album as well.

He's my best friend from college. Me and my wife and him, we met on my first day in college in 1974. He's my daughter's Godfather. He and I, we started our first band together in our freshman year in college. We met the very first day of college.

If it wasn't for Jeff Hollie, I would have never been prepared for

---

[11] Willis' wife.

[12] A Dutch cover band who performed with Hollie at a Zappa festival in Nijmegen, March 2008.

Frank Zappa. Jeff was the biggest Zappa fan in our circle. Jeff had all the albums, up to that point. He brought me up... I was at private school, from 1971 to 1974. After graduation, I was in college. Jeff, I met him on the basketball court. We go to our first orientation meeting; my wife to be is sitting across the room. So I met her and then we're hanging out in the dormitories and Jeff said, "Hey, man – are you into Zappa?" I said, "Yeah." We were into like, Yes, Zappa, Mahavishnu Orchestra, Return To Forever.

The Beatles?

Yeah, yeah, yeah. The Beatles, I love them.[13] Jeff had all the Zappa albums.

My roommate was a Yes freak. I was listening to the Mahavishnu Orchestra, Genesis, Return To Forever, The Beatles. You name it. So we'd all just sit up there smoking doobies and listen to our favourite stuff. Jeff brought me up to speed on all the latest Zappa stuff.

So by the time Frank came to our school – Washington University – and did a concert a few years later, I was on the local crew and we made eye contact. After a while, Frank takes me to his dressing room, hands me his guitar and says, "Do you know any of my shit?" And I said, "Yeah," and he said, "Well, play me something."

And I could because of Jeff Hollie. So how do you repay your best friend... I mean, if it wasn't for him, there would be no Ike Willis, okay? Because he'd always wanted to play with Frank, the only thing I could think of... all through the *Joe's Garage* sessions, Jeff was there anyway. I don't know if you've seen pictures, but there's me and Frank and Jeff in the studio. So I said, "Frank, please, please. He knows all your stuff. At least give me this. You've got to give me this. At least put Jeff on one song."

And it was on the title track [sings:] "...even if you play it on the saxophone..." – that's Jeff. I mean, how do you repay your best

---

[13] When I first sat down face-to-face with Willis backstage at Zappanale in 2002, I asked him for his top ten Beatles' tunes, and this is what he said: *I'll Be Back; I've Just Seen A Face; You're Going to Lose That Girl; Eight Days A Week; You've Got To Hide Your Love Away; I Am The Walrus; Strawberry Fields Forever; Norwegian Wood; If I Fell; In My Life.* He hopes to record a tribute album to the band at some point.

friend for doing something like that? It was the only thing I could come up with to really, really repay him for what he'd done.

Have you spoken to him lately?

Last week in Eindhoven! He lives in Amsterdam. That's the great thing. We always stay in touch. He's been in Amsterdam for fourteen years – he escaped from Washington. I told him we were coming to Eindhoven, because I hadn't seen him for a couple of years.

That's great. Now what about the project with Stu Grimshaw[14] – what happened? You performed it here a few years ago.

Oh, *Der Fremde*. Or *The Stranger*.[15]

Is it ever going to be released on CD?

It has been released!

Has it? Why was I not informed!

Yeah, yeah. I think he released it officially – either last year, or the year before last.

Really?

Oh, Stu is amazing... outstanding.

Why is it not on sale here?

I don't know.

I'm gonna have to follow this up when I get home.[16]

Yeah. In fact, I plan to touch base with Stu as soon as I get home, because I haven't talked to him for about a year or so. He just sent Hank[17] an official release of *The Stranger*. Drop Hank an email and ask him the last whereabouts of Stu. That way we'll all know, okay? Hank and I were just talking about Stu about two weeks ago.

---

[14] English-born bass player and composer who lives in Germany.

[15] Willis was Grimshaw's special guest at Zappanale in 2003, where they performed his musical for string quartet, keyboards and drum set.

[16] The author managed to track down copy No.87 of the studio recording of Grimshaw's *The Stranger* album featuring Willis, which was issued as an extremely limited edition by Extremely Serious Music.

[17] Hank Woods, Willis' manager.

It was really nice to hear that here the other year – in amongst all this great Zappa music, with the kids playing,[18] and you...

Stu is phenomenal, man. What a composer. That was some hard work, there. With the string section, the instrumentation, the singing in German and English. I haven't had to do that since Frank!

Interview conducted on Sunday 16th August 2009.

---

[18] The Paul Green School Of Rock Music.

ALBERT WING

A lbert Wing played tenor saxophone on Zappa's final world tour of 1988 – having passed the audition in 1973! He later joined the Banned From Utopia and played with Shuggie Otis[1] – both of whom he has recently toured with.

He was a one-off member of The Mar Vista Philharmonic with Arthur Barrow, Tommy Mars, Vinnie Colaiuta and the bulk of the 1988 horn section when the BBC commissioned a tribute to Zappa ten years after his passing.

Wing has been long-time friends with Ike Willis and the Fowler Brothers and in 2010 he was a willing accomplice when I was writing my *Zappa The Hard Way* book.

Here I have married some of his answers to my questions from that time to a brand new set posed specifically for this book.

Sadly, having emailed him some follow-up questions without reply, I learned that Wing had suffered a stroke on 1st February 2017 which disabled the motor functions on the right side of his body from head to foot.

Here's hoping we can one day resume our correspondence.

You tried out for Frank's band long before the 1988 tour. Tell me about that.
Bruce Fowler set up a Frank/*Be-Bop Tango* audition in early 1973. Aced it, had the gig for about a half hour - in the duration, Frank had a discussion with Herb. Long story short – it's 1987.

---

[1] Real name Johnny Alexander Veliotes, Jr., Otis is an American singer-songwriter and multi-instrumentalist, best known for his composition *Strawberry Letter 23*. He also plays bass on *Peaches En Regalia* from Zappa's album *Hot Rats* (1969). Otis is the son of blues singer, bandleader and arranger Johnny Otis (1921-2012), from whom Zappa cultivated his famous 'imperial' chin hair.

How were you first contacted about joining Frank on the Broadway The Hard Way tour?
I think Bruce or Walt told me.

Did Zappa display any signs of ill-health in 1987?
Nothing out of the ordinary then.

What was the best gig of the 1988 tour for you – and why?
Chicago – that was the night I met Randee.[2]

Sorry to be pedantic, but was that the first or second Chicago show? And would you like to tell me how you met – was it love at first sight?
Second night. I met her at the Limelight VIP room. Later we exchanged info; Randee was actually Plan B, a backline guy caught me hangin' with his little sister after Chicago 2. He told her to go home; tried calling her a little later, but then I met Randee...
     A few days later, Randee and I made plans for Burlington... she made Amsterdam-Zurich – then?

Any other good shows?
Best gig? Most memorable is more accurate... Udine, Italy – you had to be there...

I know about the problems with the house lights and the popcorn vendor during the show, but what else went on?
During the course of the concert, I remember Frank changed a few lyrics, the upshot suggesting it was over for the band. My journal on the tour was stolen by an old roommate, though unproven.

What are your memories of Mr Sting's appearance?
Appearance, aptly put.

Ed Mann says he told you all you were good musicians.
I tried to engage Sting in casual conversation - a full length mirror commanded his attention, which provided a more convivial atmosphere for him.

---

[2] Randee Pollock, who hung out with the 1988 band.

Regarding the near-appearance of Johnny Cash – did anyone else actually meet him?

No, I don't recall about anybody meeting him.

Was it fun rehearsing *Ring Of Fire*?

I did my best not to lose it; *Ring Of Fire* was that funny.

Did Scott Thunes do anything particularly unpleasant to you?

He tried to get me fired.

How and when – before the tour? At the end of it?

Before. Scott wrote a piece and asked Bruce, Walt, Kurt and Paul to rehearse it.[3] I got that.

Just excluded you from that, or asked Zappa to 'lose you'?

The exclusion. Frank said, "I like you," out of the blue, words I thought I would never hear come out of his mouth. You just had to be there to be able to understand the vibe.

There is a hilarious little vignette, post-1988, that I will one day reveal. But this is about 1988... as of now, the vignette will remain privy to me and my friend, whom shall for now remain anonymous.[4]

Any amusing on-road tales?

I remember one night, crashing in the lobby of the hotel. On average, one to two people, if they needed a place to crash, would stay with us. This night, Randee invited eight plus... I don't recall the final tally, they were still arriving as I left.

When did you last speak with Frank?

We had a private talk. This conversation happened in 1988, circa Germany/Austria, pre-Italy. Other than Frank's usual sound check banter and after Udine, we never spoke one on one ever again.

Do you know anything about the cancelled dates? Were you ever provided with an intended itinerary?

There was to be a western US tour, but nothing definite was ever

---

3 All of Zappa's horn section for the Broadway The Hard Way tour, minus Wing.

4 One of my follow-up questions asked if now was the time to reveal all.

provided.

How and where did you first meet the Fowler brothers?

I first remember the Fowlers from an early 1971 Collegiate Neophonic Concert we performed in San Diego, under the direction of Jack Wheaton[5] at Cerritos College. Dr. Fowler[6] and his sons were performing Bill's *The History of Jazz* lecture on the same program. Met Bruce in passing that day.

I remember hanging with Bill – hearing Bruce and Bill Evans[7] at the 1971 Intercollegiate Jazz Festival, held at University of Illinois at Urbana–Champaign. Amazing performances had by the both of them.

Monterey Jazz Festival 1971, happened upon Walt and Ed at a local coffee shop. Me and Walt performed with The Stars of Tomorrow combo. Walt and Stu Goldberg[8] were really burning.

1972, that's when, scholarship abundant, I moved to Utah; and the rest is history.

When were you approached about reforming Banned From Utopia, with Robert Martin taking over Bruce Fowler's previous role?

It was around February or March of 2013.

I saw you perform at Zappanale in 2013, with Mike Miller on guitar: you two have a great rapport!

That we do! Walt heard Mike play at a gig – later told me about this really great guitar player he had heard. A few days later, we went to Mike's gig; it might have been Tulagi or The Lost Knight, both clubs being the hip Boulder, CO jazz/fusion venues circa 1974- 1975.

That performance at Zappanale was amazing, seeing as how

---

[5] Jack William Wheaton (1932-2015) was a musician who won an Emmy for the Stan Kenton Collegiate Neophonic ABC Television Special Neophonic Spring and trained 84 pianists for the George Gershwin segment of the 1984 Olympics opening ceremony in Los Angeles.

[6] Jazz educator William Lambourne Fowler (1919-2009), father of the brothers Bruce, Walt and Tom.

[7] William John Evans (1929-1980) was an American jazz pianist and composer who mostly worked in a trio setting.

[8] Stuart Wayne Goldberg is an American jazz keyboard player and film composer.

that line-up had very little rehearsal.
Got in late the day before. I ended up inadvertently walking in the direction of the rehearsal, not knowing where it was. Ran in to a friend of Banned From Utopia, she said it was just two short blocks away. We really crammed a lot in such little rehearsal time.

I remember late, great drummer Glenn Leonard of Pojama People; just after the jam session bows, he said to me, "Do you remember me?" Without hesitation, I replied, "Nassau Coliseum, 1988."

That's great. We all miss Glenn. Had you worked with Ralph Humphrey before then?
Yes, I've played with Ralph on many different occasions, notably with Mike Miller's band. I used to hang out at The Etc. where Ralph performed on a regular basis.

In 2015, Banned From Utopia returned to Zappanale and you and Robert played the pre-festival gig at St. Catherine's Church in Hamburg with Frank Out![9] That was fun and included a performance of one of Robert's songs.[10] How was it for you?
Frank Out! was Out-rageous! They really brought it! Robert wrote a really great piece; let's hope for more.

Much thanks to Sebastian Knauer for his hospitality and giant support of Frank's music. I hear there is a CD of the concert?

Yes, there is.[11] Ike Willis didn't get to play with Banned From Utopia that year, but he enjoyed your show from the side of the stage. How long have you been friends with him?
Me and Ike have been friends for over 30 years – after a long spell, I finally ran in to him again at Zappanale 2015.

We've been on a few album projects in the not too distant past. He also performed with The Fowler Brothers' Airpocket for a few tours.

---

[9] A German cover band, including former members of another tribute band, Sheik Yerbouti.

[10] *Devil Dance*, based on a nightmare Martin had when he was 25 years old.

[11] *Zappa Spielt Für Bach*, Edition Nr. 8.

Are you in touch with Walt and Bruce these days? Is Bruce okay?[12]

I see Walt on occasion; in fact me, Walt and Mike Miller's Baked Potato All Stars perform a few times out of the year. I see Bruce very occasionally; he is fairly busy with his orchestration business.

How did you land the gig of playing in Shuggie Otis's band?

It was through my friend, sax/flute player and arranger, Michael Turre. He asked me to play Johnny Otis' memorial in January 2012. There I met Shuggie Otis for a very brief moment.

Later that year, Shuggie was looking for another sax player to fill out the three piece horn section. Michael suggested me. Much like Mike Miller, Shuggie and I also have a great guitar/tenor sax rapport.

What plans does Albert Wing have for the future?

Survival! Well – that's numero uno of my many TBC endeavours... the obligatory status quo – writing, performing, touring and recording. But to also "go where no tenor saxophone multiphonic has gone before." [laughs]

Okay, final question: what do you think of the three CDs Zappa released documenting the Broadway The Hard Way tour.[13]

Glad they're not vinyl!

Interviews conducted in February 2010 & November 2016.

---

[12] I had heard that Bruce Fowler had suffered a stroke.

[13] *Broadway The Hard Way* (1988), *The Best Band You Never Heard In Your Life* (1991) and *Make A Jazz Noise Here* (1991).

BOB ZAPPA

Charles Robert Zappa was born three years after his brother Frank, on 29th August 1943.

In 2015, he published his memoir *Frankie & Bobby – Growing Up Zappa*, which strives to demonstrate the affect the Zappas' early nomadic existence had on shaping Frank's later life. Bob believes the family's constant moves caused the pair to grow up as fiercely independent misfits.

The pair were clearly very close and after they fled the nest and went their separate ways, Bob talks of the anger he felt at not being around to support his brother following the December 1971 disasters in Montreux and London.

Despite their early-shared experiences, the book also sheds light on how the pair turned out so differently and on what drove Frank to become the super-creative person he was.

In 1967, Bob worked as Frank's personal assistant during the Mothers' run of shows at New York's Garrick Theater.

In the book's introduction, Bob writes, "We shared unique experiences that will disappear with me unless I make these stories public."

In the run up to publication, I asked Bob if he would submit to a short interview with me. While we had talked via Skype for the ZappaCast, we agreed it might be best to wait until after the book was out before he said any more; his only stipulation was no questions about Frank's widow or his children.

In the interim, I sent him a copy of my own *Zappa The Hard Way* book, of which he very kindly said, "You certainly know a lot about Frank and your book is an important part of his history."

Hopefully, the following interview adds a little more to the story.

I start with a typical fan question...

In *Frankie & Bobby – Growing Up Zappa*, you describe in detail the long, difficult family journey from Edgewood to Monterey in your father's Henry J[1] – which seems to have been quite significant in Frank's development. It may also have inspired the song *Kaiser Rolls*.[2] Does the 'stumbler man' mean anything to you?[3]

Questions about references in some of Frank's songs are a bit too speculative for me to try to answer. Your association with Kaiser rolls and the Henry J is pretty interesting but I wonder how many people would find that connection of interest – other than me, of course?

You'd be surprised – the various Zappa-fora are awash with such 'down in the weeds' discussions! Where you aware of Sandy Hurvitz (aka Essra Mohawk) at the time of the Garrick Theater run?

Yes, I knew about Essra – and a few others. But his relationships with other women was not a part of our story that I want readers to know.

When we spoke on the ZappaCast, you said you had no recollection of the early Zappa/Beefheart collaboration *Lost In A Whirlpool*.[4] Can you at least recall the guitars you and Frank might've used?

I don't remember which guitars were used on that recording, but I seem to recall that we had borrowed whatever we used. Maybe from the Franklin brothers[5] – but don't quote me on that.

---

[1] Henry John Kaiser (1882-1967) was an American industrialist who in 1945 co-founded Kaiser Motors, the automobile company known for the safety of their designs.

[2] From the Zappa album *FZ:OZ* (2012). Of course, it's possible that Zappa's song was inspired by small bread buns shaped like the ceremonial crown the Kaiser wore.

[3] There are references to 'stumbler men' in the songs *Kaiser Rolls*, *Village Of The Sun* and the unreleased long version of *200 Years Old*.

[4] A joint Zappa/Van Vliet composition, recorded circa. 1958, released on the Zappa album *The Lost Episodes* (1996).

[5] Carter and Johnny Franklin were members of Zappa's early group The Blackouts.

You refer to Frank's interest in necromancy and UFOs. Your comment about his deal with the devil is also intriguing.
Frank's interest in necromancy, aliens and other unworldly things was, I believe, simply part of his vast curiosity about life, death and everything in between. He also enjoyed trying to impress me and others with his bold interest in things that, at the time, were not openly discussed.

You hint that Frank may have been a synesthete. Ahmet recently claimed Frank had "an enhanced form of hearing" due to the radiation treatment he had on his sinuses as a child. Do you think there's any merit in such notions?
I don't know how Frank's hearing could have been enhanced by a radioactive nose pellet, but stranger things have happened.

Here's what Wikipedia says: *"Synesthesia is a neurological phenomenon in which stimulation of one sensory or cognitive pathway leads to automatic, involuntary experiences in a second sensory or cognitive pathway. People who report such experiences are known as synesthetes."*

Does that describe Frank's heightened sense of hearing? Hard to tell but that magic pellet could have just as easily affected his colour perception or his ability to taste. In this same vein, perception is reality.

Did you ever meet Paul Buff?
I do not remember ever meeting him.

Were you aware of Frank's brief tenure as a beat poet, writing under the pseudonym Vincent Beldon?[6]
I have a vague recollection of Frank's beat poetry period but do not remember Beldon specifically.

Tell us some more about your friendship with Dick Barber[7] – does he still 'snork'?!
Dick Barber, Bill Harris[8] and I have been friends since 1960. They

---

[6] This exchange actually took place via email on 14th October 2010.

[7] Barber was Zappa's road manager from 1967-71. He provides snorts & various vocal noises on several Zappa recordings.

[8] Harris – a prominent film critic – attended Zappanale with Bob Zappa in 2012.

were both at my wedding on 26th September here in New York. I had not seen Bill in person for over ten years, but Dick came to New York in 2014. My wife Diane and I had dinner with him here at our apartment. I am in touch with both of them by email or phone on a regular basis, sometimes daily. And at our wedding it was as though we were still high school pals, only older, slower and with less hair.

Yes, Dick still snorks! He also flies his own airplane, one that he built just before he built his house in Nevada. He is a man of many accomplishments and talents.

Were you around when Frank made that phone call to Edgard Varèse?[9]

I remember when he made it and how excited he was about it.

What is your own personal taste in music?

I listen to classical, bluegrass, Frank, of course and music from the 1940s. Like comfort food for the ears and soul.

Is it true that Frank intended to record you and Candy for his Bizarre label?

He may have wanted to record Candy but by the time he had his labels I was either in the Marines or in graduate school (I can't remember which) and quite frankly, I have no musical talent. But he always tried to include his siblings in things that amused him.

Are you still in touch with your half-sister Ann?[10]

Not on a regular basis. The last time we were together was at my mother's funeral.[11]

Have you ever used your father's book, *Chances: And How To Take Them*,[12] to bet on the baseball series?

No, I have never even read my father's book because it presumed

---

[9] On Zappa's 15th birthday, his mother allowed him an expensive long-distance call to Varèse's home in New York. At the time Varèse was in Belgium, so Zappa spoke to Varèse's wife Louise instead. Eventually Zappa and Varèse spoke on the phone, and they discussed the possibility of meeting each other. Although this meeting never took place, Zappa received a letter from Varèse which he framed and hung on his office wall.

[10] From their father's first marriage. In his book, Bob reveals that Frank and Ann never met.

[11] Rose Marie Zappa died in 2004.

[12] Francis V. Zappa's book was released via a small publisher in June 1966, and quickly disappeared. It was reprinted in 2011 by Crossfire Publications.

that anyone who did read it actually knew mathematics beyond addition, subtraction, division and multiplication – which leaves me out. Besides, I like basketball.

Do you recall the last time you spoke with Frank?
There were two special occasions: when he called to tell me about his diagnosis and once when he was going through therapy. There were many times when I called him in LA from NY but was often told he was either too sick to speak or that he was asleep.

He said he wasn't particularly interested in how he would be remembered. What do you remember most of all about him?
That as children, teenagers and young adults, we were the closest friends and shared so many experiences together that I still have vivid memories of the good and the bad times, which is why I wrote the book.

The Frank Zappa I knew is not the same person that so many people think they know. He was so much better and so much smarter and his untimely death should have been prevented.

Do you think you'll ever write a sequel – *Grown Up Zappa*, perchance?
My wife, Dr. Diane Papalia, is a retired researcher and psychology professor and the author of several widely used text books on human development. She encouraged me to finish *Frankie & Bobby – Growing Up Zappa* and we have been talking about projects that involve other periods in Frank's life and mine.

For now, though, I'm just hoping people will find this book worth reading.[13]

Interview conducted on Monday 26th October 2015.

---

[13] The second part of Bob Zappa's memoirs, *Frankie & Bobby – The Rest Of Our Story*, was published in June 2017 and lifts the lid on Gail Zappa's "increasingly irrational behaviour during the final years of Frank's life."

Candy and Bob Zappa.

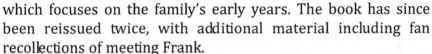

CANDY ZAPPA

Patrice JoAnne Zappa was born eleven years after her brother Frank, on 28th March 1951. In 2003, she published *My Brother Was A Mother - A Zappa Family Album*, which focuses on the family's early years. The book has since been reissued twice, with additional material including fan recollections of meeting Frank.

Patrice (better known as Candy) has sung with a number of bands in the US and Europe, including the Ed Palermo[1] Big Band and the Muffin Men. She appears on a number of tracks on Nigey Lennon's *Reinventing The Wheel* album (including on a duet with Jimmy Carl Black on the expanded version - *Reinventing The Wheel Reinvented* - issued in 2013).

She performed at Zappanale in 2002 with the Lennon / Tabacco / Zappa band and again in 2016 as a special guest of the Muffin Men and the Zappa Early Renaissance Orchestra.

In 2005, she provided lead vocals on a number of tracks on the album *Neonfire* by Neonfire.[2] The album also featured American R&B singer and songwriter Nolan Porter, who Candy married in 2007. (Porter's 1970 debut album *No Apologies* featured former Mothers Jimmy Carl Black, Roy Estrada and Lowell George. The follow-up, *Nolan* (1973), spawned the UK northern soul hit *If I Could Only Be Sure* featuring Johnny "Guitar" Watson.[3])

---

[1] New Jersey saxophonist, composer and arranger best known for his big band performances of Zappa's music.

[2] Essentially the brainchild of Greg Russo, the album also featured contributions from Napoleon Murphy Brock and The Tornadoes.

[3] John Watson, Jr. (1935–1996) was an American blues, soul, and funk musician and singer-songwriter. Zappa claimed that "Watson's 1956 song *Three Hours Past Midnight* inspired me to become a guitarist." Watson contributed to the Zappa albums *One Size Fits All* (1975), *Them Or Us* (1984), *Thing-Fish* (1984) and *Frank Zappa Meets The Mothers Of Prevention* (1985).

Having been in regular contact with Nigey Lennon since our interview in 2000, it dawned on me that she could put me in touch with Candy. After the successful 'Zappa Sings Zappa' shows with the Ed Palermo Big Band in August 2001, I plucked up the courage to ask...

First of all, how is your mother Rose Marie?
So far, mom is holding her own. She is a young 89.[4]

What was Frank's relationship with her like?
Frank loved mom but, as with any teenager, he was rebellious. He respected mom, but had his own way of dealing with mom and dad. He went to mom for more things than dad, I think.

Was the young Frank neat and tidy?
From what I can remember about him, he was usually clean and dressed neatly. I don't remember much about his room as I only went in there every so often, but it didn't seem to be unnecessarily messy.

Boys can be slobs, but I don't remember Frank as a slob. He was pretty particular about his surroundings. He was always coming and going with his friends, so it was a little sketchy as to remembering his hygiene and domestic habits!

Can you describe the house on "G" Street in Ontario, California near San Ber'dino, where Frank lived with his first wife, Kathryn J. "Kay" Sherman, in the early 1960s?
The house on "G" street was big and it smelled old. I loved it. It had a basement and an attic, a large dining room, hardwood floors, a screened in porch. Mom remembers one time they put their bed out there because it was too hot to sleep in the house. I spent many a happy time there and I have many fond memories of it.

What was Kay like?
Kay was very nice and she had lots of cats. As a young girl who loved cats, that made her okay in my book! But what went on between Frank and Kay was not my business. I only know that

---

[4] She sadly passed away three years after this interview.

when they split, Frank called mom to come and get him.[5]

Were you around when Frank made that phone call to Edgard Varèse?
I think I was too young to know about it.

What did you think of the Varèse album – and Frank's fascination with it?[6]
Unfortunately, I never heard the Varèse album. But if I could ever get a copy of it, I would definitely love to hear it.

Did you ever borrow Frank's old 45s?
No, I never borrowed them. But occasionally he would play them for me when I was little and dance with me – twirl me around – and I thought it was the best time for me.

What is your own personal taste in music and who are your biggest influences?
I love... no, wait: I LOVE JAZZ. I, of course, love Frank's music – mostly the instrumental stuff. Motown, the black sound of the 50s and 60s – in fact, Frank's music collection contained a lot of the stuff I grew to love.

I write and love songs with good melody and harmonies and as the teenyboppers on American Bandstand used to say, "I give it a 65 because you can dance to it." Good rhythms are also important.

I also love classical music and sounds that catch my attention – not so much punk or metal sounds.

Frank liked to record a lot of things – for example, his group eating breakfast (*Don't Eat There* from *Playground Psychotics*). To your knowledge, did he ever record the pre-Mothers Soul Giants either on stage or at play?
I have no knowledge of whether or not he recorded the Soul Giants.

---

5 In 2013, Sherman (now Kathryn Jones) provided an interesting insight into her time with Zappa at PBS's History Detectives website: "He loved cats! At one point in the early sixties, we had four cats and three gave birth to five kittens each. We had 19 cats of which we found homes for eight pairs and kept the rest. It was joyous. Another side of Frank that nobody knows about. He is missed."

6 Upon hearing the 1950 EMS Recordings album *The Complete Works of Edgard Varèse, Vol. 1*, Zappa became obsessed with the composer's music.

Why are you called Candy?

My brother Carl named me Candy because, as a baby, he thought I was sweet.

So you say you write your own songs?

Yes, I do write my own songs – and have recorded several and performed them too.

What kept you going to achieve your ambition?

Well, knowing that I could sing and loved doing it – in fact, Frank told me that I "sang well," coming from Frank, that was money in the bank. That was one thing. He told me to keep working and I wanted to. I like performing and no one has thrown tomatoes at me, so I guess my audiences like it too!

What will your Nigey Lennon-produced R&B album be like?

So far the *Reinventing The Wheel* CD is quite good; everyone that has heard it has given us good reviews. Any new projects we have planned are still in the works.

What were the concerts with Ed Palermo at the Bottom Line like?

Oh my, where do I begin? First of all, meeting all of those wonderfully talented musicians – and, of course, Mr Palermo himself – was incredible. Singing in front of his 18-piece band was a dream come true.

The audiences were wonderful, so supportive and attentive. New York is a fantastic place; the people were gracious and to me, very kind. It's a real charge to know that Frank's music is loved and that he is remembered so well. I was honoured to be there.

Do you have any plans to work with Ed again?

Oh God, I hope so! He has told me that I have to come back again! I would love to work with Ed on a regular basis and he has told me that if I move there I have a regular gig with his band. It could happen – don't know when – but it could![7]

---

[7] In 2016, she sang on two tracks on Palermo's bug band album, *One Child Left Behind*: Frank's *Evelyn, a Modified Dog* and Los Lobos' *Kiki And The Lavender Moon*.

How did you meet Nigey – who approached who?

A friend gave me her book, *Being Frank: My Time With Frank Zappa*. After reading it, I was totally intrigued with her and I called, left a message saying who I was. Nigey returned the call; we met for dinner at which time she presented me with a beautiful framed picture of Frank. I played her some tapes of my singing and she asked me if I would sing on her upcoming CD. The rest is history.

How did your relationship with Frank change once he became well-known?

Well, we didn't get to see each other as you can imagine. Whenever I did get to go up there to the house, it was done with an appointment because he was so busy.

I got to go to his concerts, which were always the best. We talked on the phone occasionally and I missed him horribly.

How is your relationship with your other siblings?

My other brothers and half sister Ann and I are close. Carl lives with mom and takes care of her, as do I and Bob, lives back east with his wife. Ann also lives back east and we talk quite often.

What are your memories of Don Van Vliet?

Don would come over to the house with Frank when I was playing and singing and told me he liked my voice. He wore really unusual shoes!

Ah, the Captain's fat Theresa shoes![8] I understand he has an extensive collection of sinister footwear. How about Jim Sherwood?

Jim Sherwood was a cool guy. He and Frank would also come over to our house when I was in junior high. When I would serve them coffee, I asked Jim how he wanted it and he said, "Just pour sugar in till it comes over the side." I never forgot that.

Ray Collins?

Ray 'Baby' Collins was cool, too. I got to sing with him in 1963 at

---

[8] A reference to a track on The GTOs Zappa-produced *Permanent Damage* album.

my parents' restaurant on the stage that Frank built to play his music.

I was gonna ask about The Pit – do you recall its exact address?
I only know that it was on Foothill in Upland California. The address escapes me – I don't think I ever knew it! Frank put up a stage in there and Ray Collins and some other musicians were there. That was the only time I performed on stage with Frank and Ray. I was 13 and got up to sing *Long Tall Texan*[9] and *I'm Leaving It (All) Up To You*.[10]

Wow, ten years before Donny and Marie! Aside from Nigey, have you formed friendships with any other FZ alumni?
Well it's funny you should ask: I met Bunk Gardner and Ian Underwood, Ray and I think, Jimmy Carl Black many years ago. But the other night I saw the Grandmothers at the Palace in Los Angeles and met Billy Mundi, Don Preston, Bunk – again – and Roy Estrada.

I don't hang with them as they are busy and I didn't really get to know them.

Were you as close to Frank as he was to Bobby or Carl?
I think Frank was a different kind of brother than Bob or Carl. Carl was my playmate. Bob and Frank hung together, so I didn't get to play with them a lot. I just knew that I loved them all, but Frank was so great to me. Our humour was just alike, both of us being rebellious and bent. What a combination!

When the boys would all horseplay and I wanted to get in there and play too, our dad would warn the boys to "Take care of your baby sister!" I do remember that!

Is it true that Frank originally intended to record you and Bobby for his Bizarre label?
I don't know about Bob, but at one point he was going to have me

---

[9] A song written by Nashville studio musician Henry Strzelecki (1939-2014), first released by The Four Flickers in 1959.

[10] A song written and originally performed by Don Harris and Dewey Terry in 1957. In 1974, Donny and Marie Osmond reached number one on the Billboard Hot Adult Contemporary chart with their cover version.

sing *Status Back Baby* from the *Absolutely Free* album.[11] But things beyond my control prevented it.

Did Frank make any specific references to you – lyrical or otherwise – that you particularly recall?
One night he was being interviewed on TV and he did talk about his sibling and mentioned that I was going to college and hadn't recorded anything – yet!

You were one of many who auditioned for the part of Drakma, the Queen of Cosmic Greed, in Frank's opera *Hunchentoot*. Do you remember when and where that took place?
In the early 1980s. But it was too high for my vocal range and I was totally disappointed that I couldn't do it.

Frank wasn't particularly interested in how he would be remembered, but what do you remember most of all about him?
I remember many things, but his presence was so totally intense and he cared about me and our family.

He could look at things and just know what it was all about. He was a human being who deserved to be treated well and sometimes he just wasn't.

I remember that he sought my opinion about what he did. How many people can say that about a family member? You have to remember I was eleven years younger than Frank so a lot of his activities were spent with his friends – and girls! So I can't tell too much about our life together, only what I can remember.

I wouldn't trade my time with Frank for anything.

That was very, um, sweet. Thanks, Candy!
No problem. I hope that you have a multitude of visits to your website and that what I had to say makes a little difference!

Interview conducted on Tuesday 6th November 2001.

---

[11] A version of the song, then titled *I'm Losing Status At The High School*, was recorded at Pal Recording Studios in 1963 with Paul Buff's wife Allison on vocals.

DWEEZIL ZAPPA

D weezil Zappa was born on 5th September 1969. The following month, his father's album *Hot Rats* appeared with a dedication to him.

Dweezil was a special guest guitarist on a dozen dates on Frank's last three tours in 1982, 1984 and 1988. He plays on his dad's albums *Them Or Us* (1984), *Does Humor Belong In Music?* (1986), *You Can't Do That On Stage Anymore Vol. 3* (1989) and *Trance-Fusion* (2006).

Frank produced his first solo album *Havin' A Bad Day* in 1986.

In 1991, Dweezil played a handful of live shows to support his third album, *Confessions*, which is when I arranged my first interview with him. It took place at the Holiday Inn Swiss Cottage on Wednesday 8th May, exactly one week after his first UK gig at London's Marquee. The band at that time comprised Scott Thunes (bass), Mike Keneally (second guitar), Josh Freese (drums) and his brother Ahmet (vocals).

After the *Confessions* tour, Dweezil formed a new band and project with Ahmet called "Z".

At the time of our interview, I was aware that Frank was unwell and was criticised by friends for not raising this: Dweezil was just striking out on his own with his own music and to me this didn't seem the right thing to do. He and his sister Moon would formally reveal to the public their father's prostate cancer during a press conference ahead of the Zappa's Universe concerts six months later.

So here is my first interview with Dweezil, which is largely about Dweezil. I never apologise. I'm sorry, but that's just the way I am.

First of all I want to ask you: who is Phfil Beasley?

Phfil Beasley is my alter ego – a lounge singer. Have you seen the video for *Gotta Get To You*?[1] Robert Wagner[2] plays him in the video.

Oh, he was in the *My Guitar Wants To Kill Your Mama*[3] video too – as Dick Knowse!

Detective Dick Knowse. He's now moved on to Phfil Beasley, lounge singer – with a huge pompadour.

It's just that Ahmet introduced himself as Phfil Beasley at the Marquee.

Yeah, he went out there and stole my line basically.

Okay. Who are "The Vards", who produced your first single?[4]

"The Vards" were Edward Van Halen[5] and Donn Landee.[6]

Really? I had heard that it might have been Edward Van Halen.

It was and he actually played the intro to *Mama Is a Space Cadet* – the slide guitar part.

When did you record that – you were only about..

...12 or 15, I'd only been playing nine months.

You actually played on stage with your father in 1982.

Yeah, very close after *Space Cadet*.

Has your mum got over that now!

Oh, yeah – it was never intentionally written about her.

Who are Power Tool, with whom you co-wrote a song for *Bill*

---

[1] From Dweezil's *Confessions* album.

[2] American actor, best known for starring in the TV show *Hart To Hart* (1979-1984) – and for his portrayal of Number Two in the Austin Powers trilogy of films (1997-2002).

[3] The title track of his second solo album, released in 1988.

[4] *My Mother Is a Space Cadet* (1982), produced by Frank.

[5] Dutch-American guitarist, and occasional keyboard player, who co-founded the American hard rock band Van Halen. He is considered one of the most influential guitarists in the history of rock music.

[6] American recording engineer, who has worked extensively with producer Ted Templeman. The pair worked with a wide variety of artists for Warner Bros. Records during the 1970s and 1980s, including Van Halen and the Doobie Brothers.

& Ted's Excellent Adventure[7] **– did you actually play on that?**

Yeah. The funny thing about that is, I was just messing around with the Nelson twins[8] – they put a drum machine on and I just played this guitar part. We recorded on an eight track; they took that to a studio, stole my guitar part and tried to do the song without telling me anything about it.

But I found out a couple of weeks before the movie came out – they ended up giving me a credit, but they stole the guitar solo that I had put on it originally.

That was pretty funny.

Can you tell me about *Dragon Master*?[9]

The infamous *Dragon Master*!

Yeah, Frank wrote the lyrics to it – I guess, in Stockholm.[10] I heard it in various bits and pieces, but never in an arrangement that I thought was quite appropriate for it.

Frank's not up on his thrash metal, so he suggested to me one night, "Why don't we do Dragon Master?" So I wrote basically the ugliest music that I could possibly write.

It's meant to be done as a bit of a joke, really. It's a send up of speed metal and all that stuff. It's pretty good though.

Is it going to be released in the future?

Maybe on the next record, but it's got such satanic lyrics I could get myself into trouble.

You'd be up there with Deicide[11] **and the like.**

Yeah.

Do you plan to do anymore writing together - well, that

---

[7] 1989 American science-fiction comedy buddy film, starring Alex Winter and Keanu Reeves.

[8] American singer/songwriters Matthew and Gunnar Nelson (twin sons of Ricky Nelson and Kristin Nelson). As the rock band Nelson, they achieved success during the early 1990s with their number-one hit *(Can't Live Without Your) Love And Affection*.

[9] The only song co-composed by Dweezil with his father, the first official recording of which finally appeared on Dweezil's Via Zammata' album in 2015.

[10] Frank and his band first performed a version of the song at a sound check before the 1st May 1988 concert in Stockholm, Sweden, where Dweezil was a special guest.

[11] American death metal band, formed in 1987.

wasn't actually written together as such...
Well, in a round about sort of way it was. I don't know, we often joke about doing a *Zappa Christmas Album*. But I'd like to do a guitar album with Frank – maybe that'll happen.

That'd be great.
Yeah, it'd be cool.

Do you know if there are any plans to release the version of *Chunga's Revenge* that you played on probably your last UK visit, at Wembley in 1988?
I'd heard it was gonna be out on something.

A lot of the 1988 material's coming out now, but I haven't seen any reference to that.
Yeah, it's gonna come out – it was kinda cool. I've heard it once or twice since then. I think it'll be on the next release; it was scheduled for this one, but...[12]

Are you gonna put out your guitar version of *G-Spot Tornado*?[13]
I might stick it in the middle of something.

It was a weird idea, in that *While You Were Out/Art* was done the reverse way: a guitar solo transcribed for Synclavier.[14]
I wasn't really aware of that. I'd always liked that piece of music and of course humans can only play it at half speed. But it's still more difficult than most people would... no one in their right mind would attempt to play that song!

I was surprised when I read about it in the Society Pages fanzine – I was shocked, in fact.
I think we played it okay that night; I don't recall fucking it up too badly.[15]

---

[12] It was issued in edited form on the album *Trance-Fusion* in 2006.

[13] This was one of his father's Synclavier realised compositions, which was included in Dweezil's set at the Marquee. Frank's original version can be found on his album *Jazz From Hell* (1986).

[14] *While You Were Out* is an improvised studio jam included on the *Shut Up 'N Play Yer Guitar* album (1982); the deluxe Synclavier version, *While You Were Art II*, appears on *Jazz From Hell* (1986).

[15] A more faithful rendition of *G-Spot Tornado* would be performed by Zappa Plays Zappa, circa 2007.

Now, *The Medley* – Mike Keneally was supposed to be writing out the list of all the songs. Is it 118?
Sometimes it's more, sometimes it's less; sometimes we remember songs being in there and we still count them, but they're not. I think ultimately it is 118, but at one point it was about 122.

I'd love to see that released. People I've been talking to about it who are not actually Zappa fans but know the songs, they'd love to hear that as well.
Well, I don't know if it'll be released, because it's a record company's nightmare. Also, it wouldn't be as impressive on record, unless it was a live recording – because if you just went into the studio and did the proper version of the whole thing it would lose its impact.[16]

I know you're re-writing the lyrics to *Broken Hearts Are For Assholes*;[17] it started off as *Starting Wars Is For Assholes*,[18] then *George Bush*[19] *Is An Asshole* last week – you were also gonna refer to the LAPD street beating scandal?
We did that at one point, too. It was *Daryl Gates*[20] *Is An Asshole*.

So it changes from...
...whatever is appropriate at the time. It was going to be *MC Hammer*[21] *Is An Asshole* that night, but that's a little too much of a mouthful.

---

[16] As noted elsewhere, a live version of *The Medley* was finally issued in 2015 on the *Via Zammata' Demos And Rarities* album.

[17] From Frank's album *Sheik Yerbouti* (1979). Dweezil would later issue a live recording with ZPZ that appeared on his album *Return Of The Son Of...* (2010).

[18] This interview took place just after the first Gulf War had ended.

[19] George Herbert Walker Bush, the US President who urged countries to send forces to the Gulf following the Iraqi Army's occupation of Kuwait in August 1990.

[20] Darrel Francis Gates (1926-2010) was the Chief of the Los Angeles Police Department (LAPD) from 1978 to 1992. He retired from the department following the riots that ensued after Rodney King (1965-2012), an African American taxi driver, was beaten by members of the LAPD in March 1991. Ironically, Gail Zappa would later compare herself to the LAPD when issuing cease and desist letters to Zappa fansites (Kill Ugly Radio), festivals (Zappanale) and tribute bands (Project Object) in a bid to protect and serve he late husband's legacy - making many fans feel like Rodney King.

[21] Real name Stanley Kirk Burrell, an American hip hop recording artist whose biggest hit was *U Can't Touch This* (1990).

Vanilla Ice[22] also came in for some stick.

Oh yeah – he deserves it, man.

On the subject of George Bush, it's a bit worrying that the man who was a bowel movement away from active service, was just a heartbeat away from becoming President over the weekend. So could it be *Dan Quayle Is An Asshole* next?[23]

I guess. It's really seriously whatever can fit in – we like to leave that space open. The open slot of the night.

Okay. What happened with Clitoris Records – or should I say 'Syphilis'?[24]

Oh yeah, Syphilis Records; I think I was just signed on to them so they could take a tax loss at the end of the year, because they seriously did nothing. It was like living Spinal Tap,[25] being on that label for that period.

Whom you supported, of course, earlier this year.

Yeah. That was our very first live slot, opening up for Spinal Tap.[26]

I don't know if they're ever gonna come to England.

I heard they're coming soon.

That'll be good. I'd also like to ask what happened to the Normal Life sitcom.[27] I don't know if it's ever going to be shown over here, but I understand it's been dropped now.

It was dropped a long time ago and we were glad to see it dropped because we hated working on it. We hated the people; they were

---

[22] Real name Robert Matthew Van Winkle, an American rapper whose biggest hit was *Ice Ice Baby* (1990).

[23] James Danforth Quayle was the 44th Vice President of the United States from 1989 to 1993 under President Bush. He was widely regarded as an incompetent buffoon. While jogging at Camp David on 4th May 1991, there were fears that Bush had suffered a heart attack. He was later diagnosed with atrial fibrillation related to a thyroid disease and made a full recovery.

[24] A reference to Chrysalis Records, the British record label that released Dweezil's *My Guitar Wants To Kill Your Mama* album in 1988.

[25] A parody band who spoofed British heavy metal groups, most notably in the 1984 rockumentary film *This Is Spinal Tap*.

[26] Dweezil also played guitar on the track *Diva Fever* from the band's second album, *Break Like The Wind* (1992).

[27] An American CBS TV series that aired from 21st March until 18th July 1990, and co-starred Dweezil with his sister Moon.

just the most pathetic bunch of fucking losers ever.

I've never ever seen any of it, so I have no idea.
Basically what happened was, we came up with the concept, sold the concept...

It was your idea originally?
Yeah. But then the network flipped it on us when we got into production and at that point we were still bound by contract to the project. So we had to do it.

Originally it was gonna be like The Adams Family[28] to a certain extent; you could do anything within the house, because it would be considered normal by the family. But 'normal' people would come over – you know, like neighbours – and they would be considered weird based on what was set up as the precedent for normal inside the house.

But they said, "Okay, that's great – but let's do this: let's make you really normal and have the neighbours be wacky!"

It was like, "Fuuuucck!" So...

You also appeared in a couple of films: *Pretty In Pink*[29] and *The Running Man*[30] are the two that I know of, I don't know if there were anymore. How did that all come about? I know you did a stint as a DJ on MTV...
I just did a little stuff here and there – just a way to earn a little bit of money when it's necessary. I can't really care less about it though.

You're not going to take it seriously?
Nah, it's just a job – I fucking hate actors, anyway. As people.

Have you done any sessions lately? I know you've worked

---

[28] A fictional household created by American cartoonist Charles Addams. The Addamses are a satirical inversion of the ideal 20th century American family.

[29] 1986 American romcom written by John Hughes. The film starred Molly Ringwald, who Dweezil dated at the time. His character in the film was called Simon.

[30] 1987 American sci-fi action film directed by Paul Michael Glaser and starring Arnold Schwarzenegger. It is loosely based on the 1982 novel *The Running Man* by Stephen King and published under the pseudonym Richard Bachman. Dweezil's character was called Stevie; his father in the film, Mic, was portrayed by Mick Fleetwood, drummer with Fleetwood Mac.

with Don Johnson,[31] Winger[32]...
The last session I did was on Extreme's album.[33] I did a solo...

Extreme. Did you see them at the Marquee last Thursday?
Yeah, the night after we played. I played a solo on *He-Man Woman Hater*.[34] Nuno,[35] of course, worked with me on my record.

I was wondering – as he was gonna be in town the next day – if he was gonna turn up at your show.
He came down. But no one recognised him to let him backstage – 'cause he was gonna come up and play with us.

Someone else in the audience I saw was Jeff Beck and Warren Cuccurullo was on the guest list.
He was there.

Terry Bozzio? Did I spot him?
I don't think he was there. I think he was in town, but...

Is he still with Jeff Beck, do you know?
I'm not sure, to be honest.

You did a slightly different version of *Purple Haze* with Winger to the one that you performed last week...
...just a little bit different![36]

[laughs] ...and different indeed to Frank's one, as well, which has just come out; that's quite a fun one.[37] How did the Peace

---

[31] American actor, singer and songwriter best known for his role as "Sonny" Crockett in the 1980s television series *Miami Vice*. Dweezil plays guitar on *The Last Sound Love Makes* on Johnson's 1986 album *Heartbeat*.

[32] American glam-prog metal band. Dweezil plays the left side guitar solo on a version of Jimi Hendrix's *Purple Haze* from their 1988 eponymous debut album.

[33] *Extreme II: Pornograffitti (A Funked Up Fairy Tale)* (1990), the second album by the American rock band.

[34] Dweezil plays the intro/outro guitar solos on this track from *Pornograffitti*.

[35] Nuno Duarte Gil Mendes Bettencourt – a Portuguese guitarist, singer-songwriter and record producer – appears all over the *Confessions* album, and is credited as co-producer with Dweezil.

[36] Where the Winger version was a relatively straightforward cover of the Hendrix song, Dweezil's was a 'cocktail lounge' rendition.

[37] Frank's version appeared on his album *The Best Band You Never Heard In Your Life* (1991). Recorded at a sound check on the 1988 tour, this Devo-inspired rendition features Ike Willis in *Thing-Fish* mode and segues in similar vein into a version Cream's *Sunshine Of Your Love*.

Choir thing come about?[38] You worked with Lenny Kravitz?
They just called us up and asked if we wanted to be involved and we said "Sure." It was like two days before the war started.

It's just a singing role, is it? I haven't actually heard it.
Yeah.

I don't know if it had much success around the world, but I don't think it received any airplay in this country because the BBC banned it – it was deemed too controversial for them. Some of the records they were banning were just unbelievable – stuff like Elton John's *Saturday Night's Alright (For Fighting)*... it was just weird, the list they came out with.[39]
Because of the war?

Yeah. Ridiculous. On the *Confessions* album, you've got a cover of The Beatles' song *Anytime At All*.[40] What was the idea behind that one – that's not a usual choice.
That's the main reason we did it! It's a good song, but rarely, if ever, covered. We decided it would be good for the texture of the album. I wanted to use a 12-string for a second. It's buried in there somewhere.

I was really pissed off that you played at Tower Records today and I missed it!
It was okay. The PA started to smoke in the middle of what we were doing.

So was it just you, or...
It was me, Ahmet, Mike and Scott and Josh was playing bongos.

---

[38] In 1991, Yoko Ono recorded a new version of her husband's song *Give Peace A Chance* in response to the imminent Gulf War. Helmed by Sean Ono Lennon (who penned additional lyrics) and Lenny Kravitz (who produced the record), the Peace Choir included Peter Gabriel, Bruce Hornsby, Al Jarreau, Little Richard, MC Hammer, Michael McDonald, Randy Newman, Tom Petty and Iggy Pop - as well as Ahmet, Dweezil and Moon Zappa. All three Zappas appeared in the accompanying music video.

[39] A total of 67 songs were banned from BBC airplay as the first Gulf War began, including The Bangles' *Walk Like An Egyptian*, Jona Lewie's *Stop The Cavalry* and Kenny Rogers And The First Edition's *Ruby, Don't Take Your Love To Town*.

[40] From The Beatles' album, *A Hard Day's Night* (1964).

Have you got any more gigs lined up when you go back to the States?
We do New York, Boston, Washington DC, Philadelphia, New Jersey, Los Angeles, San Francisco, Sacramento and Phoenix.

What has the reaction been so far? It was certainly favourable at the Marquee. There was a good rapport.
Basically it's been good. With this record, people are finally starting to take me seriously. The best audience that we've played for so far was the Paris audience; they really liked it quite a bit.

I've been surprised at the turn out; over here I figured no one would really be keen.

Yeah, I wondered who would be there last week. I thought it'd probably be a few of your father's fans, but it seemed to be not so many older people in there, but quite a lot of young people.
It was a mixed group. Paris was mostly young people. They're really hip to the record there. They really like it.

They like *Shoogagoogagunga*.[41]

I'm glad you said that, because I can't and wasn't going to ask you about it!
They came up, even with their French accent and then say: "Hey, dude. Don't say that, dude".

That's almost like the Bill & Ted-style speak.
To a certain extent. It's sort of like a play on Los Angeles guitar... actually, what it is, is: 'Relocated Bostonians In Los Angeles Who Learned To Say "Dude" Far Too Much' and impersonate other guitar players.

Both me and Nuno were doing that. Nuno's got a pretty heavy Massachusetts accent, so I did a bit of one as well.

Have you got any new guitar body designs? I see you've got a *Sheik Yerbouti* **one now. There's the Madonna one... but I**

---

[41] Track from *Confessions*, which is also reprised at the end of the album as *Return Of The Son Of Shoogagoogagunga*.

didn't see any of them on stage last week.
I left most of the ones with the good paint jobs at home, because I was afraid of things happening to them. We're taking out a bunch of equipment, but it didn't feel like we had enough of the proper cases to take those out and not have them get screwed up. About the most exotic one I had was the silver sparkle one. That's a cool one, though.

Is green still your favourite colour?
Yeah. I like green.

And have you met Madonna lately?
I haven't seen her for a while. The last time was at a screening and she was talking to a bunch of people. She was about as far away from me as you are. I just walked past her because she was talking to people. She stopped talking to the people and she yelled at me. She said, "Oh, great. Just walk right past without saying hello." I was like [sheepishly] "Well, I thought you were busy."

Every time I run into her, I always think that she's not gonna remember me. So, it's a bit of a shocker to be yelled at by Madonna.

Yeah, I wish I could say the same! Of the songs you played last week, there were a couple I didn't recognise. I don't know if there were any new ones. Like *The Rain Keeps Up*?
Yeah, that's sort of a new-old one; we recorded that for the *Havin' A Bad Day* album, but we never released it.

That's funny, because you didn't actually go back to the first album.
We sometimes play one or two things from there.

The set does vary quite a bit, does it?
Oh yeah. Changes every night. Sometimes we'll play *I Want A Yacht*, [42] or something like that.

---

[42] Song from *Havin' A Bad Day* that features American comedian and voice artist "Bobcat" Goldthwait. Goldthwait came to prominence as the character Zed in the *Police Academy* films.

Who does the role of Bobcat!?
No one really.

And some of the encores last week; the last one: *I Think I Love You*?
That was The Partridge Family.[43]

Oh, right. I heard it in *The Medley*.
It was very twisted.

Yeah, you were asking the audience for different styles, which was quite impressive.
But the joke is, if we get somebody to tell us what style, we go "Okay, yeah. That's the way it's going to be." But no matter what, we end it speed metal. Even if they said reggae. We'd pretend for a second, then it goes straight to speed metal.

And we also did a sort of take-off on *Bang A Gong*. A joke in the band was to do a song that absolutely nobody would clap for. Something that was so horrifying that people would just look at you and that was the song.

We laughed so hard, because it's the most inside of all jokes; it's just a reworked version of *Bang A Gong*, but Ahmet sings "Smoke a bong."

And something about stuffing rocks down his pants.
Yeah [sings:] "You know we danced, all night long. Come to my house, we'll smoke a bong; you know I love you, coz you found my missing thong. Let's, smoke a bong."

But the funny thing is, we're so anti-drug, we do songs like that because it's just a total joke to us. But people obviously think that we're on drugs when we play something like that.

Or devil worshippers, if you do *Dragon Master*.
Yeah.

I noticed in *The Medley*, there are a lot of riffs flying about. I think I spotted a Sabbath one, a couple of Deep Purple's and

---

[43] It was a number one hit single for them in the US in 1970, but only reached No.18 in the UK charts.

there's also some Led Zeppelin in there: *Kashmir*...[44]
Yeah, quite a bit of Led Zeppelin and there's Aerosmith.

But you're too young to remember those bands, surely!
Oh no. I like most of the music from that period. There's something about it. Some of it's just so stoopid, that it's great. Like *Cherokee People*, the Paul Revere & The Raiders song.[45] It's just so bad, we had to put things like that in there. *Macho Man*,[46] things like that....

It's a weird mix.
It's supposed to be the good and the bad: A musical time machine. I think it basically succeeds at that.

   If you took a cuisinart and made a pâté out of the seventies, that's what it would be.

You've also recorded, with The Fat Boys,[47] another Beatles' song.
Baby, You're A Rich Man.[48]

Which I don't think has seen the light of day?
I think it was on a soundtrack,[49] but I haven't heard that since I played on it.

   I remember that was the shortest session I ever did. I went in, they played me the song. It was tuned down a half step and my guitar I tune to A4-40. So it was like a really weird key for me to play in at that point. It was like B-flat I had to play in, because my guitar was not in tune with the track.

   I remember just playing one thing. Once I got to a certain point on the neck, I got confused as to what key I was in because it wasn't standard tuning. I started doing really weird stuff and they kept it. That was it. Just one take of the solo.

---

[44] From Zeppelin's sixth studio album, *Physical Graffiti*.

[45] The Raiders' version of the John D. Loudermilk song, *Indian Reservation (The Lament of the Cherokee Reservation Indian)*, topped the US charts in 1971.

[46] The second single recorded by the American disco group Village People (1978).

[47] American hip hop trio from Brooklyn, who emerged in the early 1980s.

[48] The b-side of The Beatles' single *All You Need Is Love* (1967).

[49] It appears in *Disorderlies*, a 1987 comedy film starring The Fat Boys and Ralph Bellamy (1904–1991).

They said, "That was it! Great. No problem. Thanks very much." Okay.

I know that, like Edward Van Halen played with Michael Jackson[50] – and now so has Slash[51] – you wanted to do a disco crossover track. Have you achieved that yet?
Well, I wanted to play on Madonna's record. But I like to play on anybody's record, really. I don't care, whoever asks me, I'll play on their record.

Actually, the last session I did – I forgot about this: I played on a punk band's record, The Vandals. On a song called *Hey, Holmes - Don't Front My Set!*[52] A good gang song. I played the most bizarre solo that I think I've ever played. It's just so ugly. The best thing. I want to play on people's record that no one would ever expect me to play on.

Like Vanilla Ice or MC Hammer?!
Yeah. Or Wilson Phillips,[53] or something. I just had dinner with them last night. That'd be funny: I wanna play on their record!

Right. I think that's about all my questions used up. So, thanks for your time.
That's no problem.

Interview conducted on Wednesday 8th May 1991.

In early 2012, I got an opportunity to ask Dweezil a couple of questions via Scott Parker, who was about to conduct a phone interview with him for Episodes 7 of the ZappaCast.

So I recorded my questions and Scott played them to Dweezil for his 'in the moment' responses.

---

[50] On the track *Beat It* from Jackson's album *Thriller* (1982).

[51] On *Give In To Me* from *Dangerous* (1991).

[52] *Hey, Holmes!* appears on *Fear Of A Punk Planet* (1990), the third album by the southern California punk rock band.

[53] American vocal group consisting of Carnie Wilson, Wendy Wilson and Chynna Phillips, the daughters, respectively, of Brian Wilson of The Beach Boys and of John and Michelle Phillips of The Mamas & The Papas. In 1990, the group won the Billboard Music Award for Hot 100 Single Of The Year for their song *Hold On*.

When I interviewed Steve Vai a few years ago, we talked about Frank's song *Solitude*. He said he thought Gail wanted you to record it. Do you have any plans to do just that?

I'm not sure if that is an accurate representation... I've never had a discussion with Gail about that song, but I know it's a little known song in Frank's catalogue... it's a song written for Gail.

It's something I could think about, but I actually haven't had that conversation with Gail. So, that's news to me!

On the version of *Stayin' Alive*[54] released on Ozzy Osbourne's *Prince Of Darkness* box set,[55] the drum and bass tracks have been re-recorded.

How did that come about?

There are certain elements in that, that I've changed on purpose.

To begin with, Ozzy sang on it and it was supposed to be on my *Confessions* record. But then Sharon[56] or somebody at the record company decided they didn't want Ozzy to be on it: they said you have to destroy that track and get rid of his vocal.

I said, "Well, that's unfortunate because I think he sounds great on it." So I put Donny Osmond on it instead of Ozzy.[57]

And then years later, they're making this box set and somebody tipped me off that they had my original track on it and they were just going to go ahead without telling me – you know, just putting it out on there.

So to make it different from the original-original version, I added some new things to it to make it specific to that box set. I've kept the original version for myself for whenever I'm going to release something – so there's the difference between some

---

[54] The disco song by the Bee Gees, originally on the *Saturday Night Fever* motion picture soundtrack (1977). Dweezil recorded a version for his third solo album, originally featuring Osbourne on vocals.

[55] Four CDs released in 2005 containing various studio recordings, live tracks, b-sides, demos, outtakes, collaborations and cover songs.

[56] Osbourne's long-time wife and manager, the daughter of music promoter and rock 'n' roll entrepreneur Don Arden (1926-2007).

[57] Frank experienced something similar when he produced a version of *Dead Girls Of London*, a song he co-wrote with Indian-born American violinist L. Shankar, for the latter's solo album *Touch Me There* (1979). The original vocalist was Van Morrison, but record company intervention prevented its release and the vocals were re-recorded jointly by Zappa with Ike Willis under the pseudonym Stucco Homes. In 2011, the Morrison version appeared on The Frank Zappa *AAAFNRAAAAAM Birthday Bundle* download album.

stuff, you know?

I just wanted to add a couple of different textures to that version that ended up on that Ozzy one.

Scott Parker: So who did the bass and drum overdubs on it?
The drums are as they were, but there's just additional programming – like midi-programming stuff – that I did.

Interview conducted in Spring 2012.

Having last sat down face to face with Dweezil in 1991, I thought it was about time to properly show him that my interviewing technique had not improved one iota in the intervening twenty-four years. So I made an approach to Tom Waring (TW) – his UK agent – ahead of Zappa Plays Zappa's sole 2015 UK tour date at the Royal Festival Hall on 18th October.

Via Zammata', his first solo album in ten years, had just been released following a successful crowd-funding campaign, so there was much to talk about.

Tom told me of a planned separate 'solo' show the day before at London's Bush Hall and that he would arrange something for that weekend.

Then the unthinkable happened: Dweezil's mother – Frank's widow – Gail passed away on 7th October.

The possibility of cancelling the Bush Hall show was discussed, but on balance Dweezil decided he wanted to push ahead – and was happy for our interview to proceed.

So without further ado, here's what happened in the Bush Hall Dining Rooms on Saturday 17 October 2015.

Although Bush Hall is a one-off solo show for now, do you think this is what you might do more of in the future – is that the plan?[58]
Yeah. But as far as tonight goes, it's not going to be a complete

---

[58] In February 2016, he would embark on a short *Via Zammata'* US tour.

solo show because we just didn't end up having time with all that transpired over the past couple of weeks. So there's gonna be a limited amount of some of my stuff and then we're gonna play the Zappa material that we won't be playing tomorrow night.

Any material from *Confessions*?
There's some from *Confessions*.

Even earlier?
We're doing *My Mother Is A Space Cadet*,[59] which we've never done before. I had to re-learn that. It's been ten years since I focused on any of my own music, in terms of writing or recording and it's been even longer than that since I focused on actually playing any of it.

Once we started rehearsing and practising some of the stuff we're gonna do tonight, it was fun because it's just a whole other thing. What's funny is to see what challenges come from it in terms of what's difficult for the band.

My own music is quirky in some ways, in terms of the arrangements. Some stuff is not as it appears: there's always something that's over the bar-line or an extra beat here or there, which is just a natural thing that happens in my style of playing: something that is easy for me to play, but the band is like "This is weird!"

They should be used to that with some of Frank's music.
Exactly.

So how much further do you think you can go with Zappa Plays Zappa? Obviously, I hope you'll do it forever, but..
There's a lot of material that we've still got to learn and there's other ways that we want to present this stuff.

I would love to be able to do almost like a Grand Wazoo style band with different orchestrations and do some of the orchestral pieces. That would be a really cool, exciting thing: to be able to go

---

59 The full set-list was: *My Mother Is A Space Cadet / Boodledang / Kidz Cereal / Flibberty Jibbet / Vanity / F.W.A.K. / Dragon Master / The Mammy Anthem / My Guitar Wants To Kill Your Mama / A Pound For A Brown On The Bus / Baby Snakes / I'm So Cute / Imaginary Diseases / Status Back Baby / Big Leg Emma / Big Swifty / The Torture Never Stops. Encores: The Evil Prince / I'm The Slime.*

ahead and play some of the things that were rock band stuff that never got an orchestral treatment, like *Sinister Footwear* for example, with a rock band at the core but have it with orchestrated parts – with a bigger brass section and all these things to bring out the colours and textures of the piece.[60]

There was of course an orchestral performance of *Sinister Footwear* in 1984, in San Francisco.
Yeah, but that didn't have a rock band. It's that combination of... *Imaginary Diseases* is a good example.

Which was the first piece I ever saw ZPZ play, at the Albert Hall in 2006.
Yeah, but that record is kind of the sound that I'm talking about. Because he had a real rock rhythm section, but then you had the extra horns and other things that were added. You could do really cool stuff with pieces like *The Black Page* and *Dog Meat*, all this kind of stuff.

So I'd like to be able to do a show that focuses on a lot of that material, which to me is the most exciting stuff of Frank's compositional work. I would focus a lot on some of those major instrumentals with a project like that.

Sounds great. Now of the tracks on you new album, *Via Zammata'*, how many were brand new songs – specifically written for it – and how many were old songs?
Well, before I set out to do the record I had a spot of time on the calendar, maybe eight or nine months in advance, where we could plan something. So as it approached, even two weeks before going into the studio, I still had not had any time to write or make any decisions about what was gonna be on the record.

So I had to listen through some stuff that I had worked on in the past to see what could work as a collection of songs. It started off with about twenty songs that were possibilities and all of them were more than twenty years old. Then, as I found a few that

---

[60] On 2nd November 2015 – a little over a fortnight after this interview – the Norwegian Wind Ensemble joined ZPZ on stage at the Sentrum Scene in Oslo to perform, inter alia, *The Grand Wazoo, Imaginary Diseases* and *Sinister Footwear*.

I felt would be good to focus on, I thought well I'll write something... I changed some parts and arrangements but the song *Funky 15* was a new composition.

What about *Truth* – is that a new one?
That's an old one, that's really old. That was originally a song with vocals. But I just decided to do it like a Jeff Beck-style arrangement.

That's one of my favourites.
Yeah, I really like the melody of that one; it reminds me somewhat of the music in the original *Willy Wonka* film.

The Gene Wilder[61] one?
Yeah. There's something about it – that's what it feels like to me when I listen to it. That one has a fretless guitar and it was a challenge to play that melody line and the solo with the fretless, but it's a cool sound.

Of course I got to work with Geoff Emerick[62] on it, so it's got that little Beatle kind of history, to a degree, because it already has that influence.

When I first interviewed you in 1991 we talked a little about *Dragon Master*. It's great to finally have your version out there. You've cleaned it up a bit though – you've left out Frank's rather 'parental advisory' lyrics at the end.
Well that crazy 'dragon masturbate', all that stuff, that wasn't in his lyrics. That was something that when we did a version with "Z", that was a thing that just became this joke – it was like "Drag! Dragon! Dragon Mast! Dragon Master! Dragon Masturbates!" None of that stuff was in there originally.

I detect Ahmet's input there.
Yeah. So none of that stuff was in Frank's original lyrics.

But even so, the lyrics that are in my version, I did also change

---

[61] Real name Jerome Silberman (1933–2016), an American actor, screenwriter, director and producer, widely known for playing the lead character in the musical fantasy film *Willy Wonka & The Chocolate Factory* (1971).

[62] English recording studio audio engineer, best known for his work with the Beatles on their albums *Revolver* (1966), *Sgt. Pepper's Lonely Hearts Club Band* (1967), *The Beatles* (1968) and *Abbey Road* (1969). Emerick recorded string quartet, brass and woodwinds for the tracks *Funky 15, Truth* and *Dragon Master* on *Via Zammata'*.

it a little bit, because there was "Dragon whore! Expose your vent! Your Master's vengeance must be spent!" A great lyric, but what I decided to do when I put this together, I wanted it to have the feeling of a classic metal tune and originally I was gonna see if I could get somebody like Rob Halford[63] or Bruce Dickinson[64] to sing it.

But the chances are good that those lyrics are not gonna be inspiring for them to want to sing it. So I just tweaked a couple of lines so that it still had the overall feel of this master of dragons, but it's something that could potentially be on metal radio.

The 1988 band did a rendition of it during rehearsals in Stockholm – you didn't use that as a reference?
The only time I ever heard it was during that sound check. Frank had put something together, but then after the sound check, that's when he handed me the lyrics and said, "You should write the music for this," because he didn't really have a riff for it. It was more like, as far as I can remember, just a chord progression type of thing – not like a blues progression, but a standardised kinda thing.

He really didn't create a major riff for it, which is what he thought it needed and that's when he said that. I used to have a version that I played in "Z" that had more speed metal and other stuff in it. At that time, I went along more with the joke of the whole thing – you know, let's put the humour at the forefront. But I did the opposite for this version.

What I wanted to do was feel like I was playing it deadly serious so that the average metal person – an Iron Maiden, Dio or Judas Priest fan – they won't hear a joke in it at all. But there are still things in it that make me laugh. There's a line in it that says, "Hate the day! Hate the light!" and I told the guy singing it, Shawn Albro, you've got to add an extra syllable to the word 'light'. He says, "What do you mean?" I said, "Like Ronnie James Dio[65] – sort of,

---

[63] English singer and songwriter, best known as the lead vocalist for heavy metal band Judas Priest.

[64] English singer, songwriter and airline pilot, best known as the lead singer of the heavy metal band Iron Maiden.

[65] Ronald James Padavona (1942-2010) was an American heavy metal singer/songwriter who fronted bands such as Rainbow, Black Sabbath and Dio.

'Hate the day! Hate the light-ahh!'" And he's like, "You mean make it cool?" And I'm like "Yes!" So it's got stuff like that, all these metal-isms that, to me, make it funny.

Tell me a little about the album title.

There's this documentary film, *Summer 82: When Zappa Came To Sicily*, where we got to trace our family heritage to this small town in Partinico, Sicily.

While we were there, we got to see the street where Frank's family emigrated from. The street was called Via Zammata'. And it was a tiny, tiny – like, not much bigger than this booth – house with a little door.

It was number 13, Via Zammata'.

So this tiny little place was where his family said, "We've got to see if there's something better than this, somewhere else," which is crazy, because it's such a beautiful part of the world. It's a nice town.

But anyway, we met all kinds of people and different relatives that we never knew about and the experience of doing that and seeing how that street was then renamed Via Frank Zappa and how our family's connected to that area, I just had the idea that when I made the record I wanted to mirror that in some way.

I wanted to have many of the elements that inspired me to make music in different ways and put them on the record – like production styles, music styles, instrumentation, all kinds of stuff. I guess the fabric of it is all rooted in 60s/70s kind of production and a little bit of 80s stuff in there. It's definitely different from my other records in terms of songwriting style, the vocals being the real driving element – in some cases, the guitar takes a real backseat in some of the songs.

Do you have any idea if *Summer 82* will be released on DVD?

Apparently it's now got some kind of distribution deal, to come out in December in Italy. They're trying to get it into some other American film festivals – so maybe next year it will come out on DVD.[66]

---

[66] The film is scheduled to be issued on Blu-Ray by MVD Visual in December 2017.

You talked about Frank's orchestral compositions. I understand you've been working on your own orchestral piece. Is that anywhere near being completed?

I have a piece that is basically done, but I recently did a thing in Montana with the LA Guitar Quartet and they asked me to write a piece of music for them.[67]

That was an interesting challenge, because they all play nylon string guitars so there's not very much variation in the timbre of the instruments. So to make a piece of music that works for four guitars is pretty hard actually – so that you can really hear all the different colours. They're very good at creating the different textures, the different playing styles and techniques.

But I think it would be more interesting to hear the piece with other instruments in the brass context and stuff like that. The piece was a challenge to write. If I'm able to do this thing I was talking about where I put a big band together and play orchestral stuff, I would then also use that same environment to play some of these pieces.[68]

It would be difficult to tour something like that though?

It would be – but you never know!

How do you feel the PledgeMusic campaign went for the album?

I had never had any experience with Pledge before. I didn't even know what it was until somebody from Pledge approached me and said, "You should try this out," and I said, "Okay, it sounds good."

There's other things called 'crowdfunding', but Pledge operates in a different way as far as I'm concerned. What you're doing there is giving people a chance to pre-order the record and be part of the record. If they're interested and they want to support it, they can see videos and blogs and other stuff.

So if you put it into the perspective of like if it was 1968 and something like this existed and people could be a fly on the wall

---

[67] *Marmux Buhdardux*, named after a character invented by his daughter Zola.

[68] On 1st December 2017, Dweezil is scheduled to present the world premiere of the full orchestral version of *Marmux Buhdardux* with the Northern Dutch Orchestra in Utrecht.

listening to Jimi Hendrix or Frank Zappa or the Beatles as they made a record, it would be the most amazing, most popular thing going.

Music has been so devalued over the years that there are only really a handful of people that still have this major attraction to music in that way – where they really want to support it and they want to see what's happening and just be a part of this thing.

That's the sort of person that wants to help with a pledge campaign. So the experience of doing it this way not only helped make the record, but it also was a positive experience on making it: you could see that there were people who were excited about what was happening and there was feedback.

Normally when you make a record it's a pretty insular kind of thing, you're just doing whatever you do and then the record comes out and people like it or they don't, or whatever.

But in this case, people are there with you during it, so it changes the way the record is made. The feeling is: everybody's part of a team and it was a fun way to do a record.

Are you aware of PJ Harvey?[69]
I know who she is.

She just did a thing at London's Somerset House where they recorded an album behind glass in a studio and you could go and watch her. You couldn't interact with her; you could just view her recording her album. Like an art installation kind of thing.
That's weird. Is the album any good?

It's not out yet.[70] Obviously, the other side of the Pledge thing is that it can help get pre-existing material released. Are there plans like that for the ZPZ 2010 live *Apostrophe* DVD, featuring George Duke?
That's the plan. I've self-financed the thing all the way through so far, but to finish it up and make copies of it and get it out there, a

---

[69] Polly Jean Harvey MBE is an English musician, singer-songwriter, writer, poet, and composer.

[70] *The Hope Six Demolition Project* was released on 15th April 2016. It was later listed in the Top 10 albums of the year in both MOJO magazine and the Chicago Tribune.

Pledge campaign would help make that happen. It's also good for awareness.

Absolutely, I had every update on *Via Zammata'* pop-up on my Facebook timeline.
Yeah. That's a really good overall performance of the material. It's captured with really good cameras, good camera work and the lighting is good.

The first DVD[71] that we made turned out pretty well, but this one to me is much, much better on so many levels of production. So I'm excited about that one.

But over the years we've filmed a lot of different shows and one of the things that I'd also like to do is make a documentary about the whole project of Zappa Plays Zappa – go back to the early days, with interviews and even when the band was just learning stuff and follow the progression of the thing. Because there's so much material, so many songs.

The first DVD had something like 26-27 songs on it and this next one has about the same with very limited overlap. I have eight or ten shows that also have all this other material, again with very limited overlap and I'm guessing there are more than 100 songs: that's a lot of material.

There's things like *Billy The Mountain*:[72] stuff that there's no footage of it ever being performed by Frank. In some cases, some of these things that we've learned, they could be the only historical document of a live visual presentation.

Parts of that are in *Son of Roxy & Elsewhere*[73] aren't they?
Yes, there's a couple snippets of that in the promo, but on that tour we did the entire *Billy The Mountain* – the 29-minute extravaganza. But there's just been so much material that we've learned over the years. I haven't kept track, but I think it's over 400 songs that we've learned.

---

[71] Filmed at two shows in Seattle and Portland in 2006, the DVD was directed and produced by Pierre & François Lamoureux and issued the following year.

[72] Originally on Frank's album *Just Another Band From L.A.* (1972).

[73] A DVD preview of a ZPZ show at LA's Roxy was uploaded to YouTube on 9th April 2009. At the time of writing, there is still only one ZPZ DVD available.

And there's a lot to choose from, with 100 albums.[74] Is there any chance that *Zappa's Universe* will ever come out on DVD?
I don't know. At the time that was a PolyGram thing.

Does Universal own that now?
I have no idea about that.

It's funny because, with my fan hat on, I wrote to your mother about that and asked if that might be on the horizon – because I thought it would be good to support what ZPZ were doing. But she said that wasn't recorded at a particularly happy period, with Frank... which hadn't really crossed my mind – as a fan, I just wanted to see it out.
My experience of what it was... it wasn't my favourite stuff – it wouldn't be high on my list of things to push through before other stuff.

What about *What The Hell Was I Thinking*?
That one I've been working on! Over the years, that thing has changed around a lot. It started as a ten-minute piece of music, with just a couple of different styles of music tossed together. Then I thought, I'll get some people to play on this and then it became "Oh, why don't I just extend it and I'll have a few other people play on it."

And then ultimately it was why, don't I try and make it the entire length of a CD, a 75-minute piece of music and get a bunch of different people to play on it, all these different styles of music. At the time that I was really working on it a lot, I also had a bunch of Frank's music thrown in as quotes – little pieces of *G-Spot Tornado*, *City Of Tiny Lites*, *Sofa*, *The Black Page* and several other little things.

Some of those appear in the extended version of *My Beef Mailbox*.[75]
Yeah. But that stuff doesn't need to be in it now because Zappa

---

[74] On 21st June 2015, *Dance Me This* became Official Release No.100.

[75] A track from *Shampoohorn*. On the brief tour to promote the album, *My Beef Mailbox* was "transformed into a large improvisational solo section." In 1995, "Z" issued a promo CD including "solos from 10 American cities edited together in no particular order."

Plays Zappa is playing specifically Frank's music. So there's a lot of stuff that arrangement wise will change.

So it's still a living and breathing project?

Yeah. I don't have any time crunch on that thing. It really is best described as an audio movie, because it's texturally changing from scene to scene, moment to moment and different guitar players are making these cameo appearances

You talked about Joe Walsh[76] doing his part in one take.

Yeah, he was very quick. He did one take with two different sounds: he did one with a talk box and one with a slide – and one take of each. He was spot on. A lot of these people who've played on it are obviously very well known, but there's new players that it would be nice to get on there too.

Guthrie Govan,[77] perhaps?

Guthrie should be on there. There's lots of great players out today. It's just a weird time for guitar, ultimately. There's a lot of players out there that technically are doing stuff that was inconceivable years ago.

Yeah, you see these little kids on YouTube that are like, wow!

Yeah. The thing is, how could it find an audience and in what form, so that it's not necessarily just like a technical precision exercise or something.

I don't play at all, but I can still appreciate that stuff.

Being that there's not radio airplay for that kind of music per se, it always fascinates me that people still take the time to get that good at that one thing that has such limited appeal. You could spend a lifetime to continue to learn how to be...

But history is littered with great artists and composers who weren't a success in their lifetimes, but became household names years later.

Yeah. It's a tricky thing, but there are a lot of great players out

---

[76] American guitarist, singer-songwriter and record producer. As well as being a member of the James Gang, Eagles and Ringo Starr's All-Starr Band, Walsh has enjoyed a successful solo career.

[77] English guitarist and guitar teacher, known for his work with The Aristocrats and Asia.

there now.

I wanted to ask you about Extraordinary Teamwork – something that was announced by the ZFT a few years ago, but the only real piece that came out of it was the Gene Simmons track, *Black Tongue*.[78]
    The idea was that you could take pieces of Frank's unreleased material and incorporate it into your own composition. For example, you could take something from the Synclavier and embellish it. That's a dream of mine!
I've never heard of the phrase 'Extraordinary Teamwork' before. It was not something that was ever spoken to me about.

Perhaps just the one press release, then. The Gene Simmons thing came out and that was it.
I never had anything to do with that press release or anything, so that's new to me. But at one point I made an effort to approach Jeff Beck to see if he wanted to do something – because he and Frank had talked about making a guitar record, or making a record at some point.

I talked to him about whether he'd be interested in listening to some tracks and working with some of the tracks but it never really went anywhere. That would be cool, though.

Absolutely. I love Jeff – I saw him at one of your shows at the Marquee. He's probably too busy working on his hot rods now. I don't want to embarrass you... too much! But can you tell me anything about the Poole family from Houston?
When I was on MTV... the Poole family, they have a lot of kids – the daughters at the time were really young – and they started writing me some letters. They were like six or seven and they knew about Frank because Brad their father was into his music.

Over the years, they've stayed in touch and all of the kids are into the music. Every time we go to Texas, some or all turn up at all the shows. It was really just that, they reached out and said, "Hey, we watch you on MTV." So I would write them back and

---

78 On his album *Asshole* (2004).

whenever I'm near wherever they are, they show up.

Brad wrote to me telling me how impressed he was by that – you'd touched their lives and how your friendship has endured since the mid-80s.
Yeah, well my experience growing up was if there was something that was exciting or interesting to me and I had a chance to pursue it or learn more about it that involved meeting somebody that was influential – like Eddie Van Halen or something – that made a big impression on me.

So if ever there's a situation where somebody reaches out in some way and says, "Oh I like what you do and I want to learn more about this," or whatever, I'm always happy to say, "Sure, I'll give you a chance." Even to the extent that when we do shows, if there's kids in the audience, I'll pull them up on stage and make them play my guitar – even if they don't play!

I was telling the band the other day – they were saying we're playing in a place we don't recognise called Hengelo. I said, "No, we've played there before."

That was where a girl came up on stage – she was about 12 – and I made her play the guitar. She didn't play guitar, but now she does because of that experience. She has stuck with it. Her dad has written to me and said, "Oh, she's really into it."

It's that kind of moment. I think it's fun to do stuff like that, because I know what it was like for me when I was a kid and I was impressionable about music. So why not?

Indeed. What about your daughters? Do they show any inclination towards making music?
My daughter Zola is taking flute in school right now and Ceylon... er, they both have guitars.

It's funny, because if I'm sitting playing guitar, which is pretty rare at home, they'll come over and be interested in what I'm doing then go, "No, no – give me the guitar. Let me show you how to do it!" And they'll just bang on it and do all kinds of stuff and I'm like "That's pretty good!"

But what they like is to turn it up really loud and put some effects on and hear it do delay – they like to see what will happen with stuff like that.

(Tom Waring): I know someone who hasn't grown out of that.

Yeah, me I think! Some time ago, Diva talked about making an album with you. A few of the tracks have been released on the 'birthday bundles', but...
We did like six or seven songs, but I don't remember how many they released on the bundles.[79]

I guess the whole thing should be released on one single thing. But what was remarkable about that was the process of doing it: she wouldn't know anything about writing songs, she never learned to play an instrument or even tried singing. But she said, "I want to make a record." And I was like "Whoa! Why?"

She just wanted to. So I said, "Okay, here's what we'll do..." The first song that we did, I interviewed her and wrote down her answers in the form of lyrics. I said these are gonna be the lyrics to the song. I'm gonna record the music for it, but you're not allowed to hear it. So when you come to sing this, you get one chance – you re gonna look at these words and whatever you do, that's the song.

I had to hide under the mixing console because I was laughing so hard. The vocal performance that she did, you can't duplicate it. It's this completely awkward, no idea when to come in, no idea what the melody is. But it's captured in such a way that there's this spontaneity to it.

There was something about that formula, once we got it, I said that's the only way you're allowed to record!

So all the songs were done that way. It's funny, because she probably could do a much more professional, better version.

But that would ruin it.
Yeah, that's not the vibe.

Are you still in touch with Nuno Bettencourt, who co-produced _Confessions_?
I haven't seen him in a while, but oddly enough I just got back in

---

[79] _Girly Woman_ and _When The Ball Drops_ appeared on _The Frank Zappa AAAFNRAA Birthday Bundle_ (2006), and _Alice_ and _Espanoza_ are on _The Frank Zappa AAA·FNR·AAA Birthday Bundle_ (2008).

touch with Paul Geary, who used to be the drummer in Extreme. Now he's a big manager of other bands like Godsmack.[80] He just reached out to me the other day. But I haven't seen Nuno for about six years or something.[81]

Haven't Extreme reformed?
Yeah, they're out playing again.

Okay. What are the chances of you working with Mike Keneally again?
Probably not anything happening any time soon.

Okay. What about the chances of reissuing your first solo album, *Havin' A Bad Day*?
Potentially... what I was thinking is at some point – because I have such limited time: when I'm not doing the Zappa Plays Zappa stuff, which obviously takes up a lot of my time, I try to spend as much time as I can with my kids. It's a challenge to get anything else done. But I'd like to refurbish my own catalogue and do something with it – though it's not a major, major priority, so we'll see.

(Tom Waring): Following up on the question about Mike Keneally: given the opportunity, who would you like to work with again – or someone that you haven't worked with already?
The one person we haven't done anything with is Vinnie Colaiuta – that would be cool.[82] I could see me doing some more stuff with Steve Vai at some point.

But the whole thing about alumni... this project was never made to create an opportunity for that – that was something that promoters wanted, so to make it happen at all, in the first year we had to use some. The way that I have always seen Zappa Plays Zappa... it's complicated to explain, but if you take Frank's core fan base that started with him, if they were ten years younger

---

[80] American rock band from Lawrence, Massachusetts, formed in 1995.

[81] I subsequently learnt that Bettencourt had 'stolen' one of Dweezil's former girlfriends.

[82] Less than two months after this interview, Colaiuta joined ZPZ on stage at the Saban Theater in Beverly Hills on 11th December 2016.

than him, up to his age and ten years older than him and they followed his whole career, at the point we started this in 2006, you're seeing an audience that's a minimum of fifty years old and a maximum of seventy.

So as it goes ten years into the future, from 2006 to 2016, some of those people aren't alive anymore.

Sadly, that's true.[83]

So the whole notion of the music being carried forward into the future is that it needs to inspire a younger generation to discover the music and play it.

What I had always said was that an audience needs to see people that didn't have an affiliation with it so they can see that it's possible and that you can show what kind of dedication is required to learn to do this stuff. Because when I was a kid and I watched these bands that Frank put together, it was like magic! Seeing them playing this stuff that's so hard, yet they're having fun.

So if you want a younger audience, you're not really gonna get that if everybody on stage is sixty plus. It doesn't matter how great the musicians are, that's just the nature of things.

I wanted to put a younger band together and focus on it that way and that's what I've been able to do.

But in the beginning, it was the promoters that wanted to turn it into a circus and make it as many alumni as possible, at all times. That doesn't sound appealing to me at all.

It's not because I don't respect those musicians, it's just for the reason that I've just described: that is not what is going to carry the music into the future.

I view this more as a repertory ensemble. If a classical ensemble is playing the music of whatever composer, they're not trying to modernise it or change it to say, "Hey, let's get this new audience to enjoy this music." They're saying, let's respect this music and play it the way it was so that generations can still be excited about this accomplishment. That's how I view Frank's music and that's

---

[83] Rest in peace: Paul Mummery, Laurie Harding, Gamma, Dave McMann and Zappo.

why we don't really do anything to adulterate it at all. That's been my approach.

I want an apples to apples comparison, as best as possible, so that if somebody hears what we do and then they hear Frank, I don't want it to sound like "Oh, it's totally a different era – it's got a rapper on" and it's got this or whatever.

Why would those changes make it better? Why would that be the thing that would get somebody into Frank's version?

That doesn't make sense to me, so that's why I never bothered with any of that stuff. But so many people tell me that if I want to get a younger audience, I've got to modernise it.

Frank's music is from the future. There's nothing that sounds like it – you don't need to modernise this.

Look at a song like *Who Are The Brain Police?*[84] It's fifty years old and there's nothing that sounds like that. So it's a challenge to get people to understand that point of view, because it's so easy for somebody to think *"Oh, all you've gotta do is use all this newfangled stuff, use computers, get a rapper, do a dance version."*

Well, that's not Frank's music: he wouldn't have done that, so why the fuck would I?[85]

(Tom Waring): We get that every year – fewer and fewer, now it's ten years on. But it's like, "Who's gonna be the guest alumni this year?"
There's a lot of people that are interested in that, but it's generally the older audience. The younger audience don't know who those people are.

But what we see a lot, especially in the States, there's a lot more younger kids that are coming to it and they know a lot about the music. They're super into the vinyl and all this kinda stuff. It's a strange thing... and there's more women!

The first year we did this, it was just a sea of guys – and a couple of disappointed wives and girlfriends, *like "Do I have to sit through this?"*

---

[84] From *Freak Out!* (1966).

[85] Interestingly, that is precisely what brother Ahmet did for a version of *Willie The Pimp* that appears on *The Frank Zappa AAA·FNRAA·AA Birthday Bundle* (2010), which features hip-hop artists DMC, Talib Kweli and MMM.

But now there's actually girls that really know the music. It's so bizarre to me to see a teenage girl to whom Frank is their favourite musician and she'll know all the music and they've got like a Frank Zappa tattoo. This is the craziest thing ever.

Back in the 1970s, most of the women only liked whatever songs that could possibly have been played on the radio. That was just the culture; that's how people get used to hearing the music.

Talking of disappointed girlfriends: in 1982, I took my then fiancée to see Frank at Hammersmith Odeon and he strode out and said something like, "How many of you guys have come here trying to impress your girlfriends so you might get a blow-job later?" I put my head in my hands, thinking "Oh no!" But she still married me and, thirty years later, we're still together! [laughs]

What's interesting and we hear it a lot too: there's a lot of women that come to the shows now with their husbands or whatever and they say I never got the music until I saw you guys play it.

There's something different about it now, because I have always just tried to make it about the music.

Frank had his own agenda with how he would give every performance – there could be political messages and there could be other social commentary, which makes the music great and all. But that's for him to do – it's not for me to impersonate Frank.

In the way that it's presented now, where it focuses on a broad spectrum of the music, it's intended to educate an audience about all of the things Frank did, so I get that from a lot of women saying I never got it till I saw you guys play it – and you guys look like you're having so much fun!

They also like seeing Scheila[86] and say, "Oh, there's a woman whose playing this stuff." There's a lot of that, that happens.

Even people that have seen Frank a bunch of times say, I know more about the music from seeing you guys play it, because we give a little back story. Also, they were totally fucked up when they saw Frank and now they're sober!

---

[86] Scheila Gonzalez, who has sung and played sax and keyboards with ZPZ since its launch in 2006.

So there's a difference in a lot of that stuff – it's a strange process.

(Tom Waring): It's a very different experience seeing it played well live and listening to it on a shitty hi-fi or something.
That has always been a part of his music: seeing it played live. It's not unlike classical music – well, it really is classical music – but when you see it with a band, all these things are orchestrated with people doing all this stuff together at the same time... I mean, it's hard enough to convince people to show up on time to go to lunch, right? So to get people on stage doing the same thing at the same moment at that one particular time to execute something, it's like a mini-miracle.

So when you see really difficult stuff, it's like "Wait a minute. First of all, how was that written? And how are they even playing that?"

That's what I saw when I would see Frank play. Even the band, we can listen to the show after and go, "Wow! I can't believe we played that!"

It's that weird thing of, even though we've learned to do it, it's still quite a feat. It's like training for the Olympics. It's hard stuff. We care a lot about the detail.

(Tom Waring): Of all of the stuff that you've learned to play with Zappa Plays Zappa, what was the toughest to learn? What was the one thing you heard back after and thought, "That was something!"?
That's happened a few times. There's some stuff that's really hard on the guitar and not necessarily that hard on other instruments. Some it's the other way around. So there's a few songs that fall into the category of super-hard.

Might *G-Spot Tornado* be one of those?
G-Spot is really hard on the guitar.

You used to play that with "Z", but you played it a lot slower than the original.
We only ever played a part of it, though; we never played the

whole song. The middle section in that is wicked. In terms of just complex rhythms and tough to play from top to bottom, *Dog Meat* is really hard... on the guitar. But I love that one.

Me too!

As a song, *Inca Roads* is incredibly hard. That's really, really hard on the guitar. *St Alfonzo's Pancake Breakfast* is super hard on the guitar.

That's the thing – some of these songs weren't designed to be played on the guitar.

They weren't ever played on the guitar! *St Alfonzo's* and *Inca Roads*, even Steve Vai never played those in Frank's band. He told me, "I tried to learn that stuff, but I couldn't do it." Because it doesn't lay out on the guitar, if you are an alternate picking guitarist, it's not possible, you just can't play it – not up to tempo, there's just no way.

I had intended to learn the melody of *Sinister Footwear*, but I didn't end up having enough time to learn it. But the band learned it and I just let them continue to play the melody because Frank never played the melody. Steve did. But I want to learn that, because that one has some hard stuff – it's probably the most demanding one of all the stuff that we've learned.

Moggio[87] is very hard. One of the things that Frank said none of the bands ever played right was...

...Ship Arriving...

...Ship Arriving Too Late To Save A Drowning Witch. That interlude in there, that's something that we plan to learn at some point. To get the performance that's on the record, there's probably seven edits from different shows. Knowing how hard that is, that's gonna be a challenge.

But there's never been anything that we've set out to learn that we weren't able to do. We only have a six-piece band at this point, so there's quite a lot of double-duty that's happening, on the keyboards and things.

---

[87] From *The Man From Utopia* (1983).

And Ben on trumpet.[88]

Trumpet... and Scheila's playing horns. Some of the arrangements sound really full for a six-piece band, for things like *Grand Wazoo*. But some people say they miss the marimba, but marimba's in there – you hear the marimba.[89] When you're watching it on stage, you see a guy hitting stuff but you're not looking over his shoulder to see what's happening.

If you hear a version of something from our tour now to how it was with a bigger band, all the textures and timbre of instrumentation, it's still there. It's exactly what it needs to be. It's just that you don't see a guy physically playing it. It's because Chris[90] can play a part and have it doubled or tripled with different instruments because it's mapped out so that as he's playing it, it's outputting several instruments at the same time. It's pretty impressive.

When he joined the band, there was talk of Chris also playing violin.

His violin chops are not up to snuff for a lot of the parts. It's okay for a couple of things, but it'd be cool to have somebody that can do all that. But there's not a lot of that in Frank's music. There was a very short period of time where he had a couple of people that played violin.

There was Ponty, Shankar, Sugar Cane Harris...

...and that other guy... hmm... in the 70s...

...Eddie Jobson. There's a monster version of *Black Napkins* with him on.

Black Napkins, that's a tune that we're probably gonna play tonight.[91] I haven't played it in forever. That's such a classic of Frank's.

---

[88] Ben Thomas was principally ZPZ's lead vocalist from 2009. In 2008, he had appeared in a ZFT authorised stage play of *Joe's Garage* at Hollywood's Open Fist Theatre – alongside former Grandmothers guitarist, Ken Rosser. A year after this interview, Dweezil replaced Thomas with female vocalist Cian Coey and David Luther on baritone lead vocals, baritone sax, keyboards and rhythm guitar.

[89] In 2012, Dweezil downsized ZPZ, releasing percussionist (and tour manager) Billy Hulting.

[90] Keyboard player/singer Chris Norton, who was added to the line-up in 2009.

[91] Because of the Bush Hall curfew, *Black Napkins* had to be cut from the set.

I named my first cat after that... a black part-Persian.

(Tom Waring): You're madder than I thought!

It's hard to play that one. The theme of it is a simple thing, but the phrasing is super hard to replicate. Then to improvise in a way that is similar to Frank's style, that makes that song extra really hard because he's doing little rhythmic twists and turns in his improvisation on the *Zoot Allures* version... yeah, it's gonna be a challenge to get back into that headspace.

(Tom Waring): And the sacred cow that you finally slaughtered, which was *Watermelon In Easter Hay*. To me, that was something else.

I saw you play that at Shepherd's Bush[92] ... but you played it in New York first?

Yeah. That was tough, man. That was very hard.[93] I mean, it's a hard song to play, but it's emotionally hard. There's a lot of that with a lot of these songs. Sometimes there's moments where I'll be playing and something will just strike me in the moment, that it's like "Wow! It didn't even feel like I played that – that came from some other place." Then it gets emotional: "Oh man, this is tough," you know? It's good though!

Interview conducted on Saturday 17th October 2015.

---

[92] On 11th November 2013.

[93] After her husband's passing, Gail revealed he had told her he did not want anyone else to perform his signature guitar compositions *Black Napkins*, *Zoot Allures* and *Watermelon In Easter Hay*. Dweezil has since played all three of these 'sacred' songs, finally debuting *Watermelon In Easter Hay* at ZPZ's New York Halloween show in 2013 – where his mother reportedly walked out.

ABOUT THE AUTHOR

Andrew Greenaway was born in Orpington, Kent, in 1958. He maintains the UK's only Frank Zappa website (www.idiotbastard.com) and has curated a half dozen Zappa-themed albums for Cordelia Records (with a seventh scheduled for release in 2018).

As well as writing *Zappa The Hard Way* (Wymer Publishing, 2010) and *The Beatles... The Easy Way: A Guide To The Official Recordings* (Wymer Publishing, 2014) Andrew has contributed to *1001 Songs You Must Hear Before You Die* (Octopus Books, 2010), *We Are The Other People - 25 Years Of Zappanale* (Arf Society, 2014) and *The Greatest Albums You'll Never Hear* (Octopus Books, 2014).

He also helped 'ghost' Anton Johnson's autobiography *King Of Clubs* (Grosvenor House, 2012) and is currently working on *The Zappa Tour Atlas* with Mick Zeuner and Klaus Kühner (slated for publication in 2018).

Andrew is one of the key contributors to ZappaCast - The Frank Zappa Podcast and co-host of Andrew & Lee's Music Emporium on SoundCloud. He also co-organises Festival MOO-AH, a biennial celebration of Zappa's music and more in Corby and is an auxiliary member of the Zappa Early Renaissance Orchestra.

Andrew has three children, three cats and lives with his wife Julie near the Thames Delta in deepest, darkest Essex. Aside from his family and music, his other interests include the Marx Brothers, Woody Allen, Kurt Vonnegut, Chelsea FC, Speedway GP, Coronation Street and having a laugh.

ABOUT THE ARTIST

Antero Valério was born in Torres Vedras, Portugal, in 1960. On the same day in 1975, he heard the albums *Hot Rats, The Grand Wazoo* and *Over-Nite Sensation*, and was amazed by the Zappa world. Still is.

Antero graduated in Visual Arts (Painting) at the Superior School of Fine Arts of Lisbon in 1988.

In 2008 he published a book of cartoons titled *Como Se Tornar Um Docentezeco*.

In 2013 Antero met the Italian Zappa-duo Inventionis Mater, and designed the covers of their albums *Does Humor Belong In Classical Music?* (2013), *Kong's Revenge* (2014) and *Zapping* (2016).

In 2014, he was invited by Andrew Greenaway to design the cover of *Weasels Re-Ripped* for Cordelia Records, and later the cover for *Sons Of Mr. Green Genes* (2016).

Antero lives and works in Lisbon. In addition to being a painter and cartoonist , he is also a graphic designer and illustrator who teaches art in high school.

You can see examples of Antero's work online at vantero.wixsite.com/antero, as well as a page of his cartoons ('Facetoons') at www.facebook.com/anterozoide/

CPSIA information can be obtained
at www.ICGtesting.com
Printed in the USA
BVOW06s1742170717
489478BV00009B/271/P